Muslims in 21st Century Europe

Muslims in 21st Century Europe explores the interaction between native majorities and Muslim minorities in various European countries with a view to highlighting different paths of integration of immigrant and native Muslims.

Starting with a critical overview of the institutionalization of Islam in Europe and a discussion on the nature of Muslimophobia as a social phenomenon, this book shows how socio-economic, institutional and political parameters set the frame for Muslim integration in Europe. Britain, France, Germany, the Netherlands and Sweden are selected as case studies among the 'old' migration hosts. Italy, Spain and Greece are included to highlight the issues arising and the policies adopted in southern Europe to accommodate Muslim claims and needs.

The book highlights the internal diversity of both minority and majority populations, and analyses critically the political and institutional responses to the presence of Muslims.

Anna Triandafyllidou is Assistant Professor at the Democritus University of Thrace in Greece, Senior Research Fellow at ELIAMEP in Athens, and Professor at the College of Europe in Bruges. Her main areas of research and teaching are migration, nationalism, and European integration. Recent books include *Irregular Migration in Europe* (2010, Ashgate), *European Immigration: A Sourcebook* (2007, Ashgate), *Multiculturalism, Muslims and Citizenship: A European Approach* (2006, Routledge), *Transcultural Europe* (2006, Palgrave) and *Contemporary Polish Migration in Europe* (2006, The Edwin Allen Press).

Routledge/European Sociological Association Studies in European Societies

Series editors: Thomas P. Boje, Max Haller, Martin Kohli and Alison Woodward

1. **European Societies**
   Fusion or fission?
   Edited by Thomas P. Boje, Bart van Steebergen and Sylvia Walby

2. **The Myth of Generational Conflict**
   The family and state in ageing societies
   Edited by Sara Arber and Claudine Attias-Donfut

3. **The End of the Welfare State?**
   Responses to state retrenchment
   Edited by Peter Taylor-Gooby and Stefan Svallfors

4. **Will Europe Work?**
   Integration, employment and the social order
   Edited by Martin Kohli and Mojca Novak

5. **Inclusions and Exclusions in European Societies**
   Edited by Martin Kohli and Alison Woodward

6. **Young Europeans, Work and Family**
   Futures in transition
   Edited by Julia Brannen, Suzan Lewis, Ann Nilsen and Janet Smithsen

7. **Autobiographies of Transformation**
   Lives in Central and Eastern Europe
   Edited by Mike Keen and Janusz Mucha

8. **Europe and Asia Beyond East and West**
   Edited by Gerard Delanty

9. **Cultural Overstretch**
   Differences between old and new member states of the EU and Turkey
   Edited by Jürgen Gerhards

10. **Social Class in Europe**
    An introduction to the European socio-economic classification
    Edited by David Rose and Eric Harrison

11. **Conflict, Citizenship and Civil Society**
    Edited by Patrick Baert, Sokratis M. Koniordos, Giovanna Procacci and Carlo Ruzza

12. **Muslims in 21st Century Europe**
    Structural and cultural perspectives
    Edited by Anna Triandafyllidou

Muslims in 21st Century Europe

Structural and cultural perspectives

Edited by Anna Triandafyllidou

Routledge
Taylor & Francis Group
LONDON AND NEW YORK

First published 2010
by Routledge
2 Park Square, Milton Park, Abingdon, Oxon, OX14 4RN

Simultaneously published in the USA and Canada
by Routledge
270 Madison Avenue, New York, NY 10016

Routledge is an imprint of the Taylor & Francis Group, an informa business

Typeset in Times New Roman by
Pindar NZ, Auckland, New Zealand
Printed and bound in Great Britain by
CPI Antony Rowe, Chippenham, Wiltshire

British Library Cataloguing in Publication Data
A catalogue record for this book is available from the British Library

Library of Congress Cataloging in Publication Data
Muslims in 21st century Europe : structural and cultural perspectives / edited by Anna Triandafyllidou.
p. cm.
"Simultaneously published in the USA and Canada"—T.p. verso.
Includes bibliographical references.
1. Muslims—Europe—Social conditions—21st century. 2. Europe—Social conditions—21st century. 3. Muslims—Europe—Social conditions—Case studies. 4. Immigrants—Europe—Social conditions—Case studies. 5. Muslims—Europe—Government relations—Case studies. 6. Europe—Social conditions—Case studies. 7. Islam—Social aspects—Europe—Case studies. 8. Cultural pluralism—Europe—Case studies. 9. Europe—Race relations—Case studies. 10. Europe—Social conditions—Case studies. I. Triandafyllidou, Anna. II. Title: Muslims in twenty-first century Europe.
D1056.2.M87M857 2010
305.6'97094—dc22 2009035226

ISBN 10: 0-415-49709-4 (hbk)
ISBN 10: 0-203-87784-5 (ebook)

ISBN 13: 978-0-415-49709-1 (hbk)
ISBN 13: 978-0-203-87784-5 (ebook)

Contents

Contributors

Valérie Amiraux is Associate Professor of Sociology at the University of Montreal where she has held the Canada Research Chair for the Study of Religious Pluralism and Ethnicity since 2007. She is on leave from her position as Permanent Research Fellow at the National Center for Scientific Research (CNRS/CURAPP). She was a Jean Monnet Fellow at the European University Institute (EUI) and coordinated the Mediterranean Programme of the EUI (1998-2001); Visiting Fellow at the French-German Marc Bloch Research Center in Fall 2003; Marie Curie Fellow at the EUI (2005-2007). Her main fields of research are sociology of religion, compared politics, Muslim minorities and discrimination. She has extensively published on Muslim minorities in Europe. Her most recent publications include 'L' "affaire" du foulard en France. Retour sur une affaire qui n'en est pas encore une', *Sociologie et Sociétés*, 2010, 41 (2), pp. 273–298; *Politics of Visibility: Young Muslims in European Public Spaces*, with Gerdien Jonker, Transcript (Bielefeld), coll. Global Local Islam, 2006.

Nynke de Witte is a Ph.D. candidate at the Faculty of Spatial Sciences of the University of Groningen, the Netherlands. She has an M.Phil. in Political and Social Sciences from Pompeu Fabra University, Barcelona and a Bachelor's and Master's degree in Human Geography from the Radboud University of Nijmegen. She worked as a researcher on the Spanish case for the EU Sixth Framework project EMILIE, A European Approach to Multicultural Citizenship. Since September 2008, she has been a researcher for the Dutch case in the EU Seventh framework project FACIT, Faith-based organizations and Exclusion in European cities.

Burak Erdenir is the Deputy Secretary General at the Secretariat General for European Union Affairs of Turkey, the governmental body which oversees Turkey's pre-accession process for European Union membership, including accession negotiations. His portfolio includes minority, immigration and identity issues, and political reforms on judiciary and fundamental rights. He also serves as the Senior Advisor to the Minister for European Union Affairs and Chief Negotiator of Turkey. He holds a B.Sc. degree from Middle East Technical University, MBA from Georgetown University and MPA from

Kennedy School of Government at Harvard University. Erdenir received his Ph.D. in Political Science and Public Administration from Ankara University. He has been teaching at Ankara University and Bilkent University as an adjunct lecturer. He is the author of *Avrupa Kimligi: Pan-Milliyetçilikten Post-Milliyetçilige* (2005). He has published articles on cultural issues and various aspects of Turkey–European Union relations.

Daniel Faas is Lecturer in Sociology at Trinity College Dublin. His research interests include migration and education, European integration and globalization, citizenship and identity politics, multiculturalism and social cohesion, ethnicity and racism, curriculum and policy developments, and comparative case study methodologies. He is author of *Negotiating Political Identities: multiethnic schools and youth in Europe* (2010) and winner of the 2009 European Sociological Association award for best article (Turkish Youth in the European Knowledge Economy, European Societies 9(4): 573–99). Dr Faas was Fulbright-Schuman Fellow in the Department of Sociology at the University of California at Berkeley (2009), and Marie Curie Research Fellow at the Hellenic Foundation for European and Foreign Policy in Athens (2006–2008) having obtained his Ph.D. in Sociology of Education from the University of Cambridge (2006). He has acted as advisor to the European Commission DG Education and Culture and consultant to the Irish Department of Education and Science. Daniel Faas is collaborator on the 'CiviTurn: Citizenship Integration in Northwest European Migration Societies' project, and Visiting Scholar at Aarhus University. He is currently supervising Ph.Ds on return migration of South Americans to Europe, Chinese migrants in Ireland, workplace equality and diversity management, and pre-schoolers construction of social selves and social organization.

Nasar Meer, Ph.D., is a lecturer in the School of Social and Political Sciences at the University of Southampton. He was previously based in the Center for the Study of Ethnicity and Citizenship at the University of Bristol and in 2005 he was a visiting fellow at the W.E.B. Du Bois Institute, at Harvard University. He has published on the topics of education, media discourse and discrimination legislation and is the author of *Citizenship Identity, and the Politics of Multiculturalism* (2010), and is co-editor of a Palgrave book series on citizenship.

Jonas Otterbeck, Ph.D., is Associate Professor of Islamology, at the Center for Theology and Religious Studies, Lund University Sweden. He has done research on Muslim discourses on Islam in Sweden and on the situation of Muslim pupils in state schools. Currently he is investigating Islamophobia in Sweden and the attitudes of Lebanese and Egyptian Muslim scholars to popular music. Otterbeck completed his Ph.D. in Islamic Studies in 2000: his dissertation is entitled 'Islam på svenska. Tidskriften Salaam och islams globalisering' (Islam in Swedish: The Journal Salaam and the Globalization of Islam) (2000). His publications include *Samtidsislam* (2010), *Islam, muslimer och den svenska* *skolan* (2000), *Muslimer i svensk skola* (1993) and the English articles 'The Legal Status of Islamic Minorities in Sweden' (2004), 'The Depiction of Islam in Sweden' (2002) and 'Local Islamic Universalism. Analyses of an Islamic Journal in Sweden' (2000), among others.

Maurizia Russo Spena specialized in Oriental Studies (Arabic language) at the University La Sapienza, Rome, receiving her Ph.D. in educational studies from the University of Rome III, where she collaborated with the Centre for Research in Intercultural Education and Training for Development and the chair of Intercultural Pedagogy, and where teaches in the master's programme on Migration Processes and Linguistic and Cultural Mediation. She has carried out research in the Middle East, Egypt and Tunisia. Her main research fields are the linguistic and cultural integration of migrants (in particular Muslims) in Italy and the mobility of labour migrants in the Mediterranean basin. She has published several research papers on these topics and has edited *Oriente e Occidente: scontro fra civiltà?* (2004) as well as a handbook for the linguistic training of future migrant workers (2008).

Sara Silvestri is an interdisciplinary political scientist with a Ph.D. from Cambridge University. Her research and publications focus on Muslim socio-political mobilization, Islamic institutions, and public policies pertaining faith communities in the EU. She is a Lecturer at City University London, where she teaches primarily Religion in International Relations and Islamism, and directs the Globalising Justice, Equality and International Law programme at the Von Hügel Institute (St Edmund's College, Cambridge University). In Cambridge she collaborates with the Muslim College, and is an associate of the POLIS department, where she previously did her post-doc. Her recent publications include: *Europe's Muslim Women: Potential Aspirations and Challenges* (KBF 2008), "Religion and Islam in the Political System of the EU (*West European Politics* 2009), "Muslim Institutions and Political Mobilisation" (CEPS 2007). Dr Silvestri has directed the Islam in Europe programme for the European Policy Centre (Brussels), has been an Associate Fellow with Chatham House (London) and a Marie Curie Fellow with the University of Paris.

Thijl Sunier is an anthropologist. He holds the VISOR Chair of Islam in European Societies at the VU University of Amsterdam. He studied Cultural Anthropology at the Universities of Utrecht and Amsterdam, and completed his Ph.D. on 'Islam in Motion: Turkish Young People and Islamic Organizations' in 1996. He participated in research on inter-ethnic relations in a postwar neighbourhood of Haarlem and conducted research among Turkish youth and Islamic organizations in France, Germany, Britain and the Netherlands; he also conducted international comparative research on nation-building and multiculturalism in France, the Netherlands and Turkey, and on Islam and modernity. Currently he is preparing research on Islamic leadership in Europe, on youth, politics, religion and popular culture as well as on historical research on Europe and Islam. He is a member of the Amsterdam School for Social Science Research

(ASSR), editor of the anthropological journal *Etnofoor*, chairman of the board of the Dutch Anthropological Association, and chairman of the Dutch Research School for Islamic studies.

Anna Triandafyllidou is Assistant Professor at the Democritus University of Thrace, Greece and Senior Research Fellow at the Hellenic Foundation for European and Foreign Policy (ELIAMEP) in Athens. She has also been Professor at the College of Europe in Bruges since 2002. She has published widely in the area of migration, nationalism and European integration. Her recent books include: *Multiculturalism, Muslims and Citizenship: A European Approach* (2006, Routledge; co-editor), *Transcultural Europe* (2006, Palgrave; co-editor), *Contemporary Polish Migration in Europe* (2006, The Edwin Mellen Press; editor), *European Immigration: A Sourcebook* (2007, Ashgate; co-editor), *The European Public Sphere and the Media* (2009, Palgrave; co-editor), and *Irregular Migration in Europe: Myths and Realities* (2010, Ashgate; editor).

Ricard Zapata-Barrero is Associate Professor of Political Theory at the Department of Social and Political Science, Universitat Pompeu Fabra (Barcelona, Spain). His main line of research deals with contemporary issues of liberal democracy in contexts of diversity, especially the relationship between democracy, citizenship and immigration. He is director of GRITIM (Interdisciplinary Research Group on Immigration, Grup de Recerca Interdisciplinari sobre Immigració, www.upf.edu/gritim) and the Master's programme on immigration management at UPF. He is currently working on different areas of research related to borders and diversity. His recent books include: *Immigration and Self-Government of Minority Nations* (2009; editor), *Citizenship Policies in the Age of Diversity* (2009; editor), *Fundamentos de los discursos políticos en torno a la inmigración* (2009), *Conceptos Políticos en el contexto español* (2007; editor), *Multiculturalism, Muslims and Citizenship: A European Approach* (Routledge) (2006; co-editor), and *Multiculturalidad e inmigración* (2004).

1 Muslims in 21st century Europe

Conceptual and empirical issues

Anna Triandafyllidou

1. Framing the 'Muslim issue'

This book explores the interaction and integration between native majorities and Muslim minorities in different European countries. Taking into account the internal diversity of both minority and majority populations, it critically analyses the political and institutional responses to the presence of Muslims and how national governments and other stakeholders promote commonality or difference.

Europe has experienced increasing tensions between national majorities and marginalized Muslim communities. Such conflicts have included: the violence in northern England between native British and Asian Muslim youth (2001); the civil unrest amongst France's Muslim Maghrib communities (2005); and the Danish cartoon crisis in 2006 following the publication of pictures of the Prophet Muhammad. Muslim communities have also come under intense scrutiny in the wake of the terrorist events in the United States (2001), Spain (2004) and England (2005). There is growing scepticism amongst European governments over the question of Turkey's accession into the European Union, a country that is socio-culturally and religiously different from the present EU-27 (European Monitoring Centre on Racism and Xenophobia 2006a; 2006b).

During the first years of the twenty-first century, politicians and academics have been debating intensively the reasons underlying such tensions and what should be done to enhance civic cohesion in European societies. One question raised by these debates is how much cultural diversity can truly be accommodated within liberal and secular democracies. Some thinkers and politicians have advanced the claim that it is impossible to accommodate Muslims in European countries because their cultural traditions and religious faith are incompatible with secular democratic states. Others have argued that Muslims can be accommodated in the socio-political order of European societies provided they adhere to a set of civic values that lie at the heart of European democratic traditions and that reflect the secular nature of society and politics in Europe. Others still have questioned the kind of secularism that underpins state institutions in Europe.

The debate has been intensive in the media, in political forums as well as in scholarly circles. In policy terms, the main conclusion drawn from such debates has been that multicultural policies have failed and that returning to an assimilation-based approach (emphasizing national culture and values) would be desirable. The Netherlands, for example, which has been a forerunner in multicultural policies since the 1980s, has now established integration courses for all immigrants (both newcomers and earlier arrivals) and recently a civic integration test for prospective migrants to take before leaving their country of origin (Ter Wal 2007; Vasta 2007; see also Thijl Sunier in this volume). In the face of mounting civil unrest and the social exclusion of second-generation immigrant youth, the French government has reasserted its republican civic integration model banning ostentatious religious symbols in schools and prioritizing labour market considerations in migration policy over migrant rights – for instance, the right to a family life (Kastoryano 2006; Guiraudon 2006).

Germany, home to one of the largest Muslim communities in Europe, is a somewhat mixed case. On the one hand, since the late 1990s the country's political elite acknowledged that Germany is an immigration country with a diverse social culture, making integration the new buzzword; on the other, the restrictive side to the liberal citizenship law implemented in 2000 led to a decrease in naturalizations (Schiffauer 2006; Green, 2005). Though integration remains the guiding principle of German migration policy, increasing pressures are put on migrants, both as individuals and as communities, to perform better in schools and in professional positions. The extent to which migrants, and in particular Muslim migrants, feel 'German' or even 'European' remains an open question (see also Daniel Faas in this volume, and Faas 2008).

Britain and Sweden are perhaps the only European countries that have not turned away from the ideals and policies of multiculturalism. Although the British government introduced a 'Life in the United Kingdom test' (a civic integration test) and civic ceremonies in an attempt to retrieve cohesion based on an inclusive understanding of Britishness, particularly in the aftermath of the July 2005 London bombings, politicians and political theorists have emphasized the importance of safeguarding multiculturalism rather than abandoning it (see Tariq Modood and Nasar Meer in this volume, and Modood 2007). In Sweden, the approach to cultural and religious diversity is predicated on a strong social welfare system and a political ideology that, though secular, has allowed for Muslims to express their identities on an individual and collective level. In recent years, however, the poor educational and labour market performance of some Muslim groups has led to a reconsideration of this model, with now a greater emphasis on individual responsibility during the integration process in the destination country (see Otterbeck in this volume).

Meanwhile, as traditional immigration countries in northern Europe exhibit deep policy contradictions when confronted with jihadist terrorism and social unrest among immigrant communities, the so-called 'new hosts' like Spain, Italy and Greece are struggling with their new realities as immigrant host countries. The European multiculturalism crisis comes at the same time that these countries are acknowledging their de facto multicultural and multi-ethnic composition. But the perceived failure of the cultural diversity approach adopted by the 'old hosts' discourages multicultural integration policies in southern Europe, and reinforces the view that immigration's economic advantages may only be reaped after immigrants become assimilated into the dominant national culture (Zapata-Barrero 2006; Triandafyllidou 2002; Ambrosini 2004). Although immigrant populations in southern Europe are not predominantly Muslim, the question of religious diversity slowly comes to the fore as these populations settle and the Muslim sectors begin expressing their particular needs and wishes (see chapters by Zapata-Barrero and de Witte, Russo Spena, and Triandafyllidou in this volume).

The question of Muslim integration is also to a certain extent hindered by the European integration process. Old and new member states strive to accept diversity within Europe as well as to define their geopolitical and cultural position within the continuously enlarging EU. National identities are under pressure by the Europeanization process – especially the former communist countries that joined the EU in 2004 and 2007 (Kuus 2004; Triandafyllidou and Spohn 2003). The question of Turkey's accession into the EU has given rise to fervent debates about the Christian (or not) roots of Europe, about the compatibility of a predominantly Muslim, albeit secular, country within the EU, and about the borders of Europe – where does Europe end effectively? In this process of identity negotiation and geopolitical reorganization within the EU, the challenge of Islam comes as one more complexity in the management of diversity in Europe, which, if anything, is less desirable and more alien than intra-European diversity. Although the EU indirectly, and sometimes even directly, supports minority protection and combats discrimination, the overall Europeanization process has certainly not made the integration of Muslims in specific member states any simpler. On the contrary, long-term Muslim residents fully integrated in their country of settlement discover they are sometimes at a disadvantage in EU member states compared with other newcomers who gain European citizenship.

The first decade of the twenty-first century is marked by considerable pessimism, particularly in comparison to the rise of multicultural citizenship ideals and policies in the 1990s, and the then general optimism regarding the accommodation of Muslim claims and needs in European societies. The current onset of a global economic crisis makes the picture particularly gloomy; the perceived competition for scarce job openings occasionally leads to xenophobic and racist incidents against people of Asian or Maghrib origin (people with darker skin). Such incidents seem to have multiplied in southern Europe during the last months.

This book responds to the need for a deeper understanding of the causes of the perceived incompatibility between European liberal democratic societies and their Muslim members. We argue that in order better to understand Muslim minority and native non-Muslim majority claims and needs, we have to look at both structural and cultural factors within each group. We need to look beyond religious affinity to the national, cultural and socio-economic features of different Muslim communities across Europe as well as their contexts of settlement in their current countries of residence. Furthermore, the book argues that in order to understand Muslim minority–native majority interaction we need to investigate the discursive processes that organize their relations and positively or negatively highlight commonality and difference.

The following section introduces the conceptual background to the country studies that follow. In particular, the notions of tolerance, pluralism, multiculturalism and integration are discussed. The third section presents the structural and cultural factors to be considered, while section four attempts to offer an overview of European Muslim populations. Section five presents the contents of this volume and explains how they are organized.

2. Secularism, tolerance and multiculturalism

The special aim of this book is to highlight, explore and assess the intertwining of cultural and structural factors in Muslim minority and native non-Muslim majority claims and needs that are often framed by media and political discourses as incompatible. In this section of the book we shall discuss briefly the main concepts on which the book rests, including the notion of minority (native or immigrant), the intertwining of ethnicity and religion as regards Muslim minority definition in Europe today, the concept of integration, and the ideas of secularism and religious pluralism. This section also proposes a conceptual–theoretical continuum along which we can place different views on how to organize Muslim minority and non-Muslim majority interaction today in Europe.

Studies in this volume are concerned with both native and immigrant Muslim populations residing in Europe. A distinction between ethnic minorities and migrant populations is generally useful in the study of ethnic politics as usually these two different types of minorities enjoy different sets of rights. Native minorities are defined as populations that historically have been established in a given territory and which have taken part in the formation of the (national or multinational) state in which they live. Usually their participation in state-building is recognized in the legal constitution and they are guaranteed special rights regarding the preservation of their cultural, religious or linguistic heritage. In some countries, there are special provisions regarding the political representation of a native minority in cases where that minority is so numerically small that it risks being left out of the political system.

Immigrant populations emerge as a result of international migration. Receiving countries assume different approaches towards these populations, some encouraging not only socio-economic but also political integration of immigrants and their offspring. Other countries have restrictive policies that keep immigrants and sometimes their second-generation offspring in a status of denizenship. Even when the members of a given immigrant group have acquired the citizenship of the country of settlement, collective minority rights do not always follow automatically. In other words, any concerns that immigrant communities may have with regard to the safeguarding of their cultural traditions or language remain ongoing after they obtain citizenship rights and usually have to be negotiated with the country of settlement.

Muslims in Europe tend to fall within this latter category of immigrant communities. Among the countries studied in this volume, Greece is the only country that has a significant *native* Muslim minority. Having said this, it is worth noting that immigrant populations who come from former colonies may be considered as an intermediate category between native minorities and immigrant groups because they have special historical, cultural and political ties with the country of settlement. In fact, in several of the countries studied here, post-colonial migrants (e.g. Commonwealth citizens in Britain, Algerians in France, Surinamese in the Netherlands) have enjoyed in the past and to this day a special status[1] as a recognition of their historical relationship with the country of settlement.

The distinction between native minorities and immigrant populations as well as the intermediate (in terms of rights and recognition) position of post-colonial minorities are pertinent here for understanding national contexts and positions towards Muslim minorities or migrant populations, but they are just one factor among many that shape the interaction between Muslim minorities and non-Muslim majorities in Europe.

The need to distinguish between different categories of Muslim populations (native vs. immigrant) eventually brings us to reflect on the linkage between religion and ethnicity for European Muslims. Indeed, Muslim residents or citizens of European countries are generally registered in national censuses and other statistical surveys in relation to their nationality or ethnicity of origin. This is actually one of the reasons why the number of Muslims residing in any one country is uncertain and can usually only be deduced by reference to nationality or ethnicity rather than religion. This lack of data on religion can be attributed both to the principle, in liberal democracies, that religion is an individual and private matter (and hence should not become the subject matter of state classifications and registers), and to a policy concern that registration of religion might give way to religious discrimination and prejudice rather than serve the populations registered.

Discussing the relationship between ethnicity and religion in general, or with particular reference to Europe's Muslims goes beyond the scope of this chapter. But the perspective this chapter proposes for analysing the situation of Muslims in different European countries makes the assumption that religion, and in particular Islam, has become a politically, culturally and symbolically important dimension of difference that often overshadows ethnicity (see also Erdenir in this volume). As Modood argues (Modood 2007), being a Muslim means having a complex identity which is subtly intertwined with numerous other aspects of an individual's identity. Although the salience of Muslim identity differs in relation to context, it has nonetheless become a significant point of difference that largely conditions the social and political experiences of Muslims both as individuals and as members of groups (Modood 1990, 2005).

This book is concerned with the interaction between Muslim minority populations and non-Muslim majorities. It is thus not a book directly concerned with Muslim 'integration'. Indeed the use of this term has been deliberately avoided in setting the framework for analysing the Muslim situation in different European countries because of the imprecision of the concept. In some countries integration is understood as a two-way process involving both 'hosting' majorities and migrant or native minorities and their respective institutions; in others, integration is understood as assimilation: a one-way process by which minorities must adapt to and eventually adopt the predominant culture and traditions. While integration remains an important subject for policy analysis,[2] the intention of this book is to study the interaction between populations, and the related institutional arrangements, policies and discourses. It seeks to highlight the internal variations of minority and majority populations as well as the intertwining of structural (socio-economic, institutional) and cultural (identity, traditions, religion, ethnicity) factors that organize the relationship between Muslim populations and national majority groups in each country.

The importance of religion in this discussion is that it poses an unavoidable challenge to European secularism, raising the question of whether European societies are truly secular or, indeed, how secular they are. Modood and Kastoryano (2006) point out the varieties of secularism that exist in European societies and show that while all European states may be considered secular to the extent that they distinguish between the public realm of citizens and policies and the private realm of belief and worship, they also adopt different institutional arrangements and different interpretations of how much distance there should be between national and religious institutions, and how religious freedom in many EU countries coexists with dominant national religious culture. Rich analytical discussions on secularism have developed recently (for instance Bader 2007; Levey and Modood 2008), casting light on the dilemmas faced by contemporary liberal democracies in dealing with religious diversity. The case studies presented in this book contribute to our understanding of how secularism exists today in the institutions and policies of various EU countries.

These case studies actually show how general constitutional principles about religious freedom and secularism may take very different practical forms when implemented in various countries. Thus in countries like Greece, the principle of religious freedom is interpreted as a negative freedom – the individual's right to exclude himself from religious ceremonies or pedagogy that take place in public institutions (e.g. schools) – rather than as an individual or collective right to have a minority religion incorporated in school life or in the workplace. By contrast, in countries like Britain, even though the Anglican Church retains some historical privileges, religious minorities are actively accommodated in their collective petitions for the building of religious temples, the accommodation of dietary needs in schools and at work, and provisions for religious education including the establishment of Muslim schools with partial state funding (Meer 2009). In France, on the other hand, the notion of religious freedom is interpreted again at the individual level but, unlike Greece, in an active manner and with more emphasis on the separation between the public and the private realm. Thus, the individual is free to choose his religion and practice it in private, but should not bring religion to the public sphere, for instance in public schools. In other words, the individual has the freedom *not to have* religion imposed upon him and the state has no official religion (in contrast to cases like Greece).

The case studies presented in this volume offer a rich source of material on which to base a consideration of how much and what kind of secularism exists or is necessary for European societies to flourish in their internal diversity. The main finding, however, seems to be that instead of an advanced or indeed absolute secularism, a notion of religious pluralism is probably more helpful, both theoretically and empirically, to make sense of what is going on in European societies. Indeed, the question is not how to accommodate Muslim needs into secular societies by making Muslims fit into a liberal conception of democracy and citizenship. Rather, there is a pressing need to pluralize the relationship between the Church and the State so as to include minority religions. In other words, the question is: what kind of policies and institutional arrangements are needed to respond to the Muslims and other religious minority groups who have not had a significant historical presence in Europe, at a time when secularism is emerging as a corollary of modernity? Rather than a change in social organization or political thought that would put into question modernity, secularism, liberalism and democracy, the best way to tackle novel claims by Muslim communities is to reconsider the nature and limits of the public sphere and how these limits are politically defined. Indeed, the type of cultural or religious difference that makes Muslim life compatible or incompatible is related to our concepts of citizenship (and related behaviours), rather than to some sort of cultural or religious 'essence' of Muslim minority groups. Moreover, citizenship attitudes are framed in actual socio-economic contexts which are part of the diversity discourse and not external to it.

Offering a state-of-the-art review of the social science and political theory literature on cultural and religious diversity and its accommodation does not belong to this chapter. The aim here is more modest but potentially more innovative. I propose a conceptual–theoretical continuum along which different concepts and normative positions can be placed. This continuum of positions is part of a larger conceptual and normative framework predicated on a moderate understanding of liberalism and secularism, as these philosophies have been shaped into concrete socio-political realities in twentieth-century Europe. This continuum ranges from a thin conception of tolerance, at its one pole, to a notion of full-fledged political multiculturalism at its other. I shall attempt below to define the two alternative poles of this continuum with a view to providing for a conceptual space within which one can place the practices and norms adopted in different parts of Europe in response to the challenges of cultural and religious diversity (see also Bader 2007).

One of the first concepts put forward to deal with religious diversity in Europe has been the notion of tolerance. In its basic form, tolerance means to refrain from objecting to something with which one does not agree. It involves that one rejects a belief or a behaviour, that one believes her/his objection to this behaviour or idea is legitimate, and that one decides to tolerate this negative behaviour along with its possible consequences (King 1997: 25). As King argues, tolerance is meaningful when the 'tolerator' has the power to suspend an act but does not exert this power. It can also be seen as a liberty which obtains only when a response that has a genuine negative motivation (to suppress the particular behaviour or action) is voluntarily suspended (King 1997).

The terms tolerance and toleration are used interchangeably to describe contexts where practices or attitudes that are disapproved of are allowed to exist. They also require that discriminatory practices or behaviours towards those who engage in the 'tolerated' practices are prohibited. In other words, tolerance may also be seen as a prohibition of discrimination.

Historically, the development of a body of theory on the subject of toleration began in the sixteenth and seventeenth centuries, in response to the Protestant Reformation and the Wars of Religion. It started as a response to conflict among Christian denominations and the persecution of witchcraft and heresy. In the sixteenth and seventeenth century, writers such as Montaigne (Langer 2005) questioned the morality of religious persecution and offered arguments supporting toleration. In the seventeenth century the concept of toleration was taken up by English thinkers such as John Milton and was further developed in the late seventeenth century by John Locke in his *Letters Concerning Toleration* and in his *Two Treatises on Government* (Kaplan 2007; Mendus 1988). Enlightenment philosophers such as Voltaire in France and Lessing in Germany developed the notion of religious tolerance further, although these ideas did not prevent intolerance and violence in early modern Europe (Zagorin 2005). Tolerance was then understood in reference to religious diversity (the dominant religion's toleration of minority religious groups), while today the concept is applied to all forms of difference including race, ethnicity, religion, sexuality and gender.

Already in the Enlightenment years, a distinction was made between mere toleration (i.e. forbearance and the permission given by adherents of a dominant religion to religious minorities to exist although they are seen as mistaken and harmful) and the higher level concept of religious liberty which involves equality between all religions and the prohibition of discrimination among them (Zagorin 2005). Indeed, this distinction is probably the main weakness or the main strength of the concept of tolerance. Some thinkers see tolerance as primarily a practical consideration, since each society or state has to set the limits of what and who it tolerates and what or who it does not tolerate; tolerance then becomes important as a way to approach issues of diversity and discrimination against minorities (for further discussion see Mendus and Edwards 1987; Mendus 1988; King 1997). Then there are others, such as Galeotti (Galeotti 2002), who propose an advanced concept of toleration that involves not only acceptance and recognition of diversity, but also a combating of negative stereotypes and identities surrounding minority groups.

In contrast, for many political theorists today and in political discourse in general, toleration of something or someone implies a negative view and hence a form of discrimination. Despite the more open and progressive origins of the concept, in current discourse, we 'tolerate' something 'bad' that we do no want to suppress for various reasons, but which we do not consider legitimate. In other words, toleration today is certainly more about 'not objecting' to something rather than about 'embracing' it.

Political scientists who are in favour of an egalitarian, thick concept of tolerance actually usually privilege the notions of pluralism and multiculturalism. Multiculturalism and the notion of multicultural citizenship (Modood, *et al.* 2006) respond to the need for a normative and theoretical perspective for dealing with diversity. Diversity may be defined as value heterogeneity (Rawls 1993), as groups oppressed on the basis of their 'difference' (Young 1990), as historic cultural communities (Taylor 1994) or as indigenous peoples and ethnicities in multi-ethnic states (Kymlicka 1995). It is generally understood that the presence of new, especially non-white, ethnic and religious groups formed by migration alongside native groups, and their quests for tolerance and recognition, is the main constituent of contemporary diversity and is challenging liberalism as well as our pre-existing notions of secularism.

Political multiculturalism is then proposed as a suitable response to the challenge of diversity in Europe today and is seen as forming an alternative pole in our continuum, in contrast to thin notions of tolerance. Tariq Modood (2007) has elaborated to a considerable degree a perspective of political multiculturalism which incorporates notions of equality, liberalism, moderate secularism and a multiple-level understanding of diversity. Modood sees as a constitutive aspect of multiculturalism the idea that the social world is made of individuals as well as groups, and that groups are as 'real' as individuals in terms of their function in the social world. He acknowledges that there are different types of social attributes that form the basis of group identities, notably race, religion and ethnicity, and hence that there are different types of 'diversity' with which a democratic and plural society has to come to terms. Moreover, he notes that not all groups experience their group identity with the same intensity or with reference to the same realms of life. Thus, some minority groups may be more concerned with socio-economic disadvantage and prioritize education and professional advancement, while other groups may concentrate their claims and actions in the cultural and symbolic realm of recognition.

Moreover, Modood notes, members of a group may experience their group identity with varying degrees of intensity and may see it as relevant in different modes and in different realms of their lives. Indeed, while (British) Muslims are often portrayed as a monolithic block of people with a strong religious identity, Modood (2007: 134) notes that:

> For some Muslims – like most Jews in Britain today – being Muslim is a matter of community membership and heritage; for others it is a few simple precepts about self, compassion, justice and the afterlife; for some others it is a worldwide movement armed with a counter-ideology of modernity; and so on. Some Muslims are devout but apolitical; some are political but do not see their politics as being 'Islamic' (indeed, may even be anti-'Islamic'). Some identify more with a nationality of origin, such as Turkish; others with the nationality of settlement and perhaps citizenship, such as French. [...] So it is no more plausible to ascribe a particular politics (religious or otherwise) to all Muslims as it is to all women or members of the working class.

Having said this, Modood, nevertheless, warns against the danger of excessive recognition of individual difference that would lead us to believe that the dominant form of life is a 'hybridic, multiculture, urban melange'. Rather, he points out that the different types and degrees of 'groupness' professed by different minorities in different contexts should alert us to the fact that a multicultural approach to accommodating diversity needs to be flexible enough to offer to each minority a mode of representation and participation in the national whole that is commensurable with its needs and wishes. This political perspective on multiculturalism, offered by Modood (2007), argues for greater recognition of and respect for minority difference, and is closely knit with socio-political realities in modern communities. In other words, while the concepts on which this approach is based remain constant – democratic liberalism, moderate secularism and religious pluralism – its actual applications, in terms of the institutions that it will be expressed through and the practices that it will inform, remain subject to the specificities of each national context and its corresponding minorities.

While Modood's perspective is not shaped by a desire to contrast or discredit notions of toleration, it offers, in my view, the most advanced normative-cum-political approach to the quest for accommodating diversity in contemporary Europe. It is at the opposite pole with respect to notions of 'thin tolerance' because of the emphasis it puts on the collective level, and the need for difference to be recognized and respected, not just as a private individual practice but in the public sphere, as a practice of groups. While Modood's ideas are informed by the British reality and historical experience, they offer a theoretical and political framework that can be applied to the experiences and challenges of most of the countries discussed in this volume.

Following from the above reasoning, I would like to propose two dimensions along which the different national approaches to dealing with Muslim minority demands are organized. The first dimension is *institutional* and refers to the relationship between Church and State. Thus we may classify the different discourses and policies concerning Muslim populations along a dimension of secularism versus religious pluralism. Absolute secularism is exemplified in the pure version of the French Republican tradition while moderate secularism is what can be found today in the Netherlands or Germany. Secularism is based on the view that citizens are equal before the State and that State and Church should be largely separated (even if hardly any country apart from France satisfies this condition). Secularism implies that religious difference can exist in the private sphere and be practised individually but that it cannot be recognized in the public space.

Religious pluralism, rather than doing away with the relationship between Church and State, seeks to pluralize it by incorporating new religions and new religious institutions and bodies in the formal institutions of the State. A relatively advanced version of religious pluralism can be found in Britain where religious groups are integrated in the conception of Britishness and where structures of participation and representation, not only of ethnic but also of religious groups, have emerged. A more moderate religious pluralism, coupled with moderate secularism, is the main approach followed by Swedish policies on Muslims.

The second dimension is *value-related* and relates also to the concept of tolerance and its varieties outlined above. To put it in simple terms: to what extent can the aim of social cohesion be achieved through a political multiculturalism approach of the kind advocated by Tariq Modood which incorporates a thick version of egalitarian tolerance (see Galeotti 2002 for instance)? Or is cultural and religious assimilation necessary for achieving social cohesion, while only a thin notion of liberal tolerance can be directed towards individuals and minority groups whose culture and religion differ from the dominant one? This seems to be the main value argument that cuts across European countries and their dealings with their Muslim populations today.

The case studies presented in this volume can tentatively be classified along these two dimensions for accommodating difference as follows in Table 1.1.

This matrix is tentative and mainly seeks to cast light on the dilemmas, institutional and value-laden, that European countries face today in their effort to accommodate the claims and needs of their Muslim populations.

3. Why structural and cultural factors?

This book adopts an induction-based approach to test and develop new arguments on the realities of Muslim minority and non-Muslim majority interaction. Few studies have addressed in a comparative framework the structural and cultural elements affecting the interaction between national majorities and Muslim immigrant minorities in Europe. Scholars have sought to assess the merits and weaknesses of the social integration models adopted by different countries like Britain, the Netherlands, France or Germany, and at times they have also compared their institutional structures, histories of migration and philosophies of integration, but they have not pursued a two-sided analysis of socio-cultural behaviour (Yazbeck Haddad 2002; Fetzer and Soper 2004; Kastoryano 2002; Maussen 2006; Favell 1998; AlSayyad and Castells 2002).

Continuing and complementing this line of enquiry, this book sets out to explore the structural and cultural parameters that condition the interaction and mutual accommodation made by Muslim minorities and national majorities in a number of European countries. We identify seven factors relating to the country of settlement which affect the interaction processes: (a) the ethno-cultural character of a nation

Table 1.1 Approaches to diversity

	Advanced multiculturalism	*Moderate multiculturalism*	*Moderate (civic) assimilation*	*Advanced (ethno-cultural) assimilation*
	Thick/egalitarian tolerance		*Thin/liberal tolerance*	
Absolute secularism			France	
Moderate secularism	Sweden		Netherlands	
Moderate religious pluralism	Britain		Germany Italy Spain	Greece
Absolute religious pluralism				

state including notions of citizenship as ethnically (*ius sanguinis*) or civically (*ius soli*) defined; (b) the colonial history (or lack of colonial experience) of a given country; (c) the religious component in the national self-concept and the relationship between Church and State in the institutional make-up of the country; (d) the role of historical Muslim minorities in the formation of the nation state and/or the symbolic or actual presence of a Muslim Other in the national self-concept; (e) the European component as part of the national self-understanding; (f) the length of immigrant settlement and experience of living together in each country; (g) social class structures and their entanglements with race, ethnicity and religion.

We also consider a set of factors that characterize the Muslim minority composition in each country, highlighting the internal diversity of Muslim populations in Europe. We look at (a) their nationality or ethnicity, (b) their branch of Islam (Sunni or Shia), (c) their rural or urban origin, (d) their reasons for migration – whether labour, family-related, asylum-seeking or study, and (e) their social class status and socio-economic background.

These two sets of structural factors are complemented by a constructivist approach to the national majority–Muslim minority interactions. We therefore examine the ways in which cultural, religious or ethnic difference is constructed and reproduced in public and political debates. We thus analyse the main arguments and dominant definitions of citizenship, national identity, difference, immigrant integration and multiculturalism with a view to highlighting how the above-mentioned structural features are reconstructed in public discourses to produce national frameworks within which Muslim immigrants and national majorities interact and accept (or reject) one another.

This constructivist perspective also takes into account the power inequality in the interactions between the two communities. It points to how difference and similarity within each community (majority and Muslim minority) and between communities are constructed and interpreted. This book argues that the national-political, socio-historical and institutional context (and the discourses developed therein) can be a dividing or a unifying factor between native non-Muslim majorities and Muslim minorities. We thus set out to explore how these social, institutional and political parameters as well as their discursive (re)construction are intertwined in each of eight European countries under study with a view also to placing each study in a European and comparative perspective and achieving a better understanding of European Muslims and the issues they face in their everyday lives.

4. European Muslims

The Muslim populations that inhabit Europe may be distinguished into two broad categories: native and immigrant. The former settled in the European continent during the expansive movements of the Ottoman and Russian empires, or are native populations that converted to Islam under Ottoman rule. Thus they are mainly found in central, Eastern and south-eastern Europe (including Albania, Bosnia, Bulgaria, Greece, the Former Yugoslav Republic of Macedonia, Romania and Serbia) and in Russia. The number of Muslims who are native to countries of the EU at this point in time remains relatively small, given that most of the south-eastern and Eastern European countries do not yet form part of the European Union.

Immigrant Muslim populations in Europe include economic immigrants or asylum seekers from Turkey, the Maghrib, sub-Saharan Africa and Asia, and have mainly arrived in Europe during the second half of the twentieth century as a result of postwar population movements. They have settled, in the vast majority, in the industrialized and economically developed countries of the European North and West (including Belgium, France, Germany, the Netherlands, Sweden and Denmark). The offspring, however, of these immigrant populations are now considered native to Europe as they are often second or third generation immigrants. We place them, however, in this second 'category' of European Muslims because they did not reside in their current countries of residence when these countries emerged as nation states. Among European Muslims of non-European origin we should include the large number of Muslims who have arrived during the last two

Table 1.2 Muslim populations in European countries

Country	*Estimate of Muslim population (including non-citizens)*	*Source*
Austria	340,000	Weishaider 2004
Belgium	320,000	Hallet 2004
Bulgaria	1 million	Bulgarian National Statistical Bureau 2001
France	5 million	Rohe 2004
Germany	3.8–4.3 million	Faas, this volume
Greece	525,000	Triandafyllidou, this volume
Italy	1 million	Kosic and Triandafyllidou 2007
Netherlands	1.1 million	Ter Wal 2007
Portugal	30,000	Leitao 2004
Romania	70,000	Iordache 2004
Spain	700,000	Gonzalez Enriquez 2007
Sweden	350,000	Otterbeck 2004
Turkey	70 million	U.S. Dept of State 2007
U.K.	1.6 million	Modood and Meer, this volume
Total w/out Turkey	***approx. 16 million***	
Total with Turkey	***approx. 86 million***	

Note: The table has been compiled by the author using a variety of sources and seeking the most recent and, to the extent possible, most accurate estimates.

decades and have settled in southern European countries, notably Italy, Spain and Greece. They originate from the Maghrib, South-East Asia or the Middle East.

European Muslims number approximately 14 million (see also Aluffi and Zincone 2004: vii). The largest Muslim populations are found in France (approximately 5 million), Germany (approximately 3 million), the United Kingdom (approximately 1.6 million), Italy (about 1 million) and the Netherlands (approximately 1.1 million).

Data on religious affiliation are not registered consistently in European countries since religion is considered to be an aspect of citizens' private lives and could become ground for discrimination. Thus in most European countries there are no reliable data on the size of Muslim populations. Table 1.2 has been compiled using the data sources available and comparing between them with a view to presenting an overview of the places of settlement of Muslims in wider Europe. This table suggests a geographical distribution of the two populations along a rough east–west axis. Native Muslims are found only in central and south-east Europe, while immigrant Muslims are concentrated in western and northern Europe. It is only in Bulgaria (1 million approx.), Greece (85,000) and Romania (70,000) where we find native Muslim minorities. And of these three countries, it is only in Greece where Muslims coexist with immigrant Muslim populations. Native Muslim minorities in Bulgaria and Romania enjoy a special status of rights and public recognition and political representation, related to and organized on the basis of their ethnic background (in Bulgaria they are Turks and to a lesser extent Pomak and Roma; in Romania they are Tatars and Turks) rather than their religion. By contrast, in Greece (see Triandafyllidou, Chapter 11 this volume), native Muslims (of Turkish, Pomak or Roma ethnicity) receive state recognition and special rights on the basis of their religious minority identity rather than their ethnicity. The chapters included in this volume, with the exception of that on Greece, deal with European Muslims of immigrant origin. Indeed, it is both the larger size of immigrant Muslim populations and their politically and culturally contested presence that have come to be the focal point of public and political discourses as well as policies for addressing Muslim claims.

5. Contents of this volume

This book is composed of 11 chapters and is organized into three parts. In Part I, Chapter 2 introduces the notions of Islamophobia and Muslimophobia in describing the situation between national majorities and Muslim minorities, while Chapter 3 discusses the proposed institutionalization of Islam in Europe as a way to address contemporary Muslim challenges from within a secular European framework. Part II investigates five host countries with large established Muslim immigrant populations: Britain, France, Germany, the Netherlands and Sweden. Their Muslim populations are largely second-generation immigrants who (with the exception perhaps of Germany) have become naturalized. These countries are also characterized by different migration experiences (post-colonial or 'guest-worker' migration) and national self-definitions (more or less ethnic/civic). This selection of 'old' host countries in Europe covers, to a large extent, the variety of European experiences and models for the accommodation of Muslim claims.

Part III includes two more case studies from countries that have recently become hosts to large Muslim immigrant populations, notably Italy and Spain. These two countries share many common features as regards their migration experience, but differ significantly in their national self-definition and historical relationship with Islam. Last but not least, Greece is included as a unique case of a European country that hosts a significant Muslim immigrant population and also a small historical Muslim community in the north of the country without, however, having yet developed an overall approach towards multiculturalism and Muslim integration.

As stated, Chapter 2, 'Islamophobia qua racial discrimination: Muslimophobia' (Burak Erdenir), explores the problematic relationship between Muslim minorities and national majorities in Europe through the concepts of Islamophobia and Muslimophobia. The chapter begins by making a distinction between these concepts. The first, Islamophobia, is an irrational fear against Islam and the values it stands for. Many in Europe believe that Islam is not compatible with the prevalent values in Europe. However, Europeans are not afraid of Islam as a faith, as such. Islamophobia might represent the age-old prejudice towards Islam; yet, it would be an oversimplification to explain the contemporary hostility towards Muslims roughly through a conflict that dates back to the eleventh century. The term Islamophobia alone would be insufficient since it assumes the dominance of religious discrimination over other forms of discrimination that may be more relevant in many cases.

The term Muslimophobia is introduced to emphasize the societal dimension of the fear. Muslimophobia is defined as distinct from Islamophobia in that it targets Muslims as citizens or residents of European countries rather than Islam as a religion. Muslimophobia is a phenomenon to be located and researched in the streets of major European cities with large immigrant populations. It is an everyday reality but also a social phenomenon. Islamophobia resembles anti-Judaism, while Muslimophobia is akin to anti-Semitism.

In the second part of the chapter, Burak Erdenir elaborates on the concept of Islamophobia as religious discrimination. This section explores the type of opposition Muslims face when expressing their religiosity in the public sphere. Erdenir distinguishes between the reactions of secular liberals and devout Christians to Muslims searching for a public space.

The third part of the chapter discusses Muslimophobia as a type of racial discrimination. Erdenir explains Muslimophobia as a sort of new racism which targets Muslims, based on identity markers like culture, lifestyle and values. Muslimophobia is very similar to anti-Semitism in the sense that both imply prejudice and discrimination towards an outside group. As a form of differentialist racism, Muslimophobia rests on the assumption that the differences between cultures are irreconcilable and therefore that Muslim values cannot adjust to liberal and secular European societies. The presence of Muslimophobia and Islamophobia in the various national cases explored in the second and third parts of this volume suggests that the internal diversity and richness of Muslim communities have become obscured by such generalizing discourses and blanket policies.

In Chapter 3, Sara Silvestri provides an overview of different manners of institutionalizing Islam in various European countries. Although there are differences from country to country, the institutional relationship articulated between religion and the secular State is the product of the age-long interaction between European governments and Christian Churches or sects. The presence of growing Muslim populations carries with it a different historical experience of the relationship between religion and State. Though post-colonial states within Muslim majority societies have attempted to impose control over the religious field in a way that is comparable to their counterparts in Europe, the resilience and reinterpretation of Islamic norms, symbols and institutions have proved that a more complex civilization-scheme is at work in determining the organization and distribution of authority in an Islamic field.

The challenges that Islam poses to the secular nature of European states is therefore a primary problem to be analysed in this chapter. A second issue that lies more deeply is the question of whether European societies are indeed fully secular or whether the challenge of Islam can help explain their only partial secularism, that is, the fact that their secular institutions are the product of a compromise between civilization-specific, 'Euro-Christian' political and religious cultures.

Yet there are internal differences within an Islamic field, due to the different origins of Muslims in Europe and to their diverse positioning vis-à-vis Islamic norms and symbols. There is, on the one hand, radical secularism and strong private commitment to Islamic norms, and on the other the desire that this commitment be made public, which would mean impinging on the post-Christian secular nature of European states and societies. This variation will be explored with examples of the complex and often contradictory ingraining of Muslim traditions in European societies, public spheres and states.

Chapter 4 (Daniel Faas) concentrates on Germany. The main goal of this chapter is to discuss the structural and cultural factors affecting the interaction between the national majority and minority Muslim communities in Germany. Faas begins with a short characterization of the Muslim community in Germany, which is for the most part Turkish. He suggests that many of the 2.6 million Turkish Muslims originate from the economically underdeveloped rural south-east Anatolia region, thus representing the 'traditional Turk' who wears a headscarf, as opposed to the 'Westernized Turk' from cities such as Antalya or Istanbul. Germany has seen a wave of inner-familial disputes between first-generation parents (representing the traditional Turk) and second-generation liberal Turks, mostly girls. In Berlin, six Turkish women were killed by family members between October 2004 and February 2005. These 'honour killings' are indicative of the identity struggle young Turks are facing.

The second part of the chapter focuses on the conditions Muslim migrants have faced in German society. Faas argues that the ethnocentric German concept of citizenship largely excluded 'foreigners' and was only liberalized under the Social Democrat-led Schröder government (1998–2005) which generally loosened Germany's hitherto restrictive approach to multiculturalism by introducing new immigration and anti-discrimination legislation and reforming the country's citizenship legislation. He thus seeks to highlight that integration has become the buzzword in recent political debates. In 2006, for instance, Chancellor Merkel (2005–present) hosted the first so-called integration summit with 86 political and societal representatives to discuss issues of German language-learning, education and job opportunities, and the equality of opportunity. An additional conference on Islam is organized every six months by Interior Minister Schäuble, to focus on the interaction between the national majority and Muslim minorities, and equal opportunity policies.

The third section of the chapter concentrates on some of the problems that minority ethnic communities, and Muslims in particular, still face despite the fact that German society has now recognized its de facto multicultural character. Faas focuses on three issues that, in his view, best highlight the interplay between the structural features of German national self-understandings and the specific features of Germany's Muslim populations. First, that Germany has not succeeded in re-conceptualizing its 'Europeanized national identity' in multicultural and multi-religious terms and still officially employs divisive terms such as 'foreigner' (*Ausländer*) or 'foreign citizen' (*ausländische Mitbürger*). Second, there are some ingrained cultural insensitivities to Muslimo- and Islamophobia (e.g. teachers talking about 'Muslim sauce' and 'non-Muslim sauce'; politicians banning headscarves from schools but not other religious symbols). Third, there is a lack of ethnic statistics and Muslim 'role models', for instance on television and in the classroom.

Chapter 5 (Tariq Modood and Nasar Meer) investigates the case of Britain and its Muslims. Though an established Muslim community has been present in Britain since the nineteenth century, mainly comprised of North African (particularly Yemeni) and East Indian sailors and merchants, the substantial part of the 2 million or so Muslim constituency results from the labour recruitment of postwar migrants who arrived from the former colonies as Citizens of the United Kingdom and Commonwealth (CUKC).

The socio-economic profile of these groups varied on arrival but included those from rural backgrounds with few skills and little education, and who became concentrated in manual labour. The skilled and qualified Indians and East Africans would, meanwhile, come to fare much better than their low-skilled counterparts in the labour market, a pattern later repeated by their children in the education system. Although there is evidence of some social mobility amongst Pakistani and Bangladeshi groups, it remains the case that the largest Muslim groups are currently concentrated in the lowest strata of employment, education and housing, and disproportionately exhibit health problems. It is as yet unclear whether the increasing change in profile and balance between South Asian and other newly arrived groups who are contributing to the Muslim constituency in Britain, such as Middle Eastern, Afghani, Somali, Bosnian and Eastern European immigrants, are affecting this socio-economic profile.

As this chapter will show, what is politically clear is that following the British Muslim mobilizations during the Salman Rushdie affair, which alerted the public mind to the presence of minorities who subscribed to a Muslim identity in the course of public self-identification, British Muslims have with increased confidence tried to navigate British equality agendas historically orientated by vectors like class, race and gender. One of the main difficulties they have faced is that the British approach to minority integration amounts to a form of multiculturalism that is underwritten by an Atlantic-centric racial equality paradigm, which has had to be contested and adapted to include Muslims as a distinctive group.

This approach to minority integration, then, amounts to a multiculturalism that has proceeded by encouraging public bodies to demonstrate that 'racial differences' are not an obstacle to participation in key arenas of British society, by promoting equal access as an example of equality of opportunity. The chapter will consider how several recent examples can demonstrate its strengths and limits compared with the increasing role of EU legal prescriptions on equality and diversity in the domestic context.

The third part of the chapter will show how these contextual factors have been increasingly foreshadowed by the events of 9/11, the accompanying 'War on Terror' and the London bombings. In linking Muslims and Islam to violence and terrorism, these events have placed an enormous strain upon Muslim communities and the equality and diversity agendas through which they have sought inclusion. Yet governmental policy and public discourse have not, on the whole, shifted away from their support and respect for 'difference'. As a result, Britain is currently experiencing a 'rebalancing' rather than a retreat in response to Muslim minority claims-making and the state's historical approach to minority integration.

Turning to another 'old' host country, Jonas Otterbeck (Chapter 6) looks at the Swedish Muslim population, which increased dramatically during the last quarter of the twentieth century. Although we have no exact statistical records for religion in Sweden, the number of individuals with a Muslim background has increased from just a couple of families in the 1950s, to 100,000 in the late 1980s, and reaching some 350,000 in 2007. The majority of Muslims in Sweden have gained admission as refugees or as family members of refugees, with only a small number as labour migrants. In Sweden we find Muslims with a plethora of different backgrounds: Turkey, the Balkans, Eastern Mediterranean, North Africa, East Africa, West Africa, Iran, Iraq, Afghanistan, Pakistan, South-East Asia, central Asia, Finland and the Baltic. There is also an increasing Swedish-born Muslim population since many young Muslims who have migrated to Sweden raise families. Approximately one third of the Muslim population is of school age or younger.

To integrate into another society, economically, socially, politically and culturally, takes time. Also, to evaluate and translate home-country educational credentials and labour-market experience can be a long process. For some of the Muslim groups this integration has gone better than for others. Bosnians are one of the immigrant groups with a high participation in the labour market despite their relatively short time in the country. For immigrants from Iraq, we find strikingly low employment rates.

Religious belonging is one of the central factors for the formation of social relations and communities, even in a strongly secularized Swedish society. To be of a different religion can create barriers and aggravate daily life, and can lead to decreased chances in the housing and labour market. Sometimes religious practices run into legal, social or educational provisions (e.g., religious rules on the slaughter of animals, religious education, school uniform, etc.), causing difficult situations for minorities. At the same time, the adjustment of Swedish society to its demographic changes is still an ongoing process.

The chapter is organized into five parts, the first of which deals with the migration history of Swedish Muslims as a framework for the chapter. It also examines the Islamic geography and Muslim demography (ethnic, national, religious diversity) of Sweden. The second part focuses on the institutional and legal incorporation (or exclusion) of the Muslim population. This is probably especially important in Sweden as the Swedish state often includes sectors perceived in other countries as typical sectors of the civil society. The third discusses the socio-economic situation, focusing, for example, on housing and labour market participation, while the fourth discusses cooperation and conflict involving Muslims. In Sweden we find some regionally influential racist parties promoting a full-scale Islamophobia, and there are examples of harsh liberal, secular leading newspapers but also some sectarian Islamic milieus. Further, we find dynamic, mixed ethnic and religious environments at, for example, upper secondary schools, interfaith cooperation and some interesting vocal Muslim profiles. The fifth part will analyse the situation as presented in the earlier parts.

Thijl Sunier (Chapter 7) analyses the situation in the Netherlands. The Dutch population with an Islamic background is just below one million and is rather mixed, even though Turks and Moroccans make up almost 75 per cent of the total. The remainder come from the former Dutch colonies of Suriname and Indonesia. Recently, the number of refugees with an Islamic background has increased, as in most European countries. The rather mixed composition of the Muslim population has had two major consequences. One is that it took a relatively long time before supranational cooperation between Muslims of various ethnic backgrounds emerged because language appeared to be a major obstacle. The second consequence concerns the representation of Islam in the public sphere. Unlike countries like France and Germany, where Muslims of one particular ethnic background form the majority, in the Netherlands (as in Britain) Islam is not associated with one particular ethno-linguistic group.

Although the majority of the former migrants can be characterized as 'guest workers' and their offspring divided into first, second and third generation, this division is hardly relevant anymore in coming to grips with the organizational landscape and the cultural and religious infrastructure of Muslims in the Netherlands. The influx of refugees and, more importantly, the so-called 'chain migration' and marital patterns have further complicated the migration picture. On the other hand, a rapidly increasing number of people with an Islamic background are now born and raised in the Netherlands, or at least arrived there at an early age. For a growing majority, experiences in the Netherlands are far more relevant than the country of their ancestors. These developments make a simple analysis along ethnic lines increasingly obsolete, or at least inadequate.

With respect to the policies towards Islam and Muslims, there are in the Netherlands two important factors that have long constituted the political agenda, the first being the very explicit integration policies from the early 1980s onwards, and the second the history of institutionalized pillarization. Integration policies have followed a winding trajectory. In the 1980s there was an emphasis on a more collectivist understanding of integration. Migrants were perceived as belonging to certain groups and categories rather than as individuals. This, however, is not to say that the Netherlands adopted any multicultural policy as is often argued. The final goal of these policies has always been assimilation, total absorption into the host society. From the early 1990s the Netherlands adopted a more individual approach to integration coined as *inburgering* (becoming citizen). The legislation based on pillarization has been the basis of the growth of Islamic schools which continues to divide politicians. For the rest, pillarization is mainly a discourse that is invoked on certain occasions.

Since 9/11, the image of Islam has deteriorated dramatically. This has not only resulted in an enormous amount of attention towards fundamentalist tendencies and deviant behaviour among young people, but also in a very strong reiteration of Dutch national heritage and its norms and values. Many of the alleged problems with Muslims are traced back to the 'era of multiculturalism'. In this chapter it will be demonstrated that both multiculturalism and anti-multiculturalism are political myths that serve certain political agendas and constituencies.

Last but not least among the 'old' host countries, France and its Muslims are considered by Valerie Amiraux in Chapter 8. The central objective of this chapter is to assess the impact of structural and cultural factors in the way Muslim citizens and non-Muslim citizens interact with each other in the French context.

France is the European Union member state with the highest number of Muslim residents. Their number is estimated to be more than 6 million, mostly resulting from migration from North African countries (Algeria, Morocco, Tunisia). Yet concerns with Muslims in France have just recently started to relate to colonial history. The first part of this chapter focuses on the complex interweaving of colonial administration of Muslim societies, migration policy and, more recently, the anti-terrorism security measures. It aims at illustrating how these different overlapping frames impact the public space in deliberating about rights, difference and equality when dealing with French Muslims.

The second part of the chapter relates the way Muslims and non-Muslims interact in France, to the change in public policies from an integrationist discourse to an anti-discrimination one. For a while (until the early 1990s), French public policies that dealt with Islam were mostly thought of as relating to migration, having as their ultimate aim the integration of the children of migrants. International events, combined with demographic, social and economic changes, have changed this picture slightly, and opened the relatively hermetic French model of integration to self-criticism: more particularly, to criticism of the archetypical republican model where citizens are considered to be equal political actors independent from any specificities (cultural, ethnic, religious). If the notion of 'integration' was the dominant reference for public policies and social scientists until the end of the 1980s, the concept nowadays is highly contested by many actors, in particular by the main targets of integration policies. However, the discussion is not limited to a national vision of practices but also highlights local variations and a margin of interpretation of national principles (in particular constitutional ones like freedom of conscience and non-discrimination).

In order to illustrate the way that Muslims appear to be challenging national cohesion or 'national identity', the third part of the chapter analyses two sets of events that led to major discussions on the validity of the French republican model of integration: one public controversy (*les affaires du foulard*) and one major episode of social contest with urban violence (*les émeutes de novembre 2005*). If the relevance of Islam in the first case is quite obvious, it is highly disputable in the second. This last part consists of a critical assessment of how the French understand their Republic to be a sufficient guarantee of equality. In particular, by looking at the interaction between Muslims and non-Muslims in the French context, the assumed value of *laïcité* as a principle organizing the peaceful coexistence of various denominations in single-ethnic societies comes into the core of the discussion: what is the place of religion in the secular project of French national identity?

The following three chapters of the book (Chapters 9 to 11) concentrate on the southern European countries that have become hosts of immigrant Muslim populations relatively recently. Chapter 9 (Maurizia Russo Spena) discusses the Italian case and the related model of integration of Muslim immigrants. As Russo Spena argues, the presence in Italy of more than 1 million people of Muslim faith raises new questions concerning models of coexistence, integration, and relations between religious communities and political authorities. On a terrain where migration policies are still uncertain and experimental and where the appearance of a second generation of migrants is a quite recent phenomenon, what becomes at stake is the idea of citizenship itself. This set of variables interacts with the process through which Muslims are coping with the tension between tradition and modernity, between the forms of democracy and the legitimacy of the institutions of the host country, between self-representation and the institutionalized forms of political representation. In question, then, is the search for a new European identity in relation to this 'other'.

The chapter is organized into three parts. The first part provides information about the Muslim presence in Italy by using statistical data and investigations which illustrate the typology of national, regional and self-professed identities of Muslims in Italy. A specific part will be dedicated to the topic of representation. The Islamic Council (Consulta Islamica), a consultative body created by the Interior Ministry, which consists of leaders of Muslim communities in Italy, is discussed as part of the Italian integration model. The second part addresses the delicate relationship between multiculturalism and identity claims, between citizenship rights and community commitments. In particular, it asks whether it is possible to integrate the claims of Muslim communities into a notion of citizenship still tied to the nation state, or whether it is necessary to update legislative and constitutional tools in order to meet their demands. The third part presents a discussion of two specific sets of issues and related controversies: the first is concerned with the display of identity and belonging on a symbolic level, as with the cross and the veil in public spaces; the second addresses more directly the structural tensions related to the Muslim presence in Italy, and more specifically the debates around the 'Value Chart' drafted this year by the Ministry of the Interior, regulating the relationship between Italian institutions and migrants.

Ricard Zapata-Barrero and Nynke de Witte discuss the situation in Spain, with its blurred representations of past and present Moors. Although Spain does not diverge from the European trend of Islamophobia, the way in which Muslims are treated as a problematic group is slightly different. The historical presence of Islam in the Iberian Peninsula for more than eight centuries has made the Moor not just the 'other' against whom national identity was built, but also an 'other' whose return is an ingrained fear. The binary opposition of Hispanic versus Moor is reproduced today through the reality of a visibly increasing presence of Moroccan migrants. It is manifested by xenophobic responses to Moroccan immigrants and the reluctance to make a place for their religion, Islam, in the public sphere. The chapter discusses the problematic encounters between Muslim minorities and Hispanic majorities by exploring two recent conflict zones: one which is general to Europe – the demand for the establishment of mosques; the other particular to Spain – the Festivals of Moors and Christians (*Moros y Cristianos*).

The chapter is organized into four main sections. The first section gives a short introduction to the composition and socio-economic characteristics of the Muslim population in Spain, the majority of whom are Moroccan immigrants, naturalized citizens and their offspring. The second section discusses how the historical bonds between religion, state and nation-building have shaped the institutionalization of Islam in Spain. It is argued that in spite of the institutionalization of extensive legal rights for religious freedom after the transition to democracy, Spanish society has been reluctant to give Muslims de facto public recognition. This reluctance, the authors argue, is based on the historical reconstruction of Maurophobia (phobia of the Moors), which makes it difficult for Hispanic majorities to accept that Muslims have a legitimate place in the public space they have struggled over for centuries. Sections three and four present a (re)construction of two case studies that are exemplary for the conflicts generated between the native Spanish majority and Muslim minorities. In section three, the opposition to the building of mosques in two localities in Catalonia demonstrates that the legal rights of Muslims to establish places of worship are only put in practice when these places are 'invisible'. The reluctance of local authorities to give Muslims a 'visible' place in the city is directly related to the electoral costs of defending Muslims' rights, who as immigrants often do not have voting rights. Section four discusses how the traditional Festivals of *Moros y Cristianos* that celebrate the Christian victory over the Moors in localities like Valencia, Andalusia and Castilla-La Mancha – became censored after the Danish cartoon affair. It demonstrates how the decision of the festival organizers to change the representation of the 'past Moor' is justified by the presence (and fear) of the 'real Moor' that is represented by Moroccan migrants. Both case studies show the difficulty of Spanish majorities to include 'new' Muslim minorities within a cultural identity and space that traditionally has perceived Muslims as 'other'.

The last of the country case chapters concentrates on Greece (Anna Triandafyllidou). Greece currently hosts a large immigrant population (accounting for 1.1 million or approximately 10 per cent of the total population) which includes an important Muslim component. Nonetheless, Greece's Muslim immigrants are in the most part Albanians (over 0.4 million) who are not particularly devout owing to their 50-year experience under a totalitarian communist regime. Other Muslims in Greece include small immigrant communities of Pakistani, Bangladeshi and Egyptian origin. Alongside the Muslim immigrants, there is a numerically small (around 85,000 people) native Muslim community in the north-eastern corner of Greece (western Thrace), mainly of Turkish ethnicity, that enjoys a special status in terms of religious and cultural rights, including the recognition of Sharia law over Greek civil law, by virtue of the International Treaty of Lausanne signed between Greece and Turkey in 1923.

During the past 18 years, Greece has followed two divergent strategies with regard to these two different Muslim populations. Since 1991 there has been a radical change in state politics and policies towards the native Muslim minority, aiming at the socio-economic integration of this minority in its local and regional context, as well as at improving inter-communal relations between local Muslims and Christians in western Thrace. By contrast, Greece has yet to develop a policy for integrating immigrants in general, or Muslim immigrants in particular.

In fact most immigrants in Greece have come from Eastern and central Europe (and to a lesser degree from Africa and Asia) as undocumented workers. During the 1990s and the early 2000s the largest part of this population has settled and through repeated regularization programmes has now largely become legal. This reality has slowly obliged the state institutions as well as public opinion to recognize that Greek society has become de facto multicultural and multi-ethnic. However this has yet to be reflected in policymaking, as immigrant integration measures are very limited, while the predominant approach remains one of assimilation rather than accommodation and acceptance of cultural diversity.

This chapter aims at explaining the interaction between native/immigrant Muslim minorities and the Greek national majority through the analysis of both the cultural and structural factors that organize this interaction. In considering cultural factors, we discuss the ethno-cultural character of the Greek nation state, the role of ethnicity and religion, as well as the idea of Europe in dominant national self-understandings. We look at the role of native and immigrant Muslims as historical or contemporary 'others'. As regards structural factors, institutional issues concerning the separation of Church and State (or their entanglement) are discussed. We also analyse the relevance of EU policies in shaping Greek state policies towards Muslims and the overall framework of immigrant and minority integration policies in the country. Last but not least we take into consideration the national, ethnic, demographic and socio-economic features of the native and immigrant Muslim populations of Greece as a set of both cultural and structural factors that affect their position in Greece.

Notes

1 Including privileged access to citizenship, relative recognition of their position and role in national history, and relative recognition of any historical racism or prejudice they have suffered.

2 See for instance Vertovec and Wessendorf (2005) or Suessmuth and Weidenfeld (2005) for a discussion of cultural, linguistic and religious diversity and integration as a concept and as a policy principle in different EU countries.

References

AlSayyad, N. and Castells, M. (eds) (2002) *Muslim Europe or Euro-Islam: Politics, Culture and Citizenship in the Age of Globalization*, Lanham: Lexington Books.

Aluffi, R. and Zincone, G. (2004) *The Legal Treatment of Islamic Minorities in Europe*, Amsterdam: Peeters Publishers.

Ambrosini, M. (2004) 'Il futuro in mezzo a noi. Le seconde generazioni scaturite dall'immigrazione nella societa italiana dei prossimi anni', in M. Ambrosini and S. Molina (eds) *Seconde Generazioni. Un'introduzione al futuro dell'immigrazione in Italia*, Torino: Fondazione Giovanni Agnelli, pp. 1–54.

Bader, V. (2007) *Secularism or Democracy? Associational Governance of Religious Diversity*, Amsterdam: Amsterdam University Press, IMISCOE.

Bulgarian National Statistical Bureau (2001) 'Census 2001', in G. Lozanova, B. Alexiev, G. Nazarska, E. Troeva-Grigorova and I. Kyurkchieva 'Regions, Minorities and European Integration: A Case Study on Muslim Minorities (Turks and Muslim Bulgarians) in the SCR of Bulgaria', *EUROREG Project Report*. Available online at: www.eliamep.gr/en/european-integration/projects-european-integration/euroreg-projects-european-integration-european-integration/project-reports-case-studies (accessed 17 November 2009).

European Monitoring Centre on Racism and Xenophobia (2006a) 'Muslims in the European Union: Discrimination and Islamophobia'. Available online at: http://eumc.europa.eu/eumc/material/pub/muslim/Manifestations_EN.pdf.

European Monitoring Centre on Racism and Xenophobia (2006b) 'Perceptions of Discrimination and Islamophobia: Voices from Members of Muslim Communities in the European Union'. Available online at: http://eumc.europa.eu/eumc/material/pub/muslim/ Perceptions_EN.pdf (accessed 16 November 2009).

Faas, D. (2008) 'Constructing Identities: The Ethno-national and Nationalistic Identities of White and Turkish Students in two English Secondary Schools', *British Journal of Sociology of Education*, 29 (1): 37–48.

Favell, A. (1998) *Philosophies of Integration: Immigration and the Idea of Citizenship in France and Britain*, Basingstoke: Macmillan in association with the Centre for Research in Ethnic Relations, University of Warwick.

Fetzer, J. and Soper, C. (2004) *Muslims and the State in Britain, France and Germany*, Cambridge: Cambridge University Press.

Galeotti, A. (2002) *Toleration as Recognition*, Cambridge: Cambridge University Press.

Green, Simon (2005) 'Between Ideology and Pragmatism: The Politics of Dual Nationality in Germany', *International Migration Review*, 39 (4): 921–52.

Guiraudon, V. (2006) 'Different Nation, Same Nationhood: The Challenge of Immigrant Policy', in Pepper D. Culpepper, Peter Hall and Bruno Palier (eds) *Changing France: The Politics that Markets Make*. Basingstoke: Palgrave Macmillan, pp. 129–49.

Kaplan, B. J. (2007) *Divided by Faith: Religious Conflict and the Practice of Toleration in Early Modern Europe*, Cambridge, MA: Belknap Press of Harvard University Press.

Kastoryano, R. (2002) *States and Immigrants in France and Germany*, Princeton, NJ: Princeton University Press.

Kastoryano, R. (2006) 'French Secularism and Islam: France's Headscarf Affair', in T. Modood, A. Triandafyllidou and R. Zapata Barrero (eds), *Multiculturalism, Muslims and Citizenship: A European Approach*, London: Routledge, pp. 57–70.

King, P. (1997) *Toleration*, London: Routledge.

Kuus, M. (2004) 'Europe's Eastern Expansion and the Re-inscription of Otherness in East Central Europe', *Progress in Human Geography*, 28 (4): 472–89.

Kymlicka, W. (1995) *Multicultural Citizenship*, Oxford: Oxford University Press.

Langer, U. (2005) (ed) *The Cambridge companion to Montaigne*, Cambridge: Cambridge University Press.

Levey, G. and Modood, T. (eds) (2008) *Secularism, Religion and Multicultural Citizenship*, Cambridge: Cambridge University Press.

Maussen, M. (2006) *The Governance of Islam in Western Europe*. A State of the Art Report, IMISCOE Working Paper, No. 16. Available online at: http://www.imiscoe.org/publications/workingpapers/documents/GoverannceofIslam-stateoftheart_000.pdf (accessed 10 June 2009).

Mendus, S. (ed.) (1988) *Justifying Toleration: Conceptual and Historical Perspectives*, New York: Cambridge University Press.

Mendus, S. and Edwards, D. (eds) (1987) *On Toleration*, Oxford: Clarendon Press.

Modood, T. (1990) 'British Asian Muslims and the Rushdie Affair', *The Political Quarterly*, 61: 143–60.

Modood, T. (2005) *Multicultural Politics: Racism, Ethnicity and Muslims in Britain*, Edinburgh: University of Minnesota Press and University of Edinburgh Press.

Modood, T. (2007) *Multiculturalism: A Public Policy Idea*, London: Polity Press.

Modood, T. and Kastoryano, R. (2006) 'Secularism and the Accommodation of Muslims in Europe', in T. Modood, A. Triandafyllidou and R. Zapata Barrero (eds), *Multiculturalism, Muslims and Citizenship, A European Approach*, London: Routledge, pp. 162–78.

Modood, T., Dhami, R. and Squires, J. (2006) *Developing Positive Action Policies: Learning from the Experiences of Europe and North America*, London: Department of Works and Pensions.

Rawls, J. (1993) *Political Liberalism*, Oxford: Oxford University Press.

Schiffauer, W. (2006) 'Enemies within the Gates – The Debate about the Citizenship of Muslims in Germany', in T. Modood, A. Triandafyllidou and R. Zapata-Barrero (eds), *Multiculturalism, Muslims and Citizenship: A European Approach*, London: Routledge, pp. 94–116.

Suessmuth, R. and Weidenfeld, W. (eds) (2005) *Managing Integration: The European Union's Responsibilities towards Immigrants*, Washington DC: MPI and the Bertelsmann Foundation.

Taylor, C. (1994) 'Multiculturalism and "The Politics of Recognition"', in A. Gutmann (ed.) *Multiculturalism: Examining The Politics of Recognition*, Princeton: Princeton University Press.

Ter Wal, J. (2007) 'The Netherlands', in A. Triandafyllidou and R. Gropas (eds), *European Immigration: A Sourcebook*, Ashgate: Aldershot, pp. 249–63.

Triandafyllidou, A. (2002) 'Religious Diversity and Multiculturalism in Southern Europe: The Italian Mosque Debate'. Available online at: http://www.socresonline.org.uk/7/1/triandafyllidou.html

Triandafyllidou, A. and Spohn, W. (2003) 'Introduction', in W. Spohn and A. Triandafyllidou (eds), *Europeanization, National Identities and Migration*. London: Routledge, pp. 1–18

US Department of State (2007) *International Religious Freedom Report, Turkey*, US Department of State. Available online at: www.state.gov/g/drl/rls/irf/2007/90204.htm (accessed 17 November 2009).

Vasta, Ellie (2007) 'From Ethnic Minorities to Ethnic Majority Policy? Multiculturalism and the Shift to Assimilationism in the Netherlands', *Ethnic and Racial Studies*, 30 (5): 713–41.

Vertovec, S. and Wessendorf, S. (2005) *Migration, Cultural, Religious and Linguistic Diversity in Europe: An Overview of Issues and Trends*, IMISCOE Cluster B6, State of the Art Report, Oxford, UK: COMPAS. Available online at: www.imiscoe.org/publications/workingpapers/documents/migration_diversity.pdf (accessed 20 December 2008).

Yazbeck Haddad, Y. (ed.) (2002) *Muslims in the West: From Sojourners to Citizens*, Oxford: Oxford University Press.

Young, I. M. (1990) *Justice and the Politics of Difference*, Princeton: Princeton University Press.

Zagorin, P. (2005) *How the Idea of Religious Toleration Came to the West*, Princeton: Princeton University Press.

Zapata-Barrero, R. (2006) 'The Muslim Community and Spanish Tradition: Maurophobia as a Fact, and Impartiality as a Desideratum', in T. Modood, A. Triandafyllidou and R. Zapata-Barrero (eds) *Multiculturalism, Muslims and Citizenship: A European Approach*, London: Routledge, pp. 143–61.

2 Islamophobia qua racial discrimination

Muslimophobia

Burak Erdenir

Introduction

Muslims have been present in Europe since the emergence of Islam itself, in the seventh century CE. There were three main waves of Islam into Europe, starting with the Moorish civilization in Iberia, followed by Muslim Tatars in the northern Slav regions, and then the Ottomans, who moved into the heart of the old continent until the beginning of the twentieth century. Europeans and Muslims also encountered each other as a result of the Crusades and European colonization efforts. Muslim immigrants of the twentieth century represent the fourth Muslim tide into Europe.

In the post-World War II era, Muslims came to Europe mainly as migrants from former colonies and guest workers from less developed countries. In the following decades many more Muslims entered Europe as refugees as a consequence of international wars, civil wars or civil unrest in their homelands. The expanding population of migrants, workers and asylum seekers emerged as a political and social problem in Europe, reinforcing already growing anti-Muslim sentiments. These newcomers were either perceived as temporary visitors or they were avoided; they were hardly ever accepted as a permanent feature of European societies. They were also confined to the margins of society and the ghettos of cities where they had limited contact with the majority.

Europeans started to discover Muslims through events that had an international impact, such as the Iranian Revolution, the Salman Rushdie affair in the United Kingdom, the headscarf affair in France, the 9/11 attacks, subsequent terrorist attacks in Madrid and London, the Danish cartoons crisis, and so forth. Through these developments the passive image of Muslims transformed into one that was aggressive.

This chapter explores the problematic relationship between Muslim minorities and national majorities in Europe through the concepts of Islamophobia and Muslimophobia. Perceptions by host societies of Muslim immigrants, which have not been free of fears and prejudices, have played a significant role in this problematic interaction. In this chapter, I aim to explain the main driving force behind the anti-Muslim sentiments by distinguishing between the concepts of Islamophobia and Muslimophobia. I begin by making a clarification in terminology. In the second part of the chapter I elaborate on the concept of Islamophobia as religious discrimination and question the role of secularism and religiosity in the reaction against Muslims. The final part of the chapter focuses on the concept of Muslimophobia so as to emphasize the societal dimension of the fear. After all, national majorities have an aversion to those Muslims who have not been able socially and culturally to integrate in the host societies. It is also a fact that the limited contact between Muslim minorities and Europeans resulted in a relationship dominated by ignorance and avoidance. I focus on the significance of Muslims' different identity markers and unfamiliar traditions in boosting anti-Muslim sentiments.

A question of terminology

Because the relationship between Islam and the West has been historically one of confrontation and conflict, it remains to be shaped by mutual hostility, stereotyping, and ignorance. According to the British historian Norman Daniel, little has changed since the eleventh century: "The earliest Christian reactions to Islam were something like those of much more recent date. The tradition has been continuous and alive" (Daniel 1980:1). The term Islamophobia was coined to define this age-old, though growing, hostility against Islam and Muslims. Although it was first used by the Orientalist Etienne Dinet in 1922, the term became much more prevalent in the 1990s, especially after its use in the much cited report "Islamophobia: A Challenge for Us All" by a British NGO, the Runnymede Trust (Cesari 2006: 5). Islamophobia could simply be defined as a "modern epidemic of an age-old prejudice towards and fear of Islam" (Sheridan and Gillett 2005: 192). However, there is no consensus on the scope and content of the term and its relationship with concepts such as racism, xenophobia, anti-Islamism, and anti-Muslimism.

Islamophobia might represent the age-old prejudice toward Islam; yet it would be an oversimplification to explain the contemporary hostility toward Muslims entirely through a conflict that dates back to the eleventh century. The Tatar Muslims' invasion of parts of Europe in the thirteenth century does not mean much for Europeans today. Even the much-debated Turkish domination of centuries does not help elucidate contemporary issues. The prejudice toward Islam might be embedded in the collective psyche of some European societies; but the present-day anti-Muslim sentiments are much more contingent. The clash between the West and Islam today is not the product of eternal religious factors; rather, it is fuelled and shaped by a myriad of contemporary issues, though voiced through a religious discourse. Issues of exclusion, segregation, prejudice, xenophobic violence, failed integration, and discrimination are not based on religious issues per se. The problematic situation Muslims face with regard to religious education, dietary laws, clothing, and observance of religious ceremonies seems to be related to their religion, but they are, in reality, social issues that end up having implications in a secular system. In other words, the clash is not between civilizations as Huntington had claimed, but more between lifestyles. The aim should be to figure out the real and material causes at the root of the conflict.

In fact, Europeans are not afraid of Islam as a faith. Their fears do not stem from any discussion based on the Qur'an, Sunna (words and living example of Prophet Muhammad), fiqh (Islamic jurisprudence), or Sharia (law derived from revelation and the example of the Prophet). The conflict is not over the accommodation of Sharia law in their respective national constitutions. For instance, the controversial issue of the status of women in Islam is less related to Islamic law than to cultural traditions. The vast majority of Europeans could not possibly know that the much-pronounced Sharia law is a modern creation and hence varies with different interpretations based on different readings of the Qur'an. Since there is no threat or pressure on the Europeans to be converted to Islam, the discussions do not question the prophethood of Muhammad, or the revelation of the Qur'an.

The phobia in European societies emanates in part from a fear of rising fundamentalist political movements in the Islamic world. The fundamentalists, in return, justify their actions by invoking Islam. Yet in reality the basis of their actions is not an eternal Islamic code. The driving force is rather the reality of their underprivileged societies at home or marginalized communities in Europe, be it socioeconomic inequality, repression by the political structure, post-colonial issues, racial/religious discrimination, or international conflict.

Islam might be disagreeable in a secular Europe where people do not have sympathy for those who openly assert their faith in the public sphere. However, anti-Muslim sentiments are rarely expressed through a purely religious dimension and Islam is hardly ever the only force at work. It would be misleading to identify Islam as the cause of the phobia and therefore the term "Islamophobia" alone would be insufficient since it assumes the dominance of religious discrimination over other forms of discrimination that may in many cases be more relevant. The fear emanates less from a resurgence of theological conflicts than from a secular and modern form of anti-Muslim sentiment.

While acknowledging the risk of concept-redundancy, the term "Muslimophobia" is needed as a way to emphasize the societal dimension of the fear accompanying Islamophobia, which the latter attributes to part of a trans-historical clash between Islam and Christianity. Islamophobia resembles anti-Judaism while Muslimophobia resembles anti-Semitism (Modood and Werbner 1997: 4). Even though there is fluidity between the two concepts, Muslimophobia is distinct from Islamophobia in the sense that the former targets Muslims as citizens or residents of European countries rather than Islam as a religion. In mainstream politics and media it is not Islam but the Muslims who are in the spotlight. The fear in Europe, in fact, emerges as a group prejudice against Muslims, or even those who are perceived as Muslims as in the case of attacks against Sikhs and Syrian Orthodox Bishops following the 9/11 attacks (Allen and Nielsen 2002). Muslimophobia is a sort of "new racism" which targets cultures, lifestyles and physical appearances of Muslims. It is a phenomenon to be located and researched in the streets of major European cities with large immigrant populations. The subsequent chapters of this book scrutinize the challenges Muslim communities face in a selection of European countries.

Studies confirm the view that in a secularized Europe religious elements do not play a prominent role in anti-Muslim sentiments. According to Richardson's study on the representations of Islam in the British press, none of the main themes were directly related to Islam as a faith (Richardson 2004: 69–93).[1] Field's analysis on opinion polls shows that anti-Muslim prejudice in Britain emanates from integration issues rather than any religious concern per se (Field 2007). Strabac and Listhaug report that both in West and East European countries the individual and contextual mechanisms and sources of anti-Muslim prejudice are similar to those of anti-immigrant prejudice in general and thus religious factors are not at play (Strabac and Listhaug 2008).[2]

The term Muslimophobia focuses on the real, material, and contingent causes of the reaction against Muslims; it explores to what extent the prejudice emanates from socioeconomic issues, power relations, political issues, international conflicts, etc. Yet it does not leave out the historical legacies that keep on shaping prejudices against Muslims and Islam in the contemporary setting. The "Muslim-" prefix stands for those contemporary reactions against Muslims, while the "-phobia" suffix takes account of the imagined, non-historical, essentialist, and irrational fears against Muslim populations.

The "-phobia" suffix of the term has created controversy among scholars (Halliday 1999; Cesari 2006; Mausen 2006) Instead of Islamophobia, Halliday prefers anti-Muslimism, while Maussen suggests anti-Muslim sentiments. According to the Merriam Webster dictionary, phobia is "an exaggerated, usually inexplicable and illogical fear of a particular object, class of objects, or situation." Islamophobia or Muslimophobia are part of an unconscious and irrational fear resulting from the presence of Islam/Muslims. They are irrational because the fear is an exaggeration of the real threat. From a psychiatric point of view, phobias are individual pathologies. Islamophobia and Muslimophobia are, however, coined as sociological terms similar to xenophobia and homophobia.

One of the most pronounced objections against such a concept is that it hampers democratic debate by creating a criticism-free zone for Islam and Muslims. Anyone criticizing the principles of Islam and acts of Muslims would be accused of being a Muslim/Islamophobe. It is essential to distinguish between academic discussions of Muslims and Islam, as opposed to discriminatory statements, prejudicial beliefs, and forms of hate speech. A point of view cannot be accused of being Muslim/Islamophobic just because it criticizes Islam or Muslims. However, even though freedom of expression in Europe is theoretically absolute, it is so only until it is shaped by its context. Every European democracy has legislation on incitement to racial/religious hatred, defamation, and blasphemy that limits the possibilities for exercising that right. Otherwise, under conditions of free speech, people have the right to criticize Islam and Muslims. The terms Islamophobia and Muslimophobia do not target legitimate criticisms such as the denouncement of human rights violations in certain Islamic countries. They are used to cover any ungrounded fear and prejudice against Muslims, their faith, and practices.

According to Maussen, since the term derives from a fear or phobia, it treats those who have Muslim/Islamophobic discourses and ideas as victims of a "mental illness" (a phobia) who should "either be cured of their 'illusions' and 'prejudices', or … should be punished for maintaining discourses which have already been 'unmasked' as false and demeaning" (Maussen 2006: 102). However, provided that we define Muslimophobia and Islamophobia as irrational fears, and as long as prejudice emanates from fear and perceptions of threat, the negative sentiment against Muslims which contains prejudice and anxiety should qualify as a phobia. The British police officer who says "he would certainly kill an innocent Asian if he was sure he would not be found out" portrays the symptoms of a pathological mind (Modood 2005: 13).[3] The officer's hatred derives from a fear, be it a fear that the "Pakis" (a derogatory term used to refer to Pakistanis) are spoiling the purity of English culture or a fear that they would take over the country. Islamophobia or Muslimophobia might not be phobias proven by psychological research or recognized by psychiatrists; nevertheless they are useful metaphors to denote the gravity of the situation.

Islamophobia qua religious discrimination

Secularization theories suggest that the complicated interaction of modernization, urbanization, industrialization, and rationalization processes has weakened the influence of religious institutions, resulting in a decline of religious values and practices in societies. Unsurprisingly, secularization started first in the most advanced industrial countries.[4] European societies experienced a decline in religious values, practices, and beliefs in the second half of the twentieth century. The steady decline in religious participation and belief in Western Europe since the 1960s is documented in the declining levels of church attendance and church membership (Norris and Inglehart 2004: 86).[5]

On the other hand, the decline in religious participation across the whole continent does not necessarily mean that Europeans have abandoned their religious beliefs completely. According to Davie, Europeans are in fact "believing without belonging" (Davie 2000: 3). As churches lose their importance, people who are in search of the meaning of life, practice their religion through an individualized spirituality in the private sphere. There might be a decline in the adherence to religious institutions but new beliefs such as the New Age spirituality are emerging in Europe. Secularization in essence stands for the differentiation between religious and secular institutions, and the declining impact of religious institutions at the societal level. Psychological secularization, which implies the differentiation of these two realms at the mental level, is as important. "Compartmentalization can be thought of as the psychological parallel to macro-level differentiation between religion and the secular" (Halman and Pettersson 2006: 34). In other words, as people differentiate their religious orientations from views on social issues, religion becomes more and more a private matter.

Meanwhile, religiosity remains the main identity marker among Muslim immigrants in a somehow secularized Europe. According to Norris and Inglehart's "existential security axiom," one of the sources of religiosity is the need for a sense of security and certainty. People who feel at risk for themselves, their families, and societies, search for religious assurance and become more religious than those who live in a safe and secure environment (Norris and Inglehart 2004: 13). Those who are not covered by the social security net, as well as minorities and the elderly, tend to retain their religiosity. This is a significant point in explaining the high level of religiosity among Muslim immigrants in a secularized Europe. Muslim immigrants are far worse off than any other group, particularly in employment, education, and housing opportunities. Unemployment rates among Muslims are almost twice as high as those of non-Muslims. Among all other religious groups, Muslims are the poorest. Since first-generation immigrants came to Europe primarily for economic reasons, their concern was to find a job and survive. Under such socioeconomic conditions it is inevitable that Muslims would search for religious assurance.[6]

Against such a background, the nature of opposition that Muslims face during their search for public space in European countries appears as "an uneven three-cornered contest between a secular hegemony; a Christianity which, albeit in a diluted way, still gives to most people their understanding of divinity and moral conduct, yet is fading as an organized religion" and Islam which has been seeking accommodation in the European sociopolitical landscape for decades (Modood 1994: 72).

As a consequence of the challenges between opposing forces, Muslims face a two-sided reaction for expressing their religiosity in the public sphere: on one side, a secular-liberal opposition for seeking openly to pursue spirituality and religious practices in twenty-first-century Europe, while on the other, the antagonism of Christians over theological and philosophical principles.

For liberals, the Muslim identity of immigrants became more disturbing at a time when religion was privatized and individualized. Growing numbers of Europeans who separate their private religious views from their opinions on social issues, perceive this as a prerequisite of a democratic liberal system and expect Muslims to internalize this type of compartmentalization. Besides, secularism in Europe is not only a lifestyle but also a political matter. Religion has been perceived as a problematic topic for its alleged compatibility problems with modern and liberal values and institutions. After all, for centuries Europe suffered much from religious clashes and eventually surpassed them by clarifying the boundaries between public and private spheres with regard to the practice of religion. The contemporary intrusion of Islam into the public realm would be the dissolution of the political system. Demands of Muslims on a variety of topics such as places for worship, properly slaughtered (halal) meat, Islamic instruction in state schools, the wearing of a headscarf, religious holidays, etc., challenge the system. Therefore, Muslims should not ask for privileges for representation and resources. Religion in general and Islam in particular "should be kept at home, in the private sphere" (Toynbee 2001).

Nevertheless, a value-free secularism does not exist in any of the European countries, including France where the Republic is called the Enlightenment Church. European societies, though secular to varying degrees, still hold deeply embedded religious elements which have an enduring effect on contemporary cultural values. The entire cultural heritage of a country, including its religious traditions, is reflected in the value orientation and institutions of that society. Cultural change on a wide array of value orientations, including family, marriage, gender relations, tolerance for differences, and professional life, is path-dependent. In any society the dominant religious traditions are transmitted to the next generations through forms of cultural socialization such as mass media and the education system, even for those who are devout secularists or who belong to minority religions. Even in Protestant countries where religiosity is at very low levels, the embedded religious elements have an enduring effect on the worldviews and cultural values. The much-cited words of an Estonian who explains the difference between the worldviews of Estonians and Russians through society's religious background reveals this fact remarkably: "We are all atheists; but I am a Lutheran atheist, and they are Orthodox atheists" (Norris and Inglehart 2004: 17). Accordingly, the Christian values embedded in the identity of European societies enjoy default recognition. Even though many secular/liberal Europeans may not be aware of this Christian heritage—which some take for granted in their daily routine—Europe's Christian legacy has its mark on the continent's values, institutions, practices, public discourse, and even public holidays. Many European countries have established Catholic and Protestant Churches. Furthermore, in the post-World War II era, Jews were incorporated as fellow citizens and the Christian civilization transformed into Judeo-Christian civilization. Jewish religious institutions and values became a part of the existing framework and discourse. Many European states granted privileges to Christianity and Judaism in a number of ways, from public funding of schools to varying degrees of tax exemption. Yet they have been reluctant to accommodate Islam with similar institutional arrangements. As a result, the boundary remains quite stable against Islam, something which becomes clearer in times of confrontation.

The permanence of Judeo-Christian discourse, values, and institutions verifies that a strict ideological secularism does not exist in Europe. As Parekh points out, "contrary to what liberals imagine, [European] public life does not and cannot rest on a uniform view of public reason" (Parekh 2006: 189). Berger goes further by questioning the secularization process: "Modernity is not necessarily secularizing; it is necessarily *pluralizing*" (Berger 2008: 23). Indeed, what we see in Europe is, rather, a pluralism that is able to accommodate different worldviews and values including those of secular/liberal, Judeo-Christian, other faith and non-faith communities at the same time. This is promising since it is a reminder that Europe has the cultural background and social mechanisms essential to extend recognition and accommodation to Muslims unless they bring unreasonable demands to this already established secularized Christian system.

Coming to the other corner of the contest, the clash between two divine religions (Christian and Muslim) has been a very controversial issue. The objective here should be to identify the anti-Muslim prejudice of devout Christians as stemming from faith-related issues. Grand narratives entangled with historical myths and theological fantasies have, for a very long time, watered down reasonable discourse on this issue. Narratives such as "Crusades," "Jihad," "Clash of Civilizations," "Islam vs. West", do not explain the divergence between the doctrines of the two faiths and the consequent implications of this divergence. They are, rather, the fabrication of a juxtaposed Islam and West through a timeless antagonism. Moreover, such rhetoric cannot justify the underlying reasons for anti-Muslim prejudice on the part of Christians in contemporary Europe.

Earlier reactions of Christians toward Islam based on biblical exegesis contained disputes over Muhammad's claim for prophecy and the nature of the revelation, condemnation of Islam's denial of the Trinity, and criticism of the Islamic understanding of Heaven, among other things. Yet until the twelfth century, the European Latin Christendom was almost entirely ignorant about the Islamic doctrine. Theologians classify 24 different misconceptions about Islam (Southern 1962: 14). After the first series of contacts between the two religions, the ignorance had transformed into an imaginative creativity based on myths about Islam. As a result of deformation of religious notions, a "religious mythical view of Islam" emerged almost entirely in contrast with Islamic teaching (Waardenburg 1998: 12). Western images of Islam contained imaginative fabrications "such as the legend that Muhammad trained a dove to peck grain from his ear while pretending to receive revelations from it" (Zebir 2000: 25). Muhammad was depicted as a "liar," "impostor", and even a "magician," Muslims as "heretics," and Islam as a "Christian heresy." Needless to say, the anti-Islam discourse has had a political–ideological backdrop which served for the creation of a conservative European/Christian identity against the Muslim "other." Christendom and Islam were two distinct religious systems, but more importantly they represented two different societies that were each, in turn, viewed as the "other." With its expanding military power, Islamic faith was the strongest oppositional force for Europeans. In short, Muslims were "heretics" but not purely for theological reasons.

On the other hand, Christianity, which was born out of Judaism as a separate faith, had doctrinal conflicts with the latter. "The Parting of the Ways" became an antagonism with time—an antagonism based on religious notions. From its very beginning Christian doctrine discriminated against Jews on the grounds of purely religious matters such as the Jewish calumny of Mary and Christ. Christianity determined the social inferiority of Jews for being collectively responsible for deicide, the killing of Jesus. This perception remained as part of the official doctrine of the Catholic Church until the Vatican absolved the Jews of deicide in 1965. If today we speak about a dominant Judeo-Christian culture in Europe, with Jewish religious institutions and values spread all over the continent, then we can claim that religious prejudice is no longer a strong social force, although anti-Semitism qua racial discrimination might still be alive. And if the "scapegoats" of Christianity, from pre-Christian to Constantinian Christian age and from the Middle Ages to twentieth-century Europe, can find more than an accommodation and recognition in a secular Europe, there should be prospects for Muslim "heretics" as ignorance for their religion dissolves through increasing dialogue.

Meanwhile, following the Second Vatican Council which abandoned the Catholic Church's traditional exclusivist stance against other religions, interfaith dialogue between Islam and Christianity has flourished. Various Christian and Protestant Churches in Europe have participated in this dialogue. Even though it took slightly longer to change the perceptions of lay Christians, the tension between Islam and Christianity as two faiths has relaxed.

Yet it is a common belief that Christians, by definition, are more prejudiced toward Muslims than seculars are. Unfolding the relationship between religiosity and prejudice, Allport and Kramer back in 1946 concluded that "there is something about religion that makes for prejudice and something that unmakes prejudice" (Scheepers, *et al.* 2002: 242). In other words, the relationship between religious commitment and prejudice is controversial and not necessarily positively associated. For instance, researchers found that Christians who are frequent church-goers tend to be less prejudiced than infrequent to moderately frequent attendees (Scheepers, *et al.* 2002: 244). A survey on ethnic minorities in Britain found that "people who said religion was important to them were much less likely to say that they were prejudiced against ethnic minorities and Muslims" (Modood, *et al.* 1997: 134). Fetzer and Soper's study on the public support for state accommodation of Muslims' religious practices in France, Germany, and Britain suggests that the religious and political divide is not between Christianity and Islam but rather between "culturally conservative" religionists, and "culturally liberal" secularists (Fetzer and Soper 2003: 250).[7] In addition to not holding prejudices toward Muslims, religiously active Christians support government policies for the accommodation of Muslims. In a twenty-first-century Europe, moderate Christians do not blame the Muslim immigrants for being "heretics"; apparently there are many contemporary issues at play.

In short, the challenge that Muslims face during their search for public space in a secularized Europe is dominated less by a clash between two religions than a secular opposition that acts with a reflex of protecting the very basis of the liberal and secular system from an unfamiliar faith that is perceived to be growing in assertiveness and visibility, and demanding recognition and accommodation in the European public sphere.

Islamophobia qua racial discrimination: Muslimophobia

After World War II and with the discrediting of race as a scientific category, the classical definition of racism based on somatic and biological differences lost its validity and the concept of "new racism" emerged in academic and political discourses (Barker 1981; Gilroy 1987). Accordingly, there has been a shift from more traditional markers of race to newer markers of cultures that are recognized as different, incompatible, and inassimilable. The otherness of "the other" is attributed to different norms, standards, customs, values, ethics, upbringing, and forms of socialization.

New racism assumes that religion is not just a private matter but it is rather about belonging by birth to a community. Even though religion is not an innate characteristic like race or sex but something acquired during an individual's lifetime, it came to be perceived by many as an identity gained at birth. Since identity, to a great extent, is about perceptions, the view of the dominant group is determinant and thus one cannot simply disengage from one's faith group by renouncing the religion. That is why, regardless of their private contemplation, people are crudely classified as Hindus or Muslims in India, and Protestants or Catholics in Ireland. Hence, a Muslim in Europe who is not practicing the religion still might be targeted as a Muslim because of that person's alleged connection to the community. This leads to the issue of the racialization of religion.

Religion and cultural traits can be the basis of racialization in the case that a common descent is believed to exist for members of a cultural group. The racial difference is perceived to emerge in religion, tradition, or lifestyle, instead of nature or biology. Modern anti-Semitism is an apparent example of cultural racism. "Jewishness" does not represent a biological category as race, yet through the course of history Jews have been racialized. In the modern era, Jews were excluded and discriminated against, not on the grounds of religious matters but rather because they were perceived as aliens threatening the national identity of European societies with their transnational religious identity. Even those who had converted to Christianity were not fully accepted by Christians since their Jewish identity was perceived as an ethnic/racial identity. Another example would be the massacre of Bosnian Muslims by people who shared the same language and culture. The latter slaughtered innocent Muslims because of their racialized identity that represented an ethnic "other."

Muslims in twenty-first-century Europe are facing a similar racialization. The concept of Muslimophobia is very similar to anti-Semitism in the sense that both stand for prejudice and discrimination against an outside group defined in a combination of religious and ethnic terms.[8] Muslims came to represent an ethno-racial group as a result of being essentialized as a monolithic identity. The belief that they belonged to the transnational, multi-ethnic community *ummah* transformed Muslims into a racial group. Muslims are perceived as an "imagined community" who believe they share a common legacy and future around common values. Brown suggests that "the idea of the *ummah* and that of the nation are remarkably similar" (Brown 2000: 79). As the perceived incompatibility between Europeans and Muslims dominates public discourse, and hostilities against the latter are on the rise, the racialization of Muslims becomes reinforced. Racism, after all, is a social construction based on the subjective perceptions of host society members that may emerge without an objective reality of a different race.

This new form of cultural racism does not emphasize the differences as explicitly as the blatant prejudices of old racism.[9] As Allen puts it, it is more about "the inferences and attitudes of everyday life rather than high-profile and widely publicised violent attacks and infringements" (Allen 2006: 96). It contains a disguised and covert version of old-fashioned prejudice. This subtle prejudice is widespread, particularly among the young, well-educated, and liberal groups who perceive Muslims as a threat to the values and norms of their society but do not express it explicitly because anti-blatancy is an established norm among those groups (Meertens and Pettigrew 1997: 55). For instance, Karakaşoğlu, *et al.* found out that German media does not present any open racism but latent racism appears in a myriad of ways. Muslim families are frequently reported in the press "in a negative context, like an example of failed integration, a criminal deed committed by a migrant or a migrant group, school failures of migrant students etc." (Karakaşoğlu, *et al.* 2006: 156). In the Netherlands, one of the countries where multiculturalism has deep roots, blatant prejudice is not socially acceptable, whereas subtle prejudice happens under cover. The shift in the manifestation of prejudice is accompanied with the change in the group it targets. Pettigrew's studies show that the Dutch have more prejudice against Turks than Surinamers, and the French have more prejudice against North Africans than Asians (Pettigrew 1998: 84). These examples indicate how prejudice is shaped increasingly by cultural rather than racial traits. Even though the racially divergent traits of Surinamers and Asians are supposed to be more pronounced, the Muslim identity of Turks and North Africans provokes a larger amount of prejudice against them. As the non-white minority groups such as African-Caribbeans and Asians become increasingly culturally assimilated in the host societies, the biological-racial discrimination they face is being transferred in the form of cultural racism to other groups such as Arabs, Turks, and non-white Muslims who are perceived to be culturally different (Modood 2005: 38).

Nevertheless, it is still a rather controversial issue whether anti-Muslim sentiments in the contemporary European context represent racial discrimination and whether Muslimophobia qualifies as racism. Wieviorka defines racism through opinions and attitudes embodied in prejudices; and behaviors and practices of discrimination, segregation, and violence (Wieviorka 1995: 37). The manifestation of these attitudes and behaviors appears in a number of studies and reports. To cite a few: in one of its General Policy Recommendations, the Council of Europe's European Commission against Racism and Intolerance reported that Muslim communities are subject to prejudice, which "may manifest itself in different guises, in particular through negative general attitudes but also to varying degrees, through discriminatory acts and through violence and harassment" (ECRI 2000). The European Monitoring Center on Racism and Xenophobia's report *Muslims in the European Union: Discrimination and Islamophobia* provides examples of residential and educational segregation all over the continent (EMCRX 2006). The report concludes that Muslims "experience various levels of discrimination and marginalization in employment, education and housing … In addition, they are vulnerable to manifestations of prejudice and hatred in the form of anything from verbal threats through to physical attacks on people and property." The much-cited report of the Commission on British Muslims and Islamophobia (1997) provides evidence of prejudice, discrimination, exclusion, and violence that Muslims have been facing across European societies. There is more than enough evidence indicating that anti-Muslim sentiments do represent more than a legitimate anxiety against the intrusion of an alien culture. In short, Muslimophobia qualifies as racism with all the characteristics of prejudice, discrimination, segregation, and violence contained in older racism, and with the structural and institutional mechanisms which reproduce that hostility.

As a form of differentialist racism, cultural racism rests on the assumption that the differences between cultures are irreconcilable and the culture of the racialized group is perceived as a threat to the host society. Muslimophobia emerges as a sort of new racism which targets Muslims based on their identity markers like culture, lifestyle, and values. One might question and criticize the principles of Islamic doctrine, let alone Islamic ideology. Islam can also become subject to satire and mockery in a liberal democracy. Yet, even though Islam as a religion or as an ideology may be criticized, the "new racism" emerging in European societies primarily targets Muslims and not their faith. Wieviorka clarifies the nature of this new racism:

> To dislike Islam to the point of violence, for example, is racist, if Muslims themselves are constructed as a natural category, and their behaviour, real or imagined, is presented as informed in some way or another by an essence, by innate attributions or an almost genetic cultural heritage. (Wieviorka 1997: 142)

Muslims are victims of racism just because of their appearance, values, norms, and lifestyle, just as the black people in America were discriminated against because of the color of their skin. This new form of racism may be connected to religion, but to the extent that Muslims are conceived as part of an immutable category based on ethnicity and birth, it is predominantly racial.

In fact, the problem with Muslims has not been their religious character so much as their unfamiliarity to Europeans. Human history has a long record of exaggerated fear over things that are incomprehensible, unknown, or unfamiliar. Strangers provoke fear as they are perceived to have habits and values alien to the dominant group and are therefore avoided, alienated, and segregated as much as possible. Contemporary European perceptions of Muslims, who have been viewed as aliens for decades, have followed a similar psychological and social route. The "other" culture is a menace that cannot exist within the society and should thus exist outside it. Segregated Muslims receive little recognition from the host societies, which is attributable to the unfamiliarity, ignorance, and insensitivity of Europeans for Muslims' concerns. This ignorance and unfamiliarity fueled a kind of hostility, a sort of racism resting on the assumption that Muslims with unfamiliar traditions and alien values do not belong to contemporary Europe. Sivanandan calls this racism, "xenoracism"; it is a type of racism "which cannot tell a settler from an immigrant, an immigrant from an asylum seeker, an asylum seeker from a Muslim, a Muslim from a terrorist" (Sivanandan 2006: 2).

Studies indicate that negative or positive views are strongly associated with the amount of knowledge of Muslims and of direct contact with them. According to contact theory, contact reduces prejudice against foreigners by enhancing knowledge, reducing anxiety and increasing empathy (Pettigrew and Tropp 2008: 922). Surveys conducted in European countries indicate that prolonged and personal contact reduced prejudice against foreigners (Myers 2005: 541). German attitudes toward Turks, Dutch attitudes toward Surinamers and Turks, French attitudes toward North Africans and Asians, and British attitudes toward West Indians and Asians improved as a result of personal contact.[10]

Interestingly, many Europeans are, more often than not, unaware of the biased nature of their attitudes and beliefs. For instance, during the Salman Rushdie affair, Muslims who found the concerned book offensive, said they were as much offended by the fact that no one in Europe seemed to understand the reason why they were offended (Brown 2006: 308). A lack of familiarity and exposure to Muslims aggravates the prejudices, which eventually triggers racism. As Modood points out, "in the European context cultural racism or culturalism directed to a racialized or racially marked group may involve an antipathy to the group because it is perceived to be an alien culture rather than merely an inferior one" (Modood 2005: 11).

The core of alienation is a belief in the incompatibility of Muslims' foreign values with liberal, secular European values. The incompatibility argument focuses particularly on issues of gender equality and sexual liberalization, including polygamy, gender roles, the wearing of headscarves, circumcision, arranged marriages, and homosexuality. In Chapter 4, Daniel Faas refers to the citizenship tests in some federal states of Germany where Muslim applicants are asked controversial questions on gender equality, homosexuality, honor killings, and domestic violence which indicate stereotypical understandings of Muslims. Norris and Inglehart claim that "The central values separating Islam and the West revolve far more centrally around Eros than Demos" (Norris and Inglehart 2004: 134). In particular, the status of women in Islamic culture is a highly controversial issue. Yet again, a prejudiced perception dominates Western views on Muslim women, and this happens through a stereotyped juxtaposition of two cultures, one inherently liberal and one inherently oppressive. Kundnani gives a perfect example of how sexism is associated with Muslims, while its occurrence among white Brits in British society is overlooked:

> [F]or example, the epidemic of domestic violence which infects all sectors of British society, and includes two women every week being killed by their partners, receives less media attention than the problem of "honour killings" carried out by Muslims. It is right that the specific justifications, which Muslim men use to legitimize violence against women is exposed. But this should not be done in such a way that combating violence against Muslim women is seen as fighting against a culture, while combating violence against white women is seen as a fight for rights. (Kundnani 2007: 40)

Religion and culture per se do not explain the presence or absence of democracy, human rights, liberties, etc. Universally recognized and accepted norms and values are not under the monopoly of any culture or society. Women's rights as an extension of human rights are a universal value and thus cannot be claimed by any particular culture. Therefore the belief that the situation of Muslim women can be explained through their religion or culture ignores the structural problems Muslim women face as part of an alienated group in Europe, in everything from education to housing opportunities, from post-colonial issues to power structures. It simply justifies differences through an essentialist cultural perspective which remains from the phenomenon of what Said called "Orientalism." This Orientalist perspective fuels racism towards Muslims on the grounds that they are different, incompatible, and inassimilable because of their particular norms, standards, customs, values, ethics, and forms of socialization.

Conclusion

The natives of twenty-first-century Europe still have a hard time recognizing that Muslims are a permanent feature of European societies. For decades Muslims were perceived as guests who would someday leave the country. They were confined to the margins of society and the ghettos of cities, with limited contact with the majority. Different country cases explored in the second and third part of this book, unveiling Muslimophobia and Islamophobia in Europe, indicate how the diversity and richness of Muslim communities have become obscured by generalizing discourses and blanket policies.

Religion had its role in the alienation and segregation of Muslims; nevertheless, the challenge Muslims face during their search for public space in Europe is dominated less by theological conflicts than by a defensive reflex on the part of secular-liberals to protect their system from a code that is unfamiliar. In other words, Islamophobia qua racial discrimination called "Muslimophobia" is much more dominant than Islamophobia qua religious discrimination. Identifying the real causes of the fear against Muslims is significant in the sense that it will help develop effective and sustainable policies.

From the outset, there is a need for more face-to-face contact, interaction, and dialogue between Muslims and host societies so as to remove prejudice, alienation, and marginalization. The contact thesis, which encourages greater interaction between different communities, has been recommended by anti-racists since the 1970s. However, European societies still lack proper contact based on firsthand experience with Muslims and non-Muslims. This should be the initial step to alleviate Muslimophobia.

At present, the gradual recognition of Muslims and the institutionalization of Islam are happening along with discrimination and hostility. But Europe has the cultural background and social mechanisms which enable the accommodation of different worldviews and values. A number of policies have been designed to accommodate the demands of Muslims in the existing secularized structure of Europe. Even though policies are shaped at the national level in most of the European countries, the visibility and recognition of Muslims is de facto happening at the local level. Muslims increasingly get involved in local and community-based activities, which enhances their contact with the local community and facilitates the dialogue between Islamic leadership and municipal authorities.

Local governments of major European cities have been more adaptive than national governments in accommodating major demands of segregated Muslims. As a result of negotiations with Muslim communities, local governments find pragmatic solutions to controversial issues from the slaughter of animals to the use of the headscarf, from the erection of mosques to burial yards. *The Economist* magazine reports a number of local initiatives, defining them as the "absorptive power of local democracy" where "Muslims and non-Muslims [are] learning to rub along, through the trade-offs of local politics" (December 4, 2008). To cite a few: in the Brussels suburb of Molenbeek, slaughterhouses have been built for the slaughter of animals during the feast of Eid al-Adha; in Leicester, Islamic burial practices are permitted; a number of French and German cities are providing lands for the erection of mosques; the city of Lyons has introduced a meatless menu to be served at primary schools taking into account Muslim students' desires for halal meat; all over Europe, Muslim representation in city councils is growing. In Chapter 5, Modood and Meer touch upon the multicultural education programs at the local level in Britain, describing these local initiatives as "municipal drift."

Nevertheless, the current level of local interaction between Muslims and non-Muslims is not sufficient for a public recognition of Muslims that is free of racism. Muslimophobia can be tackled successfully only if this limited dialogue process is backed by national multiculturalist policies that penetrate into societal perception, public discourse, and the sociopolitical landscape.

Notes

1 The themes include: military threat of Muslim countries; threat of political violence and extremism; threat to democracy posed by authoritarian Muslim political leaders and parties; and social threat of Muslim gender inequality.

2 The authors claim that their finding based on survey data from 30 European countries is the first statistically significant evidence about the increased level of anti-Muslim prejudice in Europe based on a large cross-national sample (Strabac and Listhaug 2008: 281).

3 Excerpt is from a BBC TV Documentary, *The Secret Policeman*, in which hidden cameras record a residential training course for policemen (Modood 2005: 13).

4 Norris and Inglehart explain the "American exceptionalism" to the secularization theory through the persistent socioeconomic inequalities in the United States. Even though the United States is one of the most developed countries in the world, it has high socioeconomic inequalities with a relatively weak social security net failing to cover various segments of society. As a consequence, many people who experience existential insecurity feel vulnerable and end up showing high levels of religiosity (Norris and Inglehart 2004: 106).

5 World Values Survey measures religious participation by a question widely referred to in the literature: "Apart from weddings, funerals and christenings, about how often do you attend religious services these days?"

6 The picture is changing for the second and third generation Muslims. As the socioeconomic conditions of European-born Muslims improve, they get less involved with religion. Prayer statistics indicate that the levels of secularity of West European Christians and European-born Muslims are converging. According to Malik: "In Germany only 4 percent of the European-born Muslims and not more than 6 to 8 percent of the beurs, French-born children of North African Muslim immigrants, pray regularly or fairly regularly" (Malik 2001: 103). Yet, this trend does not change the fact that the visibility and assertiveness of those Muslims who are practicing their faith is rising in Europe.

7 The study measures public support to state accommodation by asking respondents for their view on state aid to separate Islamic schools in Britain, wearing of a headscarf in the state schools in France, and instruction about Islam in state schools in Germany.

8 Yet the relative weight given to religious and ethnic terms has varied throughout history. Anti-Semitism qua religious discrimination, which is in fact anti-Judaism, has transformed into anti-Semitism qua racial discrimination as a result of the secularization process initiated with the French Revolution. The racialization of anti-Semitism had been stronger mainly because the Jews were recognized as a "people" much earlier. However, for Islam the boundaries between racial and religious hatred have become blurred. For instance, in a time when historical Islamophobia was explained through religious hatred, the medieval image of Moors was racialized (Brown 2000). Throughout history, Islamophobia and Muslimophobia have been inextricably intertwined.

9 Blatant prejudice is associated with old racism with its emphasis on fear, envy and hatred. The prejudice is close and direct. By contrast, subtle prejudice which is cool and indirect is associated with modern racism. It involves the denial of positive emotions

rather than the expression of negative emotions in which the cultural differences of the minorities are emphasized. Those who hold subtle prejudice refrain from crude and direct expressions; they prefer a covert approach, which is more socially acceptable.

10 On the other hand, prejudice does not reduce with any kind of contact. According to Allport, the contact should be supported by authorities, should be on an equal basis and requires cooperation between group members with a common goal (Allport 1954). In fact, Europeans have less prejudice against those Muslims who have similar socioeconomic status with themselves.

References

Allen, C. (2006), "United Kingdom: Final Report," *Securitization and Religious Divides in Europe, Muslims in Western Europe After 9/11: Why the Term Islamophobia is more a Predicament than an Explanation*, Submission to the Changing Landscape of Citizenship and Security 6th PCRD of European Commission, pp. 49–99.

Allen, C. and Nielsen, J. (2002), *Summary Report on Islamophobia in the EU after 11 September 2001*, Vienna: European Monitoring Centre on Racism and Xenophobia.

Allport, G. (1954), *The Nature of Prejudice*, Cambridge, MA: Addison-Wesley.

Barker, M. (1981), *The New Racism*, London: Junction Books.

Berger, P. (2008), "Secularization Falsified," *First Things*, No. 180, February, pp. 23–7.

Brown, M. D. (2000), "Conceptualising Racism and Islamophobia," in J. Wal and M. Verkuyten (eds), *Comparative Perspectives on Racism*, Aldershot: Ashgate, pp. 73–90.

Brown, M. D. (2006), "Comparative Analysis of Mainstream Discourses, Media Narratives and Representations of Islam in Britain and France Prior to 9/11," *Journal of Muslim Minority Affairs*, 26 (3): 297–312.

Cesari, J. (2006), "Use of the Term Islamophobia in European Societies," *Securitization and Religious Divides in Europe, Muslims in Western Europe After 9/11: Why the Term Islamophobia is more a Predicament than an Explanation*, Submission to the Changing Landscape of Citizenship and Security 6th PCRD of European Commission, pp. 5–48.

Commission on British Muslims and Islamophobia (1997), *Islamophobia: A Challenge for Us All*, London: Runnymede Trust.

Daniel, N. (1980), *Islam and the West: The Making of an Image*, Edinburgh: Edinburgh University Press.

Davie, G. (2000), *Religion in Modern Europe*, Oxford: Oxford University Press.

Erdenir, B. (2005), "The Future of Europe: Islamophobia?," *Turkish Policy Quarterly*, 4(3): 31–41.

European Commission against Racism and Intolerance (ECRI) (2000), *On Combating Intolerance and Discrimination Against Muslims*, General Policy Recommendation No. 5, Strasbourg: Council of Europe.

European Monitoring Center on Racism and Xenophobia (EMCRX) (2006), *Muslims in the European Union: Discrimination and Islamophobia*. Available online at: http://fra.europa.eu/fra/material/pub/muslim/Manifestations_EN.pdf (retrieved in July 2008).

Fetzer, J. S. and Soper, J. C. (2003), "The Roots of Public Attitudes Toward State Accommodation of European Muslims' Religious Practices before and after September 11," *Journal for the Scientific Study of Religion*, 42: 247–58.

Field, C. (2007), "Islamophobia in Contemporary Britain: The Evidence of the Opinion Polls, 1988–2006," *Islam and Christian-Muslim Relations*, 18(4): 447–77.

Gilroy, P. (1987), *There Ain't No Black in the Union Jack: The Cultural Politics of Race and Nation*, London: Heinemann.

Halliday, F. (1999), "'Islamophobia' Reconsidered," *Ethnic and Racial Studies*, 22 (5): 892–902.

Halman, L. and Pettersson, T. (2006), "A Decline of Religious Values?," in P. Ester, M. Braun, and P. Mohler (eds), *Globalization, Value Change and Generations: A Cross-National and Intergenerational Perspective*, European Values Studies 10, Leiden: Brill, pp. 31–60.

Karakaşoğlu, Y., Luchtenberg, S., Peter, F., and Spielhaus, R. (2006), "Germany," *Securitization and Religious Divides in Europe, Muslims in Western Europe After 9/11: Why the Term Islamophobia is more a Predicament than an Explanation*, Submission to the Changing Landscape of Citizenship and Security 6th PCRD of European Commission, pp. 143–94.

Kundnani, A. (2007), "Integrationism: The Politics of Anti-Muslim Racism," *Race & Class*, 48 (4): 24–44.

Malik, M. (2001), "Islam in Europe: Quest for a Paradigm," *Middle East Policy*, 3: 100–15.

Mausen, M. (2006), "Anti-Muslim Sentiments and Mobilization in the Netherlands: Discourse, Policies and Violence," *Securitization and Religious Divides in Europe, Muslims in Western Europe After 9/11: Why the Term Islamophobia is more a Predicament than an Explanation*, Submission to the Changing Landscape of Citizenship and Security 6th PCRD of European Commission, pp. 100–42.

Meertens, R. and Pettigrew, T. (1997), "Is Subtle Prejudice Really Prejudice?," *The Public Opinion Quarterly*, Special Issue on Race, 61 (1): 54–71.

Modood, T. (1994), "Establishment, Multiculturalism and British Citizenship," *Political Quarterly*, 65 (1): 53–73.

Modood, T. (2005), *Multicultural Politics: Racism, Ethnicity, and Muslims in Britain*, Minneapolis, MN: University of Minnesota Press.

Modood, T. and Werbner, P. (eds) (1997), *The Politics of Multiculturalism in New Europe: Racism, Identity and Community*, New York: Zed Books.

Modood T., Berthoud, R., Lakey, J., Nazroo, J., Smith, P., Virdee, S., and Reishon, S. (1997), *Ethnic Minorities in Britain: Diversity and Disadvantage*, London: Policy Studies Institute.

Myers, D. (2005), *Social Psychology*, New York: McGraw-Hill.

Nielsen, J. (1999), *Towards a European Islam*, London: Macmillan Press.

Norris, P. and Inglehart, R. (2004), *Sacred and Secular: Religion and Politics Worldwide*, Cambridge: Cambridge University Press.

Parekh, B. (2006), "Europe, Liberalism and the 'Muslim question,'" in T. Modood, A. Triandafyllidou, and R. Zapata-Barrero (eds), *Multiculturalism, Muslims and Citizenship: A European Approach*, London: Routledge, pp. 179–203.

Pettigrew, T. F. (1998), "Reactions Toward the New Minorities of Western Europe," *Annual Review of Sociology*, 24: 77–103.

Pettigrew, T. F. and Tropp, L. (2008), "How Does Intergroup Contact Reduce Prejudice? Meta-analytic Tests of Three Mediators," *European Journal of Social Psychology*, 38: 922–34.

Richardson, J. E. (2004), *(Mis)Representing Islam: The Racism and Rhetoric of British Broadsheet Newspapers*, Philadelphia, PA: John Benjamins Publishing Company.

Runnymede Trust: Commission on British Muslims and Islamophobia (1997), *Islamophobia: A Challenge for Us All: Report of the Runnymede Trust Commission on British Muslims and Islamophobia*, London: Runnymede Trust.

Scheepers, P., Gijsberts, M. and Hello, E. (2002), "Religiosity and Prejudice Against Ethnic Minorities in Europe: Cross-national Tests on a Controversial Relationship," *Review of Religious Research*, 43 (3): 242–65.

Semyonov, M., Raijman, R. and Gorodzeisky, A. (2006) "The Rise of Anti-foreigner Sentiment in European Societies, 1988–2000," *American Sociological Review*, 71: 426–49.

Sheridan, L. P. and Gillet, R. (2005), "Major World Events and Discrimination," *Asian Journal of Social Psychology*, 8: 191–7.

Sivanandan, A. (2006), "Race, Terror and Civil Society," *Race & Class*, 47 (3): 1–8.

Southern, R. W. (1962), *Western Views of Islam in the Middle Ages*, Cambridge, MA: Harvard University Press.

Strabac, Z. and Listhaug, O. (2008), "Anti-Muslim Prejudice in Europe: A Multilevel Analysis of Survey Data from 30 Countries," *Social Science Research*, 37: 268–86.

The Economist (2008), "Muslims and City Politics: When Town Halls Turn to Mecca," December 4.

Toynbee, P. (2001), "Religion must be Removed from all Functions of State." Available online at http://www.guardian.co.uk, (retrieved in December 2008).

Waardenburg, J. (1998), "Encounters between European Civilisation and Islam in History," in J. Nielsen, (ed.), *The Christian-Muslim Frontier: Chaos, Clash or Dialogue?* London: I.B. Tauris, pp. 5–22.

Wieviorka, M. (1995), *The Arena of Racism*, London: Sage.

Wieviorka, M. (1997), "Is it so Difficult to be an Anti-racist?," in P. Werbner and T. Modood, (eds), *Debating Cultural Hybridity*, London: Zed Books, pp. 139–53.

Zebir, K. (2000), *Muslims and Christians Face to Face*, Oxford: Oneworld Publications.

Zick, A., Pettigrew T. F. and Wagner, U. (2008), "Ethnic Prejudice and Discrimination in Europe," *Journal of Social Issues*, 64 (2): 233–51.

3 Public policies towards Muslims and the institutionalization of 'Moderate Islam' in Europe

Some critical reflections[1]

Sara Silvestri

Introduction

This chapter provides a comparative critical overview and assessment of the logics and mechanisms for Muslim representation in Europe as they have emerged and been consolidated in the two decades at the turn of the millennium. First, it seeks to illuminate the dual thinking behind – and the causes for – policy decisions that have led European governments to promote Muslim institutions and to engage with their Muslim populations in formal and semi-formal ways. In doing so, it questions the utilization and validity of the expression 'moderate Islam', as well as the excessive focus on 'organized' forms of Islam. After categorizing existing models of Muslim–government relations in Europe, the chapter points out the implications of this process of institutionalizing Islam, in both the short and long term, for the status of Muslim communities in Europe and for the future of Europe's secular democracies. It concludes with a call to adjust public discourse and policy approach to Islam in Europe through a methodological shift that privileges Muslims' experiences as 'individuals'.

The dual concern with Islam

The first decade of the twenty-first century in Europe has been characterized by increasing attention, on the part of state and international institutions, as well as of the general public, given to the issue of Islam. There are two dimensions to this concern. 'Internally', on a domestic political level, there is a preoccupation with the consequences of the growth of the Muslim population inside Europe. 'Externally', European foreign policy is concerned with the future of relations with the so-called Muslim world and with transnational political actors that are connected to Islam. Each of these two dimensions is characterized by a set of more specific concerns.

Internally, inside the borders of the European Union (EU) member states, awareness of ethnic and religious pluralism is growing. Scholars and policymakers have recognized that European legal and political systems should be adjusted in order fully to implement the principles of equality, anti-discrimination and freedom of religion, and better to govern ever more diverse and interconnected societies. It has also been gradually acknowledged that a transnational religion with a strong universal message – Islam – is not just increasingly visible and assertive in Europe, but has obviously become a 'feature' of Europe, since large numbers of people of Muslim faith have settled permanently in Europe and are in fact, or at least aspire to become, 'European citizens'.[2] In turn, the increasing visibility of religious symbols and the emergence of discussions around the application of Sharia law in Europe have triggered a reflection on their implications for Muslim believers and for the future of 'European values', democracy and secular-driven notions of tolerance and multiculturalism.

On the international scene, there are calls to respond to the causes and consequences of international terrorism and violence – including violence stemming from Islamist groups and ideologies.[3] Another 'external' concern for European countries is the emergence of pro-democracy reform movements in the Middle East, North Africa and Asia, which are born out of various Islamist traditions. They challenge autocratic regimes and the thin stability that they produce (Asseburg and Brumberg 2007; Pace, *et al.* 2009). The big dilemma for European actors that are interested or engaged in these regions is how to marry the search for freedom with the need for greater socio-political and economic stability (Salamé 1994; Cavatorta and Volpi 2007). Policy choices that would be obvious for promoting political participation and the empowerment of Muslim minorities 'inside' the EU might not be the best ones for dealing with Arab and Asian political actors and Islamist parties 'outside' EU borders.

In this chapter, I concentrate on the internal dimension only, since it is the one that best fits the scope of the book. This internal attention to Islam and Europe's Muslims is, however, multifaceted and context- and time-specific, and has been articulated by opinion- and policymakers in various ways. There have been general calls for the 'integration' (whether social, economic, cultural or juridical) and political participation of Muslim minorities. These efforts have combined with endeavours to steer existing Islamic institutions (e.g. mosques, schools, Sharia councils) and other forms of 'Muslim self-organization' (e.g. ethnocultural associations, advocacy groups, networks providing social services, Muslim media), in order to adapt and incorporate them somehow into European society. There have also been attempts to strengthen Muslim–government relations in Europe, both by searching for partners among European civil society actors – domestically – and by engaging in diplomatic relations with representatives of Muslim countries. A range of multi-purpose activities in the field of intercultural relations have also been promoted (Silvestri 2005a: 385–405).

Muslim–government relations

In the period spanning the 1990s and the early 2000s, the idea of Muslim–government relations often translated into attempts to establish in Europe, in a rather artificial way, consultative Muslim bodies, or councils. Such entities, which despite their aspirations never managed to be representative of the Muslim population in Europe, include people of Muslim tradition[4] who are either European citizens or long-standing immigrants in Europe. These councils are expected to function as official Islamic 'interlocutors' with European state authorities as well as with other religious and civil society groups, in a context that lacks the appropriate jurisprudence to deal with a highly religiously diversified European scene.

The idea of establishing these consultative institutions derived from the realization that the emergence of Islam in the European public sphere has been happening in a disorganized way, across an *ummah* (the global community of the faithful) that is fractured. This is because, as with Protestantism, Islam (especially in its Sunni version) is a faith focused on the direct relationship between the believer and God, and without significant intermediary figures and hierarchical structures comparable to those of the Catholic or Orthodox Churches. Moreover, the Prophet Muhammad left no instructions as to how to select his successor to lead Muslims (religiously and politically) after his death.

Enlightenment-derived notions of secularism, combined with the socio-political dominance exercised by the Christian Churches in Europe throughout the centuries, have also shaped the way bureaucracies, public authorities and legal systems, all over the continent, relate to religion, whether institutionalized or not. On the one hand, European states enthusiastically support equality and religious freedom, provided that they operate within the framework of separated private and public spheres.[5] On the other hand, the way states have developed their relations with religious groups is still shaped by corporatist models and by the traditional pattern of Church–State relations, which still reflects, if anything in this very terminology, the privileged position enjoyed until recently by the Christian Churches in this part of the world (Silvestri 2007a: 159–77).

Prior to this attempt to promote genuine 'European' Muslim institutions, channels to discuss issues and defend the rights of Muslim populations based in Europe (especially as long as these individuals were simply 'immigrants' and not 'citizens' in the countries where they were residing and working) almost automatically involved the diplomatic representation of Muslim countries (Shadid and van Koningsveld 1996). Such contacts were developed either with Muslim majority countries that 'export' migrants to Europe, or with prominent political and religious actors of the Muslim world. Saudi Arabia, Iran and the Organization of the Islamic Conference (OIC) are, for instance, three major sources of religious authority and economic influence for the Muslim (Sunni and Shia) population across the globe. This means that the Muslims of Europe did not have a chance to engage with or express directly to European society their own concerns and claims, which instead were filtered by non-European governments and institutions.

As the notion of 'intercultural dialogue' gained currency in the run up to 2008 (established by the EU as the Year of Intercultural Dialogue), a current of opinion developed in certain European countries according to which engaging in intercultural dialogue coincided with the establishment of formal mechanisms for governments to relate to Muslim communities, for instance by promoting the creation of national Muslim councils. Whereas it is important to include such initiatives as one of the many facets of intercultural dialogue, it is nevertheless crucial to realize that intercultural dialogue is not just about developing institutional and political relations that are sensitive to issues of culture, religion and identity. Intercultural dialogue entails a broader effort, implying a change in mentality directed towards a more 'human' or ethical dimension of politics (beyond concerns with power, economic interest and security); it means adopting an intercultural mindset in whatever individuals and institutions do. We could argue that intercultural dialogue succeeds in refocusing on both individual human rights and collective responsibility in a way that is in line with the concepts of 'cosmopolitan citizenship' and 'cosmopolitan democracy' discussed by Archibugi, *et al.* (1998).

The 'normalization' of 'moderate Islam'

The terrorist attacks of September 2001, March 2004 and July 2005 triggered the 'securitization' of Islam across the globe. According to the Copenhagen school, securitization is the objectification of the perception of an existential threat that leads into an exceptional response of the state (Buzan, *et al.* 1998; Bigo 2000). This process of Islam securitization did not start with 9/11. It existed in previous local and domestic tensions from the Rushdie controversy and the French *affaire du foulard* in 1989, to the northern England riots in the spring and summer of 2001, and to the intensification of migration controls across the EU following the Treaty of Amsterdam. The combination of all these factors produced 'emergency sentiments' in the non-Muslim European population, which was fearful of losing its prerogatives, and the values and traditions of individual European countries. These emotions combined with a growing Brussels-inspired procedural mentality, with the lack of legal policy and administrative instruments capable of dealing with an unprecedented level of religious-ethnic diversity in Europe, with strong religious self-awareness, and with the internal fragmentation of a (broadly speaking) acephalous religion, Islam. These factors together prompted European states to come up with a relatively easy solution, somehow inspired by existing patterns of Church–State relations as well as by a Napoleonic mechanism that had been elaborated in order to deal with Jewish minorities. This tentative solution consisted in engineering and speeding up the process whereby state agencies grant official recognition to minority religions by proactively 'institutionalizing' Islam in a 'corporatist' way, that is, by promoting the establishment of Muslim representative institutions, whether from scratch or by drawing upon existing resources and forms of self-organization.

There is an expectation that such institutions should be in place if Muslims want to 'earn' a place in the complex mechanisms of governance in EU institutions and member states. This is, first, because Muslims are perceived – and often tend to present themselves, by insisting on the unity of the *ummah* – as a bloc, as a community sharing fundamental values, sensitivities and perspectives which are often discriminated against or ignored. Second, a structural problem comes into play when we talk of Muslim engagement and representation within European states and societies; that is, the idea that Islam should 'fit in' with the criteria that regulate relations with the dominant faith groups. Such criteria are rooted in at least three basic expectations:

1 Islam should behave like an 'organized' belief, with mechanisms of representation and religious leaders in clear positions of power. This is based on the assumption that the traditional Church–State model within the secular framework of the separation between public and private spheres will work for Islam, too.
2 There is a somewhat abstract notion of 'integration' which de facto differs between various multicultural, assimilationist and mixed practices adopted by European states.
3 Muslim organizations should be representative both of the demographic and of the doctrinal characteristics of the Muslim populations of Europe.

In short, Muslim communities are implicitly expected to adopt and adapt to the existing pattern of relations between the state and ethnic and religious communities in order to engage with the social and political context of where they live. As a consequence, new forms of institutionalization of Islam (other than mosques and Islamic schools) have begun to appear in Europe, often through the direct intervention of European governments.

Elsewhere I have illustrated the specific discourses and political dynamics surrounding the emergence of Islamic institutions and in particular national Muslim councils across Europe. I took into account the perspectives, strategies and narratives of a selection of European governments and related them with those of a selection of Muslim associations and networks that operate in European countries (Silvestri 2005b: 101–29, forthcoming). Muslim councils are a relatively new invention, created with the expectation that they will constitute official interlocutors available for consultation and capable of representing the internal diversity of the Muslim communities that exist in European states, thereby acting as bridges between the grass-roots level and the state. This process inaugurates a European domestication or normalization of Islam shaped around the idea that a moderate form of integrated Islam should be supported for multiple purposes: to be more inclusive of religious-ethnic minorities, to maintain law and order, to stem radicalization, and to make sure that Muslims are properly familiarized with and incorporated in the ethos of the European countries in which they live. Ultimately, many argue that this process will construct a specifically European version of Islam or 'Euro-Islam' (cf. AlSayyad and Castells 2002).

The expression 'moderate Islam' is problematic for a number of reasons. First it assumes implicitly that Islam per se is not moderate (although what it is assumed to be exactly remains nebulous), and that it nurtures some extreme or radical qualities. Second, it appears inappropriate to use the adjective 'moderate' in relation to a religion when in fact this term normally qualifies one particular section of the wide spectrum of political activities. Third, it could produce, among Muslims, the negative impression that European society does not fully implement the principle of religious freedom and only selectively accepts 'lukewarm' Muslims. If the term moderate was to be associated with lukewarm or 'half' Muslim, then we could possibly witness, in response, an increase in deliberately radical (by this word I mean extreme, aggressive, but not necessarily violent) Muslim assertiveness.

Overall we can say that the early years of the twenty-first century have been marked by a pan-European trend, on the part of the political establishment, to promote Euro-Islam, to devise a common European pattern of Muslim institutions or mechanisms to facilitate Muslim–government relations. Many Muslims have been critical of these initiatives and have proven reluctant to participate in projects that are often directed from the top and contain a large security component. Nevertheless, the debate about these issues has promoted an interesting and positive dynamism and 'reactive' political engagement among Muslim individuals and communities in Europe. It is also interesting to note that at last across Europe, at both national and at EU level, the political community has woken up to the concerns and the needs of the Muslim individuals who reside in Europe.

Typologies of Muslim councils

Islamic commissions and councils started to emerge in Europe from the early 1990s: the Comisión Islámica de España in 1992, the Exécutif des musulmans de Belgique in 1996, the Muslim Council of Britain in 1997, the Conseil Français du Culte Musulman in France in 2003, the Italian Consulta in 2005, and the Islam-Konferenz in Germany in 2006.

Many common motivations can be found between Muslim individuals, associations and state institutions in establishing these bodies. However, the strategic mindset behind these institutions, as well as their structure and manner of function, differs according to the Muslim group(s) and the country concerned. Factors that determine these differences include: the variety of versions of Islam that exist across Europe; political ideologies; the geographical and national origins of the people involved; the socio-economic circumstances of the local Muslim population; cultural and historical features that characterize specific European countries and their approach to secularization; national and EU legal provisions concerning immigration, citizenship and discrimination; patterns of Church–State relations; conceptualization of national identity, national security and national interest; and attitudes towards foreigners and minorities in individual countries.

Another major difference determining the status, position and function of Muslim institutions in European countries is determined by the role of the state itself. Despite certain social scientists' calls for the demise of the state in the epoch of globalization (Held and McGrew 2003), the state still plays a major role in the regulation of sensitive issues such as migration flows or the modalities and limitations to the exercise of freedom of religion. Maybe this is not so evident in the Church–State relations' norms that concern the religion of the majority of the European population (Christianity), because they are so embedded in our histories, cultures and constitutions. But the crucial role of the state in setting the rules of the game is obvious in its dealings with minorities and with new religious movements. In particular, the process behind the establishment of Muslim councils in Europe shows how crucial the state is. We could in fact divide these councils into three groups, on the basis of the approach used by the state in the creation or promotion of these bodies:

1 Top-down: councils came into being thanks to a strong governmental initiative (where typically in the country concerned there were few or weak forms of self-organization on the part of the Muslim population, and Islam had been 'securitized').[6]
2 Bottom-up: councils were essentially the outcome of a strong civil society mobilization and social capital among the Muslim community, whereas the state remained officially behind the scenes while encouraging the initiative.
3 Mixed approach: in this case the formation of Muslim councils was openly encouraged by the government, which even offered some logistical structures, but did not get involved in the direct management.

Some practical examples may clarify this categorization. The Italian experience falls under the top-down approach. As organized Islam in Italy is both fragmented and weak, as well as relatively new, the Minister of the Interior established the Consulta by decree, in 2005, and personally selected those worthy of being members (Silvestri forthcoming).[7]

The British case appears to fit the second example. The Muslim Council of Britain (MCB) is a large and well-run (primarily Asian) umbrella organization but not a representative one in demographic or theological terms. Although it was never officially endorsed by the British government, it was nevertheless regarded for quite some time as a privileged interlocutor and as a protégé of New Labour (Silvestri 2005b: 101–29; McLoughlin 2005). With time, with the lead-up to the war in Iraq (see Birt 2005), and especially after the London bombings of 2005, however, the MCB increasingly lost its appeal and credibility (many ordinary Muslims began to accuse its members of being self-appointed political opportunists not caring for the young who were ending up in terrorism circles), and other competing Muslim organizations emerged, like the British Muslim Forum or the Sufi Council of Britain, which allegedly stole the support of the government (Silvestri forthcoming). However, the only time the British government attempted somehow to coordinate the different Muslim groups and movements that exist in Britain was during the post-crisis context in the summer of 2005, when it called for a taskforce on British Islam composed of a variety of people with the most diverse backgrounds to reflect upon the various aspects of Islam in Britain and on the prevention of radicalization.

Although membership of the French Conseil Français du Culte Musulman (CFCM) works by election, and membership of its German counterpart takes place by a careful system of appointments and proportional representation, both models actually appear to fall under category (c), the mixed approach. In both countries a number of separate groups were already self-organized and each government simply provided a platform to bring them together by allowing the organizations involved (and their members) a degree of independence while at the same time establishing restrictions on their membership. Membership of the CFCM is based on elections in mosques' 'constituencies', whereas for the Konferenz the German government has devised a quota system (Jasch 2007). This system attempts to reflect the diversity of backgrounds of the country's Muslim population in a very broad sense, thus also including individuals who are not practising and even people who are outspoken secularists. The Ministry of the Interior is behind these organizations in both cases, as in Italy.

None of these models is perfect or provides the right recipe to proceed. I would even argue that these councils are useful only in the short term and unnecessary in the long term because they promote a segmentation of society. However it is important to note their existence. They should be appreciated as 'experiments' on the part of governments and Muslim individuals who are trying to explore an appropriate method to organize – or, better, to 'govern', to use Foucault's term – religious pluralism. In addition, what is particularly interesting and innovative in the German case is that the architects of the Konferenz made sure that ordinary individuals of Muslim faith (and in some cases even of simply Muslim background), not affiliated with any mosque or Islamic organization, were involved. Nevertheless, leading Muslim voices in Germany (members and non-members of the Konferenz) have actually criticized this enterprise for not including religious scholars when theological matters are discussed, and for not bringing together a mix of ordinary Muslim citizens *and* Islamic scholars, and feel that the German government is manipulating the divisions that exist within Germany's Muslim communities.[8]

Caveats

A number of caveats should be spelled out in relation to these Muslim council initiatives. First, we should not take for granted that all Muslim individuals would want to identify themselves with such bodies or, indeed, may wish to be seen by society primarily through their 'Muslim' identity. In particular, individuals who are already fully integrated[9] into European society might regard these initiatives as backward steps that promote sectarian identifications.

Second, we ought to be clearer about the exact purpose of these institutions and consider the possible consequences of establishing them. Some of the initiatives analysed above have the appearance of mere window-dressing, whereas others have specific pragmatic objectives (e.g. providing a unified calendar of Islamic festivities for European Muslims, clarifying norms for slaughtering of halal meat, setting standards for the establishment of Islamic schools, making the case with local authorities for mosques and Islamic cemeteries). What if these representative bodies began to have political leverage and demanded that the Muslim faithful position themselves politically, in European societies, as 'Muslim'? Would we then see the beginning of ethno-religious consociationalism[10] in Europe? And if so, what would be the consequences?

Third, the formation of structures promoting Muslim–government relations could provoke opportunistic or hypocritical behaviour. Antagonisms could emerge among Muslim communities and leadership in order to access the governmental platform; individuals aspiring to power, visibility and leadership could become compromised by a desire for personal gain rather than by genuine interest in the well-being of their minority community. Given the variety of Islamic forms that exist in Europe, it is also possible to foresee a scenario where the Muslim actors involved in dialogue with government split into two or more strands, some working through the state, some remaining independent associations, and both claiming and fighting for authority and recognition.

The same is true for secular political parties and coalitions: their support for or opposition to Muslim issues may be totally contingent on context, time and strategic interests that tend to work only in the short term. Recent disputes in Italy and Spain are an example of the use of Islamic issues for political opportunism. In Italy, prominent voices within the centre-right political parties Lega Nord and Forza Italia have waged a demagogic vitriolic opposition to Islam and to immigration (Mangiarotti 2007).[11] State institutions and left-wing politicians that have shown support to Muslim causes in Italy and Spain[12] have been criticized by their counterparts at the centre-right for trying to undermine their political opponents, Christian forces and Catholic identity. Extreme and right-wing parties across Europe have clearly positioned themselves as defenders of Christianity in the supposed clash between Islam and the West (Klausen 2005).

European governments should be aware that these newly created Muslim councils and institutions are vulnerable to the monopolization of groups and movements that have an agenda, and which are often better organized and resourced than ordinary individuals and civil society associations. The problem here would not so much lie in the political message that Islamist groups preach – most of the fears that the actors involved in these councils might support terrorism are unfounded, as the Islamist groups that are involved in such initiatives tend to be quite liberal and have quite modest agendas, typically focused on combating discrimination and promoting religious freedom (Klausen 2005; Silvestri 2006), whereas more hard-line Islamists are not involved altogether as they reject a priori engagement with a political system that is regarded to be *Kufr* – an Arabic concept meaning 'in denial of the faith', 'disbelief', 'apostasy'. The problem is more one of guaranteeing a diversity of views among these Muslim councils' memberships. Vocal groups with a clear political agenda may, in the long term, drown out less politicized individuals in the same institution, might impose their own ideological or prescriptive religious views upon the others, and could only be pretending to speak on behalf of all the Muslim population of Europe or of a particular European country.

Finally, the amount of attention and resources that Muslims have received recently on the part of European governments and the EU for the purpose of countering radicalization could, in the long term, cause societal tensions. Competition between ethnic and religious groups in Britain, for instance, was a matter of great concern for the representatives of non-governmental organizations and local authorities that attended a conference on social cohesion in Britain in Manchester in November 2008. Non-Muslim black and Asian minority communities, in particular, felt that now their own voice and concerns were not heard, and that all the attention and public money was going to Muslims or to faith-based initiatives.[13] It is important to be aware of the existence of such perceptions and to try to prevent the emergence of such polarizations in society.

On omissions, aberrations and getting the picture straight

The analysis conducted so far inevitably leads us to broaden our critical reflection on the way Islam and Muslims have been (mis)understood and dealt with simplistically in public discourse in Europe. In scholarly investigations, as well as in policy discussions and responses to European Islam, there has been a tendency to explain Islamic religiosity, dynamics of identity politics, and the relationship between Muslim communities and the societies of settlement by relying on a series of assumptions and attitudes that in fact constitute an aberration from reality.

First, a static view of both European societies and Muslim individuals is adopted in reductionist approaches to Islam and Muslims in Europe. They are rooted in a fixed understanding of culture, identity and secularism, which lacks any historical or anthropological perspective. This entails seeing Muslims primarily through the lenses of essentialized ethnic features, their past migration history and their supposed religiosity, without acknowledging individual agency, personal evolution, the possibility of cross-fertilization between societies and cultures, and the fact that ethnic identification is often defined and redefined by specific contexts (Hall 1992; Bauman 1999).

Second, a homogenization of Islam and Muslims through reference to key concepts and norms in Islamic theology, key events in Islamic history and the ethno-national origins of the individuals concerned is also taking place. This view overlooks not only geographical and theological differences in Islam, but also the internal fragmentation and the fierce competition among Muslim communities and traditions that coexist within a very tight space in Europe. Furthermore, this view nourishes the perception that the global *ummah* poses an existential threat to Western democracies.[14]

The third aberration stems immediately from the second and consists in the obsession with the search for 'Islamic answers'. This can lead to ascribing (even forcing) 'Muslim identities' upon people and realities that have nothing or little to do with Islam, and which could often be better explained through common societal dynamics rooted in political contention, economic conditions and class, such as the French riots in the autumn of 2005 (Wihtol de Wenden 2005). The other immediate consequence of this search for Islamic answers is that of creating a self-fulfilling prophecy whereby individuals who are pigeonholed as 'Muslim' will be induced spontaneously to identify themselves as such.

Privileged attention to the 'organized' aspect of Islamic institutions and Muslim associations[15] (whether categorized as moderate or as extremist – two other highly questionable terms) can also have its drawbacks. The attempt to create appropriate avenues for consultations with the Muslim population of Europe should undoubtedly be welcomed. After all, the multiple mechanisms (all 'experimental', I would like to emphasize) that are currently in place in various European countries are the outcome of careful and context-specific considerations, in which scholars and policymakers have been engaged since the early 1990s. However, an excessive focus on organized forms of Islam and on these consultative – and, to a lesser extent, representative – bodies of Muslims in Europe can be detrimental for an open and democratic Western political system. The ordinary experiences and views of 'non-organized' Muslim individuals could be ignored by European governments, whereas the weight of Islamist networks and of newly created groups that pride themselves on being progressive or moderate could be overestimated. Furthermore, in- and out-group dynamics could be generated, thus producing the inaccurate perception that Muslim associations and national Islamic councils are the only meaningful channels through which the Muslim population of Europe can voice its concerns.

Another aberration that lies behind frequent policy approaches to Islam in Europe consists in transposing real and perceived international threats related to 'Islamist terrorism'[16] onto local situations that either constitute unlikely scenes of future violence or are conflict-prone areas, in which, nevertheless, Islam and Islamism do not play any major role. This logic can provoke a chain reaction of fears and polarization in society that would actually be based on 'non-events', that is, the absence of tangible issues and events, which is typical of the process of securitization.

Most studies and empirical approaches to the engagement of European states with their Muslim communities have actually omitted or underestimated three further crucial variables: (1) the importance of the domestic context in which Muslims live and practise their faith; it determines people's mindset and the opportunities that are available for participation in society; (2) the personal trajectory of each individual who happens to be Muslim, including their psychology, their emotional ties, their aspirations and their very personal religious experiences; (3) the social class dimension; this, more than ethnocultural differences, is likely to be a crucial determinant in social mobility, performance at school, political awareness and participation in society.

A meaningful study of Islam and Muslim communities in contemporary Europe, and of the contribution their presence makes to Europe's developing level of multiculturalism (as a reality, not as a policy) can only be conducted through a multi-tiered, interdisciplinary approach. Distinguishing between the normative dimension of the religion (Islam) and the more fluid and adaptable reality of the individuals and communities (Muslims) who practise it, is also a necessary step in order to achieve a better sense of perspective.

Notes

1 The issues addressed in this chapter were presented at – and received valuable feedback from – various academic and public policy workshops, conferences and seminars. In particular I would like to acknowledge the discussions held in Berlin and Nuremberg (with German government officials from the Ministry for Integration and the Ministry for Migration, the Migration Policy Institute, the Bertelsmann Foundation and the Weidenfeld Institute), in 2007, and at the University of Copenhagen (at the conference

organized by Nadia Jeldtoft and Jørgen Nielsen), in April 2009. All usual disclaimers apply.

2 The Muslim inhabitants of European countries with a large Muslim demographic presence (such as the UK, France, Belgium or Holland) tend to hold the legal status of 'citizens'. The majority of Muslims living in Italy and Spain (two countries that experienced only recently large influxes of individuals coming from Muslim regions of the world) and quite a few Muslims in Germany are still 'immigrants' although naturalization is increasing. Publications that stress that Islam has become a 'European' feature include: Hunter (2002); Haddad (2002); Wieviorka (2004); Cesari (2004).

3 I use interchangeably the terms 'Islamism' and 'political Islam' to indicate political movements that resort to a narrative and symbolic repertoire based on key theological and historical concepts and practices related to the religion of Islam. Such movements originated in North Africa, the Middle East and Asia at the beginning of the twentieth century, in the context of a political and ideological confrontation with the West and the consequences of decolonization. Although several groups borne out of these movements ended up implicated in bloody situations, it would be inaccurate to establish a direct correlation between faith-based political engagement and terrorism.

4 The expression 'Muslim tradition' is used here deliberately to convey a loose notion of connection with a variety of Islamic traditions and is not necessarily related to the intensity and typology of individual religious practice.

5 The assumption that it is possible to draw a clear divide between private and public sphere is, however, highly questionable because there are many features of religion and religiosity that have a 'public' face and, likewise, there are many aspects of public life that impact on personal choices and experiences.

6 On the meaning of 'securitization' see the beginning of the previous section above.

7 See also Russo Spena in this volume.

8 Source: personal conversation with conference member, June 2009.

9 By 'already fully "integrated"' I mean, for instance, people who have been fully socialized in European lifestyle, people who are happy to live and work in Europe, or young people born in Europe and who seldom, if at all, visit the country of their parents.

10 Consociationalism is a method of power sharing that is regarded as successful in maintaining stability and democracy in deeply divided societies. Lebanon is a typical example. See Lijphart 1969: 207–25.

11 This newspaper article summarizes a series of occurrences involving Lega Nord and Forza Italia (Mangiarotti 2007).

12 This was particularly apparent in the controversy around the crucifix in Italy and Spain ('Tribunale de l'Aquila: via i crocifissi dalle scuole', *Corriere della Sera*, 25 October 2003; 'Il giudice: "Via i crocefissi dalle aule" È la prima volta nella storia della Spagna', *Corriere della Sera*, 23 November 2008) and in the debate around the construction of a mosque in Bologna in 2007–2008 (cf. Allam 2008)

13 On the other hand, various scholars insist on the other side of the coin and have made the case for the need to redress specifically issues of 'religious' discrimination pertaining to Muslims in Britain. See for instance Modood and Meer (this volume) and Modood (2005).

14 On the *ummah* see the relevant section in Silvestri (2007).

15 Here I differentiate between 'Islamic' and 'Muslim': 'Islamic' refers to what pertains to the faith, 'Muslim' to what pertains to the practice.

16 For a definition of 'Islamist terrorism' versus other types of terrorism see Home Office (2009). We should warn, however, that the notion 'Islamist terrorism' is highly debatable because Islamism does not necessarily produce terrorism. Nevertheless, 'Islamist' appears more appropriate than 'Islamic' terrorism (often used by policymakers and journalists) because the former openly implies a political project whereas the latter term is more neutral in that it refers to an attribute of the faith of Islam.

References

Allam, M. (2008) 'Bologna, maxi moschea per pochi fedeli' (*Corriere della Sera*, 19 January).

AlSayyad, N. and Castells, M. (eds) (2002) *Muslim Europe or Euro-Islam: Politics, Culture and Citizenship in the Age of Globalization* (Lanham, MD and Oxford: Lexington Books).

Archibugi, D., Held, D. and Köhler, M. (eds) (1998) *Re-imagining Political Community: Studies in Cosmopolitan Democracy* (Cambridge and Oxford: Polity Press).

Asseburg, M. and Brumberg, D. (eds) (2007) *The Challenge of Islamists for EU and US Policies: Conflict, Stability and Reform* (SWP Research Paper 12, in conjunction with United States Institute for Peace, Berlin).

Bauman, G. (1999) *The Multicultural Riddle* (London: Routledge).

Buzan, B., Waever, O. and de Wilde, J. (1998) *Security: A New Framework for Analysis* (Boulder, CO and London: Lynne Rienner).

Bigo, D. (2000) 'When Two Become One: Internal and External Securitisations in Europe', in M. Kelstrup, M. C. Williams (eds), *International Relations Theory and the Politics of European Integration, Power, Security and Community* (London: Routledge), pp. 171–203.

Birt, Y. (2005) 'Lobbying and Marching: British Muslims and the State', in T. Abbas (ed.), *Muslim Britain* (London: Zed Books), pp. 92–106.

Cavatorta, F. and Volpi, F. (eds) (2007) *Democratization in the Muslim World: Changing Patterns of Authority and Power* (London: Routledge).

Cesari, J. (2004) *When Islam and Democracy Meet* (New York: Palgrave).

Haddad, Y. Y. (ed.) (2002) *Muslims in the West. From Sojourners to Citizens* (Oxford: Oxford University Press).

Hall, S. (1992) 'The Question of Cultural Identity', in S. Hall, D. Held and T. McGrew (eds), *Modernity and its Futures* (Cambridge: Polity Press, in association with Blackwell Publishers, Oxford and The Open University), pp. 273–326.

Held, D. and McGrew, A. (eds) (2003) *The Global Transformations Reader* (Cambridge and Oxford: Polity and Blackwell).

HM Government (2009) *Pursue, Prevent, Protect, Prepare. The United Kingdom's Strategy for Countering International Terrorism*, March 2009. (Norwich: The Stationary Office).

Hunter, S. (ed.) (2002) *Islam, Europe's Second Religion: The New Social, Cultural, and Political Landscape* (Westport, CT and London: Praeger).

Jasch, H. C. (2007) 'State-Dialogue with Muslim Communities in Italy and Germany – The Political Context and the Legal Frameworks for Dialogue with Islamic Faith Communities in Both Countries', *German Law Journal*, 8 (4): 341–80.

Klausen, Y. J. (2005) *The Challenge of Islam: Politics and Religion in Western Europe* (Oxford: Oxford University Press).

Lijphart, A. (1969) 'Consociational Democracy', *World Politics*, 21: 207–25.

McLoughlin, S. (2005) 'The State, "new" Muslim Leaderships and Islam as a "Resource" for Public Engagement in Britain', in J. Cesari and S. McLoughlin (eds), *European Muslims and the Secular State* (Aldershot: Ashgate), pp. 55–69.

Mangiarotti, A. (2007) 'La Lega con un maiale contro la moschea' (*Corriere della Sera*, 11 November).

Modood, T. (2005) *Multicultural Politics: Racism, Ethnicity and Muslims in Britain* (Edinburgh: Edinburgh University Press).

Pace, M., Seeberg, P. and Cavatorta, F. (2009) 'The EU's Democratization Agenda in the Mediterranean: A Critical Inside-out Approach' *Democratization*, 16 (1): 3–19.

Salamé, G. (ed.) (1994) *Democracy Without Democrats? The Renewal of Politics in the Muslim World* (London: I.B. Tauris).

Shadid, W. A. R. and van Koningsveld, P. S. (eds) (1996) *Muslims in the Margin* (Kampen, Neths: Kok Pharos).

Silvestri, S. (2005a) 'EU Relations with Islam in the Context of the EMP's Cultural Dialogue', *Mediterranean Politics*, 10 (3): 385–405.

Silvestri, S. (2005b) 'The Situation of Muslim Immigrants in Europe in the Twenty-first Century: The Creation of National Muslim Councils', in H. Henke (ed.), *Crossing Over: Comparing Recent Immigration in Europe and the United States* (Lanham, MD: Lexington), pp. 101–29.

Silvestri, S. (2006) 'The Political Mobilisation of Muslims in Europe and the EU Response' (PhD dissertation, University of Cambridge).

Silvestri, S. (2007a) 'Asserting Islam in the EU: Actors, Strategies, and Priorities', in F. Foret (ed.), *L'Europe à l'épreuve du religieux* (Université Libre de Bruxelles, 2007), pp. 159–77.

Silvestri, S. (2007b) 'Does Islam Challenge European Identity?', in L. Faltin and M. Wright (eds), *The Religious Roots of Contemporary European Identity* (London: Continuum), pp. 14–28.

Silvestri, S. (forthcoming) 'Institutionalizing British and Italian Islam: Attitudes and Policies', in H. Yilmaz and C. Aykac (eds), *Perceptions of Islam in Europe: Culture, Identity and the Muslim 'Other'* (London: I.B. Tauris).

Wieviorka, M. (ed.) (2003) *L'avenir de l'Islam en France et en Europe* (Paris: Balland).

Wihtol de Wenden, C. (2005) 'Reflections 'À Chaud' on the French Suburban Crisis', SSRC online papers on the Riots in France. Available at: http://riotsfrance.ssrc.org/Wihtol_de_Wenden/ (accessed 10 May 2008).

4 Muslims in Germany

From guest workers to citizens?

Daniel Faas

Introduction

Germany has the largest Muslim population (3.8 to 4.3 million, nearly half of whom have German citizenship) in Western Europe after France. It is also different from the other cases presented in this volume in the sense that it is home to around 2.6 million Turkish economic migrants, mostly Sunnis, from an avowedly secular country which has experience with democratic norms and has been in European Union membership negotiations since 2005.

Unlike the situation in England where Pakistani and Bangladeshi (Sunni) communities, and men in particular, tend to define their identities along religious lines (Archer 2003), Muslimness does not figure prominently in the multidimensional hybrid identities of young Turks in Germany (Faas 2009, 2010).[1] The remainder of Germany's Muslims consists of between 496,000 and 600,000 persons from the south-eastern European countries of Bosnia, Bulgaria and Albania; 292,000 to 370,000 migrants from the Middle East; between 259,000 and 302,000 from North Africa including Morocco; and smaller numbers from central Asia, Iran, South-East Asia and other parts of Africa. Unlike economic migrants from Turkey and Morocco, most German Muslims with origins in Syria, Iran and Algeria arrived as political refugees. Sunnis form the largest group amongst Muslims in Germany with 74 per cent, followed by the Alevis (13 per cent), Shi'ites (7 per cent) and small groups of Ahmadis, Sufis/Muslim mystics and Ibadis. 98 per cent of Muslims in Germany live in the former West – including Berlin, Hamburg, Cologne, Frankfurt, Duisburg and Stuttgart (see Haug, Müssig and Stichs 2009). However, in contrast to most other European countries, sizeable Muslim communities also exist in some rural regions of Germany, especially Baden-Württemberg, Hesse, Bavaria and North Rhine-Westphalia. Owing to the lack of labour immigration before 1989, there are only very few Muslims in former East Germany. Compared with other groups, Muslims are rather loosely organized. The six largest umbrella organizations – the Central Council of Muslims in Germany, the Association of Islamic Cultural Centres, the Council on Islam for the Federal Republic of Germany, the Islamic Community Milli Görüş, the Turkish-Islamic Union for Religious Affairs and the Alevi Movement in Germany – cover the activities of only around 800,000 Muslims (International Crisis Group 2007).

The internal diversity of Germany's Muslims is still relatively unclear as is the exact number of Muslims living in the country. Since most federal statistics do not employ religion as a category, it is unclear precisely to what degree Muslims as a group are marginalized in housing and employment. Although the first representative study into 'Muslim Life in Germany' (Haug, *et al.* 2009) throws some light on the socio-demographic and structural features of Germany's Muslim population, it does not yet move beyond a mainly descriptive account of religious orientations, the wearing of the headscarf and participation in educational opportunities at school. But it marks a clear departure from most previous research which focused only on Turkish Muslims.[2] Some 30 Turkish, Arab and Iranian-related organizations (up from 24 in 2004) were classified as Islamist in the 2007 federal report on extremists (Federal Ministry of the Interior 2007). In the Turkish community there is also a fairly small group who are extremely Kemalist or secularist in their attitudes, and have moved away from practising Islam, while some Turks would even classify themselves as atheists (Karakaşoğlu and Nonneman 1997).

This internal diversity amongst the Turkish populations in Germany has been vividly discussed by Ruth Mandel (2008). She highlights, for instance, that Alevites follow a mystical Sufi belief system, sharing many tenets with Shi'ism. They focus more upon the esoteric and inner purity of spirit, include women in rituals, usually do not wear headscarves and are less interested in repatriation compared with Sunnis. In contrast, Sunni Muslims in Germany adhere to the Hanefi legal code, one of the four branches of Sunni Islam, pray five times a day and strictly observe Ramadan. Sunnis speak of women's promiscuity, citing specific traits and practices, whereas Alevis proudly boast of how progressive and tolerant they are while, equally, highlighting women's participation in society and in prayer (Mandel 2008: 252). Unlike Sunnis, Alevis in Germany do not eat rabbits, which they consider to be holy animals with human-like features. Alevis, who do not necessarily subscribe to the five pillars of Islam, are constructed by Sunnis as the 'other' who also engage in incestuous sexual orgies in the dark (Mandel 2008: 254). Alevis, in turn, consider Sunnis their 'natural' enemy as a result of the repression, deportation, massacres and executions since the collapse of the Ottoman Empire. These Alevi–Sunni tensions are most evident in the politics of marriage as young people in Germany rarely marry outside sectarian boundaries (Mandel 2008: 255). This internal diversity inevitably also challenges attempts to create overarching umbrella organizations or even one single representation.

The relationship between these Muslim minorities and the German national majority was, until recently, conditioned by governmental refusals to acknowledge that the 'guest workers' were there to stay. German rather than Muslim attitudes were arguably the main factor precluding effective integration. The uncertainty of many Turkish Muslims about whether they would eventually return to their country of origin and a society-wide tendency towards social and linguistic segregation were reinforced for two generations. German policies have only changed during the past decade after it was accepted that Germany is indeed an immigration country and that its Muslim migrants are there to settle permanently. Integration has taken over as the new buzzword in political and educational debates amidst a reform of the country's citizenship law which showed a new willingness, at least in principle, to grant citizenship. The current grand coalition government under Chancellor Angela Merkel also appointed a Commissioner for Migration, Refugees and Integration as one of only three Chancellery Ministers of State (*Staatsminister*) and has, to date, hosted three so-called integration summits (*Integrationsgipfel*) with political and societal representatives to discuss issues of German language-learning, education and job opportunities. Several additional conferences on Islam (*Islamkonferenz*), organized by the Interior Minister Wolfgang Schäuble, have since also focused on the interaction between the national majority and Muslim minorities, addressing religious topics, German law and values as well as equal opportunities and employment policies. The unemployment rate for all legally resident migrants in Germany in February 2009 was more than double that for German citizens (16.9 per cent in contrast to 7.8 per cent). Migrants of Turkish origin suffer most in the labour market. In December 2007, their unemployment rate was 20 per cent (Federal Employment Agency 2009). Despite all these initiatives, laudable in principle but long overdue, the ideological struggle between the Social Democrats (SPD) and the Christian Democrats (CDU) over the meaning of the term 'integration' remains a hurdle for many Muslims in Germany, since the SPD views naturalization as a precondition of successful integration whereas the CDU mostly views integration as a precondition for naturalization.

The remainder of this chapter discusses the interaction between the national majority and Muslim minority communities in Germany. I begin with an overview of the policy responses to the Muslim presence, highlighting the shift from notions of 'foreigner politics' between the 1960s and 1990s to a politics of integration under the latest two German governments. The second part focuses on contemporary challenges posed by the presence of over 3 million Muslims in Germany. I focus my discussion mainly on the country's most visible and by far the largest Muslim community, that of the Turks. It should be noted here that most currently available research and data equate Muslims with Turks. Even in this chapter, this could not be avoided altogether given that the argument draws mainly on available evidence. In particular, I analyse their educational disadvantages, the role of (family, etc.) values and the current debates about the wearing of headscarves and Islamic religious education. The third section points towards ways of improving current policies and practices.

Policy responses to the Muslim presence

The fact that the Muslim presence in Germany is for the most part a Turkish phenomenon (around 85 per cent of German Muslims are Turks) has become evident in policy discourses and responses, the most important of which will be discussed below. In this section, I focus mainly on Muslim economic immigrants rather than Muslim political refugees. The October 1961 bilateral employment agreement between Germany and Turkey led to an influx of young male 'guest workers', many of whom were joined by their families in subsequent decades. Similar agreements were also signed with smaller Muslim countries, including Morocco (1963) and Tunisia (1965). The Turks are mainly of Sunni Muslim background and the bilateral agreement, which Şen and Goldberg (1994: 10) referred to as 'one of the most important milestones in the history of German–Turkish relations', stated that Turkish workers should return to their home country within two years. The then German government had no intention of employing 'guest workers' permanently but, because of the need for workers beyond the initially agreed end date, many of these young men continued to stay in Germany.

In 1965, the conservative-led coalition government under Chancellor Erhard responded to the presence of (mostly Muslim) migrant groups, with a 'foreigner law' (*Ausländergesetz*) granting limited rights to 'guest workers'.[3] The government, at the time, thought that 'the presence of foreigners is a temporary problem, which will resolve itself over time' (Santel and Weber 2000: 111). Throughout the 1960s, the presence of Muslims and other migrants was seen as an advantage for all sides. It secured economic growth and in this way was a precondition for Germany's economic strength. Because they took lower paid jobs, the 'guest worker' system made possible an upward shift of a large part of the German labour force and their families. Between 1960 and 1970, 2.3 million German 'blue-collar workers' became 'white-collar employees'. This was because of the constitution of 'guest workers' as a new 'sub-proletariat' (Herbert 2003: 214). Kagitçibasi (1991: 32, original emphasis) argued that:

> The migration of workers, which was desired by both country of origin [e.g. Turkey] and the host society [Germany], has nevertheless led to a marginalisation of the immigrant workers. The unclear identity of migrants was emphasised by their temporary status as *guests* as well as their socio-cultural, psychological, political, religious [Muslim] and linguistic background. The immigration … has turned into a highly complex humanitarian phenomenon with far-reaching socio-cultural, political and psychological [e.g. family-splitting] consequences.

A shift in the relationship between Muslim minorities and the German national majority was brought about by the 1973 Arab oil crisis which prompted the first-ever Social Democratic-led coalition government in Germany under Chancellor Willy Brandt to put a hold on the further recruitment of 'guest workers'. The domestic feeling towards Muslim and other immigrants changed from one that welcomed them as a pool of cheap labour to one that saw them as a threat to jobs and a drain on the welfare state. They were thus unwanted 'foreigners'. As Herbert (2003) argues, the decision to stop recruitment was also the endpoint of a debate that had lasted for several years and centred on the financial burden 'foreigners' were said to constitute if their stay was long-term or permanent;[4] foreign labour was thus seen as a purely economic factor, either contributing to the growth of the German economy or a financial burden for the social welfare systems.

Between 1974 and the early 1980s, three principles emerged under the leadership of Chancellor Helmut Schmidt (Social Democratic Party, SPD). These were: the 'integration' of those who have the right to live in Germany; the continuation of the 1973 ban on recruitment; and financial incentives to support the return of migrants to their countries of origin (Herbert 2003: 245) through the 1983 law for the 'Promotion of Readiness to Return' (*Rückkehrförderungsgesetz*). Under this law, every guest worker who left Germany voluntarily received an incentive of 10,500 Deutschmark (€5,250), but only about 250,000 migrants, mainly those of Turkish origin, responded to this opportunity (Santel and Weber 2000). Until the late 1990s, state officials continued to deploy a distinction between *us* (Germans) and *them* (guest workers); in other words, migrant workers and Muslims in particular were often perceived as inferior and addressed by terms such as 'guest worker' or 'foreigner' irrespective of the length of their residence in Germany.

Racial and religious discrimination, fuelled by youth unemployment following the fall of the Berlin Wall and the Iron Curtain, boiled over in the early 1990s into a series of anti-foreigner, anti-Muslim violence in Germany. In May 1993, four young neo-Nazi German men set fire to the house of a large Turkish family in the western German town of Solingen in the federal state of North Rhine-Westphalia. Three girls and two women died; 14 other family members were severely injured. The attack led to violent protests by Turkish Muslims in several German cities and to large demonstrations of Germans expressing solidarity with the Turkish victims. Conservative Chancellor Helmut Kohl was criticized at the time for neither visiting Solingen nor attending the memorial services. He had denounced what he called the 'condolence tourism' (*Beileidstourismus*) of other politicians. A year earlier, three Turkish women were killed in an arson attack on their homes in Mölln, in the federal state of Schleswig Holstein. Most recently, in February 2008, nine Turkish women and children died in a blaze in Ludwigshafen, a town in the state of Rhineland-Palatinate. Although the cause was said to be an electrical fault, it brought back strong memories of Solingen and renewed the tensions between Germany's largest Muslim minority and state authorities, whilst many ordinary Germans again expressed their solidarity with the victims. During a visit to the site, Recep Tayyip Erdogan, the Turkish prime minister, said he had seen Nazi symbols on the door of the house and criticized the absence of Chancellor Merkel in front of a crowd of 16,000 people of mainly Turkish Muslim origin in Cologne, which perhaps strained relations even further.

Until 1999, a form of institutional discrimination against Muslim and other migrants could be found in various specifications of the concept of citizenship in Germany (Wilpert 2003). Article 116 of the German constitution (*Grundgesetz*) defined a German citizen as a person who holds German citizenship, a spouse or descendant of persons who were settled in the German Reich (ethnic Germans), or a refugee with German ethnicity. While resettlers and refugees who migrated to Germany from foreign states qualified for dual citizenship, 'guest workers', many of whom were Muslims, did not have any right to German citizenship until 1993. Only in the aftermath of the Solingen attacks and protests was a right to citizenship granted to young immigrants between 16 and 23 years. This change created an exception to German naturalization tradition and gave legally resident foreigners a right to citizenship under certain conditions. Firstly, the children of foreigners between 16 and 23 years could be naturalized as German citizens if they had eight years of residence and six years of schooling in Germany, gave up their original citizenship and did not have a criminal record. Secondly, adult foreigners who had been legally resident for 15 years could become naturalized citizens of Germany if they applied before 31 December 1995, gave up their former citizenship, did not have a criminal record and could support themselves and their families without relying upon unemployment aid or welfare.

A marked shift in the hitherto often problematic relationship between Muslim minorities and German policymakers and politicians only occurred after 1998 with the election of the Social Democratic–Green government under Chancellor Gerhard Schröder. His administration started to loosen Germany's restrictive approach to multiculturalism by reforming the country's citizenship law and introducing immigration and anti-discrimination legislation. When the reformed citizenship law came into force in January 2000, *ius sanguinis* (citizenship by birth) was complemented by a *conditioned ius soli* (citizenship by territoriality). This legislation gives citizenship rights to children of Turkish Muslims born in Germany and who have at least one parent who has been resident in Germany for a minimum of eight years with an unlimited residence permit. These children are permitted to retain both their inherited citizenship, which they received by descent, and their new citizenship until they are of age. Between the ages of 18 and 23, they must, however, make a choice (Spindler 2002; German Government Representative for Migration, Refugees and Integration 2000). In spite of this new legislation, some discriminatory practices remain as ethnic Germans and European Union citizens are granted dual citizenship whereas Turkish Muslims and other non-EU migrants have to make a choice between German citizenship and the citizenship of their country of origin. For Turkish people, giving up their Turkish citizenship will probably mean a loss of cultural identity, which is why many continue to support the notion of dual citizenship they are still officially denied. This might explain why 'only' 280,309 Turkish citizens applied for German citizenship between 2000 and 2003. Of the 2.6 million Turkish Muslims who have applied, 840,000 have so far been granted German citizenship. This growing number of naturalizations turns guest workers into citizens and threatens to change the balance of power between insiders and outsiders (Schiffauer 2006: 94). However, recent statistics from the Federal Statistics Office (*Statistisches Bundesamt*) show a declining number of naturalizations since 2000, for Muslims as well as non-Muslims.

Paradoxically, although the German government removed the main impediment to integration by granting citizenship to most of those born in Germany after 2000, there has been increasing demand for full civic participation, from ideologically driven loyalty tests to intensified government surveillance of Muslim associations. This reflects the tensions between an ethnocultural vision of Germany that predominated until recently and a genuine, new desire to address the realities of a culturally and religiously diverse society. In early 2006, several federal states governed by the conservative Christian Democrats (Baden-Württemberg, Hesse, Lower Saxony and Bavaria) announced citizenship tests with 30 to 100 questions on German language, history, culture and postwar values. These arguably played on stereotypes of Islam and Muslim beliefs, attempting to screen views of gender equality, domestic violence and Israel's right to exist, as well as tolerance for homosexuals, Jews and blacks so as to filter out potential radicals and 'hard' integration cases. These tests, which force residents to demonstrate ideological conformity, were quickly challenged and, in the case of Baden-Württemberg, labelled 'Muslim tests'.[5] Naturalization tests are only possible for first-generation migrants but for now they affect the vast majority of Muslims who still do not have German citizenship (approximately 2.5 million). The conservative interior ministers proposed a nationwide values test, in addition to a language test, but Social Democratic interior ministers rejected this plan. In May 2006, the national conference of interior ministers compromised on some national standards, allowing 'discussion' of democratic values and a 'role-playing' exercise in civic knowledge if the civil servant dealing with the naturalization applicant deems this necessary.

More specifically, amendments to the citizenship law of 2000 came into force in August 2007 regarding linguistic knowledge, and in September 2008 regarding knowledge of cultural, political and historical aspects of Germany. The reformed law allows federal states to carry out background checks of the applicant; introduce a ceremonial component to naturalization; introduce mandatory integration courses on democracy, themes of democracy, conflict resolution in democratic society, rule of law, gender equality, basic rights and state symbols, with a test at the end (migrants with 'appropriate foreknowledge' of Germany may petition to opt out of the course and still take the test); introduce optional naturalization discussions where there is doubt regarding recognition of the free and democratic order and rule of law; and finally have the right to review a candidate's civic knowledge in other ways, such as with a role-playing exercise. Applicants who have successfully completed an integration course are now eligible for naturalization after seven years of residence (instead of eight), and those who demonstrate evidence of being integrated, after six years. Drawn from a pool of over 300 questions, the new national naturalization test consists of 33 questions including 3 on specific aspects of the federal state the candidate resides in. A candidate passes the test if s/he answers 17 of the 33 questions correctly within 60 minutes. The test can be repeated as many times as a candidate wishes to do so. Unlike Hesse, the federal state of Baden-Württemberg is the only state continuing to hold additional naturalization discussions with applicants, including questions on convictions though no longer on homosexuality. The traditionally conservative government in this state views integration as a precondition for naturalization – a particularly harsh stance which might further alienate Muslims.

Contemporary challenges to the Muslim presence

Migrant minorities, and Muslim communities in particular, face other considerable challenges despite the fact that Germany has now recognized its multicultural character. This section considers the ways in which structural features, as well as cultural and religious features, are reconstructed in current debates and challenges. These include the headscarf debate, the introduction of Islamic religious education in the German language, the educational underachievement of Turkish Muslims and the recent rise in honour killings.

One of the most prominent debates surrounds the wearing of the headscarf and Islamic religious education. In 2003, Germany's highest court (*Bundesverfassungsgericht*) ruled that the conservative-controlled federal state of Baden-Württemberg was wrong to ban Fereshta Ludin, a German teacher of Afghan descent, from wearing a headscarf in school, but declared that states could in principle legislate on such issues (Bundesverfassungsgericht 2003). Subsequently, eight federal states (Baden-Württemberg, Bavaria, Bremen, Thuringia, Lower Saxony, North Rhine-Westphalia, Saarland and Hesse) introduced legislation banning teachers from wearing headscarves. In the case of Baden-Württemberg, the amended paragraph 38 of the school law now prohibits teachers from wearing the *hijab*:

> Teachers in public schools [...] may not make statements on politics, religion or ideology that could endanger the neutrality of the State with respect to children and parents, or which may disturb the peaceful operation of the school. In particular, it is forbidden to behave in such a way as to give children or teachers the impression that the teacher is opposed to the constitutional guarantees of human dignity, equal rights according to Article 3 of the Constitution, the rights to personal and religious freedom or the liberal-democratic basis of the State. The transmission of Christian and occidental educational and cultural values is not affected by [these stipulations]. The requirement of religious neutrality does not apply to religious education, following Section 1 Article 18 of the Constitution of the state of Baden-Württemberg.

As noted above, the ban did not include Christian and Jewish religious symbols, thus showing a new form of institutionalized discrimination against Muslim communities. In contrast, the state of Berlin introduced an inclusive law banning *all* religious symbols from public institutions. Since the late 1990s, Muslims in Germany have been quite successful in claiming rights and, at the same time, Germans have been more willing to concede these rights, which are further signs of the ideological shifts that have occurred during integration. Not only did Fereshta Ludin claim a partial victory in the aforementioned decision relating to the wearing of headscarves by teachers in Germany but, in 2002, Muslims also won the right to slaughter animals according to their religious commands (halal-slaughtering). Unlike in France, students are allowed to wear headscarves in schools without any restriction. Social security funds are available for the costs of a boy's circumcision, or for the ritual washing of the body of a deceased Muslim (Rohe 2004). Policymakers and parts of the general population are finding it hard to accept this accommodation of Muslim rights.

The recent rise of Muslimophobia[6] has been part of a wider debate about national pride and xenophobia, initiated by conservative politicians. In 2001, for instance, senior members of the Christian Democratic Union (CDU) demanded that every public person in Germany must confess to be proud of Germany. Some claimed that this 'revival of the ghost of nationalism comes at a time when economy, culture and most areas of society have already moved beyond the national level towards supranational integration' (Rippert 2001). Although the main right-wing parties have been unable to surmount the 5 per cent hurdle necessary for representation in the German parliament in Berlin, they nevertheless managed their highest percentage of the vote (a combined 3.3 per cent) in 30 years in the 1998 federal elections, then dropped back to a combined 1.8 per cent in the 2002 federal elections, before rising again to a total of 2.2 per cent in the 2005 elections. Since 2005, Finland, Sweden, Denmark, the Netherlands, Belgium, Poland, Austria and France have all experienced a right-wing swing in their national governments, often on an anti-immigration, anti-Muslim platform. In contrast, at a regional level, the extremist German People's Union (DVU) received 6.1 per cent of the vote in the 2004 state elections in Brandenburg, and the right-wing National Democratic Party (NDP) received 9.2 per cent in the 2004 state elections in Saxony and 7.3 per cent in the 2006 state elections in Mecklenburg-Western Pomerania. Although the resurgence of radical parties that support nationalistic ideas and oppose immigration and the inclusion of Turkey into the EU is largely concentrated in the east, where people have expressed disillusion with the slow socio-economic reforms following Reunification (Olsen 1999),[7] there has also been a certain resurgence in the west. In 2008, the populist Citizens in Anger (BIW) party won a seat in the federal state of Bremen, having obtained 5.3 per cent of the vote in the city of Bremerhaven.

At the same time, as a result of the large number of Turkish Muslim students in German schools (approximately 700,000), several federal states have begun providing Islamic religious education in German (*Islamunterricht in deutscher Sprache*) for students of Muslim origin, alongside the Protestant and Catholic religions in German state schools (Özdil 1999; Siedler 2002).[8] One concern expressed in this debate has been that offering Islamic education alongside mainly Christian religions in state schools could lead to a 'ghettoization' of Muslim children and hamper their integration. However, without Islamic religious education in German state schools, groups could offer their more radical interpretations of Islam in private lessons; and more and more Muslim students might attend mosque-based Qur'an schools (Siedler 2002). Arguably, one of the main advantages of providing Islamic instruction in the German language in state schools is that Muslim students from different countries and cultures can learn their shared religion together. At the centre of this continuing debate about multiculturalism in Germany has been the question about the content of Islamic lessons and the extent to which Islamic organizations and communities should be allowed to shape the curriculum. The third conference on Islam in March 2008 agreed that all German state schools should offer Islamic religious education in German and that Muslim community leaders should work out a legally binding agreement with the state.[9] However, this is likely to take several years, given that Muslims in Germany are represented by no less than 15 different organizations and individuals at the conference. A more inclusive approach would have been to merge the subjects of religious education and ethics[10] and teach the major world religions to all students in the same class – a controversial strategy that was adopted in Berlin in 2006 when multi-denominational ethics lessons (not religion) became compulsory. The federal state of Hamburg has already practised 'religious education for all' under Protestant auspices as one school subject since the 1990s (Knauth 2007).[11]

Another challenge lies in the educational underperformance of migrant students, and Turkish Muslims in particular. Gang and Zimmermann (1996), for instance, compared the educational level obtained by Turkish Muslims born after 1945 who were in Germany in 1984, with the achievements of other German groups, to examine the educational attainment of guest worker children. For their study, the authors made use of the German Socio-economic Panel (GSOEP), consisting of Germans and immigrants in Germany and their families. The foreigner sample of the GSOEP contains representative households from Turkish, Yugoslavian, Greek, Italian and Spanish immigrants, who came to Germany as guest workers. From the foreigners' sample, Gang and Zimmermann kept those who were born in Germany or who arrived before the age of 16, and who in 1984 were 17–38 years old. These are considered to be second-generation immigrants (Kossoudji 1989). From the German sample, the researchers examined the same age cohort. The total sample size was therefore 4,678, with 3,895 Germans, 295 Turks, 76 Yugoslavs, 116 Greeks, 175 Italians and 121 Spaniards. Gang and Zimmermann used three measures of German educational attainment: the total years in education, schooling level and vocational training. Regarding the total years in education, the authors found that 'Germans spend the most time in German schools, on average 12.1 years, followed by Spaniards with 9.5 years, and then Greeks, Italians, Yugoslavs and Turks with, respectively, 8.9, 8.3, 8.0 and 7.6 years' (Gang and Zimmermann 1996: 5). The educational level between Germans and non-Germans, and among the minority ethnic groups, differs in that 47 per cent of Germans obtained at least a high school degree compared with only 6 per cent of Turks,[12] while 45 per cent of Germans received vocational training compared with only 17 per cent of Turks. Other minority ethnic groups fell somewhere in-between.

More recently, a survey report which built on data from the 2003 Programme for International Student Assessment (PISA) study[13] showed that the difference in school performance between migrant students and majority students was more pronounced in Germany than in almost any of the other participating countries (OECD 2006). On average, in mathematics, 15-year-olds with a migrant background trailed their native peers by 40 points, an educational deficit of about one year of study. In Germany, the gap between second-generation students and native students was nearly twice as big (93 score points) and reached 120 score points between Turkish students and German students – the equivalent of about three years of study. Paradoxically, first-generation immigrant students performed significantly better than second-generation students. This is particularly disconcerting as the latter have spent their entire school career in Germany. The mathematics performance gap between first-generation students and native students was only 71 points. The 2006 PISA study confirmed many of these findings, albeit with a focus on science (OECD 2007). The fact that Germany has some 7.3 million foreigners (guest workers and asylum seekers) and a total of 15.3 million migrants (foreigners plus refugees and resettlers of German origin) can hardly account for the fact that migrant students underperform in schools, because other immigration countries show much better results than Germany (Konsortium Bildungsberichterstattung 2006). The reasons for these gaps are complicated and include cultural factors like the fact that Muslim communities do not necessarily value education as much as other migrant communities, and structural factors around the tripartite nature of the German educational system which seems to work against students from socio-ethnically disadvantaged backgrounds.

When a 10- or 12-year-old finishes primary school, s/he is recommended in several federal states for one of the three secondary school tracks, only one of which (*Gymnasium*) grants the certificate needed to enter university. Just over 10 per cent of students of Turkish origin attend a *Gymnasium*, compared with one-third of German students; very few Turks go on to higher education – fewer than 25,000 of 235,989 Turkish 18- to 25-year-olds living in Germany were enrolled in German universities in 2004–2005, where they were outnumbered even by Chinese students (27,000) (International Crisis Group 2007: 23). Turkish students are also twice as likely as Germans to be classified as 'special education' cases, often due to linguistic disadvantages, and to be directed to a *Hauptschule*, the lowest of the secondary school tracks. Turkish Muslim students are more than twice as likely as Germans to leave school without a diploma; 25 per cent have none, compared with 1 per cent of Germans. Moreover, just 25 per cent of migrant youths participate in apprenticeship programmes, compared with 59 per cent of young Germans; foreigners, who make up 12–13 per cent of the student body, are only 4–5 per cent of the student apprentices in Berlin. Young Turks are more affected by unemployment than any other group. In some federal states, the unemployment rate within the young Muslim populations is estimated to be as high as 30 per cent (Blaschke 2004: 123). These structural inequalities have been responded to recently in the sense that some federal states, including the city states of Hamburg, Schleswig Holstein and Bremen, have abolished the vocational-track *Hauptschule* in favour of more integrated schools, whereas the larger states, including Bavaria and Baden-Württemberg, announced they would retain their tripartite systems. Cultural factors affecting educational performance include that most Muslim parents in Germany are of rural Turkish origin, without any higher education. This has been a problem for their children attending school and higher education in Germany. However, some families – especially the conservative and religiously oriented ones – tend to show more discipline and watch less television than other families with lower educational levels. Because of the emphasis placed on understanding religious books, reading had quite a high importance, which in turn encouraged children's educational aspirations (Schiffauer 2003).

Finally, Germany has seen a wave of familial disputes between first-generation parents (representing the traditional Turk) and second-generation liberal Turks, mostly girls. Between October 2004 and June 2005, eight mostly young Turkish women who broke with their family traditions and lived according to Western values (e.g. non-marital sex, own living quarters, relationships, combined job and family life) were murdered by male family members who felt that their *namus* (honour and dignity) and *seref* (reputation and prestige of the family) had been compromised. Since 1996, more than 40 girls and women of Turkish or Middle

Eastern origin who had lived in Germany for all, or most, of their lives were murdered for the same 'crime'. Many of these 'honour killings' were largely ignored by the media until 23-year-old Hatun Sürücü, born in Berlin, was shot dead in the open street on 7 February 2005 by three of her brothers who felt that she had brought dishonour on her family (Peil and Ernst 2005). Sürücü was the sixth victim among Berlin's 200,000-strong Turkish community. She had been married to her cousin eight years before in an arranged marriage, but had then run away, taking her five-year-old son with her. Her killing not only intensified the German debate about multiculturalism and integration (e.g. German language courses in kindergartens and primary schools) but also sparked a new discussion about the necessity of introducing compulsory lessons on morals and ethics, following approval of the killing by several Turkish youths at a local school. In fact, Sürücü's murder contributed to the introduction of compulsory ethics lessons in Berlin schools in 2006 following a protest by Turkish women in the streets of Berlin after her murder. In April 2006, Hatun's 19-year-old brother Ayhan was jailed for nine years and three months by a German court for shooting his sister. Two other brothers were cleared of charges of conspiring to murder her.

These 'honour killings' are indicative of the identity struggle some young Muslims are facing in contemporary Germany. Many of them feel that their community is not included in the German concept of nationhood, or national identity, and that they have been subject to discriminatory remarks because of their Muslim religion and cultural differences (Faas 2007). Auernheimer (1990: 201) has also observed that young Turkish Muslims in Germany are being marginalized and discriminated against, and face three problems:

> The culture of origin loses meaning; family strategies dominate individual life plans (familism); individuals acquire a marginal identity and positioning in relation to both cultures of reference. In Germany, Turkish youth share the first two problems with young people from other ethnic backgrounds, whereas they experience particular conflicts in relation to the third [problem] as a consequence of their positioning within racist discourse.

According to Auernheimer, the marginality of young people of Turkish origin in Germany became evident when they found themselves disparagingly identified as *alemanci* (German Turks) on their visits to Turkey. Boos-Nünning (1986) maintained that second-generation Turkish adolescents in Germany face a reference-group problem. Where they privilege the validity of their own individual perspectives, they find themselves rejected by their minority community and subject to pressures to conform to German culture and society. Those who are prepared to conform in this way, according to Boos-Nünning, run into problems with their families, but cannot count on being truly accepted into German society either because of their cultural and religious 'otherness'. Young Turks often emphasize that it is, above all, members of the Turkish community who are referred to as foreigners in Germany and that they have been singled out because of their Muslim religion and customs (Faas 2008).

The term 'foreigner' has several different connotations in the German context. First, it refers to the different citizenship status of Germans and Muslim (or other) communities. Secondly, the use of such isolating terms by the national majority sends a strong message to Muslim and other migrant communities that they are different, unwanted and not part of Germany. Arguably, this makes it extremely hard for Muslims to identify with the German nation. However, because the term 'foreigner' or 'foreign citizen' has been used frequently throughout Germany, some Turks have come to terms with their status and even use the word themselves. Finally, in purely linguistic terms, 'foreigner' can mean someone who is not a member of a group (i.e. an outsider). This is further complicated by the Turkish EU membership debate which not only splits the German political parties but is also frequently used during election campaigns. The basic point of difference is that the Social Democratic–Green government (1998–2005) has argued in favour of full Turkish EU membership whereas senior members of the Christian Democrats, including the current Chancellor Merkel (since 2005), prefer what they call a 'privileged partnership'. Ideological arguments rather than economic interests have been employed by the Christian Democrats to oppose Turkey's accession to the EU. Based upon the fact that the majority of the 74.3 million Turks in Turkey are Muslims (and would thus constitute the second largest country in the EU), it is said that Muslim Turkey does not fit into 'Christian Europe' (Blaschke 2004).

Despite the challenges Muslim communities continue to face in Germany, new subcultural traditions have emerged. This is particularly the case amongst the large Turkish community who combined a positive commitment to their ethnic and cultural background with openness to German society.[14] There has been a thriving and colourful literary and cinematic Turkish German subculture, with over a thousand works written in Turkish and dealing with Sunni and Alevi experiences in Germany (Riemann and Harrassowitz 1990); and the edited commentary by Germans and Turkish Muslims on the possibilities of integration was the first book by a major German publisher with the text given in both German and Turkish (Leggewie and Enocak 1993). In 2004, the German Turkish film *Head-On* (*Gegen die Wand*), which told the story of a marriage of convenience between two Turkish Muslims in Hamburg and thus focused upon the problems of second-generation Turkish immigrants in Germany, won the Berlinale Golden Bear and was awarded Best European Film. In November 2008, Cem Őzdemir, a German politician of Turkish descent and Member of the European Parliament, was elected leader of Germany's Green Party (Alliance 90/The Greens). He was the first German-born second-generation Muslim immigrant to be a representative in the German parliament (in 1994). At present, there are 6 Muslim politicians in the 612-strong German parliament, of whom 5 are of Turkish origin. These are Akgün (Social Democrats), Ekin Deligöz (Alliance 90/Greens), Hakki Keskin (The Left), Sevim Dağdelen (The Left) and Huseyin-Kenan Aydin (The Left), and Iranian-born Omid Nouripour (Alliance 90/Greens). Four deputies of Turkish origin are in the European Parliament. What is striking, however, is (a) that there is no Muslim representative among the centre and centre-left Liberal Democrats and Christian Democrats; and (b) the general imbalance between political representation and population. Less than 1 per cent of parliamentarians are Muslims compared with over 4 per cent of the general population. The same holds true for teachers, of whom less than 1 per cent have a Muslim or migrant background (Verband Bildung und Erziehung 2006). Today, there are also only about 600–700 Muslim soldiers in the armed forces.

Conclusion

There is insufficient information on Muslims in Germany and a general tendency to equate the notion of Muslims with Turks. Although data is mostly only available for the Turkish community, the structural factors and their influence on integration point towards a continued marginalization in employment, housing and education. Turks are in the worst situation with an unemployment rate of around 20 per cent, and in the field of education lag behind their German peers by as much as three years of study. In some federal states, according to Blaschke (2004), the unemployment rate within the juvenile Muslim population is estimated to be as high as 30 per cent. Arguably, access to the labour market amongst Germany's Muslims involves the question of employers' tolerance towards religious duties, such as the Friday prayer and the five daily prayers some observe, or the provision of the work canteen with halal food. These matters are left to the discretion of the individual employer. The low employment figures are thus indicative of a lack of acceptance and cultural awareness. Compared to many other European countries, including France (*banlieue*), and England (inner-city areas in the North), German cities show relatively lower levels of segregation but there is a concentration of migrants including Muslims in ethnic districts in central locations such as the Berlin districts of Kreuzberg and Neukölln. Migrants are disadvantaged in the housing market, but exact data concerning Muslims is also not yet available. Despite these persisting structural disadvantages, Muslims have made inroads culturally. These range from new subcultures to higher political representation, a relaxation of the *ius sanguinis* principle of citizenship since 2000, and the emergence of hybrid ethno-national (Turkish German), ethno-local (Turkish Stuttgarter) and national-European identities among second-generation Muslims of Turkish origin (Faas 2010). Although Muslims increasingly claim their rights, as evidenced in the headscarf affair and ritual slaughtering, they are still confronted with remarkable 'counter-solidarity' of the society at large which is different from the case with other minorities in Germany (Schiffauer 2004). Muslims are not just cultural but also religious 'others'. These cultural and religious factors create a hierarchy placing Spanish, Italians and Portuguese (mainly Catholics) at the top, followed by Greeks (Orthodox) and then Turks (Muslims) and other non-European Muslim-origin migrants (Mandel 2008: 90ff.).

Germany took considerably more time than other European countries to respond to the presence of Muslims. It took ten years for policymakers to address the increasing ethnocultural and religious diversity. And even when they responded in the mid-1960s, this was not the policy approach that former colonial powers like England took because England had recruited labourers who initially had the right to reside permanently in the host country. Although several European countries initially developed assimilation-based approaches, the German approach in the 1960s and 1970s was viewed as the key means of assimilating economic migrants into a monocultural conception of Germany and did not attempt to recognize diversity within the concept of national identity. What remains is that, after 50 years of migration, German policymakers still officially employ terms such as 'foreigner' (*Ausländer*) or 'foreign citizen' (*ausländische Mitbürger*) rather than acknowledging the cultural inroads migrant communities, including Muslims, have made. The recent focus on naturalization tests is also problematic in that it reflects a tendency to trace violence and sexism back to the Qur'an and Islamic culture, and gives Muslim a false choice: either embrace women's rights and other Western conceptions or remain foreigners and forgo naturalization and religious equality. The evidence from my study suggests that German policymakers need to step up their efforts to foster social cohesion and integration through a common language and citizenship, on the one hand (viewing naturalization as a precondition of successful integration), while valuing non-German cultures on the other. The latter dimension, according to Yurdakul (2009), also includes recognition of Muslim migrant associations – such as the Turkish Federation of Berlin-Brandenburg or the Federation for Democratic Workers' Associations – as forms of integration. The development of a single body to represent Muslim interests toward the German state also needs to be further encouraged but it remains questionable whether the German Islam conference is the right forum for this. For many Muslims, the journey from guest workers to citizens thus remains incomplete.

Notes

1 Other studies in Germany appear to be painting a different picture. For example, Brettfeld and Wetzels (2007) found strong religious ties amongst a majority of the Muslim population (87.3 per cent), 15-year-olds (86.5 per cent) and Muslim students (76.7 per cent). They clustered religiosity into four categories: (a) minimally religious (17.5 per cent); (b) orthodox religious (21.9 per cent); (c) fundamental religious (39.6 per cent); and (d) traditional conservative (21 per cent). This led the authors to conclude that Muslimness is important among Turks. Haug, Müssig and Stichs' (2009) survey showed that religiosity is particularly evident among Muslims of Turkish and African origin (Sunnis) whereas Muslims of Iranian descent (Shi'ites) consider themselves less religious. In contrast, I approached my interviewees in a much more open-ended way, asking questions around where they feel they belong to and what is important to them. This provided for a more rounded and complex picture of identities instead of framing questions around religiosity.

2 Germany is also part of a FP7 project entitled 'Finding a Place for Islam in Europe: Cultural Interaction between Muslim Migrants and Receiving Societies' (2009–2012). By comparing several Muslim groups in Belgium, Germany, the Netherlands, Britain and Switzerland, the project aims to move away from references to a single unified 'Muslim experience' in Europe.

3 The 1965 law was not changed until 1990, when the German parliament passed a new 'foreigner law', reaffirming the principle of *ius sanguinis*, by which only those of German 'blood' heritage received automatic German citizenship. Naturalization procedures were made easier, yet dual citizenship was still rejected at the time.

4 The government and employer organizations calculated that a 'guest worker' would generally cost around 30,000 Deutschmark (€15,000); an integrated and participating

'guest worker' who made use of the social systems would, according to state calculations, cost from 150,000 to 200,000 Deutschmark (€75,000 to €100,000) (Herbert 2003).

5 For example, Question 15 of the highly controversial, proposed test in Baden-Württemberg asked applicants if they would allow their daughters to participate in sport and swimming classes at school. Question 16 asked if they would allow their children to participate in class trips with an overnight stay. Question 9 asked directly whether the applicant would consider it progressive that men and women are equal in law and what measures the state should adopt if men would not accept this. In Question 30, the applicant was asked what they thought of homosexuals holding public office in Germany. And Question 24 asked the applicant's position with regard to 'honour killing' of women for an 'unvirtuous way of life' in order to restore 'family honour'.

6 Many of the current tensions between Muslim migrant minorities and the national German majority are not necessarily rooted in religion, but in education and other cultural areas, which is why the term 'Muslimophobia' might be better in this case than 'Islamophobia'. See also Chapter 2 by Burak Erdenir in this volume.

7 In western German federal states, with the exception of the Schill Party in 2001 in Hamburg, none of the right-wing parties were represented at a regional level between 1998 and 2005 during the left-wing period of national government in Germany.

8 In Berlin, home to the largest Turkish minority in Germany, some 17 per cent of Turkish children already attend Qur'an schools after school. In Bavaria, Islamic instruction classes were set up in the 1980s but were only available in the Turkish language.

9 Further agreements at the third Islam conference include the construction of around 180 mosques in Germany and the fight against Islamic radicalism with a view to easing some of the strained relations between Muslims and parts of the German population. Germany already has 163 mosques (the latest one was opened in October 2008 in the North Rhine-Westphalian town of Duisburg), along with 2,600 prayer rooms mostly hidden within secular buildings.

10 Religion classes are required by law in German state schools, except Berlin and Bremen. Students have a choice between Catholic and Protestant classes, with many schools also offering ethics as a multi-denominational alternative, first introduced in the 1970s.

11 The Hamburg way of 'religious education for all' is based on the fact that the Protestant Church cedes part of its curriculum space to other religious communities to exercise their influence. Although not committed to one denomination it is different from the Berlin model.

12 The different educational levels between Germans and Turks, which are at the extremes, are also highlighted by Bittner (2003). In 2001–2002, out of 417,000 Turkish pupils in German general schools, only 22,000 (5.3 per cent) attended a *Gymnasium*, 36,000 (8.8 per cent) a *Realschule* and 92,000 (22.1 per cent) a *Hauptschule*. Half of all minority ethnic pupils at *Realschulen* and *Hauptschulen* are Turkish compared with only a quarter at *Gymnasien*.

13 These OECD studies are conducted every three years amongst 15-year-old students and assess young people's performance in reading, mathematics, and science. The 2003 tests were conducted in 41 countries, 17 of which were part of a follow-up study on immigrant students' success (OECD 2006).

14 There is now an established oriental rock scene, especially in Berlin, whose style is a synthesis of Turkish oriental and Euro-American musical influences.

References

Archer, L. (2003) *Race, Masculinity and Schooling: Muslim Boys and Education*, London: Open University Press.

Auernheimer, G. (1990) 'How black are the German Turks? Ethnicity, marginality and interethnic relations for young people of Turkish origin in the FRG', in L. Chisholm, P. Büchner, H-H. Krüger and P. Brown (eds), *Childhood, Youth, and Social Change: A Comparative Perspective*, Basingstoke: Falmer Press.

Bittner, J. (2003) 'Ghetto im Kopf', available at: http://www.zeit.de/2003/36/Integration (accessed 30 January 2009).

Blaschke, J. (2004) 'Tolerated but marginalized: Muslims in Germany', in M. Anwar, J. Blaschke and A. Sander (eds), *State Policies Towards Muslim Minorities: Sweden, Great Britain and Germany*, Berlin: Edition Parabolis, pp. 106–202.

Boos-Nünning, U. (1986) 'Die schulische Situation der zweiten Generation', in W. Meys and F. Şen (eds), *Zukunft in der Bundesrepublik oder Zukunft in der Türkei*, Frankfurt: Dagyeli Verlag, pp. 131–55.

Brettfeld, K. and Wetzels, P. (2007) *Muslime in Deutschland: Integration, Integrationsbarrieren, Religion sowie Einstellungen zu Demokratie, Rechtsstaat und politisch-religiös motivierter Gewalt*, Berlin: Bundesministerium des Innern.

Bundesverfassungsgericht (2003) 'Lehrerin mit Kopftuch: Aktenzeichen 2 BvR 1436/02', available at: http://www.bundesverfassungsgericht.de/entscheidungen/rs20030924_2bvr143602.html (accessed 9 July 2009).

Faas, D. (2007) 'The Europeanization of German ethnic identities: the case of German and Turkish students in two Stuttgart secondary schools', *International Studies in Sociology of Education* 17 (1): 45–62.

Faas, D. (2008) 'From foreigner pedagogy to intercultural education: an analysis of the German responses to diversity and its impacts on schools and students', *European Educational Research Journal* 7 (1): 108–23.

Faas, D. (2009) 'Reconsidering identity: the ethnic and political dimensions of hybridity among majority and Turkish youth in Germany and England', *British Journal of Sociology* 60 (2): 299–320.

Faas, D. (2010) *Negotiating Political Identities: Multiethnic Schools and Youth in Europe*, Farnham: Ashgate.

Federal Employment Agency (2009) 'Monatlicher Analytikreport für Ausländer', available at: http://www.pub.arbeitsagentur.de/hst/services/statistik/000200/html/analytik/index.shtml (accessed 25 March 2009).

Federal Ministry of the Interior (2007) *Verfassungsschutzbericht 2007*, Berlin: Bundesministerium des Innern.

Gang, I. N. and Zimmermann, K. F. (1996) *Is Child like Parent? Educational Attainment and Ethnic Origin*, Discussion Paper 1461, London: Centre for Economic Policy Research.

German Government Representative for Migration (2000) 'Das neue Staatsangehörigkeitsrecht', available at: http://www.gesetze-im-internet.de/bundesrecht/rustag/gesamt.pdf (accessed 30 October 2009).

Haug, S., Müssig, S. and Stichs, A. (2009) *Muslimisches Leben in Deutschland*, Nürnberg: Bundesamt für Migration und Flüchtlinge.

Herbert, U. (2003) *Geschichte der Ausländerpolitik in Deutschland*, Bonn: Bundeszentrale für politische Bildung.

International Crisis Group (2007) 'Islam and identity in Germany', available at: http://www.crisisgroup.org/library/documents/europe/181_islam_in_germany.pdf (accessed 1 February 2009).

Kagitçibasi, C. (1991) 'Türkische Migranten aus der Sicht des Herkunftslandes', in P. Bott, H. Merkens and F. Schmidt (eds), *Türkische Jugendliche und Aussiedlerkinder in Familie und Schule*, Hohengehren: Schneider, pp. 31–43.

Karakaşoğlu, Y. and Nonneman, G. (1997) 'Muslims in Germany, with special reference to the Turkish-Islamic community', in G. Nonneman, T. Niblock and B. Szajkowski (eds), *Muslim Communities in the New Europe*, Reading: Ithaca Press, pp. 241–68.

Knauth, T. (2007) 'Religious education in Germany: a contribution to dialogue or source of conflict? Historical and contextual analysis of the development since the 1960s', in R. Jackson, S. Miedema, W. Weiße and J.-P. Willaime (eds), *Religion and Education in Europe: Developments, Contexts and Debates*, Münster: Waxmann, pp. 243–65.

Konsortium Bildungsberichterstattung (eds) (2006) *Bildung in Deutschland: ein indikatorengestützter Bericht mit einer Analyse zu Bildung und Migration*, Bielefeld: W. Bertelsmann Verlag.

Kossoudji, S. A. (1989) 'Immigrant worker assimilation: is it a labour market phenomenon?', *Journal of Human Resources* 24 (3): 495–527.

Leggewie, C. and Enocak, Z. (eds) (1993) *Deutsche Türken – Türk Almanlar: das Ende der Geduld – Sabrn sonu*, Reinbek: Rowohlt.

Mandel, R. (2008) *Cosmopolitan Anxieties: Turkish Challenges to Citizenship and Belonging in Germany*, Durham, NC: Duke University Press.

Olsen, J. (1999) *Nature and Nationalism: Right-wing Ecology and the Politics of Identity in Contemporary Germany*, Basingstoke: Macmillan.

OECD (Organization for Economic Cooperation and Development) (2006) *Where Immigrant Students Succeed: A Comparative Review of Performance and Engagement in PISA 2003*. Paris: OECD.

OECD (Organization for Economic Cooperation and Development) (2007) *Naturwissenschaftliche Kompetenzen für die Welt von Morgen: OECD Briefing Note für Deutschland*. Paris: OECD.

Özdil, A-Ö. (1999) *Aktuelle Debatten zum Islamunterricht in Deutschland: Religionsunterricht, religiöse Unterweisung für Muslime, Islamkunde*, Hamburg: E. B. Verlag.

Peil, F. and Ernst, S. (2005) 'Mord an junger Türkin: "Sie hat ja wie eine Deutsche gelebt"', available at: http://www.spiegel.de/panorama/0,1518,342484,00.html (accessed 9 July 2009).

Riemann, W. and Harrassowitz, O. (1990) *Über das Leben in Bitterland: Bibliographie zur türkischen Deutschlandliteratur und zur türkischen Literatur in Deutschland*, Wiesbaden: Harrassowitz.

Rippert, U. (2001) 'Stolz auf Deutschland: eine absurde Debatte', available at: http://www.wsws.org/de/2001/apr2001/stol-a11.shtml (accessed 25 Jnauary 2009).

Rohe, M. (2004) 'The legal treatment of Muslims in Germany', in R. Aluffi and G. Zincone (eds), *The Legal Treatment of Islamic Minorities in Europe*, Leuven: Peeters, pp. 83–107.

Santel, B. and Weber, A. (2000) 'Zwischen Ausländerpolitik und Einwanderungspolitik: Migrations- und Ausländerrecht in Deutschland', in K. J. Bade and R. Münz (eds), *Migrationsreport 2000*, Bonn: Bundeszentrale für politische Bildung, pp. 109–40.

Schiffauer, W. (2003) *Migration und kulturelle Differenz: Studie für das Büro der Ausländerbeauftragten des Senats von Berlin*, Berlin: Ausländerbeauftragte des Senats.

Schiffauer, W. (2004) 'Vom Exil- zum Diaspora-Islam: Muslimische Identitäten in Europa', *Soziale Welt: Zeitschrift für Sozialwissenschaftliche Forschungund Praxis* 55 (4): 347–68.

Schiffauer, W. (2006) 'Enemies within the gate: The debate about the citizenship of Muslims in Germany', in T. Modood, A. Triandafyllidou and R. Zapata-Barrero (eds), *Multiculturalism, Muslims and Citizenship*, London: Routledge.

Şen, F. and Goldberg, A. (1994) *Türken in Deutschland: Leben zwischen zwei Kulturen*, München: Verlag C. H. Beck.

Siedler, D. (2002) 'Islamunterricht an deutschen Schulen: erste Erfahrungen im nordrhein-westfälischen Schulversuch', available at: http://www.uni-leipzig.de/~rp/vortraege/siedler.html (accessed 1 February 2009).

Spindler, H. (2002) 'Das neue Staatsangehörigkeitsrecht: Ziele, Inhalte der Vorschriften und Umsetzung', in H. Storz and C. Reißlandt (eds), *Staatsbürgerschaft im Einwanderungsland Deutschland*, Opladen: Leske und Budrich, pp. 53–70.

Verband Bildung und Erziehung (2006) 'Migranten für den Lehrerberuf gewinnen: Pressekonferenz zum Weltlehrertag 2006', available at: http://vbe.de/uploads/media/03_-_Statement_Eckinger.pdf (accessed 26 January 2009).

Wilpert, C. (2003) 'Racism, discrimination, citizenship and the need for anti-discrimination legislation in Germany', in Z. Layton-Henry and C. Wilpert (eds), *Challenging Racism in Britain and Germany*, Basingstoke: Macmillan, pp. 245–69.

Yurdakul, G. (2009) *From Guest Workers into Muslims: The Transformation of Turkish Immigrant Associations in Germany*, Newcastle-upon-Tyne: Cambridge Scholars Publishing.

5 Britain

Contemporary developments in cases of Muslim–state engagement

Tariq Modood and Nasar Meer

Introduction

The concern of this chapter, as of the book as a whole, is to explore contemporary relationships between Muslim minorities and the state, with a particular focus upon structural and cultural dynamics. In this regard, the case of Britain is illustrative. This is because an analysis of political and institutional responses to Muslim 'difference' in Britain details a pattern of engagement that has evolved over time. As Modood (2006: 37) has proposed, this can be framed in terms of rising agendas of racial equality and multiculturalism to which Muslims have become central – even while they have contested important aspects of these. This implies that these developments have been neither linear nor unproblematic, for they have been marked by various crises, and, according to some authors, what this engagement has accomplished remains at best uncertain (Bagguley and Hussain 2008; Kundani 2008; McGhee 2008). It is our argument, however, that there are several significant ways in which Muslim minorities and British citizenship have been cast in potentially dynamic and mutually constitutive terms. Indeed, we suggest that, contrary to a popular insistence following the 7/7 London bombings and other terrorist incidents involving British Muslim protagonists, multiculturalism in Britain has not been erased (Meer and Modood 2009). As such we contend that any discussion of Muslim minorities in twenty-first-century Britain must not ignore these developments for they too may affect the course of future state–Muslim engagement. In order to substantiate these assertions, this chapter will begin with a discussion of the sociological and political character of British citizenship, before offering an account of the cultures and identities of contemporary British Muslim communities. It will then empirically elaborate cases of state–Muslim engagement within multiculturalist – including multi-faith – arenas, and trace the structural–cultural dynamics therein.

British multiculturalism and Britain's Muslims

While there has been a long-established Muslim presence in Britain, particularly constituted by North African (especially Yemeni) and East Indian seafaring migrants and 'lascars' (Ansari 2004), the major and most established part of

Britain's Muslim presence is the outcome of postwar Commonwealth migration. This came from India, Pakistan and Bangladesh, initially in the form of male labour from rural small farm-owning backgrounds seeking to meet the demands of unskilled and semi-skilled labour, and was later joined by families and then more urban and professional South Asian Muslim political refugees from Kenya and Uganda. These migrants from former colonies and dependent territories entered a socio-political environment that would give specific emphasis to managing group relations. As such, Britain borrowed something from the American experience but went further in focusing upon how society could achieve fair treatment for different groups, a concern that reaches beyond how these groups could blend into society (Rudiger 2007). Although lacking an official 'Multicultural Act' or 'Charter' in the way of Australia or Canada (CMEB 2000), Britain rejected the notion that the incorporation of migrants should be premised upon an uncompromising cultural 'assimilation'. It did so when the Labour Home Secretary Roy Jenkins (Jenkins 1966) defined integration as 'not a flattening process of assimilation but equal opportunity accompanied by cultural diversity in an atmosphere of mutual tolerance'. This sentiment tried to address the rights of distinct groups as well as their modes of interaction, and so was not merely concerned with the rights of individuals. This is how, at the level of Adrian Favell's (1998) 'philosophies of integration' at least, we might begin to characterize the specificity of 'British multiculturalism'.

While it is not immediately clear what this actually entailed, it is perhaps easier to ascertain that Muslims did not feature explicitly in this early multiculturalist approach, which treated postwar migrants who arrived as Citizens of the United Kingdom and Commonwealth (CUKC),[1] and subsequent British-born generations, as *ethnic* and *racial* – but not as *religious* – minorities requiring state support and differential treatment to overcome distinctive barriers in their exercise of citizenship. Under the remit of several Race Relations Acts, the state has sought to integrate minorities into the labour market and other key arenas of British society through an approach that promotes equal access as an example of equality of opportunity. Indeed, it is now over 30 years since the introduction of a third Race Relations Act (1976), which cemented a state sponsorship of race equality by consolidating earlier, weaker legislative instruments (RRA 1965, 1968). Alongside its broad remit spanning public and private institutions, the recognition of *indirect* discrimination and the imposition of a statutory public duty to promote good 'race relations', it also created the Commission for Racial Equality (CRE) to assist individual complainants and monitor the implementation of the Act (see Dhami, *et al.* 2006: 19–25). This is an example, according to Joppke (1999: 642), of a citizenship that has amounted to a 'precarious balance between citizenship universalism and racial group particularism [that] stops short of giving special group rights to immigrants'.[2] Alongside this state-centred and national focus, there is also a tradition of what we might characterize as 'municipal drift' where multiculturalist discourses and policies have been pursued through local councils and municipal authorities, making up a patchwork of British multicultural public policies in the way summarized by Singh (2005: 170):

> Historically, multiculturalism as a public policy in Britain has been heavily localised, often made voluntary, and linked essentially to issues of managing diversity in areas of immigrant settlement. The legislative framework on which this policy is based – for example, the Race Relations Acts (1965 and 1976) – recognised this contingency, giving additional resources to local authorities as well as new powers to better promote racial and ethnic equality. With these enabling powers, most local authorities with large ethnic minority populations have transformed themselves from initially being the bastions of official racism to being promoters of anti-racism and multiculturalism, and with this change the strength of local ethnic communities and coalitions has been instrumental.

Perhaps the best example of Singh's assessment of local multiculturalism is captured by the programmes of anti-racist education (Troyna 1987; Mullard 1985) and multicultural education (Swann Committee 1985) that historically have been enacted at the Local Education Authority (LEA) level. LEAs are responsible for education within the jurisdiction of county councils and metropolitan boroughs, and this includes responsibility for all state schools with the exception of those that apply for and are afforded 'voluntary aided status' (and can therefore opt out) under the terms of the 1944 Education Act. As Singh's account implies, in many multi-ethnic urban areas LEAs have actively encouraged anti-racist and multicultural initiatives in the face of – and at the cost of – some vociferous opposition (Hewer 2001), and this has, in turn, informed the national picture. Indeed, it was through debates at the local level regarding multicultural education that one of the leading public policy documents on multiculturalism arose. Entitled *Education for All*, the Swann Report (Swann 1985: 36) characterized multiculturalism in Britain as enabling

> all ethnic groups, both minority and majority, to participate in fully shaping society … whilst also allowing, and where necessary assisting the ethnic minority communities in maintaining their distinct ethnic identities within a framework of commonly accepted values.

Yet this limited multiculturalism explicitly precluded such things as state support of linguistic pluralism (in terms of teaching in the 'mother tongue' as opposed to a language like Urdu being an out-of-school subject) or the expansion of religious schools, seeking instead to make each matters of private concern. It has taken Muslim minorities decades of engagement to begin to expand such multiculturalist approaches in a way that also takes their particular needs into account, specifically by contesting this multiculturalism's secular and narrowly racial focus.

This was perhaps symbolized by the way in which the Muslim Council of Britain (MCB) developed and emerged as the main interlocutor in state–Muslim engagement, and how it achieved some success in establishing a Muslim voice in the corridors of power (Radcliffe 2004). The creation of a religion question on the national Census (Aspinall 2000), the obtaining of state funding for the first Muslim schools (Meer forthcoming) and, more broadly, the elicitation of socio-economic policies targeted at severely deprived Muslim groups (Policy Innovation Unit 2001; Abrams and Houston 2006) are illustrative examples of these successes. Inaugurated in 1997, the MCB is an expanding umbrella organization of presently over 450 local, regional and national organizations, which elects its secretary general from a central committee. Its genesis lies in the UK Action Committee on Islamic Affairs (UKACIA) which developed during the Salman Rushdie affair as the most effective means of raising mainstream Muslim voices.[3] The MCB's stated aims include the promotion of consensus and unity on Muslim affairs in the UK, giving a voice to issues of common concern, addressing discrimination and disadvantages faced by Muslims in Britain, encouraging 'a more enlightened appreciation' of Islam and Muslims in the wider society and working for 'the common good'.[4]

Backlash politics

While initial reformulations of British multiculturalism are important – especially in projecting a symbolic meaning – they remain comparatively modest when compared with the race-equality components of British multiculturalism. It is curious then, given the longevity of its *ethnic* and *racial* focus, that the fate of multiculturalism in Britain should have come to be so intertwined with the political identity of Muslims. This intertwining corresponds with how the pre-eminence of the MCB waned in the mid-2000s as it grew critical of the Iraq War and the so-called War on Terror. It has also faced considerable public criticism from both government and civil society bodies (particularly of the centre-right) for allegedly failing to reject extremism clearly and decisively.[5] Indeed, David Cameron, the leader of the opposition Conservative Party and widely anticipated to be elected prime minister in the next general election around 2010, has likened the MCB to the far-right British National Party (BNP) (Tempest 2007). Allied to these complaints has been the issue of how 'representative' of British Muslims the organization actually is – a question that has plagued it since the early days but which has had a more damaging impact upon its credibility when joined by a handful of other complaints.[6] One outcome of this political critique has been the extension to a plethora of other, though much less representative, Muslim organizations (such as the Sufi Muslim Council (SMC) and the Al-Khoie Foundation) of the invitation to represent British Muslims in matters of consultation and stakeholders. At the same time, and as is further elaborated below, newer advisory groups (such as the Mosques and Imams National Advisory Body (MINAB)) do not seek the same remit of representation as the MCB, while other older bodies such as the Islamic Sharia Council (ISC) continue to be affiliate members of the MCB.

We argue that these developments are linked to at least two further issues. The first is that Muslim claims-making has been characterized as specifically ambitious and difficult to accommodate (Joppke 2009, 2004; Policy Exchange 2007; Moore 2006, 2004). This is particularly the case when Muslims are perceived to be, often uniquely, in contravention of liberal discourses of individual rights and secularism that are made more permeable by concessions implied in multiculturalist approaches (Hutton 2007; Hansen 2006; Toynbee 2005). This is exemplified by the way in which visible Muslim practices such as veiling[7] have in public discourses been reduced to and conflated with alleged Muslim practices such as forced marriages, female genital mutilation, a rejection of positive law in favour of criminal Sharia law and so on. Each suggests a radical 'otherness' about Muslims and a non-liberality about multiculturalism, and, since the latter is alleged to license these practices, opposition to the practice, it is argued, necessarily invalidates the policy.[8]

The second reason derives from global events, and not necessarily from the acts of terrorism undertaken by protagonists proclaiming a Muslim agenda (which are routinely condemned by leading British-Muslim bodies), but from the subsequent conflation of a criminal minority with an assumed tendency inherent to the many. Indeed, in a post 9/11 and 7/7 climate, the explanatory purchase of Muslim cultural dysfunctionality has generated a profitable discursive economy in accounting for what has been described as 'Islamic terrorism' (cf. Phillips 2006; Gove 2006; Cohen 2007). The net outcome of these two issues is a coupling of diversity and anti-terrorism agendas that has implicated contemporary British multiculturalism as the culprit of Britain's security woes. Gilles Kepel (quoted in Modood 2005b), for example, has insisted that the bombers 'were the children of Britain's own multicultural society' and that the bombings have 'smashed' the implicit social consensus and multiculturalism to 'smithereens'. More recently, Prins and Salisbury (2008: 22–3) have claimed that a misplaced deference to multiculturalism, which failed to lay down the line to immigrants, has contributed to a lack of national self-confidence and a fragmenting society that has been exploited by Islamist terrorists. As Modood (2008a: 17) has argued, however, 'the simplistic linkage between home-grown terrorism and the multicultural project is unfair because it ends up blaming not just national policies but specific communities for particular outcomes'. In this case, Muslims as a whole are blamed for terrorism, for not standing up to extremism and for not integrating, which not only appears unfair 'but also divisive and so not likely to achieve the much-sought-for integration'.

Contemporary Muslim identity articulations

At the same time, and whilst Britain has undoubtedly witnessed some securitization of ethnic relations, it is not quite the case, as one commentator has suggested, that public policy solutions aimed at managing ethnic and religious diversity amount to being 'tough on mosques, tough on the causes of mosques' (Fekete 2004: 25). To elaborate our argument it is necessary to obtain a fuller understanding of the scope and nature of Muslim communities and their identifications in contemporary Britain. Based upon data from the last decennial census (2001), there are well over 1.6 million people in Britain who report an affiliation with Islam by voluntarily self-defining as 'Muslim'. This represents 2.9 per cent of the entire population and makes Islam the most populous faith in Britain after Christianity (72 per cent); more numerous than Hinduism (less than 1 per cent, numbering 559,000),

Sikhism (336,000), Judaism (267,000) and Buddhism (152,000). It is generally accepted, however, that the actual number of Muslims is higher because of initial undercounting, comparatively higher levels of fertility and subsequent inward migration. Nevertheless, a breakdown of the census data on Muslim constituencies according to ethnicity identifies 42.5 per cent of Pakistani ethnic origin, 16.8 per cent Bangladeshi, 8.5 per cent of Indian, and – most interestingly – 7.5 per cent of White Other. This is largely taken to mean people of Turkish, Arabic and North-African ethnic origin who choose the White Other category on the census form. It also includes Eastern European Muslims from Bosnia and Kosovo, as well as white Muslims from other European countries and not an insignificant and growing convert community (estimated to be over 10,000 in number, see Anwar and Bakhsh 2003). Black-African (6.2 per cent) and Other Asian (5.8 per cent) census categories dominate the remaining ethnic identification options. Even with this heterogeneity, it is still understandable – if a little misleading – that British Muslims are associated first and foremost with a South Asian background, especially since those with this background make up roughly 68 per cent of the British Muslim population, have a greater longevity in residence and have been more politically active to date.

Muslims in Britain, as in the world over, are predominantly Sunni, while the majority of the single largest group (Pakistanis) are Barelvis; the majority of the remainder are Deobandis.[9] Both these Sunni sects have their origins in the reformist movement set in motion by Shah Walliuah that came into existence in post-1857 British India, after what is commonly termed the 'Indian mutiny' but is best seen as India's first war of independence. Both these groups were concerned with ways of maintaining Islam as a living social force in a non-Muslim polity and ruling culture. The Deobandis, taking their cue from a school founded in Deoband near Delhi, came to focus primarily on education and on keeping alive in the seminaries medieval Muslim theological and juristic doctrines. They saw politics as an unequal struggle and tried to be as independent as possible from the Indian–British state. Their anti-Britishness, however, took the form of withdrawal and non-cooperation, rather than of active confrontation, but they took great care to minimize not only British and Hindu influences, but also Shia. Nevertheless, and through active proselytization, they have built up a mass following as well as an international reputation in Islamic learning. This includes a global organization named Tabligh-i-Jamaat which is represented in Britain with headquarters in Dewsbury, West Yorkshire, and which also has an active presence in Birmingham and London. The Barelvis, in contrast, are more numerous across Britain and form the core, for example, of Bradford's Muslims, but are also part of a tradition of Sufi mysticism and Indian folk religion shared by a variety of British Muslim communities. Deriving their name from Ahmed Riza Khan of Bareilly (1856–1921), theirs is an Islam of personalities; the Prophet Muhammad, for instance, is imbued with a metaphysical significance and devotional reverence that goes well beyond what some Muslims would regard as orthodox and which has been called 'the mystification of Islam' (Rahman 1982: 41). Their religious heroes are not confined to the Prophet and the early Arab Muslims but include a galaxy of minor and major saints who, contrary to more reformist Islam, can intercede with God on behalf of petitioners. Additionally, they hold dear many customs and superstitions that have no justification in the Qur'an but have been acquired from other sources.

This heterogeneity of ethnic, national and theological cleavages has led Humuyan Ansari (2004: 3) to insist that 'presumptions of Muslim homogeneity and coherence which claim to override the differences … do not necessarily correspond to social reality. A Sylheti from Bangladesh, apart from some tenets of faith, is likely to have little in common with a Mirpuri from Pakistan, let alone a Somali or Bosnian Muslim.' This is supported by Fred Halliday's (1999: 897) concern to focus analysis upon 'the intersection of identities' since:

> [I]t is easy to … study an immigrant community and present all in terms of religion. But this is to miss other identities – of work, location, ethnicity – and, not least, the ways in which different Muslims relate to each other. Anyone with the slightest acquaintance of the inner life of the Arabs in Britain, or the Pakistani and Bengali communities, will know there is as much difference as commonality.

Whilst these assessments are not without foundation, and should help counter an understanding of Muslims in Britain as a monolithic group, one of the arguments of this chapter is that certain concerns transcend Muslim difference – particularly since the (albeit slim) majority of British Muslims have not migrated to Britain but have been born here. Shared concerns are likely to encompass the ways in which to combat anti-Muslim racism, or cultivate a positive public image (heterogeneous or otherwise), or a desire amongst some Muslim parents to school their children in Islamic traditions and so on. For example, it is particularly noteworthy that while support for the present Labour government decreased amongst all minorities in the last general election, it did so radically amongst some Muslim groups. The most dramatic example of this was the defeat of the incumbent MP in the predominantly Bangladeshi London constituency of Bethnal Green and Bow by George Galloway, a former Labour MP, who led the anti-war Respect party.

One particular issue that this raises is whether a discernible British Muslim identity has given rise to a discernible 'Muslim vote' in Britain, for it is clear that Muslim organizations in the last general election campaigned on a distinctive equality agenda that drew attention to the ways Muslims have become victims of the anti-terrorism campaigns and related Islamophobia (Modood 2005a). If we continue with this example, a number of implications can be drawn from these developments that include differences between Muslim and non-Muslim ethnic minority voting patterns, as well as the extent to which Muslim political electoral participation is 'closely connected to the size of the local Muslim population [which] indicates that registration, like turnout, is affected by the forces of [Muslim] mobilisation' (Fieldhouse and Cutts 2008: 333). One example of Muslim electoral mobilization was much in evidence when the Muslim Council of Britain issued a ten-point check card to encourage Muslim voters to evaluate various politicians' positions on matters concerning both domestic and foreign policy.[10]

The reception of such a strategy by a former leading Labour politician provides a lucid illustration of the electoral impact of attitudinal and social shifts amongst the contemporary Muslims of his former constituency:

> For more than 30 years, I took the votes of Birmingham Muslims for granted … if, at any time between 1964 and 1997 I heard of a Khan, Saleem or Iqbal who did not support Labour I was both outraged and astonished. […] The Muslim view of Labour has changed. […] Anxious immigrants who throw themselves on the mercy of their members of parliament are now a minority. Their children and grandchildren will only vote for politicians who explicitly meet their demands. […] In future they will pick and choose between the parties and ask: 'What have you done for us?' (Hattersley 2005)

The central narrative running through this account is that of a confident British Muslim democratic engagement that is further illustrated by Sher Khan of the Muslim Council of Britain:

> Our position has always been that we see ourselves as part of this society. I do not think that you can be part of it if you are not willing to take part in electing your own representatives. So, engage with the process of governance or of your community as part of being a citizen of this community. We think it is imperative. (Quoted in Carter 2005)

This ethic of engagement has not been limited to electoral participation, however, for it is also observed in some key areas in which Muslims in Britain have secured forms of state recognition through processes of engagement and lobbying. This can include the provision of mortgages compliant with Islamic approaches to saving and investing, and the operation of Sharia law in civil matters more broadly. For example, the Islamic teaching that *riba* (usury or interest) is *haram* (forbidden) is a guiding tenet for some observant Muslims, but is made implausible by systems of financial products which either generate or charge interest. One alternative system which has developed organically in Britain includes an arrangement where banks buy a property on a customer's behalf but then sell it back to the customer with an additional charge equivalent to the total amount of interest. For some time, however, this incurred two sets of stamp duty (a tax which is payable to the government on the purchase of a house). This was until 2003 when the then Chancellor of the Exchequer Gordon Brown abolished this double charge, and since then the Council of Mortgage Lenders and MCB have continued to liaise with various government departments on how to make Islamic home finance products more viable in the UK.[11]

This is one example of a successful accommodation of aspects of Sharia even while Sharia councils themselves continue to be the subject of intense controversy (Modood 2008b). This was typified by the hysteria surrounding the present Archbishop of Canterbury, Dr Rowan Williams, whose public lecture on 'What degree of accommodation the law of the land can and should give to minority communities with their own strongly entrenched legal and moral codes' was met with media frenzy. The lecture included a developed and highly sensitive reflection on the reality and potential of 'plural jurisdiction', particularly in relation to the experience of and discussions about Sharia courts, their capacity to rule on such matters as family disputes and claims, and their relationship to the 'statutory law of the United Kingdom'.[12] What the media reaction to the Archbishop's lecture ignored was how, since the 1970s, some marital and inheritance disputes have been judged in Muslim arbitration boards if both parties have freely consented to such adjudication, and this has taken place under the broader remit of English civil law. Where the application of Sharia has contravened English civil law it has been rejected by the courts, as Pearl and Menski's (1988: 57–8) otherwise critical account of British traditions of positive law details:

> [T]he British legal system, with its positivist approach to what 'law' is, and what it is not, remains purposely blind to social conventions and so-called 'cultural practices' which are perceived to operate in the 'extra-legal' sphere. This fictitious, dismissive yet reluctantly tolerant attitude has in fact allowed space for the unofficial development of new hybrid rules [...] At the same time, the official legal system can afford, from a position of superiority, to keep the legal position of British Muslims under negotiation [...] in effect they are following a path which *they* consider appropriate [...] a new hybrid form of Sharia, which avoids breaking the official law of their new home.

The ambiguities of this scenario are perhaps most graphically illustrated in the machinations of the Islamic Sharia Council (ISC), an affiliate of the MCB, and one of the most prominent examples of the ways in which British Muslims are using the framework of the Sharia to resolve disputes while remaining within the bounds of British laws. This council was founded in 1982 and emerged from attempts by a group of London imams to resolve issues of conflict between British and Sharia law (Bell 2007). It consists of a bench of jurists who provide a conciliation service for disputing couples and authoritative religious legal opinions on a host of social and economic matters raised by individuals and organizations. According to Yilmaz (2001: 303–4), the council takes a pragmatic approach by allowing applicants to choose a particular school of law and they are offered legal guidance and resolution of conflicts on the basis of its perspective.

The Muslim addition to British multi-faithism

It is argued that examples of such hybrid religious-civic engagement can be drawn from Britain's multi-faith history. For while the ISC is yet to receive official recognition on a par with that afforded to Jewish Beth Din courts, for example, it is already viewed by many British Muslims as a relevant means of reconciling their legal and spiritual needs. Indeed, what the Jewish example reiterates is that British Muslim engagement with the state proceeds in a context that is characterized by an internal *religious* plurality which has been supplemented by the migration of different religious groups over the last two centuries (Filby 2006). To be sure, and in spite of maintaining a Protestant Established Church of England, the superior status of the dominant Anglican Church has consistently been challenged by other Christian denominations, not least in Scotland where the religious majority is not Anglican but Presbyterian, and which led to the creation of a Church of Scotland. Elsewhere in England and Wales, Protestant nonconformists have been vocal; and issues such as education have in the past encouraged many of these groups to 'stand out against the state for giving every opportunity to the Church of England to proselytize through the education system' (Skinner 2002: 174). The cycles of nineteenth-century migration from Ireland to London, Glasgow and the north of England have considerably expanded the Roman Catholic presence in Britain. The turn of the twentieth century, meanwhile, witnessed the arrival of destitute Jewish migrants fleeing both the pogroms and the economic deprivation in Russia (Meer and Noorani 2008). Both groups have suffered racial discrimination and civil disabilities on the basis of their religious affiliation but in due course have come to enjoy some of the benefits initially associated with 'establishment' (the identification of the Church of England with the British state). This includes allowing the Catholic Church to set up schools alongside the state and then, with the 1944 Education Act, to opt into the state sector and receive similar provisions to those enjoyed by members of the established Church; a provision which was soon extended to other religious groups, notably Jewish minorities.

Muslims then, like Hindus and Sikhs, are the most recent and numerically significant addition to this plurality to have established themselves, with varying degrees of success, as part of the 'new cultural landscape' of Britain (Peach and Gale 2003: 487–8). This is evidenced is several spheres but is made strikingly visible in what Peach and Gale (2003: 469) describe as the 'new "cathedrals" of the English cultural landscape'. By this they refer to the creation of Muslim *masjids*, alongside Hindu *mandirs* and Sikh *gurdwaras*, which have emerged through a process of dialogue between minority faith groups and British city planning authorities. One of several points of interest in the creation of these places of worship, is that out of the thousand or so that exist, the majority are in fact conversions of disused chapels, churches and other such premises (ibid.: 482). In this context it is not surprising to learn that mosque building is less controversial in Britain than it may be elsewhere on the continent, since Muslims frequently use the 1852 and 1855 Places of Worship Registration Acts, though securing planning permission to function as a place of worship or education (or both) under the Town and Country Planning Act 1971 is never straightforward (while registration is not a legal requirement, planning permission is). Similar historical settlements explain religious burial accommodations. For example, the Local Authorities Cemeteries Order 1977 empowers burial authorities to set aside any part of a cemetery that has not been consecrated for use by a religious denomination. As Ansari (forthcoming) elaborates:

> Many local authorities have responded to the expressed needs and wishes of Muslims to be able to carry out burials soon after death, and so changes have

> been made to registry office opening hours and weekend burials are carried out on request in some areas. [...] Coventry City Council has made provisions for Muslims to carry out the actual burial themselves if it is required at a weekend or on a Bank Holiday. Some burial grounds have ensured that there are specific sections for Muslims to be buried, and that the grounds are appropriately laid out. Accommodation has been made by some to comply with Muslim requirements to bury the body without a coffin.

An example of the latter includes Slough Borough Council which promises to carry out burials within hours of receipt of the necessary completed paperwork. Similar such accommodations may be found in the provision of halal meat – for while it has long been a legal requirement for animals to be 'stunned' or partially unconscious prior to slaughter, exemptions have been made for the Jewish practice of Shechita, and these were extended to the Muslim practice of Dhabh, through the Slaughter of Poultry Act 1967 and Slaughterhouses Act 1974. One of the most prominent examples of Muslim–state engagement across both multiculturalist and religious pluralist traditions is to be found in the Muslim mobilizations for Muslim schools (see Meer 2009). In this area Muslim groups achieved a watershed in 1998 when, after 18 years of a Conservative administration, a 'New Labour' government delivered on a promise in its election manifesto and co-opted two Muslim schools, Islamia School (in Brent, London) and Al-Furqan School (in Birmingham), into the state sector by awarding each Voluntary Aided (VA) status. This status prescribed an allocation of public money to cover teacher salaries and the running costs of the school. It arrived 'fourteen years and five Secretaries of State after the first naive approach' (Hewitt 1998: 22), when Muslim parents and educators had only begun to get to grips with the convoluted application process to achieve state funding, and were dealing with a Conservative government that was hostile to the idea of state-funded Muslim schools. Eleven years and another five Secretaries of State later, the number of state-funded Muslim faith schools has risen to eight. In addition to those already mentioned, this figure includes Al-Hijrah (a secondary school in Birmingham), Feversham College (a secondary school in Bradford), Gatton Primary School (in Wandsworth, South London), Tauheedul Islam Girls High School (Blackburn, Lancashire) and The Avenue School (another primary school in Brent, London).

Overarching structural and cultural factors

One salient structural factor shaping the experiences of Muslim minorities in contemporary Britain surrounds their overconcentration in particular localities where they constitute the main minorities, namely, particular regions of northern towns. These areas of early Muslim settlements were focused around older, industrial towns where the initial wave of male labourers had arrived to take up work. Outside London, other areas of settlement comprise both the east and west Midlands (Blackburn, Leicester, Birmingham), South and West Yorkshire (Sheffield, Leeds, Dewsbury and Bradford) and Greater Manchester (including Oldham and Burnley).

It has been argued that a contemporary concentration in such settlement patterns has given rise to dualistic and polarizing interactions. For example, while chair of the Commission for Racial Equality (CRE), Trevor Phillips (2005) (now chair of the Equality and Human Rights Commission (EHRC)) insisted that Britain was 'sleepwalking' into a US-style 'hard segregation', in claiming that: 'Residentially, some districts are on their way to becoming fully fledged ghettos – black holes into which no one goes without fear and trepidation, and from which no one ever escapes undamaged.'

In promoting this view Phillips has not gone unchallenged. Amongst others, the demographers Finney and Simpson (2009) have shown that the number of mixed neighbourhoods (measured in electoral wards) has actually increased rather than decreased in recent times (from 964 to 1,070) in the period between the most recent and second most recent decennial censuses. In shaping a broader pattern of dispersal rather than concentration, Finney and Simpson (ibid.) insist that there will be at least 1,300 mixed neighbourhoods by the next census in 2011 (one in five throughout England and Wales). On Phillips' more specific charge, they remind us that there is not a single ward in Britain in which the population is 100 per cent ethnic minority, and that the proportion of ethnic minorities amounting to as much as 50 per cent of the population of a neighbourhood was around 22 per cent. They have shown that there are only 14 out of over 8,850 electoral wards in England and Wales in which an ethnic minority group makes up over half the population, and that in none does a single ethnic minority account for over three-quarters of the population. In contrast there are about 5,000 wards that are 98 per cent white. Contrary to Phillips, it could be argued that where there are concentrations of ethnic minorities, this is a result of population growth rather than increasing segregation, particularly since Pakistani and Bangladeshi groups have younger age profiles. Moreover, it is of course common amongst many experiences of migration that people establish themselves in localities that allow for the sharing of resources and a general feeling of security, before social mobility facilitates a move outward (Modood 2004). The important structural component that is too frequently absent from this discussion is the change that takes place *around* such minorities, and which is no more reducible to minority cultural features than the structural elements that invited initial settlement.

A particularly stark structural component shaping the lives of Britain's Muslim minorities is their socio-economic profile which is significantly lower than for their counterparts. For example, Abrams and Houston (2006) found that Muslims have disproportionately lower incomes and higher rates of unemployment, and that they have comparatively fewer skills both in education and in vocational training. Muslim minorities are also more likely to reside in deprived housing and disproportionately suffer from bad health (see also Performance Innovation Unit (PIU) 2001; Modood, *et al.* 1997). This is illustrated by the finding that 68 per cent of Bangladeshi households live below the poverty line and about 40 per cent of Muslim children in London live in poverty (Klausen 2009: 413; see also ONS 2002a). It has, however, been argued that these features are, in truth, an ethnic phenomenon rather than a religious one since non-Pakistani and non-Bangladeshi

Muslims such as Indians and African-Asians fair much better according to these indices. What this ignores is that while ethnic origin analyses show significant variations across Muslim groups, and demonstrate that not all Muslim ethnic groups are equally disadvantaged, the most disadvantaged groups mainly consist of Muslim ethnic groups, for example Muslims with an Indian background will perform less well than Hindus with an Indian background (see Khattab, *et al.* 2006). The outcome as a whole is that Muslim minorities represent a much weaker group in the labour market and Muslims as a whole have an increased reliance on state benefits and so forth.

One important factor related to this could be deemed cultural and has to do with the greater levels of non-participation of Muslim women in the labour market. For example, according to the last census only around 28 per cent of Pakistani women and 22 per cent of Bangladeshi women are in employment (ONS 2002b). One of the most frequent explanations of this trend is to attribute it to a lack of suitable qualifications and educational training. It is significant then to note a counter-cyclical trend which reports that over the last decade Pakistani and Bangladeshi girls have become more likely than boys to achieve five GCSEs at grades A*–C[13] (ONS 2002c). This is not something limited to tertiary education for, according to Bagguley and Hussein (2007: 9), while the past two decades have seen a general expansion of participation in higher education, 'the increasing participation of South Asian women, especially those of Pakistani and Bangladeshi origin, has surpassed all expectations'. This includes a leap in the percentages of women entering university between 1979 to 2000, with an increase in Pakistani ethnicities from 1.7 per cent to 14.5 per cent, and for the same period for women of Bangladeshi ethnicity an increase from 1.6 per cent to 12.5 per cent (see also Ahmad, *et al.* 2003: discussion of 'pioneers'). In broad terms, this might be explained by migrant attitudes toward success in which ethnic minority cultural dynamics serve a positive function. This includes how 'parents, other significant relatives and community members share some general, but durable, ambitions to achieve upward mobility for themselves and especially for their children and believe that (higher) education is important in achieving those ambitions, and so prioritize the acquisition of (higher) education' (Modood 2004: 95).

State–Muslim engagement around terrorism

Perhaps the most novel and least charted present area of state–Muslim engagement, however, surrounds issues concerning the prevention of terrorism and violent extremism. Following the London bombings in July 2005, the government created seven working groups[14] comprised of representatives of Muslim communities under the terms 'Preventing Extremism Together' (PET). Though initiated by the Home Office, this would later fall under the remit of the subsequently created Department for Communities and Local Government (DCLG).

These working groups devised a series of proposals to develop practical means of tackling violent extremism. Sixty-four recommendations were put forward in a report published in November 2005, with a particular emphasis on three that could act as central planks for unfolding government strategies concerned with preventing violent extremism. These constituted, firstly, the development of a 'Scholars Roadshow' led by British Muslim organizations where 'influential mainstream' Muslim thinkers would speak to audiences of young British Muslims. The rationale behind this was that these speakers would distil effective arguments against extremist justification for terrorism in denouncing it as un-Islamic, so as to 'counter the ideological and theological underpinnings of the terrorist narrative'.[15] They included a variety of international figures, and two high-profile Muslim intellectuals to take part and remain committed to this strategy were the Swiss-born Francophone scholar, Tariq Ramadan, and the American convert Hamza Yusuf Hanson.

A second proposed plank concerned the creation of Muslim forums against extremism and Islamophobia. These could be led by key individuals and bring together members of local Muslim communities, law enforcement and public service agencies to discuss how to tackle extremism and Islamophobia in their area. The third and perhaps most long-standing recommendation, in terms of proposed structural capacity building within British Muslim communities, promoted the formation of a Mosques and Imams National Advisory Board (MINAB). To this end, a steering group of Muslim leaders has undertaken an extensive national consultation on matters such as the accreditation of imams, better governance of mosques, and interfaith activity.[16] Alongside this professional development programme or 'up-skilling' of imams and mosque officials, recommendations were also made for a national campaign and coalition to increase the visibility of Muslim women, and to specifically empower and equip them in the course of becoming active citizens.

The provenance of these working groups and their recommendations rests in a broader strategy which the British Government had been cumulatively developing since the events of 9/11. Known as CONTEST, this broad-ranging counter-terrorism strategy was launched in 2003 and comprised four components concerned with meeting the objectives of *Pursuit* (to stop terrorist attacks), *Preparedness* (to mitigate their impact where they cannot be stopped), *Protection* (to strengthen overall protection against terrorist attacks) and *Prevention* (to stop people from becoming terrorists or supporting violent extremists). It is this last objective that was given added impetus upon the news that British Muslims had planned and carried out the London bombings, and it is the objective that has most overtly sought the interactive involvement of British Muslim communities at large. It is therefore unsurprising to learn that a strategy premised upon entering, and to some extent reformulating, the life worlds of British Muslim communities has been the subject of critical debate in the study of ethnic relations more broadly (Spalek and Imoual 2007; Lambert 2008; MGhee 2008). That this intention was salient could be gleaned from the fact that immediately after the London bombing, the Home Office signalled that it would establish the Commission on Integration and Cohesion (COIC) 'to advise on how, consistent with their own religion and culture, there is better integration of those parts of the community inadequately integrated'.[17]

In this way the *Prevent* strategy signals some diffusion of formal responsibilities for policy implementation and service delivery in a way that some perceive as indicative of broader development in 'governance' practices whereby 'responsibility and accountability for a wide range of social issues is increasingly focused towards local levels, whilst at the same time centralised control in terms of resources and target-setting is maintained' (Spalek and Imoual 2007: 188). While not immediately apparent in the earlier quotation, the incorporation too of faith-based groups from within the third sector is potentially part of a novel approach of engaging with religious minorities through the practices and models of representation, stakeholders and advocacy in the consultative arena (O'Toole, *et al.* 2009). What this discussion is trying to elaborate on is the manner in which the *Prevent* agenda, in constituting part of the broad counter-terrorism strategy, appears simultaneously to be subject to at least two broader prevailing dynamics comprising:

> the implementation of anti-terrorist laws that can be used disproportionately against Muslims leading to the potential for their increased surveillance and control and thereby serving to reduce Muslims' trust of state institutions, while at the same time pursuing approaches that acknowledge, and stress the importance of, the involvement of British … Muslim communities in helping to combat extremism. (Spalek and Imoual 2007: 191)

Indeed, Spalek and Imoual (ibid.) frame these dynamics relationally in terms of 'harder' and 'softer' strategies of engagement, whereby the former may be understood as consisting of various means of surveillance, policing and intelligence gathering, and so on. The latter, meanwhile, would include the development of dialogue, participation and community feedback between Muslim communities, state agencies and voluntary organizations in a way that may serve to increase trust in 'the battle for hearts and minds'. For example, the *Prevent* strategy emphasizes, and seeks to extend to Muslims, long-established equality traditions historically orientated towards ethnic and racial minorities:

> The Prevent strategy requires a specific response, but we must also make the most of the links with wider community work to reduce inequalities, tackle racism and other forms of extremism (e.g. extreme far right), build cohesion and empower communities […] Likewise, it is recognised that the arguments of violent extremists, which rely on creating a 'them' and an 'us', are less likely to find traction in cohesive communities. (DCLG 2008: 6–7)

This builds upon recognition within government policies and legislation of Muslim religious difference that has been manifested in other ways, including measures against religious discrimination as set out in the Equality Act 2006. The tensions, then, surround the extent to which the prevailing British citizenship being extended to Muslims – through social and community cohesion agendas – is twinned with or placed within the same register as anti/counter-terrorism strategies that import or rely upon certain securitized 'hard' aspects of this dimension of state–Muslim engagement. The risk is that Muslim active citizenship is to some extent framed in terms of demonstrable counter-terrorism activities, in a way which assumes that

Muslim communities at large remain the 'locus of the issue of extremism' (Spalek and Imoual 2007: 194).

British Muslim citizenship and the rebalancing of multiculturalism

What these examples begin to illustrate is that the state of multiculturalism in Britain does not mirror the 'drastic break with multiculturalism' (Entzinger 2007: 201) recently made by the Dutch. This has seen the Netherlands discontinue some emblematic multiculturalist policies while introducing others specifically tailored to ignore ethnic minority differences. This includes the large-scale abandonment of dual-citizenship programmes; a withdrawal of national-level funding for minority group organizations and activities supporting cultural difference; reallocating the small percentage of public broadcasting time dedicated to multicultural issues; a proposed banning of the wearing of the burka in public places through an Act of parliament; and a cessation of ethnic monitoring of labour market participation (Bader 2008; Entzinger 2007, 2003; Van De Vijver, *et al.* 2006). Neither does it confirm Favell's (2008: 702) insistence that:

> [O]ur tried-and-tested narratives and models of postwar immigration in Europe – the standard discussions of immigration, integration and citizenship, based on post-colonial, guestworker and asylum models, and historical distinctions between pre- and post-1973 trends – are finished.

In contrast, what has been taking place in Britain is more like a movement from a perceived *neglect* to *affirmation* of 'Britishness' presented as a meta-membership with which all, including Muslim minorities and non-Muslim majorities, should engage. For example, the government-endorsed report entitled 'A Journey to Citizenship' (Home Office 2005: 15) chaired by the late Sir Bernard Crick has characterized Britishness as denoting

> respect [for] the laws, the elected parliamentary and democratic political structures, traditional values of mutual tolerance, respect for equal rights and mutual concern [...] To be British is to respect those over-arching specific institutions, values, beliefs and traditions that bind us all, the different nations and cultures together in peace and in a legal order. [...] So to be British does not mean assimilation into a common culture so that original identities are lost.

Similarly, the Cantle report (Cantle 2001: 10) which followed the inquiry into the civil unrest and rioting in some northern English cities, argues for a 'greater sense of citizenship' informed by 'common elements of "nationhood" [including] the use of the English language' (ibid.: 19), but equally it stresses that 'we are never going to turn the clock back to what was perceived to be a dominant or monoculturalist view of nationality' (ibid.: 18). Its lead author has elsewhere pleaded: 'let's not just throw out the concept of multiculturalism; let's update it and move it to a more sophisticated and developed approach' (Cantle 2006: 91). To this we could add the conclusions of the Home Office sponsored Denham Report (2002: 20) which stressed that 'our society is multicultural, and it is shaped by the interaction between people of diverse cultures. There is no single dominant and unchanging culture into which all must assimilate.' Indeed, Tony Blair's last speech on the topic presented this affirmation in a strong 'civic' sense in which he stated that 'the whole point is that multicultural Britain was never supposed to be a celebration of division; but of diversity. [...] So it is not that we need to dispense with multicultural Britain. On the contrary we should continue celebrating it' (Blair 2006).

The development of citizenship education is illustrative of this sentiment, and its late introduction in England, particularly when compared with North America and some European countries, is an interesting anomaly. As Kerr (1999: 204) has put it, 'the avoidance of any overt official government direction in schools concerning political socialization and citizenship education can almost be seen as a national trait', and indeed can be seen to be paralleled by the equally late adoption in England of the National Curriculum. Similarly, Sir Bernard Crick himself, as chair of the Qualifications and Curriculum Authority (QCA) commission into citizenship education, states that:

> We were the last civilised country almost in the world to make citizenship part of the national curriculum. I think we thought we didn't need it being the mother of all parliaments and a model to the world of parliamentary government; I think those ideas lingered on and long past reality. (Personal communication, 27 June 2007)

As Crick's report recommending the introduction of citizenship education put it, part of the groundswell for its recent emergence is undoubtedly a sense of 'civic deficit' epitomized by voter apathy amongst young people which the report claims 'is inexcusably bad and should and could be remedied' (QCA 1998: sec. 3. para. 10). To this end the QCA, under the commission chaired by Crick, recommended the implementation of a coordinated national strategy for the statutory requirement for schools to spend around 5 per cent of their curriculum time teaching three interdependent elements of citizenship education. These would comprise (1) social and moral responsibility, (2) community involvement, and (3) political literacy.

While these reiterate elements of the Swann Commission, they perhaps also constitute a modification of earlier approaches. Though the QCA (1998: 17) insisted upon respect for 'the plurality of nations, cultures, ethnic identities, and religions long established in the UK', there is no explicit reference to anti-racism which confirmed to some that citizenship education represents a disengagement from these issues. Osler and Starkey (2001: 293), for example, charge the QCA report with 'institutional racism' for demanding that 'minorities must learn to respect the laws, codes and conventions as much as the majority' (QCA 1998: 17–18). This they take as evidence of a 'colonial approach ... that runs throughout the report' and which 'falls into the trap of treating certain ethnicities as "Other" when it discusses cultural diversity' (Osler and Starkey 2001: 292–3.). Sir Bernard Crick repudiates the view that his committee singled out minorities, saying that

> Were not willing to give the public the view that the major thrust of citizenship was race relations. We said damn it, it's about the whole population including the majority [...] pupils should learn, respect and have knowledge of national, regional ethnic and religious differences. We were simply taking a broader view. We thought that ... all our nations' children should receive an education that would help them to become active citizens: *all* our nations' children. (Personal communication, 27 June 2007)

This need not be evidence of an assimilatory 'retreat' from anti-racism or multiculturalism, however, but something that might be characterized as a 'rebalancing' of broader discourses of anti-racism and multiculturalism. Indeed, the entire idea of citizenship education is, in itself, surely evidence of this, while the most recent comment from the government-sponsored Commission on Integration and Cohesion (COIC) (2007), *explicitly* distinguishes the definition of integration from a potentially assimilatory notion:

> Very many of the definitions of cohesion and integration offered in the response to the Commission on Integration and Cohesion (COIC) consultation spontaneously include a level of concern to distinguish integration from *assimilation*, stressing the importance for true cohesion of accepting – and celebrating – difference. Individual and group *identities* should not be endangered by the process of integration, but rather they should be enriched within both the incoming groups and the host nation. Cohesion implies a society in which differences of culture, race and faith are recognised and accommodated within an overall sense of identity, rather than a single identity, based on a uniform similarity. (COIC 2007:5 original emphasis)

With this in mind, Modood's (2007a) restatement of multiculturalism as a civic idea that can be tied to an inclusive national identity, and some of the responses this has elicited (see Modood 2007b), helps cast light upon the ways in which the COIC's aspirations might be realized and Muslims might feature in it. For not unusually among advocates of multiculturalism, Modood emphasizes the role of citizenship in fostering commonality across differences, before recasting part of this civic inclusion as proceeding through claims-making upon, and therefore a reformulating of, national identities. This is because:

> [I]t does not make sense to encourage strong multicultural or minority identities and weak common or national identities; strong multicultural identities are a good thing – they are not intrinsically divisive, reactionary or subversive – but they need the complement of a framework of vibrant, dynamic, national narratives and the ceremonies and rituals which give expression to a national identity. It is clear that minority identities are capable of exerting an emotional

> pull for the individuals for whom they are important. Multicultural citizenship, if it is to be equally attractive to the same individuals, requires a comparable counterbalancing emotional pull. (Modood 2007c)

This restatement contains at least two key points that are central to the preceding discussion. The first concerns an advocacy and continuity of earlier forms of multiculturalism that have sought to accommodate collective demands and incorporate differences into the mainstream. These demands or differences are not only tolerated but celebrated, and include the turning of a 'negative' difference into a 'positive' difference in a way that is presented in the ethnic pride currents as elements of racial equality policies in Britain. The second is to place a greater emphasis upon the unifying potential of an affirmation of a renegotiated and inclusive national identity therein. While the latter point is welcomed by some commentators who had previously formed part of the pluralistic or anti-racist left identified earlier, the bringing of previously marginalized groups into the societal mainstream is, at best, greeted more ambivalently. One example can be found in Nick Pearce, former director of the Institute for Public Policy Research (IPPR) and currently Head of the Research and Policy Unit at 10 Downing Street under Prime Minister Brown. Pearce rejects the view that religious orientation is comparable to other forms of ethnocultural belonging because this 'may end up giving public recognition to groups which endorse fundamentally illiberal and even irrational goals' (Pearce 2007). He therefore argues that one obstacle to an endorsement of multiculturalism is the public affirmation of religious identities.[18]

It is difficult, however, not to view this as a knee-jerk reaction that condemns religious identities per se, rather than examining them on a case-by-case basis, while at the same time assuming that ethnic identities are free of illiberal goals. This is empirically problematic given that clitoridectomy, for instance, is an example of a *cultural practice* among various ethnic groups and yet has little support from any religion. So to favour ethnicity and problematize religion is a reflection of a secularist bias that has alienated many religionists, especially Muslims, from multiculturalism. It is much better to acknowledge that the 'multi' in multiculturalism will encompass different kinds of groups and does not itself privilege any one kind, but that 'recognition' should be given to the identities that marginalized groups themselves value and find strength in, whether these be racial, religious or ethnic (Modood 2007c).

Conclusions

This chapter has charted the contemporary structural and cultural dynamics informing relationships between British Muslim identity articulations and the state. Traversing areas of political participation, observance of aspects of Sharia in personal and civil matters, spatial settlement and educational social mobility, and community consultation in preventing violent extremism, the chapter has elaborated how responses to Muslim 'difference' in Britain detail a pattern of engagement that has evolved over a period of time through both race-equality and multi-faith opportunity structures. In a cumulative way, developments in each have come to characterize a British multiculturalism that has, contrary to popular insistence following the London bombings, not been erased. As such we contend that any discussion of Muslim minorities in twenty-first-century Britain must not ignore these developments for they too may affect the course of future state–Muslim engagement – a point worth stressing as we stand on the threshold of a new era of Conservative electoral dominance in British politics.

Notes

1 The 1948 British Nationality Act granted freedom of movement to citizens of all formerly or presently dependent, and now Commonwealth, territories (regardless of whether their passports were issued by independent or colonial states) by creating the status of 'Citizenship of the United Kingdom and Colonies' (CUKC). Until they acquired one or other of the national citizenships in these post-colonial countries, these formerly British subjects continued to retain their British status. This is one of the reasons why Kymlicka's distinction between national minority rights and ethno-cultural minority rights is not easily transposed on to Britain (see Modood, 2007c).

2 It is important to bear in mind that the Race Relations Act does not allow positive discrimination or affirmative action. This means that an employer cannot try to change the balance of the workforce by selecting someone mainly because they are from a particular racial group. This would be discrimination on racial grounds, and therefore unlawful (see Karim, 2004/5). What in the US is called 'affirmative action' goes well beyond what is lawful in Britain.

3 See Modood (2009: 492) for a discussion of the development of the MCB.

4 See http://www.mcb.org.uk.

5 Such charges are largely circumstantial owing to the links between the MCB members and the Islamist organization Jamat-e-Islami which was founded in northern India in the 1930s by Abu A'la Mawdudi.

6 Though interestingly, its regional affiliates such as the Muslim Council of Wales (MCW) have not faced such criticism.

7 Including the headscarf or *hijab*, full-face veil or *niqab*, or full-body garments such as the *jilbab*.

8 Evidenced not only by the public and the media but also by academics and intellectuals including Christian Joppke. Writing in the *British Journal of Sociology* he states: 'Certain minority practices, on which, so far, no one had dared to comment, have now become subjected to public scrutiny as never before. The notorious example is that of arranged marriage which, to an alarming degree, *seems to be* forced marriage' (2004: 251, emphasis added). Whilst this is an important issue that must never be ignored, the evidence on which Joppke bases his assumptions remains undisclosed in the rest of the article. Although the conflation between 'forced' and 'arranged' marriages is unfortunate and misleading, the suggestion that no one has dared to comment on either betrays a surprising unfamiliarity with a British case in which pressure groups and organizations such as Southall Black Sisters and Women Against Fundamentalism (WAF) have led high profile national campaigns. The Government, moreover, has established transnational strategies such as the Working Group on Forced Marriage which has seen the creation of the Forced Marriage Unit (FMU), as well as the introduction of the Forced Marriage (Civil Protection) Act 2007.

9 This sections draws on Modood (1992).

10 See: http://www.mcb.org.uk/vote2005/ (accessed 1 September 2008).

11 See MCB press release 9 April 2003.

12 See http://www.archbishopofcanterbury.org/1575 (accessed 1 September 2008).

13 The General Certificate of Secondary Education (GCSE) is the standard qualification for students enrolled in compulsory schooling until the age of 16 years. The minimum standard for a good set of GCSEs is the possession of five at grades A*–C.

14 Clustered as follows: (1) Engaging with young people; (2) Providing a full range of education services in the UK that meet the needs of the Muslim community; (3) Engaging with Muslim women; (4) Supporting regional and local initiatives and community actions; (5) Imam training and accreditation and the role of mosques as a resource for the whole community; (6) Security – Islamophobia, protecting Muslims from extremism, and community confidence in policing, and (7) Tackling extremism and radicalization.

15 Foreign and Commonwealth Office, 'EIWG fact sheet', available at: http://www.fco.gov.uk/servlet/Front?pagename=OpenMarket/Xcelerate/ShowPage&c=Page&cid=1153388310360 (accessed 19 October 2006). The 'Radical MiddleWay' project – http://www.radicalmiddleway.co.uk – is also supported by the Home Office, and according to the DCLG over 30,000 people have so far attended the first 7 of 12 roadshows and the organizers expect more than 100,000 to attend in total (for more details see: http://www.communities.gov.uk/documents/communities/pdf/151792.pdf).

16 The steering group published a good practice guide for mosques when the Advisory Board was formally launched on 27 June 2006.

17 As outlined by Tony Blair himself. See Prime Minister's press conference, 5 August 2005, available at: http://www.pm.gov.uk/output/Page8041.asp (accessed 9 November 2005).

18 Kymlicka (2007: 54) identifies this fear as the 'liberal-illiberal' front in the new 'war' on immigrant multiculturalism.

References

Abrams, D. and Houston, D. M. (2006) *Equality, Diversity and Prejudice in Britain*. London: HMSO.

Ahmad, F., Modood, T. and Lissenburgh, L. (2003) *South Asian Women and Employment in Britain*. London: Policy Studies Institute.

Ansari, H. (forthcoming) 'The Legal Status of Muslims in the UK', draft chapter.

Ansari, H. (2004) *'The Infidel Within': Muslims in Britain since 1800*. London: Hurst & Co.

Anwar, M. and Bakhsh, M. (2003) *British Muslims and State Policies*. Warwick, England: Centre for Research in Ethnic Relations, University of Warwick.

Aspinall, P. (2000) 'Should a Question on "Religion" be Asked on the 2001 British Census? A Public Policy Case in Favour', *Social Policy & Administration*, 34 (5): 584–600.

Bader, V. (2008) 'Associational Governance of Ethno-Religious Diversity in Europe. The Dutch Case'. Paper presented at Penn Program on Democracy, Citizenship, and Constitutionalism, Conference, 9 May 2008. Available at: http://www.sas.upenn.edu/dcc/documents/AssociationalGovernanceofEthno-ReligiousDiversity.doc (accessed 19 July 2008).

Bagguley, P. and Hussein, Y. (2007) *The Role of Higher Education in Providing Opportunities for South Asian Women*. Bristol: The Policy Press.

Bagguley, P. and Hussain, Y. (2008) *Riotous Citizens: Ethnic Conflict in Multicultural Britain*. London: Ashgate.

Bell, D. (2007) 'In the Name of the Law', *The Guardian*, 14 June.

Blair, T. (2006) 'Tony Blair's On Britain Speech', *The Guardian*, 28 March. Available at: http//www.guardianunlimited.co.uk/Britain/article/0,2763,184950.00.html.asp (accessed 13 July 2008).

Cantle, T. (2001) *Community Cohesion: A Report of the Independent Review Team*. London: HMSO.

Cantle, T. (2006) 'Multiculturalism – a Failed Experiment?', *Index on Censorship*, 35 (2), 91–2.

Carter, D. (2005) 'Muslims Test their Strength as Voters and Candidates', *The Times*, 22 March.

Cohen, N. (2007) *What's Left? How Liberals Lost Their Way*. London: HarperPerennial.

Commission on Integration and Cohesion (COIC) (2007) *Our Shared Future: Themes, Messages and Challenges: A Final Analysis of the Key Themes from the Commission on Integration and Cohesion Consultation*. London: HMSO.

Commission on the Future of Multi-Ethnic Britain (CMEB) (2000) *The Future of Multi-Ethnic Britain*. London: Profile Books.

Denham, J. (2002) *Building Cohesive Communities:A Report of the Ministerial Group on Public Order and Community Cohesion*. London: HMSO.

Department for Communities and Local Government (DCLG) (2008) *Preventing Violent Extremism: A Strategy for Delivery*. London: HMSO.

Dhami, R. S., Squires, J. and Modood, T. (2006) *Developing Positive Action Policies: Learning from the Experiences of Europe and North America*. London: Department for Work and Pensions Research Report no. 406.

Entzinger, H. (2003) 'The Rise and Fall of Multiculturalism: The Case of the Netherlands', in C. Joppke and E. Morawska (eds), *Toward Assimilation and Citizenship*. Basingstoke: Palgrave Macmillan, pp. 59–86.

Entzinger, H. (2007) 'The Parallel Decline of Multiculturalism and the Welfare State in the Netherlands', in K. Banting and W. Kymlicka (eds), *Multiculturalism and the Welfare State*. Oxford: Oxford University Press, pp. 177–202.

Favell, A. (1998) *Philosophies of Integration: Immigration and the Idea of Citizenship in France and Britain*. Hampshire: Palgrave Macmillan.

Favell, A. (2008) 'The New Face of East-West Migration in Europe', *Journal of Ethnic and Migration Studies*, 34 (5): 701–16.

Fekete, L. (2004) 'Anti-Muslim Racism and the European Security State', *Race and Class*, 46 (1): 4–29.

Fieldhouse, E. and Cutts, D. (2008) 'Mobilisation or Marginalisation? Neighbourhood Effects on Muslim Electoral Registration in Britain in 2001', *Political Studies*, 56: 333–54

Filby, L. (2006) 'Religion and Belief', in *Equalities in Great Britain 1946–2006* (unpublished), Equality and Human Rights Commission (EHRC) consultation papers.

Finney, N. and Simpson, L. (2009) *'Sleepwalking to Segregation'? Challenging Myths about Race and Migration*. Bristol: Policy Press.

Gove, M. (2006) *Celsius 7/7*. London: Weidenfeld and Nicolson.

Halliday, F. (1999) '"Islamophobia" Reconsidered', *Ethnic & Racial Studies*, 22 (5): 892–902.

Hansen, R. (2006) 'The Danish Cartoon Controversy: A Defence of Liberal Freedom', *International Migration*, 44 (5): 7–16.

Hattersley, R. (2005) 'I Took the Muslim Vote for Granted – but That has all Changed …', *The Guardian*, 8 April.

Hewer, C. (2001) 'Schools for Muslims', *Oxford Review of Education*, 27: 515–27.

Hewitt, I. (1998) 'Final report', *Report: The magazine from the Association of Teachers and Lecturers*, April: 10–25.

Home Office (2005) *Life in the United Kingdom: A Journey to Citizenship*. London: HMSO.

Hutton, W. (2007) 'Why the West must Stay True to Itself', *The Observer*, 17 June.
Available at: http://www.guardian.co.uk/commentisfree/2007/jun/17/religion.comment (accessed 13 July 2008).
Jenkins, R. (1966) *Address Given by the Home Secretary to a Meeting of Voluntary Liaison Committees*, 23 May. London: NCCI.
Joppke, C. (1999) 'How Immigration is Changing Citizenship: A Comparative View', *Ethnic and Racial Studies*, 22 (4): 629–52.
Joppke, C. (2004) 'The Retreat of Multiculturalism in the Liberal State: Theory and Policy', *British Journal of Sociology*, 55 (2): 237–57.
Joppke, C. (2009) 'Limits of Integration Policy: Britain and her Muslims', *Journal of Ethnic and Migration Studies*, 35 (3): 453–72.
Karim, R. (2004/5) 'Take Care when Being Positive', *Connections*, London: Commission for Racial Equality (CRE).
Kerr, D. (1999). *Citizenship Education: An International Comparison*. London: QCA.
Khattab, N., Sirkeci, I., Modood, T. and Johnston, R. (2006) 'A Multilevel Analysis of Returns to Education in Labour Market among Ethno-religious Minorities in England and Wales', paper presented at the *European Population Conference 2006* (*EPC 2006*) *'Population Challenges in Ageing Societies'*, Department of Geography, University of Liverpool, Liverpool, UK, 21–4 June 2006. Available at: http://epc2006.princeton.edu/download.aspx?submissionId=60008 (accessed 29 March 2009).
Kundani, A. (2008) *The End of Tolerance: Racism in 21st Century Britain*. London: Pluto.
Klausen, Y. (2009) 'British Counter-Terrorism after 7/7: Adapting Community-Policing to the Fight Against Domestic Terrorism', *Journal of Ethnic and Migration Studies* 35 (3): 403–20.
Kymlicka, W. (2007) 'The New Debate on Minority Rights (and Postscript)', in A. S. Laden and D. Owen (eds), *Multiculturalism and Political Theory*. Cambridge: Cambridge University Press, pp. 25–59.
Lambert, R. (2008) 'Empowering Salafis and Islamists Against Al-Qaida: A London Counter-Terrorism Case Study'. *PS: Political Science and Politics*, 41 (1): 31–5.
McGhee, D. (2008) *The End of Multiculturalism? Terrorism, Integration & Human Rights*. Maidenhead: Open University Press and McGraw-Hill Education.
Meer, N. (2009) 'Identity Articulations, Mobilisation and Autonomy in the Movement for Muslim Schools in Britain', *Race, Ethnicity and Education*, 12 (3): 379–98.
Meer, N. and Modood, T. (2009) 'The Multicultural State we're in: Muslims, "Multiculture", and the Civic Re-balancing of British Multiculturalism'. *Political Studies*, 57 (1): 473–9.
Meer, N. and Noorani, T. (2008) 'A Sociological Comparison of Anti-Semitism and Anti-Muslim Sentiment in Britain', *The Sociological Review*, 56 (2): 195–219.
Modood, T. (1992) 'British Asians and the Salmon Rushdie Affair', in J. Donald and A. Rattansi (eds), *'Race', Culture and Difference*. London: Sage, pp. 260–77.
Modood, T. (2004) 'Capitals, Ethnic Identity and Educational Qualifications', *Cultural Trends*, 13 (2): 87–105.
Modood, T. (2005a) 'Disaffected Muslims will Make their Votes Count', *Financial Times*, 28 April.
Modood, T. (2005b) *Multicultural Politics: Racism, Ethnicity and Muslims in Britain*. Edinburgh: Edinburgh University Press.
Modood, T. (2006) 'British Muslims and the Politics of Multiculturalism', in T. Modood, A. Triandafyllidou and R. Zapata-Barrero (eds), *Multiculturalism, Muslims and Citizenship: A European Approach*. London: Routledge.

Modood, T. (2007a) *Multiculturalism: A Civic Idea*. London: Polity Press.
Modood, T. (2007b) 'Multiculturalism's Civic Future: A Response', *Open Democracy*, 20 June. Available at: http://www.opendemocracy.net/faith_ideas/Europe_islam/multi culturalism_future (accessed 19 June 2008).
Modood, T. (2007c) 'Multiculturalism, Citizenship and National Identity', *Open Democracy*, 17 May. Available at: http://www.opendemocracy.net/faith_ideas/Europe_islam/multi-culturalism_future (accessed 13 July 2008).
Modood, T. (2008a) 'Multiculturalism after 7/7: A Scapegoat or a Hope for the Future?', *RUSI*, 153 (2): 14–17.
Modood, T. (2008b) 'Multicultural Citizenship and the Sharia Storm', *Open Democracy*, 14 February. Available at: http://www.opendemocracy.net/faith_ideas/Europe_islam/multiculturalism_future (accessed 13 July 2008).
Modood, T. (forthcoming) 'Ethnicity and Religion', in M. Flinders, A. Gamble, C. Hay and M. Kenny (eds), *Oxford Handbook of British Politics*. Oxford: Oxford University Press.
Modood, T., Berthoud, R., Lakey, J., Nazroo, J., Smith, P., Virdee, S. and Beishon, S. (1997) *The Fourth National Survey of Ethnic Minorities in Britain: Diversity and Disadvantage*. London: Policy Studies Institute.
Moore, C. (2004) 'Islam is Not an Exotic Addition to the English Country Garden', *Daily Telegraph*, 21 August. Available at: http://www.telegraph.co.uk/opinion/main.jhtml?xml=lopinion/2004/08/21/do2101. xml&sSheet=/portal/2004/08/21/ixportal.html (accessed 13 July 2008).
Moore, C. (2006) 'How Cromwell Gave Us Joan Collins and Other Luminaries', *Daily Telegraph*, 17 June. Available at: http://www.telegraph.co.uk/opinion/main.jhtml?xml=/opinion/2006/06/17/do1702.xml&sSheet=/opinion/2006/06/17/ixop.html (accessed 13 July 2008).
Mullard, C. (1985) *Anti-racist Education: The Three O's*. Cardiff, UK: National Association for Multicultural Education.
Office for National Statistics (ONS) (2002a) 'Low income for 60 per cent of Pakistanis/Bangladeshis'. Available at: http://www.statistics.gov.uk/cci/nugget.asp?id=269 (accessed 28 March 2009).
Office for National Statistics (ONS) (2002b) 'Labour Market: Bangladeshis' Unemployment highest'. Available at: http://www.statistics.gov.uk/cci/nugget.asp?id=271 (accessed 28 March 2009).
Office for National Statistics (ONS) (2002c) 'Education'. Available at: http://www.statistics.gov.uk/cci/nugget.asp?id=268 (accessed 28 March 2009).
Osler, A. and Starkey, H. (2001) 'Citizenship Education and National Identities in Britain and France: Inclusive or Exclusive?' *Oxford Review of Education*, 27: 287–305.
O'Toole, T., Modood, T. and Meer, N. (2009) 'Governing Religion: The Participation of Muslims in Contemporary Forms of Governance'. Research Proposal.
Peach, C. and Gale, R. (2003) 'Muslims, Hindus, and Sikhs in the New Religious Landscape of England', *The Geographical Review*, 93 (4): 469–90.
Pearl, D. and Menski, W. (1988) *Muslim Family Law*, London: Sweet and Maxwell.
Pearce, N. (2007) *An Ambiguous Rescue Multiculturalism and Citizenship: Responses to Tariq Modood*. Available at: http://www.opendemocracy.net/faithterrorism/response _madood_4630.jsp#two (accessed 21 May 2007).
Phillips, M. (2006) *Londonistan: How Britain Created a Terror State Within*. London: Gibson Square Books.
Phillips, T. (2005) 'Sleepwalking into Segration'. Available at: http://83.137.212.42/sitearchive/

cre/Default.aspx.LocID-0hgnew07r.RefLocID-0hg00900c001001.Lang-EN.htm (accessed 18 March 2008).

Policy Exchange (2007) *Living Apart Together: British Muslims and the Paradox of Multiculturalism*. London: Policy Exchange.

Policy Innovation Unit (PIU) (2001) *Improving Labour Market Achievements for Ethnic Minorities in British Society*. Available at: http://www.cabinet-office.gov.uk/innovation/2001/ethnicity/scope.shtml (accessed 30 October 2009).

QCA (Qualifications and Curriculum Authority) (1998) *Education for Citizenship and the Teaching of Democracy in Schools*. Report of the Advisory Group on Citizenship. London: QCA.

Radcliffe, L. (2004) 'A Muslim Lobby at Whitehall?' *Islam and Christian-Muslim Relations*, 15 (3): 365–86.

Rahman, F. (1982) *Islam and Modernity*. Chicago, IL: University of Chicago Press.

Rudiger, A. (2007) 'Cultures of Equality, Traditions of Belonging', in C. Bertossi (ed.), *European Anti-Discrimination and the Politics of Citizenship*. Basingstoke: Palgrave Macmillan, pp. 41–63.

Singh, G. (2005) 'British Multiculturalism and Sikhs', *Sikhs Formations*, 1 (2): 157–73.

Skinner, G. (2002) 'Religious Pluralism and School Provision in Britain', *Intercultural Education*, 13: 171–81.

Spalek, B. and Imoual, A. (2007) 'Muslim Communities and Counter-Terror Responses: "Hard" Approaches to Community Engagement in the UK and Australia', *Journal of Muslim Minority Affairs*, 27 (2): 185–202.

Swann, M. (1985). *Education for All: The Report of the Inquiry into the Education of Pupils from Ethnic Minority Groups*. London: HMSO.

Tempest, M. (2007) 'Cameron Returns to Birmingham to Address Muslims', *The Guardian*. Available at: http://www.guardian.co.uk/politics/2007/feb/05/conservatives.religion (accessed 30 October 2009).

Toynbee, P. (2005) 'My Right to Offend a Fool: Race and Religion are Different – which is why Islamophobia is a Nonsense and Religious Hatred must Not be Outlawed', *The Guardian*, 10 June. Available at: http://www.guardian.co.uk/politics/2005/jun/10/religion.politicalcolumnists (accessed 13 July 2008).

Troyna, B. (1987) 'Beyond Multiculturalism: Towards the Enactment of Anti-racist Education in Policy Provision and Pedagogy', *Oxford Review of Education*, 13 (3): 307–20.

Van De Vijver, F., Schalk-Soekar, S., Arends-Tóth, J. and Breugelmans, S. (2006) 'Cracks in the Wall of Multiculturalism? A Review of Attitudinal Studies in the Netherlands', *IJMS International Journal on Multicultural Societies*, 8 (1): 102–18.

Yilmaz, I. (2001) 'Law as Chameleon: "The Question of Incorporation of Muslims Personal Law into the English Law"', *Journal of Muslim Minority Affairs*, 21 (2): 297–308.

6 Sweden

Cooperation and conflict

Jonas Otterbeck

Introduction

Sweden has become obsessed with its Muslim population. Blogs, newspapers, TV shows, debaters, artists, politicians, interfaith activists, academics in the social science fields, school personnel, comedians, right-wing Christians and, of course, people with a Muslim family history are active participants in an endless discourse about Muslims. Integration, criminality, honour, sexism, undemocratic thinking, rape, nativity, radicalization, etc. – everything is given a Muslim angle. And, of course, Islam and Islamophobia are hotly debated issues. This is quite remarkable when the highest estimation of the number of people in Sweden with a Muslim family history is 400,000, a mere 4.5 per cent of the total population of 9 million; there are roughly as many Muslims as there are schoolteachers in Sweden. Everyone has an opinion, though seldom a very informed one. This was not the case when I began studying Arabic, Islam and the Middle East in 1984. What has happened, and why all these strong opinions?

In what follows I will try to give a short introduction to how a Muslim presence in Sweden came about. I will further look at the socio-economic conditions of this population. Finally I will try to highlight the current debates on Muslims and Islam in Sweden, but also the collaborations in operation that are easy to miss.

But first, an observation. The constant use of the term 'Muslim' as if it were the only, or prime, identity of people with a Muslim family history is problematic in several ways. Olivier Roy (2004) points out that it is better to speak of a Muslim population than of a Muslim group; it is more reasonable to point out that a country – within its borders – has a certain number of people adhering to Islam in some way or another, rather than to say that these people share certain political, social or cultural values. Muslims adhere to several different Islamic traditions, and differences in class, language, national and ethnic background tend to colour each tradition's interpretations of Islam. Furthermore, in several contexts, identifications other than 'Muslim' are far more important.

Another factor specific to Sweden is that there are no official statistics on the population's faith. Information about religious belonging is generally considered private or unimportant, and it is seldom included in questionnaires. Thus, it is difficult to know the exact number of Muslims living in Sweden, or how Muslims fare in the housing or labour market. But one can easily find statistics about people born in, for example, Bosnia or Iraq.

A Muslim population

Sweden's transformation from a poor country with a large emigration factor in the nineteenth and early twentieth centuries to one of the most prosperous countries in the world with a fairly high immigration rate has created an interesting situation economically, politically and culturally. More than 1.5 million Swedes emigrated, mostly to the United States, between the mid-nineteenth century and 1930 (Lundh and Ohlsson 1994). During the same period the population of Sweden almost doubled (from 3.5 million in 1850 to 6.1 million in 1930), in itself a rather typical trait of countries eliciting labour migration – health and economic conditions improve and the population grows faster than the economic sector. Contrary to some other European countries, Sweden has almost no colonial history save a few co-enterprises with the Dutch in the seventeenth century. However, several Swedish investors and adventurers partook in the colonial projects of the British and the Dutch crowns. The colonial discourse – intertwined with evolutionist ideas about culture, religion and race – was well spread among the Swedish intellectual and political elite. Even though Sweden is a country in the northern periphery of Europe, racialized colonial cognitive maps are easily detected in travellers' accounts and scholarly work from the eighteenth century onwards. This includes so-called 'Orientalist discourses' on Muslims and Islam (Otterbeck 2002).

From the mid-twentieth century, in the aftermath of World War II, and with Swedish industry and infrastructure intact, a period of prosperity and immigration began (Lundh and Ohlsson 1994).

Muslim migration to Sweden was almost non-existent before the 1960s. According to often cited official statistics, Sweden had only 15 individuals of the Muslim faith in 1930 (Karlsson and Svanberg 1995). The first Islamic organization, formed in 1949 by Muslim immigrants, was called Turk-islamföreningen i Sverige för religion och kultur (The Turk-Islamic Association in Sweden for the Promotion of Religion and Culture) (Karlsson and Svanberg 1995; Otterbeck 1998). Formed in Stockholm by Tatar migrants from the Baltic countries, it was, for a long time, the only Swedish Muslim association run by migrants. The only other Muslim associations before the mid-1970s were a minor Sufi circle set up by a group attracted to Inayat Khan's teaching (Westerlund 1999), and the Ahmadiyya movement that has been active (but not very successful) in Sweden since 1956. The latter was run mainly by converts, which is not the case today due to Ahmadiyya immigration from Pakistan (Otterbeck 2000a). Ahmadiyyas are still few in number, but they do have a mosque in Gothenburg and a centre in Malmö. The mosque was founded in 1976 and was the first purpose-built mosque in Sweden.

During the 1960s, Muslims started to arrive as labour migrants from southern Europe, mainly from Turkey and former Yugoslavia. It was primarily a migration of young men who ended up in the manufacturing industries of large and mid-size cities in Sweden. There was little reflection on the religious preferences or heritage of the migrants. Due to changes in the perception of migration (calls for better control, stricter legislation from 1968 onwards) and because of economic crises in the early 1970s (like the oil crisis in 1973) it became increasingly difficult to get a permit to enter Sweden for employment (Bevelander 2004). Instead, the 1970s Muslim migration was characterized by family reunification and an occasional wave of refugees (Ugandans in the beginning of the 1970s, Iranians in the late 1970s).

Since the second half of the 1980s, refugee immigration has dominated. Almost 400,000 individuals sought refuge in Sweden between 1984 and 2001 (Bevelander 2004). It is likely that at least 150,000 of these have a Muslim family background, based on information regarding their country of origin. Refugees in particularly high numbers have come from Iran, Iraq, Somalia, Afghanistan, Bosnia-Herzegovina, Kosovo and Albania. If we stress group identity instead, some of the refugees are Palestinians, Kurds (from Iran, Turkey, Iraq), Shias (Lebanon, Iraq) and Kosovo-Albanians (from different countries in the Balkans). Since the 1980s, labour migration has been virtually nil from countries with large Muslim populations, but family reunification has been, and still is, a large part of it (Lundh and Ohlsson 1994; Bevelander 2004).

By the end of the 1980s, it is estimated that some 100,000 Muslims resided in Sweden. In 1996, the number had reached 200,000 and in 2000 roughly 350,000 (Anwar, *et al.* 2004). The latest published estimation by researchers is 400,000 in 2007 (Larsson and Sander 2007). This means that 75 per cent of those Muslims have either emigrated to Sweden or were born there in the last 20 years. It is further estimated that one-third of the Muslim population is comprised of schoolchildren or infants (Anwar, *et al.* 2004). The number of converts is often estimated at 5,000–10,000.

Muslim organizations in Sweden

There is no ethnic or national group in particular which dominates by mere size in Sweden. It was, however, Turkish and Arab Sunni Muslims who were the first to organize themselves on a larger scale and foster relations with the Swedish state as Muslims. In the 1960s, having the tradition of encouraging and sponsoring interest groups, organized sport, adult education circles and other forms of organized social life, the Swedish state offered economic grants to the so-called 'Free Churches' (mainly Protestant of different denominations).[1]

After a particularly complex discussion about dependency, marked by the suspicion of the Free Churches towards the state and the State Church, a commission presently called Nämnden för statligt stöd till trossamfund (SST, or Commission for State Grants to Religious Communities) was set up in 1971 (Ekström 2006). Soon, the Catholic and Jewish associations were included, and in the mid-1970s Orthodox Christians and Muslims became eligible for state grants.

Several observers of Swedish politics have commented on the state's far-reaching ambition to organize social life, almost to the extent that civil society agents do not exist, and if they exist at all they do so in collaboration with the government, county or municipality officials. Local projects, which in other countries might be funded by grants from religious organizations, foundations or corporations, will most likely be sponsored by one of these levels of government (Berggren and Trägårdh 2006). Further, many note the high proportion of Swedish citizens who are members of associations. For example, in 2000, as many as 96 per cent of all Swedes in the age group 25–64 were part of an association and half of them indicated that they were active members (Lindgren 2008).

SST gives each community some financial support that is calculated based on the size of the community. Often this support is used to cover rental costs, costs for an imam or the employment of administrators. There is special support to be obtained when the communities open up new areas of activities, for example women's groups, adult education or imams visiting hospitalized individuals or inmates. SST also offers courses on how to run an association (democracy, bookkeeping, formal requirements for minutes, etc.) (URL: SST 1).

The history of Muslim organizations in Sweden is difficult to sum up since several of the important actors have changed their name over the years. In this short summary, they are referred to by their most recent name.

The first Muslim organization to receive support was Förenade Islamiska Församlingar i Sverige (FIFS or United Islamic Communities in Sweden). It was formed in 1974 to fill the need among the Muslim communities for an umbrella organization. State support presupposed a national organization that would distribute economic support to the different local communities. Thus, FIFS organized all kinds of Muslim communities, including Shia and Sunni communities of different ethnic background. FIFS is still active.

Due to the sensitivity of economic matters, there were quarrels and some chose to leave FIFS and form Sveriges Förenade Muslimska Församlingar (SMF or United Muslim Communities of Sweden) in 1982. These were mainly Sunnis with an Arabic language background, but the organization also contains Shia communities. The organization today is called Sveriges Muslimska Förbund.

In 1984, a new split occurred and Islamiska Kulturcenterunionen (IKUS or Union of Islamic Centres of Culture) was formed. In 1987, it became eligible for state grants. IKUS has a leaning towards the Turkish Süleymanli interpretation of Islam, but they also coordinate quite a few Somali communities (which is obvious when reading their statutes, which, among other things, talk about actions to be taken against female circumcision and the chewing of *kat*). In IKUS there are no Shia communities. IKUS still exists, but it does not appear to be very active (Larsson and Sander 2007).

In 1988, the three aforementioned umbrella organizations joined forces in Islamiska Samarbetsrådet (IS or The Islamic Cooperation Council). Its principal function was to coordinate the collaboration with SST. Since then, two other umbrella organizations have become eligible for state grants and have become part of IS.

Svenska Islamiska Församlingar (Swedish Islamic Parishes) is the youngest of the organizations, formed in 2002 as a result of a conflict between the leaders of IKUS.

The final organization in IS is Islamiska Shiasamfunden i Sverige (The Islamic Shia Denominations in Sweden). It was formed in 1992, but was not admitted into the circle of Islamic umbrella organizations receiving state grants until 2008.

IS provides financial support for the activities of some 120 different local Muslim associations with approximately 110,000 members (URL: SST 2). Still, there are several local associations that prefer to do without the support – at times because of the criticism directed towards how the umbrella organizations are run, and at other times because other funding is obtained. Others do not want to deal with the hassle of paperwork. One of the officials at SST estimates that 75 per cent of Muslim communities are organized through the umbrella organizations supported by SST (Otterbeck 2004). There are also national organizations operating without state grants, for example different organizations for Muslim youth like Sveriges Unga Muslimer (Sweden's Young Muslims), an organization founded in 1991 which has some 10,000 registered members, and one called Bosnien-Hercegovinas Muslimska Ungdomsförbund (Bosnia-Herzegovina's Muslim Youth Association) formed in 1997 (Karlsson Minganti 2008).

Browsing through the statutes and annual reports of the different organizations, one quickly finds some patterns. Apart from the expected ritual activities, most organizations are also involved in education for children, youth and adults (Otterbeck 1999). Some of them are running or actively supporting so-called 'independent schools', the typical Swedish form of private schools. The schools are run on a plus basis. They can add to but not withdraw anything from the national curriculum. Furthermore, they are supported by the state economically and are not allowed to collect tuition fees from the pupils.

Because of this support, a bond was created between Muslim associations and government institutions. A possible effect is that specific Swedish traditions of administration – accounting for activities, rapport-making, democratic procedures and even bureaucratic administration – have been introduced to Muslims and have allowed Muslim organizations to gain a Swedish profile.

SST has also provided Muslim activists with networks outside their own contacts, and at times lobby groups have formed across religious boundaries. For example, when a new national curriculum for the first nine years of school was discussed in the early 1990s, a multi-religious lobby group was formed by persons active in SST for promoting the importance of religious values (Otterbeck 1999). The Islamic Cooperation Council and SST have given the organized Muslims of Sweden an economic platform but also provided the Swedish state with collaboration partners among the Muslims. Simply put, the state has someone to talk to but much is still to be done. As the Muslim population grows in Sweden and Muslims grow up in Sweden, it's easy to see a clash in generational perceptions of what it means to be a Muslim in Sweden (Karlsson Minganti 2008; Otterbeck 2000b).

The overall socio-economic situation

The structure of the labour market and the economic strength of the national economy are as crucial to the immigrants' integration process as local and national politics. Economic historian Pieter Bevelander has, in a number of articles and books, described how economic changes have affected the possibilities of getting a foothold in the Swedish labour market. During the 1970s and 1980s, a large number of simple jobs for unskilled labour disappeared. They were replaced by 'jobs which demanded labour with higher communicative and social abilities and which were organized on a teamwork basis' (Bevelander 1999: 461). In short, employers wanted employees with 'culture-specific social competence and language skills' (ibid.). If anything, this is even truer today.

Sweden has gone through three periods of recession during the time of Muslim immigration, in the first half of the 1970s, in the early 1990s and then again during the recent events of the global recession. It is since the late 1980s that a substantial Muslim population has formed in Sweden, coinciding with the two later recessions that have created a permanent unemployment problem. It has become a severe problem for any migrant to enter the labour market during this period. Participation in the labour market has in fact decreased during the last decades for immigrant men but not for immigrant women, even though their labour market participation has not increased as much as for Swedish-born women. This applies even for Danes, Norwegians and Germans, not to mention Turks (Bevelander 2004). On the other hand, if one looks at different regions, the difference might be more extreme. For example 69 per cent of Iraqi males are employed in Järfälla while only 13 per cent of them have a job in Sandviken. While 94 per cent of women from Bosnia-Herzegovina are employed in Sigtuna, only 40 per cent are employed in Landskrona. The main explanatory factor (but not the only one) is the structure of the local economy; the more traditional it is (manufacturing industry, etc.), the higher the employment rates (Bevelander and Lundh 2007).

Since Muslim immigration to Sweden has not been predominantly labour-based, but rather asylum-based, most migrants have not been very well prepared for the adjustment. A lack of language skills and little knowledge of the country have led to long adjustment periods. Even if one-sixth to one-fourth of migrants from Muslim-majority countries have a higher education, that education is not obtained with a future in Sweden in mind, and is often devalued in the new country (Bevelander 2004). Added to this, there are prevalent gender stereotypes about Muslim men and women (the former are considered uncivilized and the latter suppressed) which further restrict their ability to penetrate Swedish society (Otterbeck and Bevelander 2006). In a labour market requiring a high level of communication skills, these stereotypes tend to set the odds against Muslims, or encourage social and economic discrimination against them in the work environment.

A number of the Muslims who emigrated to Sweden were refugees during a period when Sweden had no recent experience of dealing with large numbers of refugees and some crucial mistakes were made. Different solutions for the first residence were tried out and included refugee camps or home-stays with relatives – but none worked out as a permanent solution. The processes to establish whether an asylum seeker had legitimate reasons to stay (or could be accepted on humanitarian grounds) took far too long for the individual asylum seeker and were criticized harshly by journalists, researchers and politicians. Few things have been as hotly debated during the last 15 years as the government's migration policies. The important thing to remember here is that quite a large part of the country's Muslim population immigrated during this rather chaotic period.

The Swedish welfare system extends to newcomers to the country who are not citizens. Housing and housing costs, food, clothes and other necessities are provided through welfare benefits by the state. In addition, language education and preparation courses for the labour market (such as IT classes) are provided. There has been an ongoing ideological debate between liberals and leftists during the last decade over whether these welfare benefits and well-intentioned adaptation courses are making immigrants passive and creating dependency, or whether they are providing them with the tools to start a new life in Sweden. It is hard to say who is right. However, it is obvious that it is fairly easy to substantiate both claims with dramatic examples.

Since statistics have refrained from covering Muslims, the only way to study the effect of religious identity is to employ figures about people originating from Muslim majority countries, which however state nothing about the religious identity and activity of the persons involved. It is reasonable to expect that both religious identity and religiosity do matter. For example the Discrimination Ombudsman (DO) in Sweden has, over the years, had several cases of discrimination against Muslim women because of veiling (when looking for employment), as featured in the DO website collection of anonymous, typical cases for reference purposes (URL: DO). It is difficult to find hard facts about Muslims in the Swedish labour market research. Economist Dan-Olof Rooth and his collaboration partners have tried to map down discrimination against Arab Muslims in a couple of articles. Their research using experimental data (like job applications) shows with great clarity that employers to a substantially high degree associate Arab Muslim names with negative traits (like incompetence, laziness, etc.) in comparison with Swedish-sounding names (Agerström and Rooth 2008; Carlsson and Rooth 2007). Stereotypical notions of Muslims and different ethnic or national groups combined with human and social capital that are not optimal create large obstacles for these groups.

Segregated housing

If economic integration is seen as the key issue by most researchers into migration in Sweden, housing is the second most common issue to look into. Like most countries with a socialist or social-democratic government, there have been large-scale building projects in Sweden with the aim of modernizing the country's housing. In Sweden the most profiled and most important project was launched in the 1960s and continued for a decade; according to the 'Million Programme' one million new apartments were to be built. In the middle of the 1970s this goal was achieved. The project created suburbs and added a new cityscape to central parts of smaller cities. Areas renowned for poverty were demolished and replaced by modern concrete apartments of a decent standard.

Built for the working class, the apartments soon became a reasonable option for migrants because of the affordable rent. Over the following decades, some of these neighbourhoods have been completely transformed in terms of ethnicity and faith. Stockholm, Gothenburg and Malmö, in particular, now have suburbs or parts of towns that consist almost entirely of families who have migrated to Sweden. As many as one-third of the foreign-born population of Sweden live in these three cities (one-fifth of the total population of Sweden live in these cities including their suburbs) (Bevelander 2004). However, Muslims also live in the medium-sized cities (30,000–90,000 population). In 2003, Muslims had formed at least one association in as many as 112 of the 290 Swedish municipalities (Otterbeck 2004). According to Bevelander, it is more likely that one will live in a neighbourhood with migrants and few native Swedes when one is also a migrant (and in particular non-European). Scandinavian immigrants, on the other hand, are more likely to live among the majority population. This has two fundamental effects: first, it becomes more difficult to connect with the networks of the majority population, thus making it more difficult to get a job (which most people get through 'contacts'); second, children are robbed of the possibility of growing up with native Swedes for peers who later on in life could become vital contacts – and of course vice versa. Luckily, many immigrants are very active in starting small-scale businesses and provide work opportunities to friends and family (Bevelander, *et al.* 2008). Another effect concerns language. Many immigrants in the so-called 'segregated areas' grow up with very few peers who have Swedish as their mother tongue. This situation has created a sociolect nicknamed *Rinkebysvenska* or *Rosengårdssvenska*, in other words Swedish from Rinkeby or Rosengård – parts of Stockholm and Malmö respectively. This sociolect is not held in high esteem in the labour market, regardless of the interest it has attracted among linguists and novelists. Added to this, several of these areas have developed a bad reputation and individuals who live there are often stigmatized by it (Ristilammi 1994; Ljungberg 2005).

To sum up, migrants from Muslim-majority countries have arrived primarily during the last two decades. They have had difficulties finding jobs and have settled in areas offering the cheapest possible housing. Because of segregation, many have a hard time making social contacts that might help them get a better chance at succeeding in the labour market. Furthermore, language skills are more difficult to acquire, both for children and adults, due to the lack of contact with native Swedish speakers. Because of the swift changes in the population of such neighbourhoods, which draw many incoming migrants and are abandoned by others when their finances improve, the schools have huge difficulties holding a good standard and are frequently given bad reviews for having a large number of failing pupils. Instead, families all too often end up being dependent on the welfare system in areas which are socially segregated. This does not apply to everyone, far from it. It is generally acknowledged that Bosnians are doing well in the Swedish labour market, but that Iraqis are not (Bevelander and Lundh 2007). Looking at it statistically, the majority of people with a Muslim family history seem to be in an unusually disadvantageous position.

Conflict and cooperation

One major concern of the majority society is how to treat Muslims in school, health care, social welfare, and in other areas where religious preferences might surface. Another concern mirrors this: the concern among right-wing reactionary and liberal groups with the claimed incompatibility of Islam and, by extension, of Muslims with Swedish society. As might be expected, this is also a major concern among Muslims – both among those who demand a right to be defined first and foremost as Muslims and who consciously Islamize as much of their social praxis as possible, and among those who simply want to live in Sweden and not be exposed to prejudices. But at the same time, yet another process comes into play. The strong focus on Muslims in society also leads to a lot of organizational collaboration and initiatives for cooperation and inclusion.

The welfare state's institutions and the Muslim other

In 1993, I was asked to write a book giving advice to teachers on how to treat Muslim pupils in school. The publishing house, dealing with pedagogical and didactic literature, wanted a teacher's manual for the Muslim mind. Refusing to write this and instead writing a book on the situation of Muslim pupils in Swedish schools that focused on contextual factors as well as differences in the Muslim population (Otterbeck 1993), gave me the opportunity to observe a change that was taking place in Swedish welfare institutions. Although designed to help cure – from a thoroughly modernist paradigm – what is considered unhealthy, uneducated or in some other way 'dysfunctional', the majority of these institutions and the professional training of their personnel had no tools to deal with the plurality of their subjects. The institutions presupposed, even stipulated, that religions, traditions and – typically for Sweden – gender roles and class were irrelevant or should be made irrelevant in health care, education and welfare (Gustafsson 2004; Otterbeck 2000b). Over the years, the system designed by the elite of the social democratic mass movement using modernism as a chrono-political moral tool, had efficiently disciplined and silenced the socially heterodox. Migration and multicultural politics challenged established systems, but the challenge was seldom verbalized, and it can be presumed that many observers and practitioners simply missed the issue at hand. Instead the focus was on questions like: will a Muslim man shake my hand? Should we accept the veil in athletics classes?

In the early 1990s the schools started to ask for help and guidelines on how to deal with the new plurality – the health and social welfare institutions followed in the late 1990s. In the twenty-first century, the urge to learn how to handle this plurality has spread to the courtrooms, which have to deal with a diversity of legal traditions inspired by Sharia law. There had actually been intense discussion before the situation was highlighted by the schools, but it centred on a stereotyped uneducated foreigner from the countryside, not on the Muslim. It was all about how to live a disciplined and correct life in modern apartments.

At the heart of the issue is the idea of social life as a contract. Nikolas Rose claims that the liberal idea of citizenship is interconnected with a disciplinary apparatus consisting of rights and obligations in an implicit moral contract. The individual citizens become obliged to honour the contract, and if they do not they will fall from grace and be exposed to the wealth of normally invisible disciplinary techniques (Rose 1999; Gustafsson 2004). Among those obligations that will not be compromised is individual freedom. Further, the importance of active individual choices is stressed. But it is not freedom to do what one wants – it is freedom from being dominated by traditions and the freedom to choose according to the modernist ideal of the collective good (Berggren and Trägårdh 2006). To legitimize a diverging standpoint, or choice, with culture, tradition or religion will only result in further compromise. Even though being highly dependent on the social democratic party, Swedish modernism is very similar to Rose's description and, if anything, goes a step further in its conscious social engineering.

A second issue surrounds multiculturalism. The Swedish state's ideology of multiculturalism has never addressed the idea of the liberal contract. Rather, it has added a multiculturalism policy layer to a thoroughly modernist state project causing confusion for the officiating practitioners who are supposed to administer the new order – on the one hand multicultural ideals, on the other modernist laws and orders. To some extent it is like having French and British political traditions fused in the same country.

We have a situation that most people are anxious to solve, a recent plurality with many newcomers not schooled according to the hidden but still crucial social contract of life in Sweden. What to do with situations that occur when previously unheard of wishes are voiced by the newcomers? Many professionals have a genuine interest and ambition to be flexible and informed, and Muslims I have interviewed are also concerned, not only about their rights but also about how to follow social and legal traditions (Otterbeck 2000b). The state supports the multiculturalism ambition. But the state also promotes an individualism reaching into the private sphere of the family (making it political and thus not private). Berggren and Trägårdh (2006: 33f) call this 'state individualism' which they see as the most typical of all Swedish socio-political traits. The state has the ambition – which is, by and large, accepted and internalized as a premise by the majority of citizens – to have a direct contract with each individual, even children, giving her or him rights and obligations regardless of (or possibly more correctly, in spite of) religion, culture, class, gender and parents. To pin down the problem: How does as a teacher promote Swedish principles of gender equality and at the same time applaud parents who promote their religious traditions and wish their sons and daughters to grow up according to religiously founded, gendered moral codes?

Most Swedish Muslims are migrants or the children of migrants and they generally lack economic strength and social networks reaching into the majority society, making Muslims more vulnerable than the average Swedish family. This makes it more likely that Muslim families will be caught up in the interest sphere of the social welfare authorities. The economically weak often get their private sphere exposed, and the well-to-do marvel at and are horrified by the trouble and strife that can be found. Through news, research and gossip, the stereotypical notions about the Muslim Other are reinforced.

The liberal fear of plurality

When it became increasingly clear that receiving migrants also meant having new religious traditions in society which, in turn, meant that new situations occurred (and not all of them viewed as enriching), some debaters and politicians turned away from the dominant patient-but-mildly-correcting style of the state. Instead, harsh rhetoric on incompatibility and threats to society was employed to voice both cynically populist and honest concerns about what was happening to society. The first wave of anti-Muslim slogans came during the economic recession of the early 1990s when a populist right-wing party called Ny demokrati (New Democracy) was founded and actually made it to parliament before disintegrating because of a lack of politically competent members. Anti-Islamic sentiments were also voiced in the same period by some charismatic Christian groups, but were soon replaced by a preoccupation with New Age ideas during the 1990s.

The anti-Muslim and anti-Islamic sentiments surfaced again at the turn of the twentieth century. The exogenous influence mainly comes from the US discourse on Islam after September 11, 2001. The other major semi-external source is the news media and the frequent international reports on Islam and Muslims connected with violence, most often as perpetrators and self-proclaimed jihadists but also at times as victims, cumulatively signifying a violent, incomprehensible world, worlds apart from the safe haven of Sweden. The Danish cartoon affair also had a strong impact (Otterbeck and Bevelander 2006).

The major endogenous causes of these sentiments are probably three: first, the (indirect) discussions about the contract mentioned previously; second, the rapid transformation of the demography in some districts in a number of Swedish cities; and third, the media attention to a series of so-called honour killings, especially the murder in 2002 of Swedish-Kurdish 26-year-old Fadime Sahindal by her father because of her life choices (Wikan 2004). The tremendous outrage of society is hard to sum up in a few sentences. It was made a national affair and she was buried with a ceremony fit for a statesman. Reporters excelled in interviewing Kurdish men (and some women) who vaguely (and on a few occasions directly) saw legitimacy in this act of killing. Many Kurds felt that Kurdish culture and religious understanding were harshly criticized, and as a positive result some young men took action and formed Sharaf's heroes (*sharaf* being a common word for honour). The organization's goal was to work against the repressive side of honour culture. It is now a nationwide organization with a counterpart of female members organized as Sharaf's heroines. Both organizations are given state support and the female section, only in 2008, was rewarded for its work by the ministry for integration and, on another occasion, by the Queen of Sweden.

With regard to the liberal discontent with Islam and Muslims, debater Andreas Malm (2009) has, in a recent book, mapped the Islamophobic discourses of the liberal right. It is an interesting read. He shows how the 'Eurabia discourse' embraced by hawkish liberals in the US and the UK has penetrated the Swedish debate. Liberal think tanks promote authors like Bruce Bawer, Bat Ye'or and Melanie Philips, and translate their texts. Their arguments pop up in editorials and blogs. The most interesting aspect of the discourse is that its conspiracy theory actually assigns intelligence and competence to Muslims, an otherwise unusual stereotype. To be able, in detail, to run all the governments of the EU (which is what is claimed that Muslims do through the European Arab Dialogue, or EAD) is an impressive feat, only second to the claim that Jews run the entire world. Otherwise, it is the visibility of Muslims that is generally considered to be the problem. It is their numbers, their pregnancies combined with their undemocratic mentality, their refusal of a Swedish/Western order, and their will for power that is threatening the Swedish state, according to this discourse. The most vulgar versions are provided by the right-wing radical groups and individuals, but the liberal groups, being much more influential, affect the general public more (Otterbeck and Bevelander 2006; Malm 2009).

The crucial problem with this discourse is its use of culture as a functional equivalent to race. Claimed cultural/religious values are presented as constants ruling the actions and preferences of Muslims – thus representing Muslims as the epitome of Otherness to modernized and individualized Swedes. This neo-racist discourse about a population already in a socio-economically weak position is, apart from being utterly vulgar, not very productive for changing the situation, or for the promotion of a liberal understanding of society.

The popularity of cooperation

Judging from this, one could easily presume that Muslims in Sweden feel alienated and are confronted by a hostile society, with widespread discrimination on a day-to-day basis. But there is another side to the coin. When talking to Muslims engaged in Muslim associations of various kinds, one hears that they often experience positive feedback and acknowledgement for their work. Below I will develop some examples about cooperation between Muslim organizations and associations and other actors.

The largest youth movement in Sweden is the scout movement (which is gender neutral in Sweden). Local branches come under six umbrella organizations, two of them secular, but four of them religious. All six work together in the Swedish Scout Council. Since 2008, one of the four religiously inspired is Sveriges Muslimska Scouter, Sweden's Muslim Scouts. Previously, the Muslim scouts were part of KFUM, the largest Christian scout organization in Sweden, but when they grew in size, they formed their own organization. All organizations cooperate in arranging national jamborees, and the Muslim organization was able, through contacts, to arrange a visit by Saudi-Arabian boy scouts to Sweden in 2006.

One of the best-organized interest groups in Sweden is the temperance movement.[2] With its roots in several different organizations and a history reaching back to the nineteenth century, the temperance movement has connections with both political and religious organizations. During the last decade, it has, on several occasions, collaborated with Muslim interest groups like the Malmö-based, Muslim-run, multimedia company Northern Light which promotes religious values, including a zero-tolerance on drugs. Together they have arranged seminars and lectures on multiculturalism and Islam. In addition, the largest temperance movement has repeatedly co-arranged seminars with the Bosnian Muslim Youth organization mentioned above; an active member of the Bosnian organization works at the temperance movement.

Even if Sweden is possibly one of the most secular countries in the world, almost eight in nine citizens pay a membership fee to a religious organization. Most Christian groups are members of Sveriges Kristna Råd (SKR), the Christian Council of Sweden, formed in 1994. SKR frequently arranges activities to which Muslim leaders are invited (especially through the SST networks, mentioned above). There is a pattern to these activities. When the Middle East appears as a particular hot spot in world news, SKR hold prayers for peace and arrange educational seminars to which Muslim leaders are invited. Also, when especially blatant Islamophobic acts are performed, a meeting is usually considered appropriate. A typical case is that of the Dialogue Group, Jews – Christians – Muslims, which was originally formed in the aftermath of the first Gulf War in May 1991 (Gunner 2002). A similar initiative to create dialogue was taken in Lund diocese in 1994. The two initiating organizations were the Swedish Church and the Christian Peace movement. It was the war in the Balkans that triggered the initiative. First a prayer for peace in the Balkans was arranged on 2 September 1993 in Lund. To this prayer, Muslims leaders (among others) were invited (Roald 2002).

Nowadays, several Churches have established Muslim dialogue partners, and the Muslim leaders who are engaged in these dialogues acquire networks with truly important agents in Swedish civil society, leading to several small-scale cooperation projects at the local level.

Another example of collaboration is the contacts between Swedish political parties and Muslim organizations. It is the Christian subgroups of these parties in particular that have been involved in these contacts. My example will be Broderskapsrörelsen, the Christian Social Democrats, formed in 1929 as a subgroup of the largest party, Socialdemokraterna, or the Social Democrats. In 1994, a group called Sveriges Muslimska Råd (SMR), the Muslim Council of Sweden, contacted the Christian Social Democrats out of a desire for collaboration. SMR is a lobby group formed by the two most dominant umbrella organizations at the time, FIFS and SMF. Its prime objective has always been to make Muslims better integrated in political and social life. The outstretched hand was accepted, and a work group was set up, headed by a Muslim man called Ahmed Ghanem who has been active in the umbrella organizations for some time. Four years later, a report about the activities was produced. Apart from the obvious seminars and meetings engaging hundreds of politicians and Muslim activists, the project included education in Swedish democratic traditions and about Islam. It was even discussed whether the Christian Social Democrats should be reformed into a multi-religious group but this was eventually rejected. Instead, Politisk Islamisk Samling (Political Islamic Coalition) was formed as a sister organization. Goals and strategies were set up in order to successfully incorporate Muslims who wanted to become politicians in the Social Democrat party, both locally and nationally. The report admits the difficulties that had to be overcome when collaborating, but also points out that at the end of the day everyone learned from the experience and things are now running more smoothly than ever before (Broderskapsrörelsen 1999). In 2008, the Christian Social Democrats adopted a multi-religious agenda, even though they have not yet changed their name.

A final, but probably the most important, point is state recognition. Since 2000, the State and the Swedish Church went their separate ways. It was a well-prepared divorce framed by the symbolic act of presenting a very ambitious translation of the Bible into Swedish prepared by the elite of Swedish biblical scholars working together with authors and poets. It also meant new legislation and the creation of a legal category for 'registered denominations'. A registered denomination can, for example, have its members' fees collected through the taxation office. Some of the Islamic organizations have applied and been acknowledged.

Before the separation of State and Church, the Swedish Church was the officially favoured partner in every case. Within the new order, there is still no doubt that the Swedish Church is the first among equals, being the largest membership-based organization in Sweden (with almost 7 million members), but it is also clear that the other denominations (including Islamic ones) have a good position in negotiations. If the state provides for a priest for the armed forces, why not an imam? And what about inmates? Support is now provided on demand in both these and other similar areas. The imams can obtain support for their work if their activity is recognized (Otterbeck 2004). This recognition of Muslim organizations as Swedish actors, valued for the work that only they can do, is something new. It invites, but also disciplines. It presupposes competence, but also the taking of responsibility. Simply put, if you are an official actor, you have to abide by the rules, and you can be held accountable if you misuse the power invested in you. As this incorporation of the imam into Swedish bureaucracy has started, voices are now rising demanding an imam-education at Swedish universities. The demand comes from two radically different positions, one from the Muslim lobby groups, stressing Muslim rights and the need for this kind of competence, the other from the political liberal right, stressing the need to control and discipline the imams through Swedish education. Nothing could be more typical of the situation than that.

Concluding remarks

All the individuals of Sweden's Muslim population have their own stories. Most are migrants, or the children of migrants, and have different reasons for migrating. They arrive from many different countries, and they end up in unique situations inside the new country. Still, some structures, which can be seen and described, affect life in the new homeland. The political system and its migration and integration policies shape the conditions these people meet. The economic strength of society and the structure of the labour market can either create openings or closures. Settling in segregated and socially stigmatized areas provides few opportunities for integration and socio-economic mobility, yet these areas continue to hold appeal because apartments there are cheap and a community of people from the same country and religious affiliation live there and provide a recognizable social framework. As far as majority sentiment is concerned, the frequency of discourses on Muslim 'otherness' and the supposed threat stemming from Islam do not help people with a Muslim family history to take an active part in society. To some extent it is reasonable to talk about structural discrimination, especially when Muslims apply for jobs or housing. Add to this a general suspicion regarding anyone who wants to align their way of life with religious values, and Muslims become suitable pray for right-wing populist parties and liberals who suspect them of not being loyal enough to the state. In an inspired metaphor at a guest lecture at Lund University, Peggy Levitt claimed that the double loyalty of some migrants (religious and national) is seen as bigamist by some in the new country of residence, leading to the same moral indignation as bigamy would do.

Being marginalized in the labour market as well as in the geography of Swedish cities, has the effect that a fair number of Muslims seek support from each other and form enclaves in Swedish society. At times, conservatism and even sectarian environments thrive. This, in turn, is enforcing stereotypes. The successful and well integrated (of which there are quite a few) are seldom used as examples of how Muslims adapt to Swedish life. Instead of understanding the difficult conditions of Muslim families as shaped by the migration experience, the lack of human and social capital, and the socio-economic situation in Sweden, many tend to prefer essentialist cultural explanations. This essentialism can also be found among Muslim leaders and activists seeking authority as representatives of the plurality of people with a Muslim family background.

At the same time, different levels of Swedish society have started to include Muslim organizations (sometimes on an equal basis). It is possible to talk about a structural inclusion as a result of the design of Swedish legislation and multicultural policies. Civil society organizations, like the scout movement, temperance movement and different Church organizations, have included Muslims or are cooperating with Muslim organizations. Furthermore, influential political parties (or their subgroups) collaborate in different projects with organized Muslim groups. Finally, the state has started to recognize that a demographic change has taken place and is trying to provide the same service for Muslims that it provides for other believers in, for example, health care, prisons and the military. A preliminary observation is that conflicts seem to lead to cooperation, i.e. dialogue ensues whenever Muslims are targeted in the Swedish media as victims or perpetrators. If focus is only put on one aspect, the complexity of the situation is lost.

Activist Muslims have engaged themselves in organizations according to typically Swedish patterns. Associations on the local level have joined umbrella organizations in order to get support from the state through SST. This relation has in itself created personal contacts and led to different kinds of collaborations. Typically, associations and organizations are formed by individual enthusiasts and often go through periods of being run undemocratically. Strong wills and different interests have split umbrella organizations; nevertheless, this has given more people the chance to come in contact with the authorities. Earlier preferences and networks formed in other countries are slowly exchanged with or complemented by Swedish ones.

In the future, it will be interesting to see if the claims by Muslim activists to represent everyone who can be called Muslim will succeed or if they will fail and lead to a situation where only those who are activist Muslims accept the proposed leadership while others either identify with majority society or find other ethnocultural or national values to centre around.

Observing Swedish society today, it is easy to find very harsh expressions of discontent and contempt regarding Muslims. At the same time, collaborations are taking place all over Sweden to normalize the Muslim presence. It is hard to say which is the predominant trend. They are simultaneous and both can be seen as logical expressions of the construction of the state.

Notes

1 The Free Churches are the non-state Churches of Sweden. They have played an important role in Swedish religious, political and social life, not least in mid-size cities and in the countryside since the nineteenth century.

2 The modern temperance movement grew out of Christian, Socialist and union-based engagement and associations that all addressed the issue of living a sober life, abstaining from alcohol (Lindgren 2008).

References

Agerström, Jens and Rooth, Dan-Olof (2008) 'Implicit Prejudice and Ethnic Minorities: Arab-Muslims in Sweden'. Working paper IZA DP No. 3873 at IZA. Available at: http://www.iza.org/ (accessed 16 June 2009).

Anwar, Muhammad, Blaschke, Jochen and Sander, Åke (2004) *State Policies towards Muslim Minorities: Sweden, Great Britain and Germany*. Berlin: EditionParabolis.

Berggren, Henrik and Trägårdh, Lars (2006) *Är svensken människa? Gemenskap och oberoende i det moderna Sverige*. Stockholm: Nordstedt.

Bevelander, Pieter (1999) 'The Employment Integration of Immigrants in Sweden' *Journal of Ethnic and Migration Studies*, 25 (3): 445–68.

Bevelander, Pieter (2004) *Immigration Patterns, Economic Integration and Residential Segregation: Sweden in the Late 20th Century*. Current Themes in IMER Research, no. 2. Malmö: Malmö University Press.

Bevelander, Pieter, Broomé, Per, Dahlstedt, Inge and Schölin, Tobias (2008) *Företagare i Skåne – kartläggning och analys av inrikes och utrikes födda företagare*. Malmö: MIM.

Bevelander, Pieter and Lundh, Christer (2007) 'Employment Integration of Refugees: The Influence of Local Factors on Refugee Job Opportunities in Sweden'. Working paper IZA DP No. 2551 at IZA. Available at: http://www.iza.org/ (accessed 16 June 2009).

Broderskapsrörelsen (1999) 'Delaktighet, Identitet & Integration'. *Rapport 4/99*. Unpublished Report by the Christian Social Democrats.

Carlsson, Magnus and Rooth, Dan-Olof (2007) 'Evidence of Ethnic Discrimination in the Swedish Labor Market Using Experimental Data' *Labour Economics*, 14 (4): 716–29.

Ekström, Sören (2006) 'Staten, trossamfunden och samhällets grundläggande värderingar – en bakgrund', in SST (ed.), *Samfunden och bidragen*. Stockholm: Proprius.

Gustafsson, Christina (2004) *Muslimsk skola, svenska villkor*. Umeå: Boréa.

Gunner, Göran (2002) 'I Gulfkrigets spår: Ett exempel på religionsdialog i svenskt perspektiv', in M. Stenmark and D. Westerlund (eds), *Polemik eller dialog? Nutida religionsteologiska perspektiv bland kristna och muslimer*. Nora: Nya Doxa, pp. 71–82.

Karlsson, Pia and Svanberg, Ingvar (1995) 'Moskéer i Sverige: En religionsetnologisk studie i intolerans och administrativ vanmakt' *Tro & tanke*, 7/95: 5–107.

Karlsson Minganti, Pia (2008) *Muslima: Islamisk väckelse och unga muslimska kvinnors förhandlingar in genus i det samtida Sverige*. Stockholm: Carlsson.

Larsson, Göran and Sander, Åke (2007) *Islam and Muslims in Sweden: Integration or Fragmentation? A Contextual Study*. Berlin: Lit verlag.

Lindgren, Åke (2008) 'Folk i rörelser: Om nykterhetsrörelsen och andra folkrörelser i Sverige efter 1970' in Å. Lindgren (ed.), *Nykterhet i rörelse: Nykterhetens och nykterhetsrörelsens utveckling efter 1970*. Stockholm: Sober, pp. 137–61.

Ljungberg, Caroline (2005) *Den svenska skolan och det mångkulturella – en paradox?* Malmö: Malmö University Press.

Lundh, Christer and Ohlsson, Rolf (1994) *Från arbetskraftsimport till flyktinginvandring*. Stockholm: SNS.

Malm, Andreas (2009) *Hatet mot muslimer*. Stockholm: Atlas.

Otterbeck, Jonas (1993) *Muslimer i svensk skola*. Malmö: Gleerups.

Otterbeck, Jonas (1998) 'The Baltic Tatars: The First Muslim Group in Modern Sweden', in K. Junefeld and M. Peterson (eds), *Cultural Encounters in East Central Europe*. Stockholm: FRN, pp. 145–53.

Otterbeck, Jonas (1999) 'Skolan, islam och muslimer', in I. Svanberg and D. Westerlund (eds), *Blågul islam? Muslimer i Sverige*. Nora: Nya Doxa, pp. 157–74.

Otterbeck, Jonas (2000a) *Islam på svenska: Tidskriften Salaam och islams globalisering*. Stockholm: Almqvist & Wiksell International.

Otterbeck, Jonas (2000b) *Islam, muslimer och den svenska skolan*. Lund: Studentlitteratur.

Otterbeck, Jonas (2002) 'The Depiction of Islam in Sweden' *The Muslim World*, 92 (1 and 2): 143–56.

Otterbeck, Jonas (2004) 'The Legal Status of Islamic Minorities in Sweden', in R. Aluffi Beck-Peccoz and G. Zincone (eds), *The Legal Treatment of Islamic Minorities in Europe*. Leuven: Peeters, pp. 233–54.

Otterbeck, Jonas and Bevelander, Pieter (2006) *Islamofobi: En studie av begreppet, ungdomars attityder och unga muslimers utsatthet*. Stockholm: Forum för levande historia.

Ristilammi, Per-Markku (1994) *Rosengård och den svarta poesin: en studie av modern annorlundahet*. Stockholm: Symposion.

Roald, Anne Sofie (2002) 'Religionsdialogiska perspektiv: En fallstudie av en dialoggrupp i södra Sverige', in M. Stenmark and D. Westerlund (eds), *Polemik eller dialog? Nutida religionsteologiska perspektiv bland kristna och muslimer*. Nora: Nya Doxa, pp. 83–97.

Rose, Nikolas (1999) *Powers of Freedom: Reframing Political Thought*. Cambridge: Cambridge University Press.

Roy, Olivier (2004) *Globalized Islam: The Search for a New Ummah*. New York: Columbia University Press.

Westerlund, David (1999), 'Euro-sufism – universalister och konvertiter', in I. Svanberg and D. Westerlund (eds), *Blågul islam? Muslimer i Sverige*. Nora: Nya Doxa, pp. 85–106.

Wikan, Unni (2004) *En fråga om heder*. Stockholm: Orfront.

URLs

Discrimination Ombudsman (DO): http://do.episerverhotell.net/t/news____1079.aspx (accessed 19 May 2009).

Nämnden för statligt stöd till trossamfund (SST) 1: http://www.sst.a.se (accessed 9 May 2009).

Nämnden för statligt stöd till trossamfund (SST) 2: http://www.sst.a.se/download/18.3e8d58c211f8378233080009349/Uppfoljningrapport2.pdf (accessed 9 May 2009).

7 Islam in the Netherlands, Dutch Islam

Thijl Sunier

Introduction

In 2008 there were almost one million people with an Islamic background in the Netherlands, comprising about 6 per cent of the total population. Turkish Muslims constitute the largest group (372,000), followed by Moroccans (335,000), Surinamese Muslims (45,000), Pakistanis (50,000), Iraqis (45,000), Afghans (38,000) and Iranians (30,000). The remaining Muslims come from Somalia and other African countries, with a relatively small number from Indonesia – about 10,000 according to estimations – and a small proportion from other East Asian countries. There are about 12,000 converts to Islam in the Netherlands. Nominally, Islam constitutes the second largest religious denomination in the country (CBS 2008). Unlike countries such as France and the UK, the overwhelming majority of Muslim migrants come from countries that had no colonial relations with the Netherlands. From the early 1960s onwards, labour migrants from Turkey and Morocco were hired by industries in the Netherlands. Most of them had a rural background and found work in low-wage and unskilled sections of the labour market, which were in the process of fundamental restructuring after World War II.[1] The idea was that most of these temporal 'guest workers', as they were called, would return to their home countries once the restructuring process was completed.

As we know, this return migration never took place in most cases. From the mid-1970s onwards many guest workers brought their families to Europe and settled in the old neighbourhoods in the main cities of the country. Today, the majority of these former migrants with an Islamic background work and live in the south-western part of the country in cities like Rotterdam and The Hague. The capital city of Amsterdam and the industrial southern city of Eindhoven also have relatively large migrant populations.

Almost half of the population with an Islamic background belongs to what official statistics call the 'second generation', that is, people born in the Netherlands with at least one parent born abroad. Although this has nothing to do with religion, the position of the second generation plays a crucial role in the present debate on integration in the Netherlands. The categorization of migrants in terms of statistical figures causes enormous confusion. Official statistics on labour market position, educational performance and the socio-economic status of the population indicate

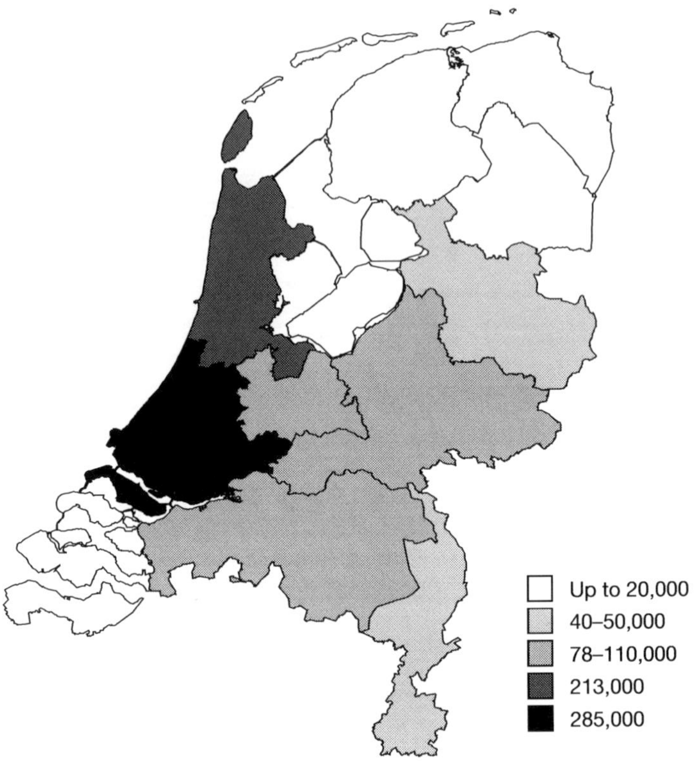

Figure 7.1 Number of Muslims per province (see squares).

Source: IHSAN (a Muslim organization).

that there are two fundamental categories: autochthonous, denoting people of Dutch origin, and allochthonous, denoting people of non-Dutch origin (see also Geschiere 2009). The latter category is divided into Western and non-Western allochthonous. Although this is an extremely vague statistical category without clear delineations, let alone any explanatory power, it serves as the basis of official policy reports. In the public eye, Muslims and non-western allochtonous are practically similar categories (see CBS 2008).

According to official statistics, with respect to type of secondary education, there is still a significant difference between autochthonous and non-Western allochthonous pupils. Around 50 per cent of the first category has followed only pure vocational training, compared with 70 per cent of the latter (CBS 2008). Taken over a longer period of time, however, the rapid improvement in educational performance of young non-Western allochthonous pupils is remarkable,[2] even though the public debate continues to focus on the relatively small proportion of young males performing badly, or not finishing school at all.

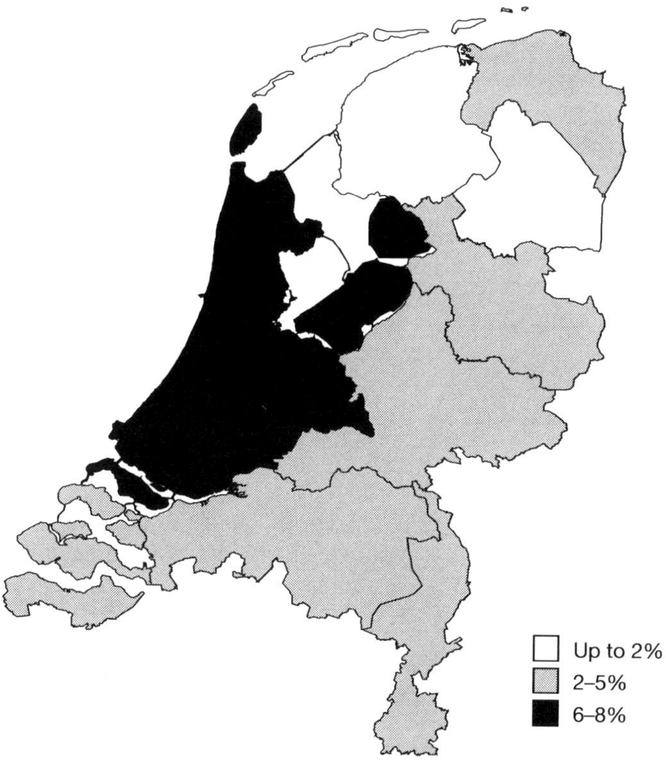

Figure 7.2 Percentage of Muslims per province (see squares).

Source: IHSAN (a Muslim organization). Figures are taken from the report by WRR 2006.

When we look at the labour market position there is an increase in the proportion of non-Western allochthonous people working in regular jobs. Their overall position in the labour market, however, is still weak despite their improved educational performance. In particular, even highly educated individuals of Islamic background were often denied jobs after 9/11. Discrimination continues to be a very powerful factor with regard to unemployment.

This influx of guest workers also ushered a 'new' religion into the Netherlands – a trend that, for a long time, went unnoticed. Initially, Islamic practices remained hidden behind the walls of the boarding houses where the migrants lived. On special religious holidays such as Ramadan, Muslims were sometimes able to make use of factory halls or churches in order to perform their religious duties. It was only on these occasions that the public sensed their presence. Today, Islam has been firmly institutionalized in Dutch society.

As of 2009 there are over 500 mosques in the Netherlands (Maussen 2009), although the precise number is difficult to estimate. Since 1988 the government has not registered houses of prayer because such a registration, it is argued, would infringe the constitutional freedom of religion. Municipalities do have local statistics when they develop policies relating to mosque-building, but these are far from complete or reliable. The number of mosques serves as a yardstick of the alleged 'Islamization of space' and is thus prone to wild speculation. The majority of MPs in the Dutch parliament deny the constitutional freedom of worship and demand a greater control over the building of mosques, as well as a thorough investigation of their activities beyond religious services. There is even a majority that asks for a control over the religious services. Since 9/11 there are continuous allegations by journalists that some imams are preaching hatred and violence. They often refer to the reports issued by the Dutch intelligence services about these matters.

The majority of mosques (220) in the Netherlands are of Turkish origin, while some 100 are Moroccan and the remainder are of other origins. There is a small but increasing number of mosques that are not organized along ethnic lines, but refer to their members as Dutch. The vast majority of mosques are Sunni; only about ten mosques are Iranian and have a Shi'ite background. Approximately 35–40 per cent of migrants from Turkey have an Alevi background.[3]

At present there are more than 40 Islamic schools in the Netherlands, while the first Islamic primary school opened in 1998.[4] In addition, Muslims, through a number of consultative bodies, can exert influence on policymaking at a local level. Despite all the drawbacks and limitations, Islam has gained a foothold in Dutch society over the past 25 years. Yet it is certainly not the institutional dimension of the settling process that accounts for the fact that the presence of Islam in Dutch society has turned into a highly sensitive and much debated issue. Islam has become 'super visible', a hyper-reality, to paraphrase Baudrillard (1994). It is the image of Islam rather than the actual developments that determines the political climate. There is hardly a day when the media does not cast attention to events related to Islam. These events, which do not even take place but resonate in the media, determine to a large extent the place of Islam in Dutch society. It has seriously affected the political landscape in the Netherlands on a national as well as local level.

Since the early 1980s the Dutch public discourse on migrants has increasingly been centred on the concept of integration (BiZA 1999; Engbersen and Gabriëls 1995; WVC 1993; Schinkel 2007). Integration policies on their part have almost completely become conflated with issues related to the presence of Muslims. In order to understand the nexus between immigration, integration and Islam, we first have to take a closer look at how integration policies came about. This will give us a clue as to why the 'demise of multiculturalism' is tied up so much with a particular image of Islam. It also sheds light on the shift of Islam from an invisible to an undesirable phenomenon.

Islam and Dutch political culture

Integration has specific connotations in the Dutch context. It is generally referred to as the path individual migrants have to follow in order to take part fully in the central institutions of Dutch society (housing, labour and education), regardless of ethnic differences. The key term in this integration debate is '(individual) participation', leading to full citizenship. Through a coherent programme of economic and educational measures, structural inequality between migrants and native Dutch should be resolved. Once this is accomplished everybody can take part in society on an equal basis. The idea behind it is the assertion that with material equality, ethnic differences become irrelevant and may eventually fade away completely. The Dutch term 'allochthonous' contains all these elements. Principally speaking, it refers not to culturally distinct collectivities but to equal yet distinct individuals. In the early 1980s, however, the government adopted a political agenda that granted a certain degree of cultural autonomy to migrants and their cultural institutions. There was a widely held trust that these associations and structures would become obsolete. However, these early integration policies should not be confused with multiculturalism. There is a widespread misunderstanding about the alleged multicultural underpinnings of these policies. It is true that the government had a lenient attitude towards cultural diversity and has stated in policy reports that cultural and religious identities are important human prerequisites. It is also true that the government subsidized cultural and even religious activities, but this has always been a temporal arrangement. It should be understood as technical and pragmatic rather than matters of principle. The final goal has always been total absorption (assimilation) of immigrants into the Dutch moral community.

Although this is now considered to be the ideal mode of civic incorporation, Dutch political history, particularly the history of pillarization,[5] has fuelled a debate about a complementary, more collective path towards migrant integration. Although pillarization lost most of its saliency, structural and legal remnants do still play a role as an integrative device in the Dutch political culture. As a consequence, an ongoing debate is taking place in the Netherlands about the question of whether these typical Dutch political arrangements offer Muslims the opportunities to integrate into Dutch society on a more collective basis and whether an 'Islamic pillar', reminiscent of the 'traditional' pillars, can be considered as a viable option.

The argument put forward here is that although the possibilities for Muslims to set up a religious infrastructure are generally conditioned by constitutional rights such as the freedom of religion, the separation of Church and State, the equality of all religious denominations and, not least, legal provisions related to pillarization, specific aims with regard to minority policies have become increasingly important in determining these possibilities. In addition, I argue that the position of Islam in Dutch society cannot properly be understood without taking into account the mediatized images that dominate present debates and negotiations.

In order to show this, I distinguish four analytical dimensions of the integration of Islam: institutional, political, ideological and mediatized. Although these dimensions are closely related to one another, each follows its own logic.

The institutional dimension

With respect to the institutional dimension, the central question regards the extent to which Muslims can claim equal treatment based on formal and legal provisions laid down in the Constitution and other legislation. In other words, what possibilities do Dutch legal arrangements offer Muslims to live according to their religious convictions and to build up a religious infrastructure?[6] Two legal aspects are relevant: constitutional principles and the aforementioned legal remnants of pillarization.

In the Netherlands formal and legal equality of *all* religious denominations in conjunction with the 'non-recognition principle' constitutes the central element in the relation between State and Church. Although the origin of this equality principle dates back to the beginning of the twentieth century, the thorough revision of the Constitution in 1983 gave a new impetus to this principle. Formally, all financial relations between the State and the Church were broken off (Hampsink and Roosblad 1992: 9). From then on all religions are considered legally equal (including 'new' religions such as Islam and Hinduism). 'Non-recognition' is not stated explicitly in the law, but does constitute an important element in the Dutch version of religious equality. It actually implies that religious denominations, from a legal point of view, can never acquire a privileged position vis-à-vis other religious denominations. In practice, however, there are of course privileged positions and implicit differences.

The present-day position of religion can be defined by three legal principles: (1) equality of all religious denominations, (2) freedom of religion and (3) separation of Church and State. The first principle implies that all religions, irrespective of their historical link to the Dutch state, are equal and should be treated accordingly. This may sound trivial, but as we will see further on, the principle of equality produced intriguing discourses about the special position of religious minorities. The second and third principles imply that the state should not interfere in religious affairs and should consider religion a private pursuit.

More important though is that constitutional principles interfere with the Dutch history of pillarization. Although the system lost most of its function decades ago due to secularization, the idea that all religious denominations should have an equal share and should be treated equally is still valid. It is through this principle that Muslims can claim equal treatment such as the right to found religious schools. The level of religious autonomy that existed in the heyday of pillarization, however, has been completely replaced by a strict top-down governmental control mechanism. This shift has manifested itself gradually in the growth of Islamic confessional schools (Sunier 2004). As more Islamic schools opened their doors, the government and politicians expressed a growing concern about their possible negative effect on integration. Here, the legal principles of the freedom of schools are interfering with certain political goals.

The political dimension

As far as the institutional dimension is concerned, equal treatment is granted through established (or adapted) legal provisions with regard to the 'new' religions. As we have seen, however, these provisions must be regarded as including conditions. The actual interpretation of these principles, and therefore the level of religious equality, is a matter of political decision-making and political power. Although constitutional principles and the system of pillarization offer Muslims legal opportunities to establish a religious-cultural infrastructure, it is clear that the system contains a built-in mechanism of preferences towards established religions, particularly Christianity. What these preferences are and how they pan out can only be traced by a close observation of the process of political decision-making at a local level. Thus, we see that the foundation of schools with an Islamic identity is monitored much more closely and restricted by conditions and limitations than for other confessional schools. But this is also clearly visible in the organization of society. It is still not widely accepted that Muslim employees can follow their own celebration days – they have to take a day off because society follows the Christian calendar. In that respect, Christianity still plays a decisive role in the make-up of Dutch society. Last, but not least, the present political landscape reveals that an overwhelming majority of the population are in favour of stricter regulations against the spread of Islamic institutions.

Since the mid-1980s discussions about the relation between the State and the Church in the Netherlands have been influenced greatly by the arrival of immigrants (WRR 1989). When we analyse the way in which political decision-making about 'new' religions has developed over the past 25 years, it becomes apparent that the government based its decisions on considerations relating to the societal positions of these immigrants and the priorities of the integration policies, rather than on principles regarding the ('neutral') relation between Church and State. Muslims are defined as migrants, rather than as citizens with a specific religious identity. Dutch integration policies aim at lifting the economic, social and educational deprivation of migrants. The idea is that equality is not just legal rhetoric; it should be accomplished through an active intervention by the government. In some situations this has proved to be beneficial for Muslims. They could well argue that special treatment and extra support from the government in setting up religious institutions could be interpreted as a means to increase their integration and positive participation in society. Actors thus actively apply these principles in different ways in different situations.

In general, the extent to which Muslims (and other religious denominations) are able to set up their own infrastructure is thus the outcome of a political process, or rather a political interest struggle. It is an ongoing negotiation process about definitions, guiding principles and conditions in which the influence of (in this case) Muslims on decision-making procedures is of vital importance. In fact the extent to which Muslims are able to exert influence on decision-making can be considered as a measure of their integration. In short, the position of migrants is highly determined by their position in the political arena and their degree of political leverage in society.

The position of Muslims in the Dutch political arena is on the whole rather weak. There is still a large proportion of Muslims who do not have Dutch nationality. They only have voting rights on the municipal level. Formal politics offer as yet hardly any perspective, not in the least because Muslims have not yet managed to exploit these channels properly.[7] But even if they had managed to do so, they are too few in number to exert any substantial influence on political decision-making.

In such situations a strong extra-parliamentary lobby seems to be an adequate alternative. Setting up interest organizations is thus a crucial condition. In the Netherlands there is a widespread system of non-governmental organizations and institutions which form a layer between the government and the citizens. It consists of welfare institutions, societal pressure groups, professional groups, trade unions, advisory boards, local residents' interest groups, but also various kinds of religious organizations. Although this layer is part of civil society and can be found in other European countries as well, the Dutch version can be conceived of as an important additional democratic and integrative device. It is an aspect of the typical Dutch consultative society. It is crucial that organizations and institutions that are part of this layer have achieved a certain degree of recognition in order to be able to take part in consultation procedures. Many of these organizations have a well-established position and are recognized by government as partners in decision-making procedures. The main advantage of such a system is that it is not a part of the formal political structure. Recruitment and participation is open to any societal category. Muslim organizations that have been able to establish good contacts in a neighbourhood and cooperate with other local institutions, for example, can gradually become part of the system and the consultancy structure. This layer of non-governmental organization thus constitutes a potential means for Muslims (and other migrants) to exert influence. The effect, both in a positive and in a negative sense, of this structure can be observed recently in the negotiations following problems with young Moroccans in a neighbourhood in Amsterdam. Although these problems had nothing to do with Islam, Islamic spokespersons did play a crucial role in settling the conflict. There are two shortcomings to this, however: on the one hand there is a tendency to overemphasize the role of religion in these kinds of neighbourhood conflicts, and on the other hand there is always reluctance on the part of the Dutch authorities to grant religious actors a role in these negotiations because it would infringe upon the separation of Church and State.

Overall, since recognition as consultancy partners is mainly a matter of achieved privileges through long-term lobby and negotiation, Muslim representative bodies have not always reached an adequate level of recognition so as to be fully accepted and able to exert substantial influence. Yet although today's Muslim representative bodies may lack an adequate level of recognition, their mode of representation and their functioning towards the outside world fits perfectly into the Dutch consultative democracy.

If we consider developments with respect to those organizations set up by Muslims, it is clear that increasingly they are reflecting Dutch political culture. This becomes apparent when we look at the ways in which Muslims joined forces in order to set up religious institutions. From the end of the 1960s to the mid-1970s, acquiring suitable premises for prayer was the main focus of collective action among Muslims, who initially sought temporary accommodation for important religious occasions such as Ramadan. In this phase, Dutch intermediaries, especially churches, played a crucial role. In fact it was not collective action by Muslims but collective action *for* Muslims. At that time, Muslims themselves were not even seeking this. The Dutch intermediaries felt Muslim 'guest workers' might need these facilities for the duration of their stay (Landman 1992; Sunier 1996).

It was only after some time that cooperation began to emerge among Muslims in order to set up premises for prayer. Initially Muslims of different nationalities worked together, but later the cooperation was mainly among Muslims of the same nationality (Landman 1992; Rath, *et al.* 1996; Shadid and van Koningsveld 1992). Money was collected from the believers to purchase premises, and thus the first mosques came into being. Religious services were led by ordinary believers with a knowledge of Islam who were chosen from the community.

It was clear that the need for religious accommodation on the part of the ordinary believers was closely connected at the time to their orientation towards their country of origin. These premises were not just religious facilities; they also served as gathering places for people who saw themselves as temporary passers-by who would soon return to their home country (Rath, *et al.* 1996).

Most of the associations founded at that time were very local initiatives, and were far from professional. For a short time, collective action acquired a more egalitarian modus. Dutch brokers more or less faded into the background, but there were hardly any representatives among the Muslims and the organizational means were still poorly developed. Due to practical problems such as language barriers and the fact that Islam was inextricably linked to loyalties towards the country of origin or to specific ideological movements, any cross-national cooperation between Muslims of different ethnic background was (and still is) very hard to achieve (Landman 1992).

Between the mid-1970s and 1980s, leaders and representatives of Muslim organizations made several attempts to set up one overarching representative body for all Muslims. Those first attempts, however, failed due to the aforementioned fragmentation and the absence of any unified pursuit. But equally important was the fact that the Dutch government at that time did not see any necessity to consult Muslims collectively. Muslims were considered to be migrants and as such they could apply to the established Turkish or Moroccan welfare organizations for migrants. More often than not, the representatives of these welfare organizations were anti-religious. Moreover, the government had already established contacts with these migrant representatives but they were not very willing to cooperate with Muslims. At that time Muslim organizations were suspected of having links with extreme right-wing organizations such as Moroccan Amicales and Turkish Grey Wolves (LAKAF 1980).

In 1989 new attempts at cooperation were made. This time circumstances had changed considerably. First, Islam had become a main point of concern for the government (see page 132). Several advisory reports had been published in the eighties about the necessity of consulting Muslim representatives on matters concerning religious provisions. At that time the government was ready to take over some of this responsibility (Landman 1992: 250). The immediate trigger for renewed cooperation between Muslim organizations, however, was the Rushdie affair and the subsequent turmoil created by the reaction of Muslims all over the world. Soon after this, the Islamic National Committee (ILC) was founded. Muslims in the Netherlands feared that the backlash of the affair, and not least the very negative tone in the media, would harm their delicate relations with the government and the public. The Committee, representing the vast majority of Muslim organizations in the Netherlands, officially distanced itself from the fatwa of Khomeini and from the demonstrations held in The Hague and Rotterdam. Some consultation meetings were held between the Committee and the government, but this did not lead to a regular consultation. Again, the government thought that there was no need for such a platform. Within a few months the Committee was dissolved.

In the 1990s several national umbrella organizations came into being, but until now no regular consultations with the government have taken place. When we consider the issues that have been raised and the political agenda of these organizations, there is, however, a remarkable shift from internal matters such as relations with the country of origin and the creation of religious accommodation, to matters concerning the position of Muslims *in* Dutch society. Much more attention has been given to the political representation of Muslims in all kinds of Dutch institutional settings. Aims and means have been gradually tuned to Dutch political culture. To the outside world these organizations tend to represent themselves more and more as types of Dutch welfare professionals. This shift in strategy is mainly attributable to ideological factors.

In the post 9/11 climate the political leverage of these consultative bodies has waned considerably. Overall, representative bodies have conceded much of their bargaining power to the more performative spokespersons who use the media rather than the negotiating table to make their case. The third and fourth dimensions that follow are generally more flexible, fuzzy and unpredictable, and account to a large extent for this shift.

The ideological dimension

Integration of Muslims in Dutch society is not only determined by legal, structural and political factors, but also by existing ideas about the character of the Dutch nation and the definition of citizenship. With regard to this dimension the integration process can be depicted as an ongoing struggle between Muslims and society about social boundaries, identity and recognition. The ideological parameters of this dimension are determined by what Schinkel calls the 'dream of unity and order' of governments and political elites (Schinkel 2007: 42).

With respect to the integration process of Muslims, a mechanism of definition, allocation and attribution is at work. The definition of 'Muslim' depends on the specific political conjuncture. Over the years, a growing number of Muslim representatives have attempted to convince the government and society that they constitute a separate (religious) category in society, but that this does not prevent them from taking part in that society. The unwillingness on the part of the government to acknowledge this, is related to ideological images about the character of the Dutch nation and to specific problematic definitions that have been adopted over the course of recent years. The bottom line in this mode of thinking is that the (Christian) Dutch society was well on its way to becoming a modern secularized society when large numbers of immigrants entered the country bringing a different religion with them. These immigrants asked for provisions which society had already done away with.

Until the end of the 1970s, the religious background of migrants did not play any significant role in debates about their position in society. As far as background was concerned, migrants were defined in terms of ethnic origin, but this had no political consequences. Migrants were primarily seen as temporary labour forces who would return to their countries of origin. Officially the Netherlands was not an immigration country. Policies were based on this idea of temporariness. Migrants were temporary guests. Their cultural background was irrelevant.

Towards the beginning of the 1980s a turning point was reached. For the first time the government acknowledged that the idea of temporariness was unrealistic. The majority of the migrants were there to stay permanently.

An important aspect of this new discourse was that a relation was constructed between integration and cultural background. 'Guest workers' were renamed 'ethnic minorities', 'cultural minorities' or 'ethnic groups' and, later on, 'allochthonous'. In other words, a shift in the definition of the situation took place. From being an economic category migrants turned into a cultural one. Since structural integration was the central aim of the new policies, culture became the single most important criterion by which integration came to be measured.

This, however, did not mean that cultural background was on the whole neglected, far from it. In the path to full citizenship the relevance of culture and religion for the people concerned was recognized as a psychological outlet, a 'sacred canopy', to paraphrase Peter Berger, that functioned as a means to avert tensions caused by living in a strange environment. But as such, culture was also considered a barrier that slows down the pace of integration. Migrant organizations were considered to function as a bridge between the individual migrant and society, ensuring the migrant's smooth integration into it. The idea that the Dutch nation is a nation apart from its cultural and religious communities was expressed in the declaration that the articulation of culture is legitimate as long as it does not inhibit participation on the national scale. Only for the time being should the government be lenient towards cultural specificities.

Migrant organizations gained more significance during the integration process. They were politically and ideologically incorporated into the government's policies. Also, Islamic organizations were considered important immigrant organizations, and their activities were judged by their effects on the integration process. I call this the 'migrantization' of Islamic organizations.

This new attitude towards migrants took shape at a time when dramatic events were taking place in the Islamic world, such as the revolution in Iran and the assassination of the Egyptian president, Anwar el-Sadat. These events caused a flurry of publications about Islam and its adherents. Suddenly migrants from countries like Turkey and Morocco were 'discovered' to be Muslims. A new cultural category emerged: Muslim migrants. For the sake of convenience people with a completely different background were lumped together under the heading of 'Muslim culture'. Since it was, above all, Muslims who faced problems of deprivation with respect to housing, labour and education, 'Muslim culture' took on a specific meaning.

Islam increasingly became the explanatory factor, not only for specific (collective) behaviour of Muslims, but for all kinds of societal problems they faced: When one wants to know what goes on inside the head of a Muslim then one should study Islam. All other possible explanations were in fact reduced to 'Islam'. One can find numerous publications and statements by politicians in which this line of thinking is expressed. One of the leaders of the Dutch liberal party considered Islam the main threat to European liberal civilization. In 1991 it was a growing belief that Muslims should be monitored carefully (Rath and Sunier 1994).

The image of Islam was increasingly tied up with the notion that order had to be established, and declarations of how this process was being hampered by Muslim assertiveness. With respect to this image, there are generally two analytically separate ideological representations to be distinguished. The most widespread but harmless one is the idea that Muslims are the least integrated migrants. They are seen as passive, fatalist people who are introverted and face difficulties catching up with the pace of modern society. For that reason they easily fall back to their faith. One of the main objections to the foundation of Islamic schools, for example, was that they cause the undesirable isolation of young children. Islam forces rules upon them that inhibit their participation in society.

The origin of this image is related to the so-called 'rural bias'. The majority of the first-generation Muslim migrants had a rural background. They stand for the archetype 'Muslim'. Rural habits and Islamic prescriptions were amalgamated into a representation of the religion as a whole. But although cultural differences were considered significant, there was a certain inclusiveness and compassionate undertone to the image. Muslims are not excluded as a separate category; it is their faith that enforces rules upon them. But these problems can be overcome through systematic socialization. The boundary may be a temporary one, provided certain conditions are fulfilled. This may explain the strong pedagogical underpinnings in Dutch integration discourses.

Towards the end of the 1980s, and more or less as a direct consequence of the Rushdie affair, a new type of image made its way into the public discourse. This image is far from harmless and links Muslims in the Netherlands to the violence in the Middle East. Muslims are conceived of as a fifth column that may be a threat to society. The ongoing debate about growing fundamentalism among migrants, the alleged connections between Muslims in the Netherlands and fundamentalist groups in the Middle East, and the strong orientation of Muslims towards their country of origin, are all the result of this image. Muslims were depicted as outsiders who can never become part of Dutch society.

It will come as no surprise that 9/11 and subsequent events, particularly the murder of filmmaker Theo van Gogh, have greatly contributed to the development of this exclusivist rhetoric into a dominant discourse. Today we cannot understand the complex ideological mechanisms at work with respect to the position of Muslims in society unless we take into account the fourth dimension of the fabric of integration, namely the role of the modern mass media.

The mediatized dimension

It is always the case – by definition – that we are informed about Islam through mediatized information. The ubiquitous public eye has become the principal vehicle through which struggle and negotiation evolve. Whether it be the controversies about the building of a mosque, the discussion about the quality of Islamic schools, the question of whether or not MPs with an Islamic background can be trusted as loyal servants of the state, or whether a lawyer can wear a headscarf – it is through these kinds of high-profile events that we become informed. It is, however, a mistake to assume that these events are just part of the hype that conceals the 'real' process of integration and that we should therefore concentrate on these *longue durée* processes. While in many instances negotiations about the acquisition of rooms for prayer take place quietly and without trouble, in other cases the negotiations are boisterous and conflict-ridden, and it is through the latter that the public, politicians and policymakers become alerted and dragged into the issue. Sometimes it is even non-events that shape contentious situations, for example there was public turmoil about expected uproar by Muslims in the Netherlands following the release of the movie *fita* by the extreme right-wing politician Geert Wilders in 2008. But the uproar never took place. Again, mediatized high-profile events are not just odd cases in a sea of silent diplomacy, they are the constitutive narratives of the national imagination. Events are made up of narrative threads and aesthetic and performative moments in which the story of the nation is being told. In such events the nation is being reformulated and renegotiated (Handelman 1998).

Muslims in twenty-first-century Europe

In the numerous writings on the position of Muslims in twenty-first-century Europe, there is often a tendency to consider 9/11 as a watershed, a fundamental breach with the (often multicultural) past. I personally very much doubt this. It is certainly true that 9/11 has made the political, social and ideological parameters of the debate much more explicit and outspoken. At the same time, it is too simple and also too easy just to discard the long-term developments that have determined the present situation. As I have shown in this chapter, with respect to the Dutch situation, political decision-making has increasingly become based on considerations and priorities with regard to policies concerning minorities and not least on images of the character of Islam. In the 1980s this proved to be partially beneficial for Muslims, but since these policies in the 1990s shifted more and more to an individual level of integration, the conflation of 'Muslim' with 'migrant' has become more and more counterproductive in the eyes of many Muslim representatives. It has also become a serious drawback when it comes to constitutional rights of Muslims. Today the idea of the 'foreignness' of Islam, which is rooted in the migrant background of Muslims, has been sublimated into a discourse in which any link between Muslims and the outside world is considered dangerous. Where the world is in a global flux, Muslims cannot but comply completely with a narrow national Dutch project. Although Muslims are formally able to make use of the legal opportunities in order to build their own religious infrastructure, they have to seek commonalties, rather than emphasize religious boundaries. The paradox here is that in order to be accepted as Muslims, they have to make themselves invisible as Muslims to the outside world. Talal Asad has eloquently captured this paradox when he argues that the public sphere is never an empty space for carrying out debates. Any entrance to a pre-existing public realm will disrupt existing public assumptions about the character of that public sphere (Asad 2003: 185). In the case of the Netherlands (and in many other countries for that matter) the initial basis of the integration project – tackling the social and economic inequality of migrants – has turned into a mechanism of exclusion.

Notes

1 The majority of migrants from Turkey come from rural areas around the cities of Kayseri and Konya in central Anatolia. The majority of migrants from Morocco come from the northern Rif area.

2 For example the proportion of non-Western allochthonous pupils enrolling in higher education, denoting university and professional education, has doubled since 1995. Today the proportion of non-Western allochthonous and autochthonous students is almost the same (CBS 2008).

3 Alevis in Turkey live for the most part in central parts of Anatolia. There is a very remote link between Alevism and Shi'ism, but Alevis have adopted a heterodox version of Islam.

4 The Dutch educational system has two main types of schools: public schools and confessional ones. The school system is a good example of Dutch 'contained pluralism'. The state is responsible for the curriculum and the educational aims. Thus every pupil in the Netherlands should have the same basic curriculum in the same type of school. In addition, confessional schools can give religious lessons according to their religious convictions. The status of public and confessional schools and the general material resources they have at their disposal are the same. Confessional schools have their own administrative board, whereas public schools are administered by the state. The Dutch school system has its origin in the so-called 'school struggle' that took place at the beginning of the twentieth century. At the moment there are 12 'recognized' confessions. They have been granted principal rights to set up a school. Although secularization has found its way even to many confessional schools, the system is still one of the most delicate issues in Dutch politics (Sunier 2004).

5 The origin of the Dutch pillarization structure dates back to the Dutch history of religious emancipation at the beginning of the twentieth century. Pillarization was in fact the unintended consequence of strategies in which socio-political organization, ecclesiastical structure and religious ideology were interwoven (Stuurman 1983: 307). The pillar system implied a society completely fragmented into confessional pillars, at the top of which was a closely collaborating elite who dominated the whole system. After World War II the system gradually lost its function and in most sections of civil society a process of decategorization took place. Pillarization was the result of specific political conjunctures and cannot simply be applied to new situations like the case of Muslims.

6 In the 1980s when collective notions of integration were still in vogue, numerous articles were published about the possibility of including certain aspects of Islamic law in Dutch legislation (see Van Bakelen 1984; Rutten 1988; Vestdijk-Van der Hoeven 1991).

7 Rath (1984; 1990) has argued that all attempts to set up an Islamic party failed till now, due to lack of support. Since then the situation has not changed considerably. Most Muslims tend to vote for existing parties, but most political parties are not willing to

include Muslim issues in their programs. Quite the contrary. Since 9/11 for any political party it is strategically speaking not very clever to ask openly for special provisions for Islam. It may cost votes in the present anti-Islamic climate.

References

Asad, T. (2003) *Formations of the Secular: Christianity, Islam, Modernity*. Stanford: Stanford University Press.

Bakelen, F. A. van (1984) 'Implementatie van het recht van de islam in de Nederlandse wetgeving en jurisprudentie', in F. A. van Bakelen (ed.), *Recht van de islam. Teksten van het op 3 juni 1983 te Leiden gehouden Symposium*. Groningen: RIMO, pp. 19–42.

Baudrillard, J. (1994) *Simulacra and Simulation*. Ann Arbor: University of Michigan Press.

Centraal Bureau voor de Statistiek (CBS) (2008) *Jaarrapport Integratie 2008*. Den Haag: CBS.

Engbersen, G. and Gabriëls, R. (eds) (1995) *Sferen van Integratie: Naar een gedifferentieerd allochtonenbeleid*. Amsterdam: Boom.

Geschiere, P. (2009) *Perils of Belonging: Authochthony, Citizenship and Exclusion in Africa and Europe*. Chicago, IL: Chicago University Press.

Hampsink, R. and Roosblad, J. (1992) *Nederland en de islam*. Nijmegen: KUN.

Handelman, D. (1998) *Models and Mirrors: Towards an Anthropology of Public Events*. New York: Berghahn Books.

Landelijk Aktie Komite Anti Fascisme (LAKAF) (1980) *De grijze Wolf en de halve maan*. Utrecht: LAKAF.

Landman, N. (1992) *Van mat tot minaret: De institutionalisering van de islam in Nederland*. Amsterdam: VU Uitgeverij.

Maussen, M. (2009) 'Constructing Mosques: The Governance of Islam in France and the Netherlands'. Amsterdam: ASSR.

Ministerie van Binnenlandse Zaken (BiZa) (1999) *Kansen krijgen, kansen pakken: Integratiebeleid 1999–2002*. Den Haag: BiZa.

Ministerie van Welzijn Volksgezondheid en Cultuur (WVC) (1993). *Investeren en Integreren. Het WVC-minderhedenbeleid*. Den Haag: Min. van WVC.

Rath, J. (1984) *Migranten, de Centrumpartij en de deelraadsverkiezingen van 16 mei 1984 te Rotterdam*. Leiden: COMT.

Rath, J. (1990) 'Politieke participatie', in H. B. Entzinger and P. J. J. Stijnen (eds), *Etnische minderheden in Nederland*. Amsterdam: Boom Meppel, pp. 123–40.

Rath, J. and Sunier, T. (1994) 'Angst voor de islam in Nederland?', in W. Bot, M. van der Linden and R. Went (eds), *Kritiek: Jaarboek voor socialistische discussie en analyse 93–4*. Utrecht: Stichting Toestanden, pp. 53–63.

Rath, J., Penninx, R., Groenendijk, K. and Meyer, A. (1996) *Nederland en zijn islam*. Amsterdam: Het Spinhuis.

Rutten, S. (1998) *Moslims in de Nederlandse*. Rechtspraak Kampen: Kok.

Schinkel, W. (2007) *Denken in een tijd van socialehypochondrie: Aanzet tot een theorie voorbij de maatschappij*. Kampen: Klement.

Shadid, W. A. R. and Koningsveld, P.S. van (eds) (1992) *Islam in Dutch Society: Current Developments and Future Prospects*. Kampen: Kok Pharos.

Stuurman, S. (1983) *Verzuiling, Kapitalisme en Patriarchaat*. Nijmegen: SUN.

Sunier, T. (1996) *Islam in beweging: Turkse jongeren en islamitische organisaties*. Amsterdam: Spinhuis.

Sunier, T. (2004) 'Naar een nieuwe schoolstrijd?' *BMGN*, 119(4): 552–76.

Vestdijk-Van der Hoeven, M. (1991) *Religieus recht en minderheden*. Arnhem: Gouda Quint.

Wetenschappelijke Raad voor het Regeringsbeleid (WRR) (1989) *Allochtonenbeleid*. Den Haag: WRR

Wetenschappelijke Raad voor het Regeringsbeleid (WRR) (2006) *Geloven in het publieke domein*. Amsterdam: Amsterdam University Press.

8 From Empire to Republic, the French Muslim dilemma[1]

Valérie Amiraux

Introduction[2]

France has long been acknowledged as a principle destination country for migrants[3] where the process of incorporation (known in French as '*intégration*' until the mid-1990s) is framed by two pillar principles: republicanism and secularism (*laïcité*).[4] Where France was once viewed as the prototypical model of republican integration, it is now viewed as simply one model among others, including those of Britain and Germany. The convergent elements of these historically different traditions could certainly be better addressed, in particular when looking at what could be called Muslim politics, that is, the set of rules, political decisions and provisions addressing the needs expressed by Muslims. As has occurred in other European settings, Islam and Muslims have become priorities on the political agenda, as a result of both domestic dynamics and international events. The main distinction between France and its European neighbours lies in a different definition of nationhood (ethnic versus territorial, if comparing France and Germany) and with the development of a multicultural conception of politics, articulating race and ethnicity as central criteria for the implementation of justice in the British context. In recent years, and in particular following the transposition of European anti-discrimination provisions, the French political formula of incorporation is not very radically challenging when compared with other European 'philosophies of integration' (Favell 1998). Indeed, it has been described recently as convergent with other historically defined Anglo-Saxon traditions of accommodation and recognition of ethnic diversity (Amiraux, *et al.* 2008).

The questions raised by the presence of Muslims in France was (as in most other EU countries) conceived as a consequence of migration waves that lasted up to the end of the 1980s and have slowed down since then. These Muslim migrants, in their majority, came from the former French colonies of North Africa and the sub-Sahara region. The issue is nowadays defined more as a post-migration issue even if migration moves continue to contribute to the demographic evolution of the Muslim population.[5] In 2004–5, the official numbers were the following: 1.5 million immigrants came from North Africa (an increase of 17 per cent compared with 1999), mostly from Algeria and Morocco, while a comparable 1.4 million persons originated from other parts of the world. For the most part, these people came from

Asia (48 per cent, of which 16 per cent came from Turkey) and sub-Saharan Africa (40 per cent). Natives from sub-Saharan Africa were 570,000 in 2004 – a 45 per cent increase if compared with 1999. Seven out of ten of these persons came from a country that used to be administered by France.[6]

Though Islam is undeniably the second religion in France, opinions diverge regarding the exact number of Muslims living in France, which could be anywhere between 3.5 million and 7 million. This uncertainty about the numbers is *per se* a first indication of an important dimension that characterizes the French context, namely, the refusal to legitimize the elaboration of public indicators helping to identify the population according to its identity markers (not only religious, but also ethnic and racial, for instance). This Muslim population with a post-colonial migration background has in large part acquired French citizenship[7]. The 'Islam and Muslims' question is thus simultaneously considered to be a political, social and cultural question. Lately it also encompasses security aspects, though well before 9/11 and roughly since the mid-1990s, that have intensified with the 2009–10 public discussions related to the legitimacy of the presence of women wearing the burqa in public spaces. All these interrelated issues have appeared to expose French society to the complex challenge of having, on the one hand, to continue to promote equality as part of the republican project of integration, while simultaneously safeguarding the religious aspect of individual identity.

In France, the public discussions surrounding the 'Islam and Muslims question' is mostly related to the way secularism as a principle had to be reaffirmed as a core value and a regulatory principle.[8] It has also been shaped recently as a post-colonial issue, bringing back the internal contradiction of the long-term history of the republican French ideals: producing the conditions for equality and freedom among citizens,[9] while having treated people differently during the colonial period. The issue of Islamophobia, which we here briefly define as hostility towards the culture, religion and believers of Islam, made a relatively recent entry into the public discussion, compared for instance to the British context, but the existence of religious discrimination as distinct from ethnic discrimination still remains something both stakeholders and Muslim leaders do not investigate seriously.[10] As Muslims have been 'going more public' since 2001,[11] questions of representation and the difficulty (or social cost) of presenting oneself as Muslim are indeed a constant reminder of the historic basis for this stigmatization dating to the colonial period, which has long remained at the periphery of French historiography. Suspicions regarding Muslims and Islam as a faith, for instance, are part of an old republican tradition from long before 9/11 (Geisser and Zemouri 2007). A reading of the administrative vocabulary provides further evidence for this (Le Pautremat 2003; Laurens 2004).

This chapter aims at explaining the interaction between Muslim populations and French society through the analysis of the cultural and structural factors that shape this interaction, with a strong emphasis on history. We therefore at this point need to review the hypothesis of continuity between the colonial imagination, discourse and practice, on the one hand, and their contemporary counterparts on the other, in dealing with diversity in France. To do this, we will first consider the treatment of Islam as a religion by public authorities back in the colonial experience, then at later attempts to control the Muslim religion by public authorities, and at the hostility of the Republic to particular figures seen as typifying the day-to-day problems of interaction between society and Muslim otherness. Secular France (with 5 million Muslims, of whom 3 million are French) differs indeed from other European contexts where Muslim populations have settled, mostly by virtue of the increasingly passionate and almost visceral nature of the debates that have taken place over the past 20 years about Islam and Muslims, with most of those taking part voicing intense emotions (hatred, scorn, resentment, love, admiration) and enthusiastic militancy, that have been again illustrative of the general irrationality of the national identity discussion since summer 2009. The main purpose of this chapter is to suggest that the categories assigned from a religious point of view to Muslims have themselves become sources of discrimination in the public arena, marking them as 'deviant' from norms of behaviour for citizens of the Republic. These endure in the republican context in France because they have been preserved by the historical account linking the colonial Empire with the larger history of the French Republic. In this chapter, I wish to identify a series of nodes or key points in migration history, politics of integration, and Muslims and Islam as part of being a French citizen with multiple identities. What are the specific policies implemented towards Islam and Muslims? This leads us to a further important point assembling a historical perspective on the situation of Islam and Muslims: that there is a historical pattern of mistreatment of Islam and Muslims,[12] which changed from an institutional point of view only recently (2003, the year during which the CFCM was created, elected and implemented[13]) and still is, from a social and more inter-subjective perspective, the background for hostile and somewhat racist attitudes that lead to the unequal consideration and possible discrimination of Muslim French citizens.

Problems of numbers and categories

Before entering into our argument, it is essential to give a brief account of demographics. Let's start with two numbers: first, that Muslims are estimated to represent between 3.5 million and 7 millions Muslims in France;[14] second, that one out of three French people has at least one foreigner among his/her ancestors – in Paris it is one inhabitant in seven.[15] What do these numbers indicate? To begin with, they highlight the historical diversity of the French population, indicating also that migration is part of the family history of one-third of the Parisian population. Additionally, they illustrate how far France is from knowing about the religious identity (self-declared) of its population (foreign and national), for Muslims but for others as well.[16] Globally and in relation with the ethnic and colour blindness policy perspective, knowledge about the origins and belonging of the national population is based on proxies that work as indicators of the demographic situation without really allowing for a discussion of their relevance.

The first numbers (speaking of 3.5–7 million Muslims potentially settled in France) reflect the uncertainty, not to say the ignorance (as in the range 3.5 to 7 and 1 to 2) when trying to map the real numbers of Muslims in France, and of any population of believers whatever denomination they may be affiliated with. For instance, when trying to assess how many Muslims are living in France, there are usually two tendencies. The first, based on statistical regression, grounds the assessment on the idea that ethnic criteria can be used for determining who the Muslims are. The ethnic criteria is often based on the place of origin of the parents or the grandparents –that is, of the first person who moved to France. Practically, this means that the last individuals registered as members of a family with a Muslim background, and living on French soil, would be considered *ex ante* Muslim. This is usually the kind of statistical regression that is done starting from public statistics where the origin of the first migrant is available. Of course, this is done in complete ignorance of the most recent account of the sociology of religion insisting on the volatility of belonging, the individualization of the relation to one's religious family heritage and the multiplicity of identifications that can lead an individual to convert and to change religions several times in his/her life, especially in a non-Muslim surrounding. What matters though is rather the migration trajectory as the place of birth of the elders. The categorization of people as French opens a Pandora's box of issues over the validity of nationality as a criterion by which to identify whether or not certain individuals have a particular relationship to cultural or ethnic groups. The genealogical criterion does not properly reflect the migration dynamics that impact on the life of people.

In other type of surveys, not based on the census, which are conceived by people aware of the limits if this ethnic statistical regression, the criteria for identifying Muslims relies on what we call an institutional perception of what defines a believer – that is, his/her relationship to practice and more generally to worship.[17] Practice refers here to an institutional reading of religious belonging where religion is associated with faith and worship – that is, with practices related to collective rituals, fasting, consuming halal food or praying. Many illustrations of this trend, the most recent one being the quantitative study published in 2005 by Brouard and Tiberj (Brouard and Tiberj 2005) that – while useful for qualitative scholars unable to produce quantitative data and relying in most cases on qualitative typologies, because it offered a point of comparison with non-Muslim populations – ended up being quite vague in the definition of the categories used to situate the individuals of the sample, and still relied on an institutional definition of people's belief (places of worship as indicators of practices) crossed with ethnic origins (names, country of origin of the parents, place of birth). This can be interpreted as a sign of a larger problem that is dominating the field of study of religious diversity and in particular of Muslims minorities in France. This problem is mostly a definition issue.

The Muslim population in France is, in 2009, quite heterogeneous. This statement stems from the considerable amount of qualitative and often descriptive literature on Muslims that has developed since the 1980s. What is known about Muslims in France is the way they settled in the country over an extended time span (Kepel 1986; Leveau, Kepel 1988; Cesari 1994), the number of places of Muslim worship (Frégosi and Boubeker 2006), the complex network of associations that are active in it (Godard and Taussig 2007; Laurence and Vaisse 2006; Geisser and Zemouri 2007), and the extreme variety of profiles (Césari 1994; Venel 2004;

Weibel 2000). A particularly vast literature has developed since the 1990s around the issue of gender relationships and the headscarf (Gaspard and Khosrokhavar 1995; Lorcerie 2005; Guénif and Macé 2004). Two trends of research have to be mentioned. The first one connects to Muslim voices so as to enrich knowledge about Muslims from the inside. The second is linked to the emergence of a Muslim NGO activists' front that has published several reports dealing with stigmatization and discrimination of Muslims in France.[18] The literature by scholars and academics has been recently joined books written by Muslims or writers with a migrant background who take their distance with the public discussion focusing on Islam and activism (Bouzar 2004; Bouzar and Saïda 2003; Chouder *et al.* (2008); on this literature see Amiraux, 2006). This 'authentic testimony literature', as in other European countries such as Germany or the Netherlands, has emerged following the intensification of the discussion on headscarves in public schools. It has contributed to the constitution of a map of Islamic voices, mostly female, that have not yet really found a way to the public stage. When they have done, they have defined the limits of a quasi-normative iconography of good versus bad Muslims that relies on a strong gender differentiation. The women wearing the full head-to-toe headscarf – called 'voile integral' or 'burqa' in the French debates – embody the climax of this gender differentiation.

The ties binding the colonial Empire to the French Republic: one history, many stories

In the public challenges experienced by Muslims living in France today,[19] issues of portrayal and self-presentation are at work, inviting direct links to be made with colonial history, otherwise a fairly peripheral factor in the historical account of the nation.[20] The persistence of colonial images of people whose countries of origin have since gained their independence, and the echoes of these attitudes in the debate over integration and citizenship have been central to work in social sciences since the end of the 1990s, and to political views (Breviglieri 2001). For some people, post-colonialism is recognized everywhere, expressed either through political condemnation (such as the movement for Indigènes de la République [Indigenous People's Movement]), or through mockery (Stavo-Debauge 2007). Others see the focus on colonial history and its insertion into the present debate on racism and discrimination to be based on the theory that 'contemporary forms of the social issue would be racial, since they would originate in practices and ways of thinking from the colonial era (Saada 2006: 64).[21] Post-colonial approaches in France are dominated by an accusatory tone, capitalizing on the trajectory followed from indigenous to immigrant, and stressing both amnesia and culpability in regard to the republican colonial past. A few voices are raised against such 'facile indignation' (Stavo-Debauge 2007) summoning up the 'colonial imagination which neatly combines in the memory [...] both guilty soul-searching and self-critical exoneration' (Merle and Sibeud 2003). Hostility to the exploitation of the past is understandable, particularly in the face of attempts to make it an overarching explanatory cause and the tendency to turn the past into a national heritage.

It is not a question of reducing a complex colonial experience of difference and individual classification to a simple account of racism and exclusion that casts Muslims as victims today, as they were under colonial rule. The artificial insertion of a causal relationship between the way in which the Muslim religion was administered in Algeria in 1830, and the organization of its representation in France in 2003 is not the issue. The work on the 'post-colonial' approach undertaken recently in France rarely focuses on the religious issues. Nonetheless, the way in which these Muslim issues are framed invokes the idea of suspicion, the need to control people and places (Geisser and Zemouri 2007), the subversive potential of Islam and the Muslims as a primary source of insecurity and public disorder. They appear as tangible continuities, located especially within the administrative vocabulary (Le Pautremat 2004). Sarah Mazouz provides a subtle account of how, in the naturalization ceremony she describes in Doucy, even at the point of transition from foreigner to French citizen, there remains a kind of embarrassment associated with the intrinsic paradox of the republican ritual. Through the confusion of representatives of the public authorities in attendance, this ritual becomes a real test of qualification:[22]

> At the very moment the newly naturalised citizens are actually integrated, assimilated, they are still being spoken of and marked out as different and illegitimate. […] There is a real paradox involved, since the way in which these ceremonies are constructed, and the reappropriation by the State's representatives of categories of law marks even more boldly the boundary separating those things that are given by right, and those things that are never given by right.' (Mazouz 2008)

Muslim policies and *laïcité*

While the dream of an ideal colonial Empire is cast in the image of the Third Republic (Bancel, *et al.* 2003), the colonial experience does not prove to be a reliable implementation of republican ideals. Conquest was indeed in the name of republican principles, particularly the universal egalitarian project, but it brought about a coexistent set of dissonant practices, with the inequality among citizens of different status being one of the best known. The end of the nineteenth century marked the seminal moment in the republican mystique projected into the colonial experience.[23] Colonial practice as regards religion embodies these ambivalences. The Separation Law of 1905 thus becomes a factor in the rhetoric of the civilizing emancipatory mission in the colonies, and a resource for colonial domination. Indirect in its spirit as in its letter, the law of 1905 will never actually apply to Muslim religious associations created all the same under the terms of the 1907 decree. 'At this time, the ulemas highlighted the inherent contradiction of the Republic ready to turn laïcité into a dogma in France itself, and to distort it in Algeria as soon as the control of the indigenous population was at stake' (Achi 2007). Despite being one of the foundation stones of the Republic and its political culture, *laïcité* rings hollow in the colonial context, in particular in Algeria (Achi

2004: 81–106). It would not be applied in Algeria until 1947 (although it was transposed by decree from September 1907) and became a point challenged by Muslim reformers. There are therefore different wordings, drafted mainly on the republican citizenship model, and practices, depending on whether they are used for France or the colonized territories. In mainland France, the Third Republic put in place a democratic process integrating the various components of the French population, while in the extra-European world that the French Republicans aim at dominating, the vision of advancing civilization is formed as and justified by an exceptional colonial situation.[24] These contradictions are brought to a climax in the Algerian context, and made possible by the volatility of legal regulations relating to citizenship. Until 1946, indigenous Algerian people, although of French nationality, were denied citizenship (and hence voting rights) even though in French legal tradition race and ethnicity are not categories for awarding citizens' rights.[25] In Algeria, a French *département*, there is a two-tier citizenship process, depending on the group concerned – French Muslims or French from France.

There has never been a uniform policy towards Muslims in lands under colonial rule. Tensions between the republican project and the complex and unequal architecture of the colonial administrative system became ever more complex with further conquests and clashes with very disparate environments in the various territories (Egypt, Morocco, Tunisia, and Algeria). French Muslim policy was therefore not officially established until 1890 and implemented mostly during the following century. As a product of the twentieth century, it remains haunted by the idea that everything associated with Islam is potentially subversive and a risk to the unity of the French Empire. To put it briefly, the aim of the policy for Islam was mainly to create systems of control for protecting the republican project and the colonial Empire from the threat of 'Islam' in every area of society. The Algerian conquest was the ideal incarnate of France's Arab policy, where a strategic assimilation was made of new territories into French law, while the status of indigenous people was kept separate (French but not citizens). The status of '*Français Musulmans d'Algérie*' (French Muslims from Algeria, hereafter FMA) is the most typical illustration of the bifurcation between citizenship and nationality in the French colonial context.[26] In the end, it contributed to 'making citizenship irrelevant as criteria of national identity' (Kepel 1994:135).[27] Later on came the '*politique des égards*' (consideration politics), a term used at the end of the nineteenth century to describe the French practice, within its colonial control policy, of making use of some of the indigenous people, and respecting traditional institutions.[28] The Muslim policy, a kind of '*policing of souls*' (Lyauzu 1994: 61) thus combined the expertise of university academics, particularly orientialists, with that of the administrative authorities of the Muslim territories of the French Empire, and from 1910, that of the indigenous people (Laurens 2004: 251–80). The Arab Bureaux, from 1833 in Algeria, and the Interministerial Commission for Muslim Affairs (CIAM), created by the decree of June 1911, thus relied on local contacts to mediate with central authorities. Managed initially by the Ministry of Foreign Affairs (Morocco, Tunisia and Syria administrator) and the Ministry of the Interior (responsible for Algeria), CIAM had the task of further integrating French Muslim policy. It was designed as a coordination department, in which indigenous representation was a constant issue from 1915.[29] The posts of Muslim advisers ('intermediaries able to convey the grievances and complaints of the Muslim people'[30]) were created in 1931 as trustworthy vectors with the mainland: it was very important to show that the Republic was not hostile to Islam.

The obsessive control and organization of the Muslim religion in accordance with republican principles, which came to the surface during the 1980–1990s, is therefore not just an invention of the Fifth Republic. It had a much longer history than that, despite having had different aims in the past. After independence, during the mass labour migrations in the 1970s, a period of relative laissez-faire temporarily prevailed, where the pragmatic vision of the issues involved intersected with security concerns and diplomatic attitudes towards the Arab world. From 1989 to 1990, the period culminating in the establishment of the CFCM in 2003, there were alternating periods of tension and of harmony marking the progress of the institutionalization of representation for Islam.[31] For many Muslims involved in the consultation process set up by Jean-Pierre Chevènement, when he was Minister of the Interior (from 1997 to 2000), discussions with public authorities bore signs of colonialism. The accusation of illegitimacy that hangs over Muslim religious needs, or rather the suspicion of disloyalty that follows them, emerges in the definition of the legislative framework in which discussions take place. The invitation offered to representatives of the Islamic religion to 'join us at the table of the Republic'[32] was difficult to accept in January 2000 because of the '[d]eclaration of intent on the rights and obligations of members of the Muslim faith in France', subsequently renamed the '[l]egal principle', which affected the foundations governing relations between public authorities and the Muslim religion in France. The advisers responsible for Islam who succeeded one another alongside the ministers from 1989 alternated between idealists (desiring to 'civilize the Muslims') and pragmatists (assuming 'a sociological and demographic realism') explains Vincent Geisser (Geisser and Zemouri 2007: 71–99). There were mixed feelings among the representatives included in the consultation process, with some of the younger ones experiencing the invitation from successive Ministers of the Interior as a 'paternalistic, colonial command', while the older ones swung between feelings of helplessness and distrust.[33] The 18 months during which Sarkozy, then Minister of Interior, succeeded in getting Muslim leaders and associations to sit down and together organize a national board to represent them in the dialogue with the state about the conditions of worship, witnessed a rather long and infuriating process taking place. It came to a rather inconclusive end in April 2003 with a first mandate to a freshly elected board of Muslim representatives. Indeed, Muslims were finally represented in a centralized institution (CFCM) based on a coordination of regional boards (CRCM). On 19 April, Sarkozy made a speech during a yearly Muslim fair that took place in Le Bourget (close to Paris) during which he solemnly praised Muslims for having achieved this unique result,[34] and made a series of statements reminding Muslims of the way to become 'des Français comme les autres' in a manner that does not require them to receive any different treatment as far as their religious traditions are concerned.[35]

The 'homo islamicus' (Tezcan 2007: 51–74) emerging at the junction between public regulation and the requirements of Muslim associations in this process of institutionalization is a Janus figure, as it was in the colonial context. One face is the product of the institutional adoption of the Muslim religion as worship, cast in the bronze of civic *virtù* and loyalty to the Republic. The other face, the face of challenge, is that of resistance to the pressure on representatives of Islam to conform when they sit down at the table of the Republic. Over and above the altercations and scuffles among the various representatives of Muslim associations and federations (Frégosi 2005: 99–114), increasing supervision by public and political authorities observed over the period 2002–3 will be maintained. The story of the relationship between the French state (colonial and post-colonial) and the Muslim religion is *in fine* one of interference rather than neutral indifference. While state interference may be desirable for the sake of ensuring common freedoms, this would only be risk-free if there were guaranteed to be no arbitrary intervention in the lives of vulnerable people (Pettit 2004).

The indigenous and Muslim citizens in antithesis?

The tension between principles and ideals, on the one hand, and praxis and action, on the other, also appears in daily life. The problem of the coexistence of multiple definitions of the good can then lead to the appearance of unease, hostility, discrimination or even explicit racism. Other than at the institutional just outlined, the start of the twenty-first century has seen the emergence of a renewed iconography of deviation from the republican ideal, no longer a fantasy but in male and female figures that typify behaviours considered hostile to the Republic. The connection is made between an iconic fantasy of otherness, and a much more ordinary unease, arising from day-to-day interactions between people ignorant of or unfamiliar with Islam. This daily discomfort does not lead us away from the central hypothesis of this chapter (that of the continuity between pre- and post-colonial imagination, discourse and practice in handling Muslim otherness in France). Rather, it makes its typical content more ethnographic than historiographic, considering the way in which the 'governmentality' of the body (in the sense of the struggle engaged to control modes of integration and social reproduction between state and organized social forces, via the governance of the bodies of young female and male Muslims) highlights lines of continuity in the stigmatization of particular practices.[36]

There are two standard reconstructions of the figure of the 'other' in the colonial context: that of the 'savage' and that of the 'indigenous' person (Bancel and Blanchard 2008: 149–62). This combination of fantasies is embodied in the archetypes of the Muslim savage (the barbarian) portrayed as the opposite of the civilized, Catholic white man.[37] More specifically, among the many faces of the native, 'that of the horseman of the Maghrib, perpetuating a magnificent tradition of the brave "Arab" warrior, firmly establishing its function, perception and the fears it inspires (particularly Islam) in the narrow political field' (Bancel and Blanchard: 150) is situated in the world of politics and protest, launching a stereotype still operating in very similar ways today. The Arabs' skill in combat, brought under control by the Republic, and the notion of their violent nature and uncontrollable impulses, remain enduring elements in a historical pattern of stigmatization during which the 'indigenous Muslim' does not appear to be quite as 'teachable' as he has been depicted. In passing, we should note that, in this context, Islam is understood more as culture than as theology, or even as a lack of culture or ignorance. The 'Arab boy' (the product of Maghrib immigration), painted vividly in the media in the last few years as a troublemaker and source of danger within and outside his own community, 'is a ghost from the colonial past [...] one of the avatars of the indigenous immigrant who becomes the Muslim'(Guénif 2006: 118), sometimes welcomed in colonial times, but now despised.[38] The idea of Arab cruelty, an archetypal pillar of colonial culture, is now fostered by new scenes of confrontation around barbarous sexual practices which dominate the news[39] – though very different from the transnational repertoire suggesting the connection between Islam and terrorist violence.[40] Stigmatization here revolves around the incapacity of men to control their rough nature, 'their inability to interiorize in their own bodies the rules of propriety and courtesy that have always governed interaction between men and women, the expression of the French exception' (Guénif 2005: 204). In this context, Zinedine Zidane's head butt during the World Cup final in 2006, a public breach of sporting rules and codes, was for some the admission of an inability to control personal emotions, a complete distortion of the noble behaviour expected of the best athletes. Yasmin Jeewani emphasizes the orientalist and especially the animal imagery invoked by journalists of the international media to describe and interpret the event, concluding that the sportsman's performance was a failure in terms of integration (Jeewani 2008: 11–33). The same construction is also found elsewhere in the media coverage of this event, typically of a racialized image of the heterosexual Arab man (here a Kabyle), one of whose vocations is to protect the honour of the women in his family, insulted by the player in the opposing team. Nacira Guénif, in her analysis of the various stances towards the controversy over the wearing of the headscarf in 2003–4, provides a subtle description of the reassuring, successfully integrated characters, the '*beurette*' (slang term for a liberated Arab girl) and '*the lay Muslim*', in contrast to their negatively connoted opposites (the bearded fundamentalist and the young, veiled woman) (Guénif 2006: 111). The individual miraculously saved by sport (Z. Zidane) or the exceptionally successful student (Rachida Dati appointed Minister of Justice by Sarkozy in May 2007) were found to be fallible, and described as entangled in their 'roots', causing them to become transgressors rather than conformists in the lay moral context, even though Islam is not one of the identities either claims. The tension reaches its peak between the concrete formality of citizenship inherent in basic rights and principles, and the ideal citizen who has never taken root, to the point of abstraction, which in some eyes is an admission of incompetence. Between the cult of virginity and the inclination to rape, the danger of the indigenous individual, his lack of submissiveness and his resistance have gained the upper hand, independent of his gender, it should be said. Gender equality is in some way achieved through ordinary racism, which from now on does not stigmatize just the male figure (the Muslim Arab), but also his female counterpart (the young veiled woman). For men and women, the ''integration gap' for these post-colonial French people does not result from their social inadequacy, nor from their failure to adapt to the employment market. It lies within their own bodies, in their inability to submit to the rules of self-control required by the civilizing process in France'(Guénif 2006: 120).

The stigmatization of the Islamic headscarf over the past 20 years follows similar lines. There have been many phases in the argument, focused on the wearing of the headscarf in France, from the politicization to the 'juridicization' of discussions on either side (Amiraux 2009; Bowen 2006; de Galembert 2008). The consensus that dominated in 2003–4, when the controversy on wearing of the headscarf in state schools came to a head, was marked by the assumption that the headscarf is a polluting factor, damaging to the Republic and to the young women who wear it. Its presence offends several principles seen as central to the balance of the republican plan: it exports private signs into the public space, thereby identifying religious affiliation; the believer's identity takes priority over the citizen's identity, fracturing equality among students by introducing a visible, distinguishing feature; it thus harms the school's civic mission and leads to 'school à la carte' in which authorities other than teachers are involved; finally, the Islamic headscarf foils religious freedom by offending the freedom of conscience of others (Laborde 2005: 327–8). For the defenders of the lay republican stronghold, the headscarf is therefore an obvious sign of a threat to public order and to the symbolic ecology in which the sensitivities of the citizens are shaped and make sense. Separation of Church and State remains the main thrust of the Act of March 2004, onto which are grafted arguments relating to the protection of young veiled women and republican values, of which the school is the main channel of transmission.

The public controversies questioning the legitimacy of wearing the Islamic headscarf in public schools since 1989 illustrates the implementation of a governance of bodies that is very much anchored in the republican tradition of control of private space (Iacub 2008). The public obsession with the headscarf results from the convergence of different dynamics, from politicization to judicialization of the debates (Amiraux 2007; Bowen 2006; Lorcerie 2005; De Galembert 2008). Schools are no longer sanctuaries. Reading the headscarf controversies as a 'normative account of the relationships between citizenship and identity'. Laborde distinguishes two forms of criticism, mostly from the political left. One the one hand, culture-blind universalism was blamed for being an ideological mystification perpetuating the structure of post-colonial domination (Laborde 2001). The type of discourses this criticism ends up producing can best be illustrated by the Indigènes de la République movement, or the MIB (Mouvement de l'Immigration et des Banlieues). On the other hand, says Laborde, culture should be understood as an integral part of individual identity that cannot just be left behind when discussing political participation or going public. This second criticism of the French republican tradition pushes towards a more multicultural republicanism, considering the recognition of cultural elements of distinction as part of an egalitarian public sphere. For the defenders of the republican fortress, the headscarf embodies the threat to public order and the symbolic urban ecology through which citizens make sense of their experience. The governance of private manners and of modesty is not a new tradition of republicanism. Marcella Iacub, examining the secularization of civil law, illustrates how the erection of a 'wall of modesty/decency' between the private and the public spaces in nineteenth-century France led state authorities to govern previously purely private issues of sexuality and modesty (Iacub 2008). This tension has been exacerbated with the passing of the March 2004 law on religious signs in public schools: if religion should remain a private matter in the secular Republic, should the legislator and the state take care of it?

In secular republican France, the personal and private sphere makes no difference, politically speaking, to the way in which the state understands those it administers. In all secular, liberal democracies, religion is confined to the world of the personal and private. It may briefly be said, therefore, that secularism, from which *laïcité* has partially been derived, emerges from a liberal desire to protect individual freedoms as well as the various concepts of the good cohabiting in a pluralist society. The heart of secularism in a liberal context consequently incorporates religious freedom, equality of all citizens and state neutrality into a common plan. *Laïcité* in France is proposed in turn as a way for the administration to regulate differences in the public space, or as a context for recognizing[41] and even accommodating a real social pluralism. The contemporary version of *laïcité*, however, goes further than the nodal benchmark for separation. French *laïcité* combines two important factors: on the one hand the part played by institutions in implementing equality and neutrality, and on the other the 'doctrine of conscience', which lays down behavioural codes and standards for the attention of both religious organizations (internal laicization) and individuals, who are expected to exercise religious reserve in public (Laborde 2001: 716–35). These are therefore the infra-political foundations of republican attitudes that make justice and tolerance possible, not just through the law itself but also through a deeply etched ethical sense within a personal political culture.

In the end, Muslims in France stand at the crossroads of two contradictory commands: one requiring personal invisibility, eulogizing 'the invisible immigrant' (Noiriel 2007), the other inviting gratitude for the equality of treatment given to the various denominations in the country. The expectation of invisibility combines with the liberating plan for privatizing cultural identities in the name of equality for all in the citizen's public space, free of emotional attachment to contingent cultural features. This invisibility remains ambiguous and has even some legal consequences. For instance, while the concept of discrimination (including discrimination over the religious belonging of the victim) became a central notion of the legal and political arena in terms of promotion of equality and respect for differences, it has remained largely ignored and absent from the discourse about Muslims and Islam in France. This has been recently changing, in particular thanks to the legal interpretation given by the Halde (Haute Autorité de Lutte contre les Discriminations et pour l'Égalité) on specific circumstances (Ast 2010). So the acknowledgement of a continuous hostile feeling towards Muslims has been treated distinctively from the practices of discrimination vis-à-vis Muslims. This pertains to a certain logic of the political philosophy of integration and equality in France: religion is private, intimate and invisible. When dealing with Muslims though, the question becomes: do they have something more (or something less) than an ethnic minority? Significant forms of identification for particular groups of people individually and collectively are thus maintained in the absence and denial of recognition or invisibility. As Joan Stavo-Debauge explains, with regard to black people in France, this constitutes 'the most paradigmatic of experiences of humiliation, scorn and denial. Being invisible means being excluded from full, authorized membership of a community or even of a situation. It also means not being considered as someone who can participate by right to make a contribution that may be recognized and welcomed for its own merits by the other participants in the community.' (Stavo-Debauge 2007). The invitation to recognition itself comes from a European convergence of attitudes around multiculturalism and the fight against discrimination as a political means of handling diversity. This second point is also equivocal in the French context, where among the attributes discredited by the republican model of integration and conquest, religion takes pride of place. The 'indigenous Muslim tends to become a Muslim client, the subject of all the concerns of the public authorities, to the points of becoming trapped in religious identity at the expense of other social memberships'(Geisser and Zemouri 2007: 11).

Some conclusions

Islam's place in France is still not stable. Its fate is decided on the basis of a number of issues (historical, political, legal, social) which all converge on an apparent loss of trust in the lay republican system. As Habermas describes in conversation with the Pope Benedict XVI, the lay (or for Habermas, the 'secular') state relies on assumptions of uncertain reliability and durability. The inclination to the common good assumes more than simple obedience to law and involves a more costly undertaking in terms of political virtue, he explains; it is not possible to act only through interest or constraint in order to deploy values such as those of solidarity, tolerance and recognition. The consistent historical hostility to particular expressions of diversity, even in the innermost recesses of the personal life of individuals, raises echoes of an unacknowledged nationalism around the republican discourses and its publicly expressed hostile reflexes. The thoroughly modern, anti-Muslim racism that characterizes European public opinion relies in the French context on republican universalism, 'the new incarnation of post-colonial imperialism, which makes Islam into the "other" who cannot be assimilated, confusing the self-determination of the autonomous subject with the subjectivity of the white, European male' (Laborde 2001: 721). The current French context, as far as Muslims' incorporation is concerned, can probably best be defined as a moment of simultaneous invention of vocabulary and categories to fit in with a new European governance that has made of discrimination a central term in the development of a politics of difference, and the redefinition of a political grammar to articulate this new situation with a longer historical perspective (Fassin 2002; Amiraux and Simon 2006). Since 2006 this evolution has taken place in a slightly tense context, marked by the virulent public discussions (2003–4) that concluded with a law banning conspicuous religious signs from state schools (March 2004), urban riots all over France that lasted three weeks (November 2005) and lastly the upsurge of a wide discussion opposing experts and politicians on the legitimacy of adopting the collection of ethnic data in public statistics.[42] The challenge for political leaders and public agencies seem to be a double headed one, underlining the evidence of, first, the growing gap between historical narratives and practices, and second, the conflict between ideal political principles and their pragmatic implementation.[43]

Historically, post-revolutionary republicanism was established in France particularly around the recognition of the need to privatize cultural factors, especially religion, so that all citizens are treated equally in the public domain. Freedom of conscience, mutual incapacity for both politics and religion, equality of religion and personal belief before the State form some of the fundamental benefits of this republican plan, which also represents itself as secular. In theory, the keystone of the structure (meaning the set of rules and institutions governing the framework of its application) lies in the neutral practice of power and exercise of public authority. Neutrality then becomes the indicator of the political reality of *laïcité* in its capacity to face constant protests and claims (Koussens 2008). In practice, a separation from these ideals is gradually viewed as a normal state of affairs, with the tensions around issues relating to politics to be discussed in multicultural France contributing to the assumption that *laïcité* would naturally be a factor in a national political culture that is constantly under threat, but at the same time always an ideal goal towards which to aim. In other words, *laïcité*, more honoured by some in the breach than in the observance, remains a founding concept of the republican spirit, a shared conviction, despite its many possible interpretations. Since March 2004, the passing of the law regarding the wearing of symbols or clothing demonstrating religious affiliation in state schools and colleges, in application of the principle of *laïcité*, has made it a 'moral fact' in the sense of a mandatory '*rule of behaviour to be penalised*', independent of the diversity of consciences forming a society.[44] In at least one sector of public life, breaching *laïcité* is therefore now punished.[45] Is this enough to maintain the primary meaning of the post-revolutionary secular plan for peace-making and reconciliation?

Over the past years, French politics of difference have been a mixture of hesitation, inconsistency and faithfulness to historical ghosts and abstract principles. The most apparent elements in recent evolution are the institutional responses by the state to integration-related issues in terms of anti-discrimination policy – more and more use of categories and references to the law and to the European perspective – and a new visibility of collective mobilization around questions of recognition. The current context is illustrative of the tensions resulting from the temptation to remain at a high level of abstraction rather than switch to more local levels of observation of social difficulties. 'The citizen is not a concrete individual. One does not meet the citizen. It is a subject of law' (Schnapper 2004: 27). There is a need to invent a new type of tie binding individual citizens to the political, since national belonging (citizenship) is increasingly disassociated from cultural belonging. Citizenship and nationality are not equivalent. Many scholars have used quantitative or qualitative approaches to illustrate this non-equivalence (Duchesne 1997; Safi 2008). The republican paradigm needs to be somehow updated so that elements of multiculturalism can be introduced, starting with the recognition of the cultural and ethnic diversity of French society also in the statistic approach of diversity.

The present is nevertheless characterized by certain positive elements. First, state authorities are more and more active in regulating private religious issues of certain groups of people, with migrant background or/and Muslims.[46] Second, the conjunction of international events (9/11) with top-down input from transnational political institutions (the European Union) in the implementation of equality of treatment of all religions accelerated in April 2003 the creation of a board of representatives of Islam as a religion (Godard and Taussig 2007). However, even if this institutionalization of the Islamic representation has granted more space to a discussion of Muslim issues in the public sphere (Amiraux and Jonker 2006), it did not 'neutralize' the stigmatization and racialization (Fassin and Fassin 2006) of Islam-related elements of diversity that can be observed in today's France. The historical permanence of hostility towards certain forms of diversity, even when purely part of the private life of individuals, echoes an unspoken nationalism. Anti-Muslim racism, common all over Europe, in France is based on republican universalism. A rigidity of ideas and principles when dealing with citizenry and 'what it means to be a French man or woman' continues to dominate the public image of the French nation, which perceives itself as universal and abstract. French MPs from different political backgrounds have voiced several positions in favour of an extension of the current March 2004 law to 'the public space' at large.[47] The discussion of how to be *laïc* in a pluralist France has still a long way to go. The recent 2009 re-opening of a discussion related to the wear of the burka in France further confirms the iconic place of Muslims, more particularly Muslim women, in this endeavour.[48]

Notes

1 The author wishes to thank Joanna Waller for her translation into English of most parts of this chapter.

2 This chapter was drafted before the French debate on the 'national identity' started during Fall 2009, and the parallel work conducted by the Mission d'information parlementaire sur le port du foulard integral sur le territoire, which was already implemented in June 2009.

3 For a historical synthesis see Noiriel (1988).

4 There is always hesitation when coming to the translation into English of words such as *laïcité* and into French of word such as race or ethnicity. The way categories are defined/selected/applied are never neutral processes. Laicity is increasingly used to refer to the separation between State and Church as a condition for freedom of conscience and equality of rights. "Secular state" or "secularism" is the translation given by the Council of Europe and other international institutions, and mostly the one preferred by lawyers too. These are institutional uses of the word that do not encompass sociological perspectives on 'secularization processes' for instance (further definition can also be found in Baubérot 2007: 19–20).

5 For updated data see www.insee.fr (Institut national de la statistique et des etudes économiques (INSEE)).

6 See INSEE 1999 census, updated through the yearly census survey (INSEE 2004 and 2005), http://www.recensement-1999.insee.fr/RP99/rp99/page_accueil.paccueil (with English version), updated through the yearly census survey (2005 to 2009),

available at http://www.insee.fr/fr/bases-de-donnees/default.asp?page=recensements.htm

7 There is no official data cross-referencing religious identification with the national origin of the prime migrants. For mid-2004, 2 million immigrants were said to have French nationality, i.e. 40 per cent of the total number of migrants. They acquired nationality through marriage or naturalization. See *Enquête annuelle de recensement*, INSEE 2004.

8 This chapter was written before the national debate on the national identity was launched by Minister Besson in October 2009, and before the publication of the report by the parliamentary mission regarding the wearing of the burqa in France (January 2010).

9 Article 1 of the French Constitution 1958 states: 'France shall be an indivisible, secular, democratic and social Republic. It shall ensure the equality of all citizens before the law, without distinction of origin, race or religion. It shall respect all beliefs. It shall be organized on a decentralized basis. Statutes shall promote equal access by women and men to elective offices and posts as well as to professional and social positions.'

10 The current context of discussion about ethnic statistics may change that position. Comité pour la mesure de la diversité et l'évaluation des discriminations (COMEDD) under the direction of François Héran, *Inégalités et discriminations. Pour un usage critique et responsable de l'outil statistique*, présenté à M. Yazid Sabeg, commissaire à la diversité et à l'égalité des chances, 3 February 2010 (available at: http://www.scribd.com/doc/26484593/Inegalites-et-discriminations-COMEDD-2010).

11 Going public refers here to the simultaneous intensification of discourses on the incompatibility of Islam and democracy, Islam and secularism, the increased designation of Muslims as potential suspects following 9/11, the politicization of the notion of Islamophobia and the establishment of a double-standard discourse regarding Muslim mobilization in European contexts at large.

12 Impressive work has been carried out by historians on that matter: first on the different juridical categories invented to cope with the variety of status in the Muslim societies under French administration; second, to point out the non-application of the 1905 law on separation in part of the colonized territories, i.e. Algeria (though a French department). On the post-colonial categorization and its impact on housing policies for instance, see de Barros (2005).

13 CFCM stands for *Conseil Français du Culte Musulman* (French Council for the Muslim Religion) that, since 2003, is a representative institution of Muslims, both at the national and regional levels, in matters mostly related to practices, ritual and institutional life.

14 This '*querelle des chiffres*' has been going on for years among scholars studying Islam and Muslims in France. A good illustration is the first chapter in Kaltenbach and Tribalat (2002). For a recent update on Muslims in France (with statistics), see Godard and Taussig (2007).

15 The data comes from Atelier Parisien d'urbanisme (APUR), *La population étrangère à Paris*, n. 7, janvier 2003 which is a synthesis of a larger survey conducted by APUR for the Paris City Hall.

16 There are no statistics for Catholics, Protestants, Jews, Sikhs, Buddhists, only estimations.

17 This has to do with the legal framework on religion in the French context where religion is barely defined independently from worship.

18 Probably the more active on the subject of religious discrimination and Islamophobia are Comité 24 mars et libertés; Collectif Contre l'Islamophobie en France (CCIF).

19 By this 'public confrontation' I mean the overlapping of several different processes operating at a number of levels. First of all, there is the historical and sometimes imaginary connection drawn between Islam and the French Republic, in terms of their incompatibility, particularly around values of equality and *laïcité*. Then there is the gradual ethnicization over the past 20 years (since 1989) of the denominational difference of Muslims living in France to the point where factors of insecurity become inculturated, at the international level as well as with regard to internal policy. This movement may

for instance be associated with the phenomenon of Islamophobia. Finally, as a corollary to these, there is the generalized suspicion of all Muslims, demanding of them demonstrations of loyalty and knowledge of the rules, down to the most mundane interactions of daily life. The initial aspects of this analysis have been described in Amiraux (2004: 209–45).

20 The political foundations of social science discussions are indisputable. Several authors have recently developed these themes, to the point of speaking of state xenophobia, particularly as regards the creation of the Ministry of National Identity and Immigration. 'By "xenophobia", we mean all the speech and actions that tend to identify the foreigner as a problem, a risk or a threat to the receiving society, keeping him or her distanced from this society, whether before arrival but preparing to come, or after arrival, or even once settled for some time. This preliminary definition can be further refined into a government xenophobia with a history, characteristics and specific forms of expression, distinct from the far right's anti-establishment xenophobia which Europe has been experiencing again for over two decades' (Valluy (2008: 12); *Asylon* (2008); *Journal des Anthropologues* (2007); *Raisons Politiques* (2007).

21 For views on recent developments in French debates about these issues, see *Genèses* (2003) edited by Alexis Spire and *Genèses* (2007) edited by Emmanuelle Saada.

22 It is hardly surprising to learn that an abusive (in the sense of beyond the scope of the law) extension of the law of March 2004 imposing the principle of *laïcité* in state schools resulted in women being banned from wearing veils in city halls when receiving their citizenship decree from an elected representative or assistant. In this regard, see resolution 2006–131 5 June 2006 from HALDE (Haute autorité de lutte contre les discriminations et pour l'égalité) [High authority for the fight against discrimination and for equality].

23 On the subject of the weaknesses of the French model of integration, a more contemporary expression speaks of the violence of the abstract universal, which excludes rather than integrates, while helping to stigmatize the 'other' (see Khosrokhavar 1996: 113–51).

24 The French term 'civilization' shares its legacy in the French colonial context with its equivalent in the British context. The English term 'civilization' emerged around 1830, and its later use in the plural (1860) was contrasted with the idea of 'barbarians' and 'savages' (Williams 1983).

25 Williams (1983).

26 The Indigenous People's Code was imposed in Algeria in 1881. It was repealed in 1946. The indigenous Muslims, who therefore had French nationality but not citizenship, then became French Muslims. The ruling of March 1944 applying the principle of equal rights and duties to French Muslims and non-Muslims was only very tardily applied, and during the Algerian war legal distinctions continued to be made among categories of French citizens, with the law and its usage relating to various practices (see Spire 2003: 61).

27 Algerians, though of French nationality, did not have the right to vote and were, to use the contemporary word, denizens. This denial of citizens' rights applied while race and ethnicity were not legitimate categories in the matter of civic rights. After 1946, French citizenship was extended to all persons living on French territory, but the distinction between civil and personal status survived in colonized Algeria, and the French Muslims in Algeria were those who did not renounce their religion but were French citizens.

28 In the act of surrender in 1830, the French authorities undertook to respect local customs, particularly retaining a personal status founded on religious law, and identifying the various denominations present in Algeria. Following the Crémieux decree of October 1870, indigenous Jews from Algerian *départements* became French citizens, with only the Muslims retaining their indigenous status.

29 We used the work of P. Le Pautremat (2003), on this point.

30 'It is impossible for us to claim any immediate influence over people to whom we are

strangers. In order to handle them we need intermediaries: we have to give them leaders, otherwise they will choose their own. I preferred the ulemas and doctors of the law: first, because they were natural leaders, secondly because they were interpreters of the Koran and our greatest obstacles have been and will continue to be found in religious ideas, and thirdly because these ulemas have gentle ways, they love justice and they are guided by a fertile moral conscience. [...] I have involved them in my administration. I made use of them to speak to the people.' Extract from *Mémoire sur l'administration intérieure de l'Egypte* de Bonaparte, quoted by Laurens (2004: 54).

31 The institutionalization of Islam in April 2003 resulted in the formation of a representative authority, the CFCM, a part-elected, part-nominated body. For a useful summary, see Laurence and Vaisse (2006: 135–62); Zeghal (2005).

32 The expression is taken from Jean-Pierre Chevènement when he was Minister of Interior (1997–2000), and has been used almost liturgically since then by his successors.

33 Geisser and Zemouri 2007: 86–7.

34 'C'est une victoire pour les musulmans de France qui ont témoigné ainsi de leur volonté de vivre leur religion dans la paix et le respect des valeurs de la République. La France est la première démocratie à avoir accompli ce progrès. Il vous appartient maintenant de le faire vivre.' (Sarkozy 2003).

35 The precise illustration dealt with the obligation to be bare-headed in photographs on official ID documents: 'La loi impose que sur une carte nationale d'identité, la photographie du titulaire soit tête nue que ce soit celle d'une femme ou d'un homme. Cette obligation est respectée par les religieuses catholiques, comme par toutes les femmes vivant en France. Rien ne justifierait que les femmes de confession musulmanes bénéficient d'une loi différente', ibid.

36 For a parallel account of the stigmatization of personal practices associated with religion (prayer, wearing the headscarf) and their integration in sport, see Silverstein (2004: 121–50); Guénif (2005: 199–209).

37 Perhaps more interesting than particular details of national history is the image of Islam that existed in medieval Western Europe and has altered little since. On the long history of the construction of mutual images, inspired by an ideological confrontation, by animosity and hatred (Islamophobia, as it is now called), as well as by love or fascination, see Daniel (1993); Goody (2004); Dakhlia (2005).

38 Post-colonial studies in France have not yet examined issues of gender in depth. In his splendid work *Desiring Arabs*, Joseph Massad outlines a history of gay tourism to expose the interactions between issues of 'culture', sexual practices and colonial power. He supports Stoler's criticism of Foucault: 'why have we been so willing to accept his history of a nineteenth century sexual order that systematically excludes and/or subsumes the fact of colonialism within it?' A. Stoler (1995) quoted in Massad (2007: 7).

39 Referring here to the media coverage of mass rape, also known as 'gang-bangs'. See Muchielli (2005). On popular imagery and the stigmatization of the 'Arab boy' as a violent, polygamous heterosexual, a circumciser of women, see Guénif and Macé (2004).

40 On the media construction of these characters, see Delthombe (2005).

41 'that is, a *laïcité* which while respecting the separate independence of the State and religion, and taking care to ensure the fundamental principles of liberty and non-discrimination implied, acknowledges the social, educational and civil contributions made by religions and incorporates these into the public sphere' (Willaime 2006: 89).

42 Again a series of public reports in respect of the French tradition on controversial issues: 'Report of the Reflection Committee on the Constitution Preamble' (*Rapport du comité de réflexion sur le Préambule de la Constitution*, December 2008). Commission Yazid Sabeg and its report on the promotion of diversity and equality (May 2009).

43 For an update on the field of discrimination see Amiraux and Guiraudon (2009).

44 Durkheim later states that the moral facts follow rules that are distinguished by two features: society responds in the event of an action deviating from the moral rule to

which it must conform; the reaction follows the breach of the rule 'with a real need'. And further, 'the only possible progress is that which society makes collectively' (Durkheim 1893: 16, 19).

45 'So the reality of an obligation is certain only if it is manifested by some sanction', ibid., p. 20.

46 One thinks for instance of the hardening of the laws dealing with family reunification, of the public campaigns against 'forced/arranged marriages' (two practices that are definitely not synonymous but still confused), of the unanticipated effects of new migration policies in Europe (Guild 2008).

47 By a decision on 27 June 2008 (Mme Machbour, n°286798), the French Council of State denied French nationality to a Moroccan woman living in France, married to a Frenchman and mother of three children, because it considered her religious practice as radical and incompatible with the core values of French community. See also the draft Law n. 1121 proposed on 23 September 2008 by Jacques Myard banning burqas in public.

48 See Koussens (2009); Laborde (2008b).

References

Achi, Raberh (2007) '"L'islam authentique appartient à Dieu, 'l'islam algérien' à César": La mobilisation de l'association des oulémas d'Algérie pour la séparation du culte musulman et de l'Etat (1931–1956)', *Genèses*, 4 (69): 49–69.

Achi, Raberh (2004) 'La séparation des Eglises et de l'Etat à l'épreuve de la situation coloniale: L'Etat colonial et l'usage politique de la dérogation dans l'administration du culte musulman en Algérie (1907–1959)', *Politix*, 17 (66): 81–106.

Amiraux, Valérie (2004) 'Expertises, savoir et politique: La constitution de l'islam comme problème public en France et en Allemagne', in Bénédicte Zimmermann (ed.), *Les sciences sociales à l'épreuve de l'action*, Paris, EHESS, pp. 209–45.

Amiraux, Valérie (2006) 'Speaking as a Muslim: Avoiding Religion in French Public Space', in Valerie Amiraux and Gerdien Jonker (eds) *Politics of Visibility: Young Muslims in European Public Spaces*, Bielefeld, Transcript Verlag, pp. 21–52.

Amiraux, Valérie (2007) 'Religious Discrimination: Muslims Claiming Equality in the EU', in Christophe Bertossi (ed.), *European Anti-Discrimination and the Politics of Citizenship: France and Britain*, Basingstoke and New York, Palgrave-Macmillan, pp. 143–67.

Amiraux, Valérie (2009) 'L' "affaire du foulard" en France: Épure d'un fait social ou, retour sur une affaire qui n'en est pas encore une', *Sociologie & Sociétés* (Autumn).

Amiraux, Valérie and Jonker, Gerdien (2006) 'Introduction: Talking about Visibility – Actors, Politics, Forms of Engagement', in Valerie Amiraux and Gerdien Jonker (eds) *Politics of Visibilities: Young Muslims European Public Spaces*, Bielefeld, Transcript Verlag, pp. 9–20.

Amiraux Valérie, and Guiraudon, Virginie (2009) 'Discrimination in comparative perspective: policies and practices', *The American Behavioral Scientist*, 12: 1–2.

Amiraux, Valérie and Simon, Patrick (2006) 'Immigrants and Integration in France. There are no Minorities Here: Cultures of Scholarship and Public Debate on', *International Journal of Comparative Sociology*, 47: 191–215.

Amiraux, Valérie, Kirszbaum, Thomas, Lépinard, Éléonore and Sabbagh, Daniel (2008) Les approches anglo-saxonnes et française de la lutte contre les discriminations ethniques: convergences et divergences des normes, instruments et mobilisations dans l'accès au logement, à l'enseignement et au droit, DREES/MIRe report, October, unpublished.

Asylon (2008) 'Institutionnalisation de la xénophobie en France' (special issue), *Asylon*, 4.

Ast Frédérique, 'L'apport du droit à la non-discrimination à la protection du pluralisme religieux. Regards croisés des jurisdictions et de la HALDE', posted on http://www.droitdesreligions.net (accessed 8 February 2010).

Atelier Parisien d'urbanisme (APUR) (2002) *La population étrangère à Paris: elements de diagnostic sociodémographique à partir des données du recensement*, Diagnostic local d'intégration de la Ville de Paris.

Bancel, Nicolas and Blanchard, Pascal (2008) 'Civiliser: l'invention de l'indigène', in Pascal Blanchard and Sandrine Lemaire (eds), *Culture coloniale: La France conquise par son Empire, 1871–1931*, Paris, Editions Autrement, pp. 149–62.

Bancel, N., Blanchard, P. and Vergès, F. (2003) *La République coloniale: Essai sur une utopie*, Paris, Albin Michel.

Baubérot, Jean (2007) *Les laïcités dans le monde*, Paris, PUF ('Que sais-je?').

Bouzar, Dounia (2004) *Monsieur Islam n'existe pas: Pour une désislamisation des débats*, Paris, Hachette.

Bouzar, Dounia and Kada, Saïda (2003) *L'une voilée l'autre pas*, Paris, Albin Michel.

Bowen, John (2006) *Why the French Don't Like Headscarves: Islam, the State, and Public Space*, Princeton, NJ, Princeton University Press.

Breviglieri, Marc (2001) 'L'étreinte de l'origine: Attachement, mémoire et nostalgie chez les enfants d'immigrés maghrébins', *Confluences Méditerranée*, 39: 37–47.

Brouard, Sylvain and Tiberj, Vincent (2005) *Français comme les autres? Enquête sur les citoyens issus de l'immigration africaine et turque*, Paris, Presses de Sciences-Po.

Césari, Jocelyne (1994) 'L'islam dans l'immigration: un bilan de la recherche', *Pensée*, 299: 59–68.

Chouder, Ismahane, Latrèche, Mohammed and Tévanian, Pierre (2008) *Les Filles voilées parlent*, Paris, Éditions La Fabrique.

Comité pour la mesure de la diversité et l'évaluation des discriminations (COMEDD) under the direction of François Héran, *Inégalités et discriminations. Pour un usage critique et responsable de l'outil statistique*, présenté à M. Yazid Sabeg, commissaire à la diversité et à l'égalité des chances, 3 February 2010. Available at: http://www.scribd.com/doc/26484593/Inegalites-et-discriminations-COMEDD-2010).

Dakhlia, Jocelyne (2005) *Islamicités*, Paris, PUF.

Daniel, Norman (1993) *Islam et Occident*, Paris, Le Cerf.

Delthombe, Thomas (2005) *L'islam imaginaire: Les musulmans de France à la télévision, 1975–2003*, Paris, La Découverte.

Duchesne, Sophie (1997) *Citoyenneté à la française*, Paris, Presses de Sciences Po.

de Galembert, Claire (ed.) (2008) 'Le voile en procès', *Droit et Société.*

De Barros, Françoise (2005) 'Des "Français musulmans d'Algérie" aux immigrés: L'importation de classifications coloniales dans les politiques de logement en France (1960–1970)', *Actes de la Recherches en Sciences sociales*, 159 (September): 26–45.

Durkheim, Émile (1893) *Social Division of Labour*, Paris, Alcan.

Fassin, Didier (2002) 'L'invention française de la discrimination', *Revue française de science politique*, 52 (4): 395–415.

Fassin, Didier and Fassin, Éric (eds) (2006) *De la question sociale à la question raciale:Représenter la société française*, Paris, La découverte.

Favell, Adrian (1998) *Philosophies of Integration: Immigration and the Idea of Citizenship in France and Britain*, London, Macmillan.

Frégosi, Franck and Boubeker, Ahmed (2005) 'Les enjeux liés à la structuration de l'islam en France', in Rémy Leveau and Khadija Mohsen-Finan (eds), *Musulmans de France et d'Europe*, Paris, CNRS Editions, pp. 99–114.

Frégosi, Franck and Boubeker, Ahmed (2006) (eds) *L'exercice du culte musulman en France. Lieux de prière et d'inhumation*, Paris, La documentation française.

Gaspard, Françoise and Khosrokhavar, Farhad (1995) *Le foulard et la République*, Paris, La Découverte.

Geisser, Vincent (2005) 'L'islamophobie en France au regard du débat européen', in Rémy Leveau and Khadija Mohsen-Finan (eds), *Musulmans de France et d'Europe*, Paris, CNRS Editions, pp. 67–9.

Geisser, Vincent and Zemouri, Aziz (2007) *Marianne et Allah: Les politiques françaises face à la 'question musulmane'*, Paris, La Découverte. pp. 15–41

Godard, Bernard and Taussig, Sylvie (2007) *Les musulmans en France: Courants, institutions, communautés: un état des lieux*, Paris, Robert Laffont.

Goody, Jack (2004) *L'Islam en Europe: Histoire, échanges, conflits*, Paris, La découverte.

Guénif, Nacira (2005) 'La réduction à son corps de l'indigène de la République', in Nicolas Bancel, Pascal Blanchard and Sandrine Lemaire (eds), *La fracture coloniale*, Paris, La découverte, pp. 199–209.

Guénif, Nacira (2006) 'La Française voilée, la beurette, le garçon arabe et le musulman laïc: Les figures assignées du racisme vertueux', in N. Guénif (ed.), *La République mise à nu par son immigration*, Paris, La Fabrique, pp. 109–32.

Guénif, Nacira and Macé, Éric (2004) *Les féministes et le garçon arabe*, Paris, éditions de l'aube.

Guild, Elspeth (2008) 'Les étrangers en Europe, victimes collatérales de la guerre contre le terrorisme', in Didier Bigo, Laurent Bonelli and Thomas Deltombe (eds), *Au nom du 11 septembre … Les démocraties à l'épreuve de l'antiterrorisme*, Paris, La Découverte.

Iacub, Marcella (2008) Par le trou de la serrure: Une histoire de la pudeur publique XIX–XXIè siècle, Paris, Fayard.

INSEE (Institut national de la statistique et des études économiques) (1999) Available at: http://www.recensement-1999.insee.fr/RP99/rp99/page_accueil.paccuei

INSEE (2004) *Enquête annuelle de recensement.* Available at: http://www.insee.fr/fr/bases-de-donnees/

INSEE (2005) Available at: http://www.insee.fr/fr/bases-de-donnees/

INSEE (2006) Borrel, Catherine, *Enquêtes annuelles de recensement 2004 et 2005. Près de 5 millions d'immigrés à la mi-2004*, INSEE, n. 1098, août 2006. Available at: http://www.insee.fr/fr/themes/document.asp?ref_id=ip1098&reg_id=0

Jeewani, Yasmin (2008) 'Sport as Civilizing Mission: Zinedine Zidane and the Infamous Head-butt', *Topia. Canadian Journal of Cultural Studies*, 19: 11–33.

Journal des Anthropologues (2007) 'Identités nationales d'Etat' (special issue), *Journal des Anthropologues.*

Kaltenbach, Marie-Hélène and Tribalat, Michèle (2002) *La République et l'Islam: Entre crainte et aveuglement*, Paris, Gallimard.

Kepel, Gilles (1986) *Les banlieues de l'Islam*, Paris, le Seuil.

Kepel, Gilles (1994) *A l'ouest d'Allah*, Paris, le Seuil.

Khosrokhavar, Farhad (1996) 'L'universel abstrait. Le politique et la construction de l'islamisme comme une forme d'altérité', in M. Wieviorka (ed.), *Une société fragmentée: le multiculturalisme en débat*, Paris, La découverte, pp. 113–51.

Koussens, David, (2009) 'Sous l'affaire de la *burqa* … quel visage de la laïcité française?', *Sociologie et Sociétés.*

Laborde, Cécile (2001) 'The culture(s) of the Republic: Nationalism and Multiculturalism in French Republican Thought', *Political Theory*, 29 (5): 716–35.

Laborde, Cécile (2005) 'Secular Philosophy and Muslim Headscarves in Schools', *The Journal of Political Philosophy*, 13 (3): 305–29.

Laborde, Cécile (2008a) *Critical Republicanism: The Hijab Controversy in Political Philosophy*, Oxford, Oxford University Press.

Laborde, Cécile (2008b) 'Virginity and Burqa: Unreasonable Accommodations? Considerations on the Stasi and Bouchard-Taylor Reports', *La vie des idées*, 30 October. Available at: http://www.laviedesidees.fr/Virginity-and-Burqa-Unreasonable.html (accessed 22 May 2009).

Lacoste-Dujardin, Camille (1993) *Ils disent que je suis une beurette*, Paris, Fixot.

Laurence, Jonathan and Vaisse, Justin (2006) *Integrating Islam: Political and Religious Challenges in Contemporary France*, Washington DC, Brookings Institution Press.

Laurens, Henry, 2004, *Orientales II: La IIIème République et l'Islam*, Paris, CNRS Éditions.

Le Pautremat, Pascal (2003) *La politique musulmane de la France au XXème siècle. De l'Hexagone aux terres d'Islam*, Paris, Maisonneuve et Larose.

Leveau, Rémy and Kepel, Gilles (1988) (eds) *Les musulmans dans la société française*, Paris, Presses de la FNSP.

Lorcerie, Françoise (2005) *La politisation du voile: l'affaire en France, en Europe et dans le monde arabe*, Paris, L'Harmattan.

Lyauzu, Claude (1994) *L'Europe et l'Afrique méditerranéenne, de Suez (1869) à nos jours*, Paris, Éditions Complexe.

Massad, Joseph A. (2007) *Desiring Arabs*, Chicago, IL, Chicago University Press.

Mazouz, Sarah (2008) 'Une célébration paradoxale: Les cérémonies de remise des décrets de naturalisation', *Genèses*, 70: 88–105.

Merle, Isabelle and Sibeud, Emmanuelle (2003) 'Histoire en marge ou histoire en marche? La colonisation entre repentance et patrimonialisation', Proceedings of the conference *La politique du passé: constructions, usages et mobilisation de l'histoire dans la France des années 1970 à nos jours*. Available at: http://histoire-sociale.univ-paris1.fr/Collo/Merle.pdf (accessed 10 June 2008).

Muchielli, Laurent (2005) *Le scandale des tournantes*, Paris, La Découverte.

Noiriel, Gérard (1988) *Le creuset français, Histoire de l'immigration (19ème–20ème siècles)*, Paris, Seuil.

Noiriel, Gérard (2007) *Immigration, antisémitisme et racisme en France (XIXe–XXe siècle): Discours publics, humiliations privées*, Paris, Fayard.

Pettit, Philip (2004) *Républicanisme: une théorie de la liberté et du gouvernement*, Paris, Gallimard.

Raisons politiques (2007) 'Choisir ses immigrés?' (special issue), *Raisons politiques*, 26.

Saada, Emmanuelle (2006) 'Un racisme de l'expansion: Les discriminations raciales au regard des situations coloniales', in Didier Fassin and Eric Fassin (eds), *De la question sociale à la question raciale? Représenter la société française*, Paris, La découverte, pp. 55–71.

Saada, Emmanuelle (2007) 'La parole est aux Indigènes' (special issue), *Genèses*, 69 (4).

Safi, Mirna (2008) 'The Immigrant Integration Process in France: Inequalities and Segmentation', *Revue française de sociologie*, 49 (5): 3–44.

Sarkozy, Nicolas (2003) 'Intervention de Monsieur Nicolas Sarkozy, ministre de l'Intérieur, de la sécurité intérieure et des libertés locales – Le Bourget', 19 April. Available at: http://www.interieur.gouv.fr/sections/le_ministre/interventions/archives-nicolas-sarkozy/19-04-2003-20eme-uoif/view

Schnapper, Dominique (2004) *Guide Républicain*, Paris, La documentation française.

Silverstein, Paul A. (2004) *Algeria in France: Transpolitics, Race and Nation*, Bloomington, Indiana University Press

Spire, Alexis (2003) 'Semblables et pourtant différents. La citoyenneté paradoxale des "Français musulmans d'Algérie" en métropole', *Genèses*, 53 (December): 48–68.

Stavo-Debauge, Joan (2007) 'L'invisibilité du tort et le tort de l'invisibilité', *Espacestemps.net, Actuel*, http://espacestemps.net/document2233.html (accessed 10 June 2008).

Tezcan, Levent (2007) 'Kultur, Gouvernementalität der Religion und der Integrationsdiskurs', in Monika Wohlrab-Sahr and Levent Tezcan (eds), *Konfliktfeld Islam in Europa*, Baden-Baden, Nomos Verlag (Soziale Welt), pp. 51–74.

Valluy, Jérôme (2008) 'Quelles sont les origines du ministère de l'Identité nationale et de l'Immigration?', in *Cultures et conflits*, 'Xénophobie de gouvernement, nationalisme d'État', 69. Available online at: www.conflits.org

Venel, Nancy (2004) *Musulmans et citoyens*, Paris, PUF.

Weibel, Nadine (2000) *Par delà le voile. Femmes d'islam en Europe*, Bruxelles, Complexe.

Willaime, Jean-Paul (2006) 'Séparation et coopération Églises-État en Allemagne', in Alain Dierkens and Jean-Philippe Schreiber (eds), *Laïcité et sécularisation dans l'Union européenne*, éditions de l'Université de Bruxelles, pp. 89–105,

Williams, Raymond (1983) *Keywords, Vocabulary of Culture and Society*, Oxford, Oxford University Press.

Zeghal, Malika (2005) 'La constitution du Conseil Français du Culte Musulman: reconnaissance politique d'un Islam français?', *Archives de sciences sociales des religions*, 129.

9 Muslims in Italy

Models of integration and new citizenship

Maurizia Russo Spena

Introduction

The presence of more than 1 million foreign citizens of Muslim faith in Italy raises a series of questions about how they ought to be integrated or made to coexist with the majority domestic group, and what sort of relationship should be established between the two, as well as between Italian institutions and organized Muslim communities. The focus of discussion is not just Italy's relations with migrant citizens and an understanding of their demands, but also the constitutive relationship between, on the one hand, the beliefs, lifestyles and claims of migrants, and, on the other, the notions of citizenship, rights, inclusion and coexistence that frame the European-Italian perspective.

The settlement of new citizens in Italy has been a complex process. Along with the various tensions and forms of exclusion it has given rise to, this process has also brought to light a series of contradictions lying at the heart of Italian society regarding social representations and the different ways in which economic, legal, cultural and affective relations are produced.

At stake in discussions over how to resolve such tensions and contradictions are the present dynamics of migration and globalization as well as the state's definition of needs, rights and belonging. But there are also contradictions that exist within Islam itself: the conflicts between tradition and modernity, forms of democracy and the legitimacy of power, and conflicts between self-representation and other forms of representation. A further significant question is the search of Muslim communities for an authentic European and Western identity as part of their historical, political and cultural relationship with alterity. The overall question of migration, in fact, forces us to rethink the categories we use in comprehending our own identity, and to deconstruct our political, institutional, social and cultural understandings.

The chapter consists of three parts. The first provides information about the Muslim presence in Italy, drawing on statistical data and research which illustrates the national, regional and confessional differences of Muslims in Italy. The second part addresses the delicate relationships between multiculturalism and identity claims, and between citizenship rights and community commitments. In particular, it considers whether it is possible to integrate the claims of Muslim communities into a notion of citizenship that continues to be bound to the nation state, or whether it is necessary to update legislative and constitutional instruments in order to meet their demands. The third part focuses on the question of representation. In particular, it analyses the experience of the Islamic Assembly (Consulta Islamica), a consultative organ set up by the Interior Ministry consisting of leaders of Muslim communities in Italy. It also directly addresses the structural tensions related to the Muslim presence in Italy, more specifically the controversies over the Charter of Values, which regulates the relations between Italian institutions and migrants.

A breakdown of the Islamic presence in Italy

The presence of Islam in Italy is a relatively recent social and cultural phenomenon which has much to do with the increasing number of Muslim migrants arriving and settling in Italy since the 1980s. Given the complex and multiform nature of contemporary Islam it would be difficult to provide an exhaustive portrait. That said, it is worth attempting a general typology and classification of Italian Islam that draws primarily, but not exclusively, on variables linked to the dynamics of migration. While it would be possible to trace some tendencies and structural characteristics across migration flows, we need to take into consideration the impact of quantitative and qualitative changes in recent years upon a number of foreign communities in Italy. The multi-ethnic composition of Italian Islam, the stable presence of families, the question of women and members of the second generation, the issues of naturalization and conversion, the diverse geographical distribution and the types of settlement are all variables that have recently acquired greater importance and which frame any analysis of such phenomena. Empirical research on Islam in Italy has often been unable to keep pace with political and institutional debates and the (often misleading) public image of Islam in Italy created by the media. The overestimation of the number of Muslims residing in the country is only one example.

In order to represent the situation in a more numerically accurate manner, it is necessary to draw on the classificatory approach used by different organizations and institutions to study and describe the phenomenon of Islam in Italy. The choice of this approach immediately raises a major methodological question regarding the definition of the Muslim subject: how and to what extent is a religious and confessional identity a personal claim to be drawn from interviews? Indeed, religious identity is not a straightforward demographic indicator. A second question, which is of a rather epistemological nature, concerns the ways in which we understand complex ideas about ‘religious identity’, ‘believing’, ‘belonging’ and ‘culture of origin’ in the context of shifting population masses. The presence of contested, plural, redefined and renegotiated identities in the receiving societies themselves makes it even more difficult to arrive at appropriate definitions.

The most common method of religious classification for migrants is to refer exclusively to the official or majority religion in a migrant’s country of origin. In other words, it is based on national and not on ethnic and/or confessional criteria, which leads to a degree of ambiguity in the interpretation of data if one intends to construct a typology around religious or cultural parameters. This type of data needs to take into account the increasingly significant presence of children born or schooled in Italy, migrants who have acquired Italian citizenship, and converts to Islam.

This issue also affects the description of pluralism within Islam and its subdivision into confessional communities, legal schools, national and supranational networks. The available information is often the result of censuses carried out by the Muslim communities themselves or research conducted in specific fields, and therefore cannot be generalized.

The difficulty of defining religious identity has led to a reflection on the need to combine methodological and conceptual tools from diverse disciplinary approaches in order to conceive and describe Islam in all its social, religious and cultural complexity. The most significant research on Islamic migration in fact draws on a range of contributions from the social sciences, anthropology, law (especially case studies of emergent controversies between legal systems), as well as linguistic studies (such as the role of Arabic in the languages of migrants and in the spoken Italian itself) and ethnographic research which has focused on particular regional situations, ethnonational and specific confessional groups, or questions of age and gender (in other words women, youths and members of the second generation).

According to the annual Caritas/Migrantes report,[1] there are approximately 1,250,000 Muslims in Italy, comprising more than 30 per cent of the total migrant population. The majority of these Muslims (58.4 per cent) originate from countries in the African continent. Christianity is the principal religion of migrants in Italy (with over 2 million followers); of these, Orthodox Christians represent the largest group (1,130,000), followed by Catholics (775,000) and Protestants (140,000). The relative size of each religious group reflects, and will indeed continue to reflect, the shifting flows of global migration (Caritas/Migrantes 2008).

The most recent official statistics regarding the foreign resident population in Italy is instead provided by Istat (Istituto Nazionale di Statistica) and was published in the Annual Report.[2] According to Istat, in January 2008 the foreign resident population in Italy stood at 3,432,000, corresponding to 5.8 per cent of the total Italian population and exhibiting a 17.8 per cent rise in comparison to the previous year. The five main countries of origin, in descending order, were Romania (more than 600,000 individuals), Albania (around 400,000), Morocco (around 366,000), China (more than 150,000) and the Ukraine. Overall, Eastern Europe represents the area of origin of more than half the total of non-Italian citizens resident in Italy, followed by North Africa (and in particular Morocco, Tunisia and Egypt) at almost 18 per cent and Asia (16 per cent). People from the remaining geographical areas of origin comprise less than 9 per cent (Istat 2008).

The immigrant population is spread, albeit unevenly, throughout the country. Approximately 61 per cent of the population is concentrated in the north, while 25 per cent is located in the centre and 9 per cent in the south. Lombardy in the north is the region with the highest immigrant population, followed by Emilia-Romagna and Veneto. In the centre, there is a particularly high concentration of foreign citizens in Umbria.

The majority of resident permits issued in Italy are long-term and not temporary, and for the most part are for work (60.6 per cent) and family (31.6 per cent) purposes. According to the data of Inail (the National Institute for Industrial Accident Insurance) over 7 per cent of immigrants are employed in the agricultural sector, while around 35 per cent work in industry (which includes 15 per cent in the building sector). The service sector remains the main source of work, employing almost 54 per cent, including 10 per cent in hotels and restaurants, 11.7 per cent in business services such as cleaning and 11.3 per cent in domestic work (Istat 2008).

The statistics also reveal that just over half of all immigrants (50.4 per cent) are women. The foreign population is younger than the national average: over 50 per cent of immigrants are between 18 and 39 years old. In 2007 63,000 babies of foreign parental origin were born (the equivalent of 11 per cent of all births in Italy), with the highest concentration in the centre-north. Thirty per cent of the approximate 770,000 foreign minors arrived in Italy as a result of family reunification, almost 600,000 are enrolled in schools, while 14,500 are unaccompanied minors.

From this general portrait provided by statistical information on immigration, Italy's Muslims can be seen to reflect the great geographic and geopolitical diversity of Islam, partly because the formerly dominant Maghribi component (Moroccan in particular) no longer represents the absolute majority of migrants in Italy. 'Simplifying, we could say that four out of every ten foreigners present in Italy are Muslim, and of these one will be Moroccan, one Albanian, one from the following countries (Tunisia, Senegal, Egypt, Pakistan and Bangladesh) and one from another nation, such as Algeria, Somalia, Iran or India' (Di Leo 2004: 123). With regard instead to the internal pluralism of Islam, producing numerically accurate data for Shi'ites in Italy is particularly difficult, unless reference is made to those immigrants originating from countries with a Shi'ite majority (above all Iran). The city where they are most active and culturally present is Naples, where there is a centre frequented mainly by Italian converts. There is also a significant Muridi confraternity as a result of the Wolof majority among Senegalese immigrants (it is estimated that about two-thirds of Senegalese in Italy – over 60,000 – are members of the Muridiya, which makes it the largest Sufi confraternity in Italy).[3] Other Sufi confraternities include the Tijaniya, widespread above all among the Maghribi communities, and the Turkish Jerrahi-Halveti confraternity, which is based in Milan. Finally, the Tablighi Jamaat, despite not possessing any centres in Italy, has a prevalent North African following which is not always in accord with the Indian and Pakistani origins of the movement.

The phenomenon of a Muslim migration possessing specific identity and cultural claims, has perhaps only fully started to emerge during the last decade. According to a study conducted in 1997,[4] the Muslim population in Italy was relatively young (with an average age of 33), primarily male with the exception of migrants originating from the Horn of Africa (Di Leo 2004), and was comprised of individuals who had yet to establish stable and definitive migration plans, while continuing to be strongly linked to their countries of origin (demonstrated by the importance of nationally based organizational networks).

> The presence [of Muslims in Italy] has evolved as a result of substantial

> migration flows, which since the 1950s in particular, have headed towards northern European countries and have mainly originated from Africa and Asia countries where Islam is the main religion or at least very widespread. (Pacini 2000: 21)

Research conducted in 2000 (and analysed in Allam and Gritti 2001) on a sample of approximately 500 Muslims consisting primarily of married males with children, discovered that most Muslims were educated to either an intermediate or advanced level (almost 30 per cent had a degree or a specialization and almost 45 per cent had a high school diploma), approximately 80 per cent of these had received their qualifications in their country of origin and 10 per cent in Italy; 57 per cent understood Italian well, about 26 per cent used computers and 14.4 per cent regularly bought a newspaper. According to this research, those who decide to emigrate appear to possess a higher level of education compared with the rest of the population in their countries of origin, so that their migration project reflects a degree of purpose and not just opportunity (Allam and Gritti 2001: 81). The same research discovered that about 35 per cent of Muslim immigrants were students at the moment of departure while 7.3 per cent were unemployed or in search of their first employment. White-collar workers, blue-collar workers and self-employed ranged between 7 and 8.5 per cent.

The stratification of occupational positions is usually a telling measure of a community's integration. However, breaking down the data for Muslims is a particularly complex task due to the general instability of employment (despite its regulation through government work quotas[5]) and the lack of a statistical link between employment and religion. The general impression is that Muslim immigrants do not differ that much from the majority of other foreign citizens who work either in factories and small firms or as domestic workers (although social care tends to be provided by people originating from countries where Christianity is the main religion). According to Istat, the overall foreign workforce numbers 1,502,400 and resides primarily in the north of the country (63 per cent), and to a lesser degree in the centre (25.6 per cent) and south (11.4 per cent). This means that one out of every four new employees is a foreign citizen. The majority of foreign workers are employed in low-skilled and unskilled work (29.5 per cent and 43 per cent), while the number of white-collar and skilled workers is much lower (18.2 per cent and 9.3 per cent) (Istat 2008).

Nevertheless, private enterprise and self-employment, particularly for the more stable communities in Italy, has started to become a significant characteristic of migrant labour. According to Istat, foreign entrepreneurs represent 2.8 per cent of entrepreneurial activity in Italy, with a peak of 3.6 per cent in the north-west. In 2007, one in three new businesses in Italy had a foreign owner, while two out of ten foreigners were self-employed.

The social and ethnic networks of migrants, in terms of initial material and practical assistance and linguistic and emotional support, play a fundamental role in creating niches for occupational independence. These networks are able to match labour demand and supply, above all in the poorer regions, and they balance the informality (if not outright irregularity) of the immigrant presence with the labour needs of a disorganized Italian job market (Ambrosini 2003).

A key example is the so-called 'ethnic business', in which a sizeable portion of immigrants conduct specialized activities that are linked to occupational and professional traditions of their country of origin. In the case of Muslims, this type of business primarily entails commerce and catering. If we consider Istat data for three of the principal national communities of the Muslim population, we discover that one-sixth of Moroccan workers in Italy are concentrated in the industrial sector, one-sixth are in cleaning services and a further one-sixth in itinerant trading; Egyptians appear to be much more inclined to work in the catering sector, both as owners of restaurants and as employees (with a total of around 7,000 workers), while the ten main occupations of Tunisian workers include low-skilled agricultural workers (with more than 10,000 employees), artisans and semi-skilled workers in the building trade (over 7,000) and low-skilled construction workers (roughly 2,500 employees).

Models of integration and dialogue between generations

When Italian Islam is discussed, especially in sociological studies, reference is usually made to its distinctiveness in comparison with the rest of Europe. Its main characteristics, according to Allievi and Dassetto (1993) are:

- The lack of identification of Islam in Italy with a single national or ethnolinguistic origin (as is the case in France, Great Britain or Germany)
- The rapidity of arrival and settlement, and the increased public visibility of the Muslim immigrant community
- The widespread condition of irregular status among Muslim immigrants (which ultimately extends to all immigrants due to the restrictive laws of recent years)
- The diverse nature of the settlement of migrants depending on the region of residence and the type of employment
- Their lower exposure to the Italian system in the country of origin prior to migration (besides perhaps in former Italian colonies such as Eritrea and Somalia)
- The significant role played by converts (particularly visible and influential in negotiations and in social and cultural production)
- The scarce number of associative representatives or spokespersons who are able to provide mosques with a more relevant religious and social role in local society.

In addition, Italian Islam remains fundamentally *first generation*, although the significance and role of a new, younger generation of Muslims is increasing. The settlement and stabilization of families is, indeed, a relatively recent trend. Moreover, the sorts of claims collectively made by communities appear to be more directed at the recognition of their faith, identity and symbols in public spaces, than at competing for equal opportunities of access to resources, the job market and social policies.

In fact, the needs of the Muslim community are rarely met with a unified, structured response from the Italian state. On the contrary, demands tend to be resolved on a case-by-case basis and through particular relations established with local institutions and administrations. Responses to Muslims' needs and claims have varied from outright examples of racist discourse in the electoral campaigns of the Northern League to positive changes in response to specific requests of small community groups (for example, the creation of a prayer room in a local area because of an increase in the number of Muslim employees concentrated in the same economic district).

Such contradictions enable us, in my opinion, tentatively to describe Islam in Italy in terms of a minority. *Muslimness* has continued to possess multifarious and fragmented characteristics as a result of two dimensions – one internal, the other external – that shape the very process of its incorporation:[6]

1 Those who emigrate do not constitute a fixed, univocal mass of people, but are embodied subjects who reinterpret and recodify their own sense of identity and belonging according to the context in which they find themselves;
2 The rise of Islam in Italy is essentially linked to processes of immigration (and therefore shares its fundamental characteristics) and, consequently, is bound to the policies for integration and inclusion that Italy has pursued in recent decades.

The question of whether Italy can be considered a country that does not follow a specific model of integration – at least not to the extent to which cultural and assimilation politics have been defined and systematized in other European countries (reference is usually made to the respective cases of Great Britain and France) – has been the focus of intense debates in the media, in the political arena as well as in academia. Numerous scholars[7] have underlined how the Italian case amounts to an 'implicit' model, largely characterized by a spontaneous, ad hoc approach to the governing of labour recruitment (Bonifazi, *et al.* 2008). This approach has, over the years, delegated the management of the social, economic and cultural inclusion of migrants to local administrations and civil society organizations.

Another typical characteristic of the Italian 'model' (or lack thereof), concealed behind a public discourse that continues, somewhat paradoxically, to insist on describing Italy as a 'country of recent immigration', is the unsystematic and, at times, arbitrary nature of its practices. Given the absence of a common, articulate model, there has been a tendency towards seeing emergency measures as the norm and of representing the arrival of immigrants in terms of invasion. This latter point has strongly conditioned relations between institutions and migrants, and the perception of migrants among the host society.

The focus on the politics of security, recently exploited as an electoral banner and currently used as a means of defending and controlling public consensus, is a worrying sign of growing institutional racism.[8] In public debate, the idea of 'integrable diversity' (therefore tolerable and assimilable) is that which is not perceived or represented as a threat to the constituted cultural and social order. Inclusive action is prevalent and aimed at integrating immigrants into economic and productive structures but excludes the possibility that they might negotiate specific demands regarding their religious and cultural diversity. Moreover, this diversity is not only experienced as a threat, but is subject to value judgements and mechanisms of subordination.

Islam, experienced both as an international media phenomenon and, in recent decades, as a form of organized migration, disturbs society as a result of its visible differences and, at times, particular demands.

The entrenchment of identity and cultural autism are the products both of restrictive and exclusionary migration policies and of the explicit racism and Islamophobia within public discourse. To the extent that Islam tends to safeguard its key ideas about religion, culture and civilization, integration is regarded as unfeasible.

Interesting aspects about the issue of identity among Muslims in Italy have emerged from different investigations over the last decade. According to a survey conducted by the Italian daily *La Repubblica* in 2000,[9] a sense of national and religious identity was stronger among Muslim immigrants than other foreigners (55.7 per cent of Muslims responded 'I feel like a member of my country of origin/ of my religious faith', as opposed to 46.8 per cent of the other immigrants); while on the question of integration, the vast majority of Muslims interviewed (about 74 per cent) replied that they 'accept Italian values, while maintaining their own identity'.

More recently, the part of the 2008 Makno inquiry commissioned by the Interior Ministry (*Una Ricerca Sociale sull'Immigrazione*), which explored the opinions and attitudes of Muslim immigrants (64.6 per cent of the sample of immigrants resident in Italy were interviewed in a qualitative study using focus groups and individual interviews), found that interviewees referred exclusively to symbolic and relational aspects when explaining the difficulties they encountered living in Italy. Their responses can be grouped as follows:

- At the level of values: there is the risk of 'losing the values of one's culture' (30.2 per cent), 'there is too much freedom in Italy' (21.8 per cent), 'we do not believe that our religion is accepted' (13.8 per cent), 'Muslim women do not feel at ease in public' (12.7 per cent);
- At the level of practices: it is difficult to 'respect religious practices' (39.5 per cent), it is difficult to 'find appropriate food' (28 per cent), in schools it is difficult to 'educate your children with your own values' (17.5 per cent).

There was, however, a significant percentage of respondents who instead claimed 'not to experience difficulties' (23.2 per cent). In fact, only 25.7 per cent of Muslims interviewed believed that 'Italians treat Muslim immigrants worse than other immigrants'. If we examine the motives for such an assertion we note that the highest percentage (almost 40 per cent) replied that 'they are afraid we might be terrorists'.

It is notable that already from the 1980s, the migration of Muslims to Italy that resulted from bilateral and readmission agreements[10] did not define itself according to the country of origin, but through reference to confessional identity. This process has led to a reinvention of ways of being Muslim in Europe (Dassetto 1994: 3).

The concept coined by Dassetto of a new 'Muslimness' in countries of immigration highlights the idea of Islam as a vehicle of inclusion for foreign citizens in European societies. Outside the traditional ecumenical territory of Islam, immigrants negotiate and redefine its symbolic space. It is in Islam where individuals can find a community, an identity, a sense of belonging, an ideological reference point, a social and supportive network, and a reminder of languages, symbols and collective myths.

When processes of integration are not truly inclusive and precisely because relations among social actors are always 'double-sided' (Lewin 1980), there are two possible risks:

1 That inequalities along ethnic lines are produced (for instance, access to job opportunities, social mobility, housing and health care) which add to existing social inequalities;
2 That disadvantaged ethnic minority communities are created which in turn reject the external context and turn to deviant practices, thus entering a process of 'downward assimilation' (Portes 2001).

In fact, what we might define as 'second-generation' Islam is an Islam that has evolved in Europe (and is therefore European) and bears a composite (but not contradictory) amalgam of culture and civilization (Dassetto 2004).

Young Muslim women and men born and raised in Italy have often expressed an ambivalent sense of belonging that has been reflected in conflicts with families and communities of origin. The experiences of women have perhaps been more disruptive. As a result of their entry into the labour market and because of their multiple social relations, they have begun to liberate themselves from the role assigned to them in the family. In short, the people of the second generation have sought to synthesize community and identity references with the wider reality in which they live, work and begin new life projects.

Young Muslims tend to find themselves torn between the need to be a part of Italian society and access all the possibilities that this offers them, and constant references to the mythical place of origin. Because of their deeper ties to Italy and Europe, in comparison with their parents, they do not just claim the right to difference in Italian society, but also the right to equality (Frisina 2007).

An interesting study by Ambrosini and Molina (2004), which attempts to build a phenomenology of the second-generation migrants in Italy, outlines a number of discontinuities, such as the rejection of the subaltern integration accepted by their parents and the specific search for identity that fluctuates between two opposite desires: to be inside, and to be outside. These are seen to generate clashes at an individual, family, social and cultural level, and ultimately to culminate in radical conflicts, both with the symbolic universe of the community of origin and with the host society.

In a country like Italy, which is still trying to resolve the complex relationship between different models of integration, the young generations must resolve, through forms of conflict and negotiation but also through their very existence, the exclusion/inclusion dialectic, and in doing so open up a space of dialogue around the significance of belonging so that they can design a future of possible relations between the two worlds.

Dialogue and representation: the Assembly and the Charter of Values

The role of foreign communities in the destination countries (for instance in terms of their ability to connect networks) can strongly condition people's migration projects and increase their chances of benefiting from the integration policies of receiving countries.

> In particular, the membership of a network allows a potential migrant to access two fundamental types of resource: cognitive resources and normative resources [...] At the same time, migration is both a 'network-creating' and 'network-dependent' process, in the sense that on the one hand individual decisions have the effect of generating sets of relations, and on the other, these same relations then influence successive decisions. (Zanfrini 2004: 88–9)

The networks of contacts indirectly encourage the migration chain by minimizing the costs and the physical, emotive and symbolic strains of migration. Especially during the arrival phase, community membership represents the key space of congregation and group formation. This community 'in exile' codifies and interprets norms which are, in turn, used to maintain control within the group.

This represents a sort of 'double integration': on the one hand the natural incorporation into the community of origin that has been reconstituted in exile, and, on the other, the laborious encounter with the host society (Carchedi 2000). In the specific case of Islam, the transnational religious dimension often overlaps with the formation of ethnical and national networks.

The intrinsic plurality of forms within Islam, which are the product of different historic, regional, political and cultural processes, means that Muslims in Italy have often struggled to find a unified voice in their negotiations with the state and their claims for recognition in Italian law. The collective expressions of Islam vary greatly, from informal groups that gather in places of worship, to associations organized along ethnic and national lines, and then to more official Muslim organizations considered to be valid representatives of Islam in the eyes of the Italian state but which ultimately represent a small, albeit visible and conscious, minority.

The first public manifestation of Italian Islam occurred in Northern Italy during the 1970s following the request by Muslim students (who had formed USMI – Union of Muslim Students in Italy) to have spaces for worship. The subsequent and gradual proliferation of Muslim organizations reflected both a rise in the numbers of Muslim immigrants settling in Italy and the plurality and complexity of affiliations within Islam. Principal groups involved in negotiations with the Italian state and society include UCOII (Union of Islamic Organizations and Communities in Italy), the Islamic Cultural Centre of Italy (which is based at the mosque of Rome and is recognized as an institutional body), COREIS (Islamic Religious Community, which mainly represents a group of converts) and UMI (Union of Muslims of Italy, which is famous for the media stunts of its leader Adel Smith). ADMI (Association of Muslim Women in Italy) and GMI (Young Muslims in Italy) are both recently formed organizations that make specific requests regarding youth and gender issues. There are also numerous groups linked to confraternities, formal and informal associations organized along ethnic and national lines, and groups that reflect the geographical distribution of immigrants (primarily in main cities, but also at the provincial and rural level).[11]

Muslim immigration in Italy has therefore experienced a wide range of collective organization. A division appears to have opened up between, on the one hand, an archetypal model and original value system in *dar al-islam* and, on the other, the multiplicity of social practices, identity forms and gathering places established in the 'land of exile' (*dar al-hijra*).

The need for institutional representation and recognition has faced obstacles from both Muslims and the Italian state. In the former case, the difficulties of reaching an agreement[12] have stemmed, first and foremost, from a leadership struggle within European and Italian Islam, but also out of the very way in which Islam, as a religion without an institutional centre, is socially and culturally organized. Community organizations hence play a key role in negotiations with the state and accentuate elements of Islam's spatial and temporal separateness that turns into a protective strategy in the land of exile.

The Italian state, meanwhile, has tried to avoid confronting the problem of Muslim state-recognition by claiming that there is no credible negotiating partner that fully represents the world of Islam. Behind this excuse lies the (often ungrounded) fear that it would have to deal with Muslims' demands for special and separate rights, in other words negotiate with subjects who appear not to recognize the basic foundations of the state.

Moreover, the state has sought to resolve its relationship with Muslim communities solely at the level of recognizing cultural and religious difference.[13] The key points of contention have been considered by both centre-right and centre-left governments alike as questions of cultural endangerment.[14] These points include: the training of imams, the regulation of the slaughter of meat, the construction of places of worship, the recognition of festivities, the right to burial, the regulation of prayers during work time, tax breaks for charity work and the possibility of benefiting from the eight per thousand funds,[15] the opening of Islamic schools, the recognition of marriages, the teaching of religion and Arabic in schools, and spiritual care in prisons and hospitals (Dusi 2007).

Established by the centre-right Berlusconi government with a decree dated 10 September 2005,

> the Assembly for Italian Islam is a consultative body of the Interior Ministry that conducts research which formulates positions and proposals for the purpose of encouraging institutional dialogue with the Islamic communities in order to identify the most adequate solutions for a harmonious inclusion of Islam within the national community with respect to the laws of the Italian Republic. (Statute of the Assembly article 1)

The Assembly is the only institutional body promoting formal dialogue with the Muslim communities. In the plethora of local, provincial and regional public spheres where the relationship between the majority and minorities is discussed, Muslims are represented either at an ethnic-national or macro-regional level. The bodies for inter-religious dialogue established at a local level, despite their relative visibility in the media, involve associations which are essentially delegated the task of building positive relations between the major denominations in Italy. Moving in the same direction is the Youth Assembly for Religious and Cultural Pluralism, set up by the Interior Ministry in 2006, which has the objective of formulating proposals for raising awareness and encouraging harmonious relations between different cultural and religious groups in Italy.

Since its inception, the Assembly, which was retained by the centre-left Prodi government (2006–2008), has instead served to highlight the different identities that make up the variegated world of Italian Muslim associations (the 16 members belong to diverse groups and were directly summoned by the minister) and, through the recognition of 'moderate Islam', to keep the supposedly more threatening world of the mosques under control (or at least this was how the participation of UCOII[16] in the Assembly was interpreted).

In fact, rather than resolving the problem of including Islamic communities (and their potentially critical standpoints) in Italian society, the Assembly has instead debated theoretical questions considered to be points of division between the West and Islam: terrorism, gender equality, war, international conflicts and religious freedom.

Paradoxically, the idea of the Assembly was originally based on the model created by Nicolas Sarkozy, as French interior minister, to open a channel of dialogue with moderate Islam with the aim of reducing violence in the suburbs.[17] Bearing in mind the differences with French Islam, which is more consolidated and structured within society, the Italian version of the assembly instead aimed to obtain a deeper understanding of the debate within Italian Islam, and to provide it with the most democratic forum possible (Dusi 2007). In spite of the very debatable role that this body has played, it is worth considering critically the structure and functioning of the Assembly.

This means in particular focusing on the aspects of representation (which are not exclusive to Muslim organizations but characterize migrant associations in general) such as the crisis of traditional forms of representation and their public recognition, new forms of participation, and the crucial question of power; how this is managed from the inside and the effectiveness of the associations' mediation with the outside world.

If it is true that the setting-up of the Assembly reflected the Italian state's recognition of the need for a meeting point with Muslim communities, a series of problems nevertheless emerged which concerned the representation of Islam, the role assigned by the Italian state to the participating communities, and the evolution of the body itself:

- By creating a specific forum for discussing the inclusion of Muslim communities in Italian society, these communities are attributed special status in contrast to other migrant communities and their diversity is emphasized. The forum thus risks being experienced purely as a space where claims to specific interests are appeased and not as a place of mediation;
- Such bodies have a purely consultative character; the procedure risks running counter to the promotion of processes of more effective participation;
- Its members have not been freely elected but rather have been chosen by the Interior Minister from a wide range of associations and leading Muslim figures; this logic of co-optation meets both the internal requirements of native (political, labour-based and religious) organizations and the need of the institutions themselves to identify reliable interlocutors in order to interpret and discuss the demands of the communities;
- It could be asserted, perhaps harshly, that those who sit at the discussion table and are faced with the task of making Islam visible in the public sphere ultimately represent the organized leadership of Islam which has greater resources at its disposal, manages sections of the communities at a material and spiritual level, and provides welfare and charity for their members. The network of mosques, undoubtedly less transparent but which is self-managed and organizes numerous spaces and services on the grass-roots level, is given much less representation. The question is whether a body like the Assembly is really able to guarantee visibility and a voice to the entire range of Muslim communities;
- Islam as a religion does not possess an institutional centre: there are many geographical and national differences in terms of membership and ways of living according to the religion, from Senegalese Murids to Turkish confraternities. Those who claim to represent Islam cannot therefore fully capture the complexity of Italian Islam;
- It is declared that the Assembly was set up to resolve integration problems regarding Muslim immigrants, but there is a large component of converts among the representatives on the Assembly,[18] who have greater visibility and more contractual power, but less influence upon Muslim immigrant communities. The everyday practice of Islam in Italy and the instrumental use of religion among migrants as a general strategy of inclusion and self-identification have yet to be seriously explored in research, much less to be taken into account by policymakers;[19]
- The Italian imams are often self-ordained or elected on the basis of trust because they possess certain characteristics and expertise (such as knowledge of Arabic and of the canonical texts, moral integrity or some affiliation with

> important figures in the world of Islam). In other words, they have rarely received official training in an Islamic school or university. They are more usually recognized leaders of communities who act as mediators between members of communities/associations and the host society and its institutions. They exercise a double function: they elevate their own personal status, often already acquired in their countries of origin, by reinstating a power hierarchy among compatriots and, at the same time, they guarantee the internal stability of the community and reinforce a level of dialogue with the outside world. The imams appear, in the eyes of the immigrant communities, to be guarantors of traditional ideas about public and private behaviour, female demeanour, family cohesion, education, and the relationship between society and the state. As a matter of fact, the image of Islam that they spread, precisely because it is one of exodus, is only indirectly affected by the deep and often bitter debates over the relationship between tradition and modernity that take place in Muslim majority countries.

In September 2008 the current Minister for EU Policies Andrea Ronchi announced his intention to resume the activities of the Assembly for Islam and to focus on the discussion about coexistence. The Assembly had stopped meeting after the previous Interior Minister Giuliano Amato (who originally had given it his full support in spite of the fact that the body had been instituted by the earlier government led by Berlusconi) submitted to its members the final text of the Charter of Values.[20]

The drawing-up of the Charter of Values of Citizenship and Integration in Italy has reignited an age-old political, media and academic debate about the relationship between the guarantee of universal rights and the particular identity and cultural claims of foreign citizens in Italy. It is also reflected as part of the unresolved dilemmas in migration policies.

Caught between respect for the public institutions of the host society and allegiance to their own communities, Muslim immigrants in Italy necessarily challenge the immediate reality of Italian national life (through the public nature of their symbols and rituals) as well as the abstract sphere of laws and values. The Charter of Values, adopted by the previous centre-left government, attempted to deal with the social and symbolic conflicts produced by the coexistence of different cultures in the same country by establishing a basic framework for conducting a balanced and positive dialogue between the Italian population and foreign citizens.

Already in 2005 the European Commission had produced a ‘Common Agenda for Integration’ which underlined the necessity of ‘emphasizing civic orientation in introduction programmes and other activities for newly arrived third-country nationals with the view of ensuring that immigrants understand, respect and benefit from common European and national values’ (CEC 2005: 5). ‘Charters of Values’ have thereupon been drawn up in a number of European countries. While they are not legally binding, they emphasize the principles that should regulate and govern the process of migrants’ inclusion in society. In other words, they amount to declarations of principles which orientate institutional activity with regard to integration policies.

According to the intentions of its drafters, the objective of the Italian Charter is to encourage the integration and regulation of the foreign presence in the national community, through the communication of the core ideas of Italian culture and society within the frame of cultural and religious pluralism. It provides general guidelines for orienting the government's relations with immigrant and religious communities in a state of mutual respect for the principles of the Charter and for its policies on integration and social cohesion. In addition, the Charter asserts Italy's commitment to the principle that every person, from the moment he or she enters Italian territory, should enjoy fundamental rights regardless of gender, ethnicity, religion and social conditions. At the same time, every person who lives in Italy must respect the values upon which society is based, the rights of others, and the civil duties required by law.[21]

The text therefore talks about constitutional values and principles that should regulate coexistence in Italy. So far so good. But while, on the one hand, it indeed has the merit of addressing all communities in Italy (it was translated into all the principal immigrant languages and was promoted through extensive consultation with organizations working in the field), in reality it appears more like an effort to conceal the lack of real desire to resolve conflicts with Muslim communities over values and cultural matters.

Moreover, if one reads the opening words of the Charter, there is an explicit reference to Italy's particular religious and cultural heritage: 'Italy is one of the most ancient countries in Europe whose roots are in the classical culture of Greece and Rome. It developed under Christianity, which permeated all aspects of its history and, together with Judaism, prepared the way to modernity and the principles of freedom and justice' (Charter of Values 2007). There is no sign of the contribution of other societies, worlds and cultures, and no reference to the history of cohabitation with numerous other populations who had varying levels of contact with Italy.

Apart from the emphasis placed on fundamental and inalienable rights which Italy is committed to respecting, a browse through the text suggests only more allusions to a presumed conflict with Muslim culture and society[22]:

- 'Marriage is founded on the equality of rights and responsibility between husband and wife, and for this reason is of a monogamous structure. Monogamy unites two lives and makes them co-responsible for all that is done together, starting with the rearing of children. Italy prohibits polygamy as a violation of women's rights, also in accordance with the principles affirmed by European institutions' (article 17);
- 'The basis of conjugal union includes the marital freedom for children, and thus prohibits forced or child marriages' (article 18);
- 'Italy is a lay country founded on the recognition of total individual and collective religious freedom' (article 20);
- 'Freedom of religion and conscience includes the right to hold or not to hold a religious faith, to practising or not to practise, to change religion, to spread it by convincing others and to gather in confessional organizations. The freedom

of worship is fully guaranteed as long as it does not infringe criminal law and the rights of others' (article 23);

- 'Drawing upon its own religious and cultural tradition, Italy respects the symbols and signs of all religions' (article 25);
- 'In Italy no restrictions are placed on a person's dress as long as this is worn out of free choice and is not detrimental to one's dignity. Items of clothing that cover the face are not acceptable because they impede the recognition of the person and prevent them from entering into relations with other people' (article 26);
- 'Italy is committed to a peaceful resolution of the principal international crises, in particular the Israeli–Palestinian conflict which has been dragging on for a long time' (article 30).

The Charter of Values claims to set down the basic principles of a social pact. It was set up, in fact, during a period of social alarm around immigration-related topics, which was not only the result of public order issues and social and cultural conflicts, but also, and especially, due to the unprecedented dramatization of the question in the mass media. There is no doubt that in recent years this uneasiness has permeated political discourse from left to right.

The most striking contradiction is that while the Charter attempts to build a set of necessary universal parameters of integration (ultimately conceived in terms of assimilation), the underlying tendency is instead to hypostatize the identity of individuals and communities, by tying them to their cultures of origin. The image of Islam conveyed in the document is therefore monolithic and not at all plural, and its followers do not seem to be intersected by any of the subjective and objective contradictions experienced by migrants.

The Charter seeks the ambitious goal of regulating the entire range of demands that Muslim citizens place upon the Italian state and society, at the risk of turning these into an indistinct hotchpotch. In fact, the requests raised by the Muslim community – those that concern informal, associative and identity spaces, and those that instead involve a balance between institutional, state and value frameworks – need to be treated separately.

The Charter is only one instrument which establishes a clear relationship between immigration policies and the process of integration. Here the possibility of full inclusion in a new context appears to be linked to the capacity of individuals and identity groups to accept the dominant values and principles upon which such societies are regulated. Among the necessary criteria for the acquisition of Italian citizenship is the need to possess knowledge of the 'Italian language' and 'the essential elements of national history and culture' as well as 'the principles that regulate our society'. These elements therefore become diriment. The emphasis is on duties and no longer on rights (such as that of learning the language of the host country), which the foreign citizen should be able to exercise in multicultural societies. As a result of the Charter, the following has been observed:

> The outcome could be defined as a post-constitutional system in which the

> Constitution continues to wield superficial respect but is demoted from a higher law to a partial system: it is incapable of binding all holders of public power and informing the entire law-making process and is therefore turned into an object of complements and integrations. (Colaianni 2007: 9–10)

In view of such considerations it is clear that the presence of more than one million Muslim citizens in Italy should make us not only reflect on the ways in which the 'threat' posed by diversity is used in media, political and, at times, academic debates, but also on the extent to which this idea acquires a normative value, and is thus able to influence opinions and mould the attitudes of society as a whole.

From research examining the perceptions and attitudes of Italians towards immigrants, Cotesta (2002) observes that out of 1,200 Italian interviewees, negative responses tended to prevail among men aged over 30, particularly in the north-east of the country, among those with a low level of education, among believers and churchgoers, among those who do not vote in elections and the electorate of the centre-right, above all the Northern League, and among those not involved in voluntary work. The most recent report on immigration by the Interior Ministry (published in 2008)[23] indicates a certain amount of concern among Italians about Muslim immigration and, consequently, about the coexistence of values, traditions and cultures perceived to be extremely different.

In particular, 55.3 per cent of Italians interviewed believe (combining the responses 'I totally agree', 'I partially agree') that the integration of Muslim citizens in Italy creates more problems than the integration of immigrants from other countries, insofar as they bear more visible social, cultural and religious differences and as a result of their distance (spatial as well as socio-cultural) from the rest of the population. About 28 per cent of Italians believe that the specific problem lies in 'the intolerance towards Catholicism', while almost 25 per cent speak of 'critical attitudes about Italian culture' and 15.6 per cent feel that there is an 'intolerance towards the Italian way of life'. Worryingly, 17.2 per cent of respondents think that a key issue is 'the fear of terrorist attacks', 8.3 per cent that Muslims 'consider anyone who does not believe in Islam as an infidel' and 7.6 per cent that Muslims 'want to Islamicize Italy'. Once again, the problems seem to revolve entirely around cultural and religious questions (viewed in terms of a threat to one's security) and not in terms of competition in acquiring jobs or accessing resources and services. Moreover, the lack of cultural integration would appear to be due to the attitudes of Muslim immigrants and not to Italian society or the policies of Italian national and local governments.

On the theme of mosques in Italy (which is a highly topical issue today, following a series of blockages on construction, especially by mayors in northern Italy), about 40 per cent of Italians agree that Muslims should have a place of worship, although 11 per cent believe that these should be self-funded (but note this is in fact the norm, because local councils simply provide planning permission) and 5.4 per cent feel that there should be a similar equal treatment of Catholic or Christian churches in Muslim countries; 31.4 per cent (to varying degrees and giving different reasons) 'do not agree'. Not surprisingly, the level of knowledge of the societies and cultures of Islamic countries among the Italian population is quite low: almost 78 per cent of respondents, if we combine the 18.8 per cent who replied 'I'm not interested in knowing anything about them' and the 59.1 per cent who claimed to know them 'superficially'.

Conclusions

It is not just the model of integration that needs to be reconsidered, but also the notion of citizenship, which has become highly disrupted through the re-evaluation of social and cultural identity.

Access to citizenship and the consequent recognition of the status of the citizen should not be treated as a strictly technical and legal matter, but as a political and cultural problem, insofar as it has come to frame not only the politics of inclusion of the migrant population, but also to serve as a measure of the quality of democracy in Italy and the state's relationship with identity, rights and governance.

The political debate about, on the one hand, the universality of laws and rights which aim to accommodate difference, and, on the other, the expression, even within legal praxis, of such alterity, is marked by a deficiency of substance: eventually people are expected to be able to integrate by themselves – to be adaptable to different contexts and find ways to integrate themselves in the labour market and society. Take, for example, the system through which one acquires Italian citizenship, which is still regulated on the basis of *jus sanguinis*. Children (including those born in Italy) follow the fate of their parents, for whom the assignment of citizenship[24] is subject to the 'verification of the real cultural, linguistic and social integration of the foreigner in the territory of the state'.[25] Since 2007 a number of Italian municipalities, including Rome, have begun to experiment with citizenship training courses that aim to provide immigrants with a basic knowledge about the concept of citizenship, the Italian Constitution, the political system of the republic and the organization of the state.

With the introduction of the notion of 'mild law', Zagrebelsky (1992) underlines how the founding principles of a constitution today cannot be taken as absolute values. Rather, these must be considered compatible with other coexisting principles, in order to maintain a constitution's unity and integration. The substitution of citizenship based on *blood and wealth* with a citizenship *based on residence* moves beyond the legal idea of citizenship to encapsulate a set of subjective questions, desires and practices that challenge Italian institutions and society. Such a perspective underlines the difficulty of identifying legal instruments able to protect rights and the real possibility of collective mobilization to have these same rights publicly recognized (Mezzadra 2001).

Notes

1 The annual dossier compiled by the Catholic organization Caritas/Migrantes on immigration in Italy uses, among other sources, the official data of the Interior Ministry.

2 The estimate of almost four million foreign citizens in the Caritas/Migrantes dossier is

higher than the estimate given by Istat because it not only registers official residents but all others sojourning on Italian territory.

3 See the studies by Schmidt di Friedberg (1994) and by Piga (2000).

4 This is to be found in the Murst 40 per cent (1997) project "The religious phenomenon in international relations". For a discussion of this research, see Ferrari (2000).

5 It must be remembered that the arrival of immigrant workers in Italy is regulated by annual quotas published in the decree on immigrant flows and that existing immigration legislation ties residence to an employment contract. For 2009 the quota stands at 150,000 individuals.

6 This category is borrowed from sociology to mean 'integration', an ambivalent term that implies, in its current use, also the assimilation of subjects within a dominant culture. In this chapter, the term 'integration' is understood as the complex constitutive process of inclusive 'interaction'. See Zanfrini (2004); Gallissot and Rivera (2001); Filtzinger (1984).

7 Giovanna Zincone (2000) speaks of 'reasonable integration' while Vittorio Cotesta (2007) speaks of 'subordinate inclusion'. Given the peculiarities of southern European countries, the idea of a 'Mediterranean model' has been discussed (Cassata, Martire, Strozza, Vitello and Zindato (2008)).

8 The current government has proposed the so-called 'security package' (Bill of Law no. 733), which, among various restrictions regarding immigration, proposes to make irregular entry and stay a crime.

9 Its results are partially presented and discussed in the essay by Di Leo (2004).

10 The agreements between states have gone hand in hand with the desire to cooperate for dealing with the phenomenon of illegal immigration.

11 For a detailed analysis of Islamic organizations in Italy, see Allievi and Dassetto (1993).

12 On this point, see Bastenier and Dassetto (1993); Guolo (2000); Cilardo (2003).

13 The establishment of inter-religious discussion tables and the declared urgency for a bill of law on religious freedom (proposed by the previous centre-left government) head in this direction.

14 See Pacini (2000).

15 Eight per thousand refers to the system by which the Italian state, on the basis of choices made by taxpayers, shares out 0.08 perfect of the total amount raised by income tax among the state and various religious confessions.

16 The Union of Islamic Communities and Organizations in Italy was founded in 1990 with a declared link with the Muslim Brotherhood movement. There has been much debate about its legitimacy of participating in institutional discussions due to its controversial positions, especially on international matters. For example, Egyptian journalist Magdi Allam, who lives and works in Italy and recently converted to Christianity, declared in 2005 that the banning of UCOII should be seriously considered, passing through a breach that had already been opened up at a political and institutional level. It should be remembered that UCOII signed the Charter of Values.

17 I am referring here to the *Conseil Français du culte musulman*, active since 2003.

18 In the last census of the Interior Ministry, there were more than 10,000 Italian converts to Islam. On this issue, see Allievi (1999).

19 According to data of the Interior Ministry, only 5 per cent of the total Muslim population attends mosques on a regular basis.

20 The participants in the discussions about the Charter of Values signed a Declaration of Intent to set up the Federation of Italian Islam, and have collaborated over the last year with the Academic Council, chaired by Carlo Cardia, professor of Ecclesiastical and Canonical Law, and with representatives of the Mosque of Rome.

21 The decree was made public by the Gazzetta Ufficiale della Repubblica Italiana, n. 137, on 15 June 2007.

22 All quotations in Italian have been translated into English by the author.

23 See Makno inquiry (Ministero dell'Interno 2008).

24 It should be noted that the acquisitions of citizenship in 2007 were almost 40,000 (Istat 2007).
25 Bill with regard to citizenship law reform (Bill of Law 04/08/06)

References

Allam, M. and Gritti, R. (eds) (2001), *Islam, Italia. Chi sono e cosa pensano i musulmani che vivono tra noi*, Milano: Guerini e Associati.

Allievi, S. (1999), *I nuovi musulmani. I convertiti all'Islam*, Roma: Edizioni Lavoro.

Allievi, S. and Dassetto, F. (1993), *Il ritorno dell'Islam. I musulmani in Italia*, Roma: Edizioni Lavoro.

Ambrosini, M. (2003), 'Per un inquadramento teorico del tema: il modello italiano di immigrazione e le funzioni delle reti etniche', in M. La Rosa and L. Zanfrini (eds), *Percorsi migratori, tra reti etniche, istituzioni e mercato del lavoro*, Milano: Franco Angeli, pp. 9–23.

Ambrosini, M. and Molina, S. (2004), *Seconde generazioni. Un'introduzione al futuro dell'immigrazione in Italia*, Torino: Edizioni della Fondazione Giovanni Agnelli.

Bastenier, A.and Dassetto, F. (1993), *Immigration et espace public. La controversie de l'integration*, Paris: L'Harmattan.

Bonifazi, C., Ferruzza, A., Strozza, S. and Todisco, E. (eds) (2008), 'Immigrati e stranieri al censimento del 2001', *Studi emigrazione*, XLV, 171, Roma: Cser, pp. 519–730.

Carchedi, F. (2000), 'Le associazioni degli immigrati', in E. Pugliese (ed), *Rapporto immigrazione: Lavoro, sindacato, società*, Roma: Ediesse.

Caritas/Migrantes (2008), *Immigrazione: Dossier Statistico 2008. XVIII Rapporto*, Roma: Idos.

Cassata, L., Martire, F., Strozza, S., Vitiello, M. and Zindato, D. (eds) (2008), 'L'integrazione come processo multi-dimensionale. Condizioni di vita e di lavoro degli immigrati', *Studi emigrazione*, XLV, 171, Roma: Cser, pp. 657–97.

CEC (2005), *A common agenda for integration: framework for the integration of third-country nationals in the European Union*, Bruxelles: European Commission.

Cilardo, A. (2003), 'Globalizzazione e internazionalizzazione. Le bozze di intesa tra la Repubblica Italiana e le Associazioni islamiche in Italia', *Studi emigrazione*, XL, 151, Roma: Cser, pp. 583–98.

Colaianni, N. (2007), 'Una "carta" post-costituzionale?', *Stato, Chiese e pluralismo confessionale*. Available online at: http://www.statoechiese.it/images/stories/papers/200706/colaianni_carta.pdf (accessed November 2009).

Cotesta, V. (2002), *Lo straniero. Pluralità culturale e immagini dell'Altro nella società globale*, Roma-Bari: Laterza.

Cotesta, V. (2007), *Le migrazioni nella società globale*, Roma: Anicia.

Dassetto, F. (1994), *L'Islam in Europa*, Torino: Edizioni della Fondazione Giovanni Agnelli.

Dassetto, F. (2004), *L'incontro complesso: Mondi occidentali e mondi islamici*, Troina (En): Città aperta edizioni.

Di Leo, F. (2004), 'Il nostro Islam in cifre', *Limes*, (Il nostro Islam) 3: 121–30.

Dusi, E. (2007), 'Il fantasma della Consulta', *Limes*, (Il mondo in casa) 4: 149–56.

Eve, M. (2003), 'Le disuguaglianze etniche', in M. Eve, A. R. Favretto, C. Meraviglia (eds), *Le disuguaglianze sociali*, Roma: Carocci.

Ferrari, S. (ed) (2000), *Musulmani in Italia. La condizione giuridica delle comunità islamiche*, Bologna: Il Mulino.

Filtzinger, O. (1984), *Integrazione di bambini stranieri nel settore prescolastico e scolastico nella repubblica Federale di Germania*, Roma: ITAL-UIL.
Frisina, A. (2007), *Giovani musulmani d'Italia*, Roma: Carocci.
Gallissot, R. and Rivera, A. (eds) (2001), *L'imbroglio etnico. In dieci parole chiave*, Bari: Dedalo.
Guolo, R. (2000), 'La rappresentanza dell'Islam italiano e la questione delle intese', in S. Ferrari (ed), *Musulmani in Italia. La condizione giuridica delle comunità islamiche*, Bologna: Il Mulino.
Istat (2007), *Rilevazione trimestrale forze di lavoro*, Roma.
Istat (2008), *Rapporto Annuale: La situazione del Paese nel 2007*, Roma.
Lewin, K. (1980), *I conflitti sociali: Saggi di dinamica di gruppo*, Milano: Franco Angeli.
Mezzadra, S. (2001), *Diritto di fuga: Migrazioni, cittadinanza, globalizzazione*, Verona: Ombre corte.
Ministero dell'Interno (2008), *Rapporto Makno: Una ricerca sociale sull'immigrazione*, Roma.
Pacini, A. (2000), 'I musulmani in Italia: Dinamiche organizzative e processi di interazione con la società e le istituzioni italiane', in S. Ferrari (ed), *Musulmani in Italia. La condizione giuridica delle comunità islamiche*, Bologna: Il Mulino, pp. 21–52.
Piga, A. (2000), 'Un universo sufi cangiante, criptico e poliedrico: la Qadiriyya, la Muridiyya e la Tijaniyya: tre ordini mistici nel Senegal contemporaneo', in M. I. Macioti (ed), *Immigrati e religioni*, Napoli: Liguori.
Portes, A. and Rumbaut, R. G. (2001), *Legacies: The Story of the Immigrant Second Generation*, Berkeley: University of California Press.
Schmidt di Friedberg, O. (1994), *Islam, solidarietà e lavoro. I muridi senegalesi in Italia*, Torino: Edizioni della Fondazione Agnelli.
Zagrebelsky, G. (1992), *Il diritto mite*, Torino: Einaudi.
Zanfrini, L. (2004), *Sociologia delle migrazioni*, Roma and Bari: Laterza.
Zincone, G. (ed) (2000), *Primo rapporto sull'integrazione degli immigrati in Italia*, Bologna: il Mulino.

10 Muslims in Spain

Blurring past and present Moors[1]

Ricard Zapata-Barrero and Nynke de Witte

Introduction

While following the general European trend of Islamophobia,[2] the construal of Muslims as a problematic group in Spain is based on a revival of the centuries-old discourse of Maurophobia (phobia of the Moors). This chapter will argue that the historical construction of Spanish national identity in opposition to the Moor is crucial in order to understand the difficulties of public recognition of 'new' Muslim minorities (especially Moroccan immigrants). In spite of the extensive legal rights granted for religious freedom, Spanish society has been reluctant to make a place for Muslims in the public sphere, and to incorporate Islam within its secular – though culturally speaking Catholic – identity.

The chapter illustrates how the Moroccan Muslim minority is being reproduced as the religious and cultural 'other'. It will highlight the importance of several structural features that are crucial for understanding the specific characteristics of non-Muslim majority-Muslim minority interactions in the Spanish case. In relation to the host society, we emphasize the role of the historical Muslim presence in the formation of the state and nation, which has shaped the state's relationship to religion, as well as a specific religious national self-definition and related notions of citizenship. With regard to the characteristics of the Muslim minority we stress the importance of the nationality of the majority of Muslims in Spain (Moroccans), which is important for understanding their construal as a threat.

The first section gives a short introduction to the composition and characteristics of Muslims in Spain. Section two discusses the main structural factors that have allowed or constrained a public recognition of Islam, focusing on the historical Spanish experience with Islam in the Iberian Peninsula and related processes of state-building, nation-building and evolving relations between state and religion. Sections three and four examine how these structural factors are reproduced in discourses around conflictive interactions between Muslim minorities and Spanish majorities. The third section describes the difficulty faced by Muslim communities in establishing mosques and presents the discourses of different actors involved in the conflicts around mosque establishment in two towns in Catalonia. Following the main argument of the chapter, section four illustrates how the representation of the 'past imagined Moor' in the traditional festivals *Moros y Cristianos* (Moors and Christians) in Valencia is contested by the presence of Muslim immigrants. The conflicts around mosque establishment and the controversy around 'the Muhammad' doll in the Festival of Moors and Christians demonstrate in different ways the difficulty of including 'new' Muslim minorities within a cultural identity and space that has traditionally perceived Muslims as the 'other', in terms of 'not us' or even 'against us'.

The Muslim population of Spain

There is little statistical information about the current Muslim population of Spain.[3] The Observatorio Andalusí, an institute associated with the Union of Islamic Communities in Spain (Unión de Comunidades Islámicas de Espana/UCIDE) estimates the Muslim population at 1,145,424, representing 2.5 per cent of the population. The majority are Sunnis, following one of the four major Sunni legal schools, especially the Maliki School. There is a small minority of Shi'a Muslims who follow the Jafari School. Moroccan immigrants, naturalized citizens and their offspring make up the largest group of Muslims in Spain, but there are also Muslim immigrants from Algeria, Pakistan and several sub-Saharan African countries, in addition to a small group of Spanish converts (Observatorio Andalusí 2007).

Migration from Morocco since the late 1980s has made Muslims visible in Spain. The number of Moroccan foreign residents has increased from 74,886 in 1995 to 672,864 in June 2008.[4] The majority originate from northern parts of Morocco, especially the (rural) RIF area, and have settled in Catalonia, Madrid, Murcia or Andalusia (Berriane 2004). The Moroccan immigrant community is relatively young (on average, men are 29 and women 26 years old) and three-quarters fall in the economic active age cohort.[5] Like other immigrant nationalities, Moroccans often have temporary jobs for which they are overqualified, and work in sectors of the economy where salaries are low and working conditions harsh. While most Moroccan women work in the (usually domestic) service industry, Moroccan men are divided among the agriculture, construction and service sectors. Compared with other immigrant nationalities, Moroccan immigrants have the highest unemployment rates and several studies have demonstrated the presence of discrimination against them in the labour market (Colectivo Ioé 1995, 2003).

Structural factors: historical bonds between religion, state and nation, and the institutionalization of Islam

Unlike the position in some other European countries, Islam is not a new religion in Spain. The presence of Muslims in the Iberian Peninsula for more than eight centuries (from 711 to 1492) makes the reactions of the receiving society to Muslim immigrants different from those of other European countries (Alvarez-Miranda 2005; Zapata-Barrero and Qasem 2008). This section will show how this historical experience with Islam has conditioned state-building, shaped the construction of Spanish national identity and conditioned the development of the state's relationship to religion.

The building of the Spanish state started with the Christian *Reconquista* of the Iberian Peninsula at the end of the fifteenth century. *Reconquista* refers to the process by which the Catholic kings (Queen Isabel and King Ferdinand) of Aragón-Catalunya and Castilla-León in northern Spain managed to retrieve the southern part of the Iberian Peninsula from the Muslims. After the Christian victory in 1492, with the fall of the city of Granada, the kings expelled, persecuted and forced conversion of Muslims, Jews and gypsies in their territory, thereby rendering Spain an exclusively Catholic territory. The Muslim presence ended completely in 1609 with the expulsion of the *moriscos* – Muslims who had converted to Christianity – after the *Reconquista* (Zapata-Barrero, 2006: 145).

Within the process of building a mono-confessional Catholic state, Spanish national identity was built upon a negative perception of the Muslim in general and the Moroccan in particular, considered in pejorative terms as 'the Moor' (*el moro*) (Zapata-Barerro 2006: 143). The representation of the Moor in the propaganda of the *Reconquista* disqualified Islamic religion, and created stereotypes of Moors as being impure, treasonous, false, cruel, cowardly, and so on (Martín Corrales 2002). This negative perception of the Moor would be reconstructed in other phases of Spanish history, and result in Maurophobia. Spanish identity was built upon a political notion of *Hispanidad*, the idea of a community bound by linguistic (Spanish) and religious (Catholic) criteria. The year 1492 in that context not only marked the end of the Muslim presence in Spain, but also saw the start of the Spanish Catholic conquest of America (Zapata-Barrero 2006: 143–7).

The link between the state and Catholicism was not challenged to the same extent by the Reformation and/or anti-clerical movements in the nineteenth century as it was in other parts of Europe. The most important 'secular' interruptions in the history of the Spanish state before 1979 took place during the First Republic (1873–4) and Second Republic (1931–9). While the Catholic Church started to embrace transnationalism as a response to secular nationalism, the Spanish Church emphasized the historical identification of Spain with Catholicism (De Busser 2006: 284–5). This emphasis on the religious nature of the Spanish nation state eventually paved the way for the national Catholic ideology of the Franco regime (1939–1975), where *Hispanidad* was reconstructed as a symbol of homogeneity and unity (González Antón 1997: 613). The first challenge to the strong bonds of religion and politics came not from society, but from the Second Vatican Council (1962–5) which advocated not only religious freedom and separation of State and Church, but also criticized the Spanish political regime for maintaining its religious ties (Tamayo 2003). The consequent crisis instigated a process of depoliticizing the Spanish Church. The state responded with a new law on religious freedom (1967), but only after Franco's death did relations between the state and the Catholic Church change more radically (De Busser 2006).

With the transition to democracy, Spain transformed from a mono-confessional Catholic state to a non-confessional state. Article 14 of the 1978 constitution guarantees religious equality, and Article 16 provides for religious freedom and the freedom of worship for individuals and groups, and guarantees that 'no faith shall have the character of a state religion'. Although this altered fundamentally the ties between the Catholic Church and the state, the Catholic Church did not lose all its privileges. Several agreements were negotiated between the Holy See and the state before the new constitution was established, which informed the arrangement of disestablishment. In these agreements, which were only made public in 1979, the Catholic Church managed to preserve some of its privileges, like its legal position, the validity of Catholic marriages by civil law, religious education, tax privileges and financial support by the state.[6] In order to provide 'other' religions equal opportunities, the Constitutional Law on Religious Freedom of 1980 established the possibility for other communities with 'firm roots' (*arraigo*) to obtain privileges, by signing treaties with the state, similar – but not equal – to those with the Holy See.[7] Islam was declared a 'firmly rooted' religion in 1989, five years after Protestantism and Judaism.

The continued relevance of the discourse of *Hispanidad* is also apparent in the legislation for citizenship acquisition in 1985, which combines *ius soli* (birth in territory) and *ius sanguinis* (descent). Those born in Spain with at least one parent also born there, acquire citizenship automatically at birth. Second-generation immigrants with foreign parents can obtain Spanish citizenship after one year of residence and first-generation immigrants may acquire Spanish citizenship after a certain period of residence, depending on their nationality. Most first-generation immigrants have to be resident for ten years to be able to apply for Spanish nationality (except asylum seekers who can apply after five years of residence). However, this is reduced to only two years for those with a preferential nationality and, if they can claim some historical link with Spanish nationality, just one year. The preference groups are: Latin Americans, Portuguese, Filipinas, Andorrans, Guineans and Sephardic Jews. *Moriscos*, who like Sephardic Jews were expelled after the reconquest of *Al Andalus*, are not included in this list (Código Civil, articles 17–26, Law no. 36/2002, October 2002) (Zapata-Barrero 2004: 54–62).

The political transition to democracy favoured the development of Muslim associations, especially by Spanish converts in Andalusia. The first 'new' prayer halls, however, were established in the 1980s by Moroccans, sub-Saharan Africans and Pakistanis (Moreras 2002: 53). In 1989 various associations of Spanish converts – financed by various Middle Eastern countries – created the Federación Española de Entidades Religiosas Islámicas (FEERI). In 1990, associations of naturalized citizens originating from Middle Eastern countries formed another federation, UCIDE, which is close ideologically to the moderate wing of the Muslim Brotherhood. In 1992, the two federations were forced to join into a national organ that was established to represent the Muslim community in Spain – the Islamic Commission of Spain (Comisión Islámica de España – CIE) – which has been until today the main interlocutor for the government.

In 1992 a Cooperation Agreement was signed between the state and the Islamic Commission of Spain, which started the construction of an institutional position for Muslims as a religious minority in Spain (Jefatura del Estado 1992). Although '[t]he agreement was superimposed on heterogeneity of models and initiatives for association present among Muslims in Spain' (Moreras 2002: 59), it has provided Muslims in Spain with several legal rights and benefits. The content of the agreement includes, for example, the right to set up Muslim schools and to receive instructions in Islam in public schools; the right to celebrate Islamic holidays; the right to have Muslim marriages recognized under civil law; the legal protection of mosques; legal status for religious leaders and imams; tax relief for religious activities, and prescriptions for halal food.

In spite of this rather extensive legal recognition, Muslims in Spain suffer from a lack of de facto recognition and accommodation of their religious rights. One of the most important issues is the establishment of places of worship. Although there is no official register of mosques, it is estimated that there are between 350 and 500 mosques and oratories in Spain (Moreras 2004: 413; Bastante 2006). The only legal requirement for Islamic communities to open and/or build a prayer hall is the consent from the Islamic Commission of Spain. In the struggle between both federations (FEERI and CIE) for the right to represent Muslims in Spain, both have sought support from new Muslim immigrants.[8] Local Muslim immigrant communities have sometimes made use of membership in one of the federations to obtain legal status and make public claims for religious infrastructure (Moreras 2002: 59–60). The Arabist Martín Muñoz (2003: 119) estimates that 70 per cent of the Moroccan oratories are managed by a religious association (that might be, but does not have to be inscribed in the Spanish Islamic Commission), while some 30 per cent are not registered at all, thereby lacking the fiscal advantages and legal recognition provided by the 1992 Agreement. Internal fragmentation and problems of representation, especially at the local level, have complicated public claims-making of Muslims (Moreras 2002: 61). But as the opposition to mosque establishment described in the next paragraph will demonstrate, what is probably more important is the reluctance of Spanish local authorities to make a place for Muslims' religious infrastructure in the public space. Similar struggles of the Muslim minority with public authorities include demands for Muslim cemeteries or spaces to allow funeral rites (Martín Muñoz 2003: 119), the demand for halal food in public buildings, the wearing of headscarves in schools and Islamic education. The lack of Islamic education in public schools is especially striking in the context of Roman Catholic teaching being offered – though recently made optional – in all public schools.

Conflicts around mosque establishment: two case studies in Catalonia

The most important *conflict zone* between Muslim minorities and Spanish majorities is in the subject of building mosques and/or opening oratories.[9] While 'oratory' (*oratorio*) is often used to refer to Muslim prayer halls established in existing private buildings (like garages or offices), mosques (*mezquita*) refer to the specific architecture of Muslim prayer halls that makes Islam visible in public space. Plans for building mosques have opened up debates about the actual meaning of public space. Protest against building mosques and the opening of oratories has been widespread in recent years, especially in Catalonia. Between 2001 and 2006 there have been at least 18 cases of protest in Catalonia, compared with only 7 other cases in the rest of Spain during the same period.[10]

The relatively high number of Muslims living in Catalonia might create more demand for places of worship, but it does not explain why other autonomous communities with similar percentages of Muslim immigrants, like Andalusia, Madrid or Valencia, have not experienced similar levels of opposition. The most likely answer is that Catalonia – unlike the other three – has no large purpose-built mosque. The Islamic Cultural Council of Catalonia (Consejo Islámico Cultural de Cataluña) has made several requests for the building of such a large mosque in Barcelona, and in December 2006 there was a petition of 50 imams with the same request, in addition to the request for 'descent' oratories (Casals 2006; Playà Maset 2006). In spite of these demands for a purpose-built mosque, the Catalan government seems to prefer small neighbourhood oratories that are more easily controlled. These oratories, however, have not been free from tensions either, as will be noted in the conflicts around Muslim places of worship in two towns in Catalonia: Premiá del Mar and Badalona.[11]

Premiá del Mar

Premiá del Mar is a small town north of Barcelona where Muslim immigrants make up only 4.4 per cent of the population. It became the object of confrontation in 2002 after the local Muslim community (Asociación Islámica At-Tauba) declared its desire to build a mosque in the centre of the town. The demand was a direct consequence of the closing of an oratory used by the Muslim community since 1987. After several complaints about noise, the judicial authority ordered its closure in November 2001, because of its incompliance with security requirements. The City Hall promised the Muslims an alternative place of worship, and in February 2002 a provisional agreement was made to use a public school until June 2002.

Meanwhile the Muslim community bought a plot of land assigned for cultural service use in the centre of the town, and applied for a licence to build a mosque. When the news of this building project spread, the local population mobilized in opposition to the plan, starting with the collection of 5,554 signatures. In response to the local protest, the City Hall proposed that the mosque be built in a less centrally located area: an industrial park on the outskirts of the town. Yet this only relocated the site of protest, as neighbours in the destined area collected some 700 signatures against the plan. The Muslim community was not happy with the proposed solution either and negotiations between both parties broke down. When the City Hall ordered the Muslim community to leave the school, the community found itself without a place of worship, and used the plot in the centre of town for the Friday sermon, as a form of protest. This public form of demonstration triggered the first street protests by neighbours on 19 April 2002.

When the City Hall approved the building of a mosque in the town centre on 26 April 2002, a protest by neighbours was held on the same day. A spokesman of the Platform for Premià (including different neighbour associations) made it clear that mosques were not welcome: 'We do not want any mosque in Premiá, has that not become clear after 20 years?' and 'let them pray in their homes' (Pérez 2002).[12]

Other protestors used different arguments, like the fear that their property would become devalued and the migration of 'autochthons' (Vives 2002). It was also feared that the construction of a mosque would attract Muslims from elsewhere, which would turn the zone into a 'Muslim ghetto' and increase conflicts between local citizens and Muslim immigrants. Still others pointed out that Muslims do not want to be integrated or cannot be integrated (Gabinet d'Estudis Socials 2002: 25). The protests were publicly supported by the right-wing populist leader Josep Anglada and his 'Platform for Catalonia' (Plataforma por Cataluña). Using a language designed to trigger xenophobic reactions, he emphasized the threat of a Muslim 'invasion' and the need to defend 'our identities, customs and culture' (*ABC*, 20 May 2002).

In support of the Muslim community, an opposition group called 'Premiá for peaceful coexistence' (Coordinadora Premià per la Convivència) was formed, consisting of several groups, including SOS Racism. It organized a counter-protest on 12 May, mobilizing some 1,000 demonstrators. On Saturday 18 May, large demonstrations were held by two neighbourhood groups, one led by Josep Anglada and the other by a group of youngsters from Antifascist Action. Some 8,000 signatures were collected against the building of the mosque, next to a petition that demanded the mayor's resignation. The conflict had now reached the attention of the regional and national media and the Catalan government (*Generalitat*) got involved to mediate a solution. Eventually the Muslim community agreed to start negotiations anew, and an agreement was reached on 5 September 2002 to use an abandoned school building for a period of 15 years, while freezing the licence for constructing a mosque until a final solution was reached.

Badalona

Badalona is a municipality located in the Barcelona Metropolitan Area with some 221,000 inhabitants and a Muslim community of around 10,000 people. After several complaints from neighbours, the City Hall decided to close one of the two oratories in the municipality (in the neighbourhood of La Pau) on 23 February 2005, because of the lack of a proper licence and the oratory's non-compliance with security requirements. At the beginning of March, the City Hall and the Muslim community agreed to move the prayer hall to a factory in an industrial zone (in the neighbourhood of Congrés), at the border of the municipalities of Badalona and Santa Coloma. The agreement included an arrangement for a provisional oratory while the factory was adapted for its new function. The imam of the closed oratory explained that he was not very enthusiastic about the location, 'being moved away from the people, as if we have leprosy', but that at least it was a solution (González 2006).

Soon afterwards, however, neighbours living a short distance from the industrial area collected almost 4,000 signatures in opposition to the transformation of the site. With the help of the property owner of the industrial building, the neighbours were able to block the plan. The argument of the property owner is an exemplary reconstruction of the discourse of Mauropobhia: 'The neighbourhood has been invaded by moors […] and has left the Spaniards a minority in their own neighbourhood' (González 2006). As in Premiá del Mar, neighbours feared that the construction of a mosque in Badalona would attract Muslims from adjacent areas and argued that Muslims do not truly want to integrate and are often delinquent. Moreover, the president of the neighbourhood associations made it clear that if the City Hall continued with their plan, 'there will be clashes with the Muslims' (González 2006).

In July 2005 the City Hall of Badalona suspended the concession of a new licence for the opening or extension of all religious centres and prayer halls for a year, in order to investigate the state and accessibility of religious buildings, and the locations planned for religious temples. In addition, the City Council promised to create a regulation for the opening of religious rooms and spaces. On 25 February 2006 the Muslim community – now without a prayer hall – assembled at the municipality square in front of the City Hall, and prayed there as a form of protest. In July 2006 the City Hall approved a regulation for the opening of oratories, restricting the capacity of prayer halls to a maximum of 70 people, in order to prevent large agglomerations, and allowing larger prayer halls only in industrial areas. At the same time, it changed (without consent of the People's Party) the destination of a plot of land at the periphery of the town (in the neighbourhood of Montigalà) from social to religious usage.

The local People's Party, claiming that the mayor had suggested the possibility of the construction of a great mosque, started collecting signatures against the cession of land. Stimulated by the People's Party (Partido Popular), various neighbourhood associations created the platform 'No to Mosques on Public Land' (*No a la mezquita en terrenos públicos*), claiming that the public land should be used for social housing or day-care centres and not for the construction of a mosque. In the meantime, the urban commission of the Catalan government (*Generalitat*) got involved as well, freezing the reservation and change in use of the plot by introducing a bureaucratic procedure that required modifications in the General Metropolitan Plan and a process of appeal.

In January 2007, two months before the local elections, the local People's Party further politicized the issue by presenting some 20,800 signatures (with help from the Platform) to the City Hall in protest of the supposed construction of a mosque in Montigalà. The president of the party argued that the Muslim minority had been given preferential treatment and affirmed that his party, if elected, would assign the public lands to preschooling facilities or centres for elderly. Moreover, he claimed that 'the Muslim community should solve their own problems, without help from the public authorities' (Benvenuty 2007a). The president of the Junta Islamica Catalana publicly contested this argument, stating that in other municipalities '[the People's Party] does assign terrains for Catholic Churches, but when dealing with Islam they talk of laicism' (*Europa Press*, 16 January 2007). The president also accused the party of 'demonization and creating fear of Islam', and argued that the denial of a fundamental right which is 'not negotiable' showed a 'lack of democratic maturity' and 'palpable Islamophobia' in Spain and Catalonia (*Europa Press*, 16 January 2007). Some support for the Muslim community came also from the Catholic parishes in Badalona and Sant Adrià de Besos, where posters were found that probably reflect the most 'progressive' discourse regarding the incorporation of Muslims:

> Whether we like it or not, actual Badalona, and much more so in 10 years, will be profoundly plural and intercultural, and this needs to be reflected in daily life. In an integrated Badalona the existence of Muslim oratories should be normal. Those who come need to adapt to a lot of things; we too need to adapt. (Benvenuty 2007b)

Meanwhile, Muslims from Badalona have to go to other municipalities to pray on Fridays, while the City Hall has put the issue on hold until the Catalan government comes up with regulations (*La Razón*, 31 December 2006; Orduña 2007).

Sources and causes of resistance to mosque establishment

The conflicts around mosque establishment in Premiá del Mar and Badalona shared several characteristics. In both cases the closure of an oratory left the Muslim community without a place of worship. After the demand for the building of a purpose-built mosque, neighbourhood associations were the first to mobilize in opposition, by collecting signatures and/or organizing street protests. They were supported by right-wing groups and political parties of the opposition who took advantage of the protests to gain political support. Local authorities, in turn, often 'adopt an "understanding" position towards the local inhabitants, no doubt because of the electoral cost of defending Muslims' claims' (Zapata-Barrero 2006: 149). In the words of the imam in Badalona: 'the problem with us is that we are not allowed to vote. [...] the local authorities do not care about us' (Gonzáles 2006). The Muslim communities turned to silent protest, by praying in the open air. They were supported in their claims by human rights groups and in the case of Badalona by Catholic parishes.

While opposition from neighbours, stimulated by right-wing political parties, draws on xenophobia and maurophobia, local authorities use more tacit discourses when obstructing mosque establishment. Lack of safety, or the reluctance to change the formal 'designation' of a building in urban plans are commonly used as arguments to oppose the opening (or demand the closure) of oratories. Extending planning or construction permits are the most common way for local authorities to prevent or delay the building of mosques. And if granted a permit, this is preferably at the periphery of town, out of sight of public life. These actions demonstrate that the legal right of Muslims to establish places of worship is only put in practice when these places are rather 'invisible' or not part of public space. This is the case for oratories, which are often located in private garages, offices and apartments, and also the solution used for the establishment of mosques, as in Premiá del Mar, where the Muslim community was transferred to a school that was not in use. As Muslim immigrants often have no voting rights, as a result of the discriminatory citizenship regime, local authorities have no political incentives to defend their rights.

Opposition to the building of mosques is found in many European countries (see for instance Cesari 2005; Maussen 2006), but the degree and type of opposition varies from place to place. In countries like Spain and Italy, opposition is strong, it is argued, due to the relatively recent immigration of Muslims. Migration flows from Morocco to Spain, however, cannot be said to be a recent phenomenon anymore. What is striking about the case studies described here is the issue at stake: the reluctance to recognize Islam as a legitimate religion in the public sphere. While in Spain there is still a strong reluctance to make place for Islam to begin with, elsewhere in Europe debates have shifted towards the conditions of mosque establishment (i.e. the architecture, the presence of a muezzin, public finance, etc.). As the spokesman of the only oratory open in the Badalona municipality explains: 'We are happy to pay for the terrain and the construction work, the only thing we ask the City Hall for is where' (Benvenuty 2007a). In spite of the secularization of both state and society,[13] exclusive discourses of Maurophobia and *Hispanidad* are reconstructed in opposition to mosque establishment. Even in Catalonia, which is an odd case in terms of the political discourse of *Hispanidad* (because of its divergence from the dominant language and culture), there is no place for Islam in the supposedly secular public sphere. Denying Muslim migrants a public place in the city reignites the idea that Spanish identity and space is defined in opposition to the presence of Muslims, both in the past and in the present.

Festivals *Moros y Cristianos* (Moors and Christians)

The annual festival *Moros y Cristianos* celebrates the Christian triumph over Islam during the Spanish Reconquest, by the symbolic re-enacting of local victories over Moorish armies. It can be witnessed in almost 400 localities in Spain, mostly in the Autonomous Communities of Valencia, Andalusia and Castilla-La Mancha. According to Harris (1994: 46) the historical origins of the festival can be traced back to the victories of Jaime I between 1244 and 1245, and the rebellion that followed in the region where the Treaty of Almizra was signed in 1244 to establish the borders between the expanding kingdoms of Aragón-Catalunya and Castilla-León. The dramatized battles became only occasional after the reconquest of Granada in 1492. Its yearly celebration in some places since the late sixteenth century is explained (Harris 1994: 46) as a culmination of different traditions, including the *soldadescas* (mock battles) of local militias that, in the late sixteenth century, guarded the coast against the Turkish navy and Berber pirates, and the much older annual procession of local patron saints or the Virgin (Harris 1994: 46). Over time, tourism has increased the popularity and the number of places where the Festival is celebrated.

The celebration consists of a symbolic battle for territory (sometimes commemorating a specific local battle) among Moorish and Christian military units that can last for several days, resulting in a victory for the Christians. 'In the festivals, the Moors are defeated in combat and then converted to Christianity, or, in the case of some villages on the coast of Alicante, they are "symbolically" thrown into the sea' (Flesler and Melgosa 2003: 153). In the festivals, the Moor is characterized by two stereotypes: 'One portrays him as an exotic, sensual being admired for his courage as a warrior and for his outstanding scientific and artistic creativity and sophistication. The other one depicts him as a treacherous, violent and cruel figure that wants to seize territories away from the Christians' (Flesler and Melgosa 2003: 152). The oppositional narrative of the performances in the festivals is found not only in the contra-distinguished categories of Moors and Christians, but also in the depicting of an 'essential Christian right to the land, while explaining away the presence of the Moors as something temporary and inconsequential' (Flesler and Melgosa 2003: 154). During the festival both Moors and Christians parade their troops through the village and act like owners of the castle by defending it from attacks from the invading other. Although during these ceremonies the two groups take turns in the role of 'guest' and 'host', 'invaders' and 'invaded', in the end the Christians are the 'native' owners of the territory (Flesler and Melgosa 2003: 155).

Participants in the festivals argue that it makes no difference whether they perform as Moor or Christian, something which is often displayed as a sign of reconciliation. For example, the official columnist of the festival in Alcoi argues that 'centuries ago the Alcoi citizens surpassed the differences between Moors and Christians: we show off the one as much as the other. Nevertheless, the Moorish group is the one with more prestige because its ostentation is more exotic' (Gallardo 2006). The president of the Junta Mayor de Fiestas de Moros y Cristianos de Elda argues that by 'taking things out of their context' you get controversial results. In the festivals, he argues, 'Christians dress like Moors, atheists represent Christians and the white skinned are painted black' (*El Periodico de Cataluña*, 4 October 2006). Flesler and Melgosa (2003: 156) argue that the indifferent attitude to both categories can also be understood as a way of accepting 'the inevitability of being a "guest" in one's "own" place'. Indeed, representations of past and present Moors (i.e. Moroccan immigrants) are often clearly separated. The former group (past Moor) is admired in the festivals, while the latter, Moroccan immigrants who exist as 'real' guests in the country, are discriminated against and accused of 'invading' the country (as the conflicts around mosques demonstrate). In some instances the 'imagined past Moor' is mixed up with the 'real present Moor'. The association that organizes the festivals in localities in Valencia and Alicante, for example, notes that immigrants who have settled in the province also take part in the festivals, 'and not always as the group that identifies them' (Marínez and Antolín 2006).

The representation of the 'imagined' Moor in the festivals became blurred with the present 'real' Moors most clearly after the Danish cartoon affair.[14] The publication of the cartoons of the Prophet in the *Jyllands-Posten* and its subsequent reactions in European and Middle Eastern countries did not create much polemic in Spanish society. The cartoons were not reprinted in the main daily newspapers and the government publicly condemned their publication. It did have a direct effect though on the practices in the festivals. While the majority of potentially offensive elements in the festivals had already been removed after a recommendation from the Vatican Council II in 1968, some acts that were used to represent the 'defeated' Moor became the objects of debate after the cartoon affair. This is especially the case for 'the Muhammad', a dummy made of cardboard that in some places is used as a banner of the Moorish army and symbolically killed to symbolize Christian victory by beheading or burning it (Ruiz Sierra 2006; Marínez and Antolín 2006; Gadea 2006).

After the Danish cartoon affair, organizers of the festivals in Beneixama and Boicarent avoided these last representations of 'the Muhammad', in order not to offend Muslims. In these towns the festivals normally conclude with an act in which a dummy of more than three metres in height, with Arabian clothing and called 'the Muhammad' is burned on the last day by exploding fireworks through its head. Although it is stressed that 'the Muhammad' is just a doll that symbolizes the Moorish army and does not represent the Prophet or the Muslim community (Ruiz Sierra 2006; *ABC*, 4 October 2006), the organizers in both towns decided not to include the act in the festivals that year. In the past the organizers used the argument of tradition to justify controversial issues in the festivals, for example the exclusion of women from performances (Flesler and Melgosa 2003: 164). Removing 'the Muhammad' therefore highlights the sensitive link between past and present Moors after the Danish cartoon affair. Although 'the Muhammad' might be interpreted by the organizers and participants of the festivals as merely an identity symbol of the Moorish army, its burning as a symbolic closure act celebrates the victory of Catholic Spain through the expunging of Muslims and Islam from Spanish territory.

In October 'the Christians' of Alcoi (the largest and most publicized Festivals of Moors and Christians) proudly head the traditional parade of *Hispanidad* on Fifth Avenue in New York (Gallardo 2006). It was during this time that the first critique from the Muslim community in Spain on the festivals was heard (Martínez 2006). The president of Federación Española de Entidades Religiosas Islámicas (FEERI), who is also an imam in Malaga, demanded the elimination of the festivals, criticizing the image they give to Muslims (Martínez 2006; Marínez and Antolín 2006). While he makes a direct link between the representation of past and present Moors, the four local associations that are part of FEERI in Valencia (where most festivals take place) do not agree with their president. The Centro Religioso Islámico de Valencia, for example, argues that criticizing the parades means 'to take them out of their context', and thereby pleads for the separation of past and present representation of Moors. A similar interpretation comes from the Consejo Islámico de Valencia which also disqualifies the president's statements, because it would 'create an artificial' debate based on 'a lack of knowledge of the Festivals' that had developed 'without any offensive spirit towards Islam' (*Las Provincias*, 5 October 2006). The president of the Islamic Community of Alicante also claimed that the festivals did not represent any attack on Islam or the Prophet: 'We see it as a feast and it should be understood like that', but he believed it 'wise' of the municipalities of Bocairent and Beneixama to eliminate the blowing up of 'the Muhammad' doll in order to prevent conflict (*El Periodico de Cataluña*, 4 October 2006). Finally, the president of the Consejo Islámico Valenciano argued that the festivals should be maintained because they were in fact a demonstration of *convivencia* (peaceful coexistence) (*Las Provincias*, 6 October 2006).

While the representatives of Muslim communities in the region do not seem to have any problems with the festivals, the local participants and organizers do change protocols because they are afraid of violent reactions from the Muslim community. Several articles have criticized this change of protocol, claiming that the burning of 'the Muhammad' has disappeared from the Festivals only out of fear of radical Islam (see for example Gundín 2006). This fear could be said also to have reached the political sphere, when the Popular Party (PP) presented a legal proposal in order to pressure the government to recommend the festivals of Moors and Christians to UNESCO for protection (Martínez 2006). The act of self-censorship thus reproduces Moroccan immigrants as a threat to Spanish society.

Conclusion

The construction of differences in interactions between Spanish majorities and Muslim minorities should be understood within the context of the historical presence of Islam in the Iberian Peninsula for more than eight centuries. As we have seen, the religious component in the self-identification of Spanish majorities is reproduced in the context of interactions with Moroccan Muslim minorities. While Hispanic identity over time has become more cultural and linguistic than religious, it is still being constructed in opposition to the category of the Moor – traditionally referring to Berbers from North Africa. The binary logic of Hispanic versus Moor is reproduced today in the context of the increasing presence and visibility of Moroccan migrants. As a result, in spite of Muslims' extensive legal recognition, there is a large gap between legal and de facto recognition of the religious rights of Muslims.

The two case studies demonstrate how this structural feature of self-identification characterizing the Spanish host society is reconstructed in interactions between Moroccan Muslim minorities and Spanish majorities. The opposition to Muslim places of worship highlights the deep-rooted resistance towards the visibility of Muslims and their religious infrastructure within public space. Local authorities are reluctant to guarantee Muslims the right to establish places of worship, due to a strong social and often politicized discourse of Maurophobia. Expressed fears for an 'invasion' of Muslims and the 're-Islamicization' of Spain explicitly draw on the historical presence of Muslims in the Iberian Peninsula. To deal with the legitimate claims from the Muslim community, on the one hand, and the opposition of citizens, on the other, local authorities often opt for the accommodation of prayer halls in private spaces (like oratories) or at the periphery of urban space. Excluding Muslims from visibility in public space reflects the reinforcement of the exclusive nature of Spanish historical self-definition and therefore a reluctance to redefine Spanish national identity in the face of an increasing presence of migrants with different cultural and religious identities.

The festivals of Moors and Christians celebrate the Christian victory over Moors, thereby reproducing the idea of Christians being the 'native' heirs of the territory. In contrast to the concealment of places of worship of contemporary 'Moors' (Muslim immigrants) from the public, during the festivals the 'imagined Moor of the past' obtains huge visibility, as both an exotic and barbaric figure. The self-censorship instigated after the Danish cartoon affair demonstrates the problematic interaction between representations of present and past Moors, as changing the representation of the 'past Moor' is justified by the presence (and fear) of the 'real Moor'. Today, as opposed to the time of the *Reconquista*, the freedom of religion within the context of Spanish liberal democracy makes the idea of 'Christians' being the only legitimate heirs of the territory problematic. Interactions between Muslim minorities and Spanish majorities today, therefore, present not only a challenge of accommodating religious diversity, but also that of reconstructing national identity (Zapata-Barrero 2009). The question is therefore not *if*, but rather *when* Spanish society will be ready to accept their cultural and religious 'other' as part of the Spanish 'self'.

Notes

1 This chapter has its origins in a report prepared for the sixth European Framework project: *A European Approach to Multicultural Citizenship: Legal Political and Educational Challenges* (EMILIE) Contract no. CIT5-CT-2005-028205 -WP2 Spanish report on migration and multiculturalism discourses (April 2007). (www.upf.edu/gritim)
2 See for example International Helsinki Federation for Human Rights 2005: 120–1; European Monitoring Centre on Racism and Xenophobia 2006.
3 Article 16.2 of the Spanish constitution does not provide for official census of religious confessions (http://www.congreso.es/funciones/constitucion/indice.htm).
4 Anuario Estadístico de Extranjería 1995, Ministerio de Trabajo y Asuntos Sociales; Informe trimestral 30 de junio de 2008, Ministerio de Trabajo y Asuntos Sociales (http://extranjeros.mtin.es/es/InformacionEstadistica).
5 Statistical Yearbook of Immigration 2006, State Secretariat for Immigration and Emigration, Permanent Observatory for Immigration (http://extranjeros.mtin.es/es/InformacionEstadistica/Anuarios/Archivos/Anuario_Estadistico_Inmigracixn2006InglesInternet.pdf).
6 The different agreements can be found in Boletín Oficial del Estado BOE (The Official Spanish Bulletin) no. 300, 15 December 1979.
7 The Spanish state continues to have an asymmetrical relationship with the Catholic Church. One of the most disputed legal issues has been the direct financial support. A legislative change in September 2006 stopped direct state payments to the Church, but increased the voluntary contribution from 0.5 to 0.7 per cent. For voluntary contributions two options are available to taxpayers: the Catholic Church and social work.
8 According to the Observatorio Andalusí (2007) UCIDE represents some 70 per cent, and FEERI some 10 per cent of the Islamic communities in Spain.
9 The term 'conflict zone' comes from Zapata-Barrero (2006 and 2008).
10 Of which 2 in Andalucía, 1 in the Baleares, 1 in Castilla y León, 1 in Extremadura, 1 in Galicia and 1 in Valencia. To identify cases of opposition to the building of mosques and/or opening of oratories information has been collected from the yearbooks of SOS Racismo (2002–2006) and daily newspapers.
11 The sources used to reconstruct the course of events in Premia del Mar are: *ABC*, 27 November 2001; Pérez, 2002; Vives, 2002; Gabinet d'Estudis Socials, 2002; SOS Racismo, 2002: 239–40; SOS Racismo, 2003: 214–19; Zapata-Barrero, 2003: 6; Motilla, 2004: 88. For the reconstruction of the Badalona case: *EFE*, 28 July 2005; SOS Racismo, 2006: 208–9; González, 2006; Sales, 2007; De Barros, 2007; Ayuso, 2007; *El País*, 13 January 2007; Benvenuty, 2007a, 2007b, 2007c.
12 All quotes originally in Spanish or Catalan have been translated by the authors.

13 According to the latest statistics, 77.4 per cent of Spanish people consider themselves Catholic, but only 2.5 per cent of those attend church several days a week, 15.1 per cent attending almost every Sunday, 11.3 per cent attending once a month and 56 per cent almost never. Although Catholic religious practice has decreased considerably in Catalonia, religious values continue to be important as a tradition, and as a cultural expression.

14 See, among others, Blomart (2006), Kunelius, *et al.* (2007), Mouritsen, *et al.* (eds 2009).

References

Álvarez-Miranda, B. (2005) 'Muslim Communities in Europe: Recognition of Religious Differences in Britain, Germany and France', Michigan Paper Series. Available at: www.umich.edu/-iinet/euc/Academics/MichiganPaperSeries.html (accessed 20 January 2009).

Berriane, M. (2004) 'Los focos migratorios marroquíes y la emigración hacia España', in B. López García and M. Berriane (eds), *Atlas de la inmigración magrebí en España*, Taller de Estudios Internacionales Mediterráneos, Observatorio Permanente de la Inmigración, Ministerio de Trabajo y Asuntos Sociales, pp. 128–30.

Blomart, A. (2006) *Getting it Right: Lessons of the 'Cartoons Crisis' and Beyond, EuroMeSCo Annual Report*. Bruxelles: European Commission.

Boletín Oficial Del Estado (BOE) (1979) 'Acuerdos del Estado Español con las Confesiones Religiosas: Con la Iglesia Católica (Santa Sede)', *BOE*, 300: 28782–28783.

Busser, C. de (2006) 'Church–state relations in Spain: Variations on a National-Catholic theme?', *GeoJournal*, 67: 283–94.

Cesari, J. (2005) 'Mosque Conflicts in European Cities: Introduction', *Journal of Ethnic and Migration Studies*, 31(6): 1015–24.

Colectivo Ioé (1995) 'Discriminación contra trabajadores marroquíes en el acceso al empleo', in Colectivo Ioé and R. Pérez Molina, *La Discriminación Laboral a los Trabajadores Inmigrantes en España*, Geneva: Internacional Labour Organization, pp. 1–59.

Colectivo Ioé (2003) 'Experiencias de discriminación de minorías étnicas en España – Contra Inmigrantes no-comunitarios y el colectivo gitano', European Monitoring Centre on Racism and Xenophobia, Ref No. 2002/02/01. Available at: http://www.sp.upcomillas.es/sites/mtas/Lists/Documentos/Attachments/58/EUMC.pdf (accessed 20 January 2009).

European Monitoring Centre on Racism and Xenophobia (2006) *Muslims in the European Union: Discrimination and Islamophobia*. Available at: http://eumc.europa.eu/eumc/material/pub/muslim/Manifestations_EN.pdf (accessed 20 January 2009).

Flesler, D. and Melgosa, A. P. (2003) 'Battles of Identity, or Playing "Guest" and "Host": The Festivals of Moors and Christians in the Context of Moroccan Immigration in Spain', *Journal of Spanish Cultural Studies*, 4(2): 151–68.

Gabinet d'Estudis Socials (2002) *Estudio del conflicto de la mezquita de Premiá de Mar*, Barcelona: Centro de Referencia en España, Observatorio Europeo contra el Racismo y la Xenofobia (EUMC).

González Antón, L. (1997) *España y las Españas*, Madrid: Alianza.

Harris, M. (1994) 'Muhammed and the Virgin, Folk Dramatizations of Battles Between Moors and Christians in Modern Spain', *The Drama Review*, 38 (1): 45–61.

International Helsinki Federation for Human Rights (2005) 'Spain', in *Report on Intolerance and Discrimination against Muslims in the EU: Developments since September 11*. Available at: http://www.ihf-hr.org/viewbinary/viewdocument.php?download=1&doc_id=6242 (accessed 20 January 2009).

Jefatura de Estado (1992) 'Ley 26/1992, de 10 Noviembre, por la que se aprueba el acuerdo de cooperación del estado con la comisión islámica de España', *BOE*, 272.

Kunelius, R., Eide, E. and Hahn, O. (2007) *Reading the Mohammed Cartoons Controversy: An International Analysis of Press Discourses on Free Speech and Political Spin*. Bochum: Projekt Verlag, Bochum and Freiburg.

Martín Corrales, E. (2002) *La imagen del magrebi en Espana una perspectiva historica, siglos XVI–XX*, Barcelona: Bellaterra.

Martin Muñoz, G. (2003) *Marroquíes en España, Estudio sobre su integración*, Madrid: Fundación Repsol.

Maussen, M. (2006) 'The Governance of Islam in Western Europe: A State of the Art Report', IMISCOE Working Paper, no. 16. Available at: http://www.imiscoe.org/publications/workingpapers/documents/GovernanceofIslam-stateoftheart_000.pdf (accessed 20 January 2009).

Moreras, J. (2002) 'Limits and Contradictions in the Legal Recognition of Muslims in Spain', in W. Shadid and P. S. Van Koningsveld (eds), *Religious Freedom and the Neutrality of the State: The Position of Islam in the European Union*, Leiden: Peeters, pp. 52–64.

Moreras, J. (2004) 'La religiosidad en contexto migratorio: partencias y observancias', in B. López García and M. Berriane (eds), *Atlas de la inmigración magrebí en España*. Taller de Estudios Internacionales Mediterráneos. Observatorio Permanente de la Inmigración, Ministerio de Trabajo y Asuntos Sociales, pp. 412–15.

Motilla, A. (2004) 'La protección de los lugares de culto Islámicos', in A. Motilla (ed.) *Los Musulmanes en España. Libertad religiosa e identidad cultural*, Madrid: Trotta, pp. 79–106.

Observatorio Andalusí (2007) 'Estudio demográfico de la población musulmana', Explotación estadística del censo de ciudadanos musulmanes en España referido a fecha 31/12/2007. Available at: http://mx.geocities.com/hispanomuslime/estademograf.doc (accessed 20 January 2009).

SOS Racismo (2002–2006) *Informe Anual sobre el racismo en el Estado español*, Barcelona: Icaria.

State Secretariat for Immigration and Emigration (2006) *Statistical yearbook of Immigration*, Madrid: Ministry of Labour and Immigration. Available at: http://extranjeros.mtin.es/es/InformacionEstadistica/Anuarios/Archivos/Anuario_Estadistico_Inmigracixn2006InglesInternet.pdf (accessed 20 January 2009).

Tamayo, J. J. (2003) *Adiós al la cristianidad: la iglesia católica española en la democracia*, Barcelona: Ediciones.

Zapata-Barrero, R. (2003) La politització de la immigració durant la companya de les eleccions municipals del 25 de maig de 2003, Discurs polític i social a Barcelona, Premià de Mar i Vic, Barcelona: Universitat Pompeu Fabra. Available at: www.upf.edu/gritim (accessed 20 January 2009).

Zapata-Barrero, R. (2004) *Multiculturalidad e inmigración*, Síntesis: Barcelona.

Zapata-Barrero, R. (2006) 'The Muslim Community and Spanish Tradition: Maurophobia as a Fact, and Impartiality as a Desiratum', in T. Modood, A. Triandafyllidou and R. Zapata-Barrero (eds), *Multiculturalism, Muslims and Citizenship: A European Approach*, New York: Routledge, pp. 143–61.

Zapata-Barrero, R. (2009) 'Dynamics of Diversity in Spain: Old Questions, New Challenges', in S. Vertovec and S. Wessendorf (eds), *Backlash Against Multiculturalism in Europe: Public Discourse, Policies and Practices*, London: Routledge, pp. 73–93.

Zapata-Barrero, R. and Qasem, I. (2008) 'The Politics of Discourse Towards Islam and Muslim Communities in Europe', in P. Mouritsen and K. E. Jørgensen (eds), *Constituting*

Communities: Political Solutions to Cultural Conflict, Hampshire: Palgrave Macmillan, pp. 73–93.

Newspapers

(2001) 'Presentan 5.500 firmas en contra de una mezquita en Premià de Mar', *ABC*, 27 November.

(2002) 'La ultraderecha aprovecha los brotes racistas para crear un partido en Cataluña', *ABC*, 20 May.

(2005) 'Cataluña centros religiosos. Badalona suspende un año concesión licencias centros religiosos', *EFE*, 28 July.

(2006) 'Carod anuncia una ley de centros de culto para profundizar en la "laicidad sana"', *La Razón*, 31 December.

(2006) 'El Consejo Islámico de Valencia descalifica las declaraciones del presidente de la FEERI, Félix Herrero, sobre las fiestas de moros y cristianos', *Las Provincias*, 5 October (www.Weblslam.com) (accessed 20 January 2009).

(2006) 'La comunidad islámica de Alicante celebra que Mahoma no arda en fiestas', *El Periodico de Cataluña*, 4 October.

(2006) 'La comunidad islámica, con las fiestas de Moros y Cristianos', *ABC*, 4 October.

(2006) 'Todas las mezquitas de Valencia se oponen a la propuesta de Herrero para suprimir la fiesta de moros y cristianos', *Las Provincias*, 6 October (www.Weblslam.com) (accessed 20 January 2009).

(2007) 'El PP recoge firmas contra la construcción de una mezquita en Badalona', *El País*, 13 January.

(2007) 'La Junta Islámica acusa al PP de Badalona (Barcelona) de 'demonizar el Islam' por recoger firmas contra una mezquita', *Europa Press*, 16 January.

Ayuso, G. (2007) 'El PP reaviva la polémica sobre la aperture de mezquitas en Badalona con una campaña de recogida de firmas', *El País*, 16 January.

Barros, M. de (2007) 'La ubicación de una mezquita en terreno público divide a los vecinos de Badalona', *ABC*, 17 January.

Bastante, J. (2006) 'La España que reza a Alá', *ABC*, 3 July.

Benvenuty, L. (2007a) 'Mezquitas en el aire. Badalona lleva un lustro buscando un emplazamiento para los rezos musulmanes', *La Vanguardia*, 21 January.

Benvenuty, L. (2007b) 'Católicos de Badalona apoyan la construcción de una mezquita', *La Vanguardia*, 23 January.

Benvenuty, L. (2007c) 'Tension', *La Vanguardia*, 8 October.

Casals, D. (2006) 'Los imanes de Cataluña reivindican una gran mezquita en Barcelona. Los musulmanes piden lugares de culto legales y "dignos"', *El País*, 11 December.

Gadea, L. (2006) 'Pueblos valencianos suprimen de las fiestas actos ofensivos a Mahoma', *El País*, 2 October.

Gallardo, À. (2006) 'Los cristianos de Alcoi desfilarán por Nueva York sin los moros', *El Periodico de Cataluña*, 6 October.

González, R. (2006) 'Una mezquita en Badalona', *La Insignia*, 12 May (Weblslam.com).

Gundín, J. A. (2006) 'Ni moros, ni cristianos. Lo criticable es que se suprimen partes de la fiesta por miedo al islamista y no por convencimiento, gusto estético o madurez', *La Razon*, 6 October.

Marínez, D. and Antolín, A. (2006) 'Los barullos de Mahoma' *ABC*, 8 October.

Martínez, D. (2006) 'Zaplana ampara a los "Moros"', *ABC*, 14 October.

Orduña, C. (2007) 'Una ley para los cultos no católicos', *El País*, 4 January.

Pérez, M. (2002) 'El Ayuntamiento de Premià aparca el proyecto de la mezquita y cede una escuela a los musulmanes', *El País*, 27 June.

Playà Maset, J. (2006) 'Los imanes reivindican mezquitas dignas', *La Vanguardia*, 11 December.

Ruiz Sierra, J. (2006) 'La quema de Mahoma desaparece por temor en las fiestas valencianas', *Periodico de Cataluña*, 1 October.

Sales, F. (2007) 'Mezquitas en Cataluña. Las catacumbas del Islam. Una red de 160 locales diseminados por Cataluña se convierten los viernes en oratorios', *El País*, 21 January.

Vives, J. (2002) 'La mezquita de Premià. La construcción del templo origina un agitado debate ciudadano', *La Vanguardia*, 27 April.

11 Greece

The challenge of native and immigrant Muslim populations

Anna Triandafyllidou

Introduction

Greece currently hosts a large number of immigrants (accounting for 1.1 million or approximately 10 per cent of the total population), a considerable proportion of whom are Muslim. Greece's Muslim immigrants are in the most part Albanians (over 0.4 million) who are not particularly devout Muslims given their socialization for over 50 years in a totalitarian communist regime (see also Tsitselikis 2004b). Other Muslims in Greece include small immigrant communities of Pakistani, Bangladeshi and Egyptian origin. Alongside Muslim immigrants, there is a numerically small (around 85,000 people) native Muslim community in the north-eastern corner of Greece (Western Thrace), mainly of Turkish ethnicity, that enjoys a special status in terms of religious and cultural rights including the recognition of Sharia law, in derogation to Greek civil law (Tsitselikis 2004a, 2004b; Basiakou 2008).

Over the past 18 years, Greece has followed two divergent strategies with regard to these two different Muslim populations. Since 1991 policies towards the native Muslim minority of Thrace have aimed at the socio-economic integration of this minority in its local and regional context and the improvement of inter-communal relations between Muslims and Christians in the region. The measures that have been taken mainly address citizenship rights at the individual level and the combating of socio-economic discrimination against minority members. By contrast, as regards Muslim immigrants, Greece is yet to develop a policy concerning their social integration at the individual or collective level (Tsitselikis 2004a; 2004b; Triandafyllidou and Gropas 2009).

The lack of appropriate integration policies for Muslim immigrants is, however, part of the wider lack of an integration policy towards economic migrants who have arrived in Greece during the past 20 years. The large majority of these immigrants are, however, Christian (Orthodox mainly and to a lesser extent Catholic) and originate from eastern and south-eastern Europe and Eurasia. Most immigrants arrived as undocumented workers. After three large regularization programmes, they have largely been converted into a legal population and many have settled in the country. While this reality has slowly obliged state institutions and public opinion to recognize that Greek society has become de facto multicultural and multi-ethnic, it is yet to be reflected in policymaking for immigrant integration. The few initiatives or policy programmes enacted are based on a rationale of assimilation rather than recognition of cultural diversity (Gropas and Triandafyllidou 2009). Religious diversity resulting from immigration has emerged as a challenge only during the past few years, as Asian Muslim groups have increased in size and have started raising claims regarding their religious needs (e.g. the need for a Muslim burial ground, for an official mosque in Athens, and generally for a more institutionalized dialogue with Greek authorities).

This chapter aims to explain the interaction between native and immigrant Muslim populations and the Greek national majority through the analysis of both the cultural and structural factors that organize this interaction. As regards cultural factors, the ethnocultural character of the Greek nation state, the role of ethnicity and religion, as well as the idea of Europe in dominant national self-understandings are each analysed as part of this discussion. I further look at the role of native and immigrant Muslims as historical or contemporary 'others'. As regards structural factors, institutional issues concerning the separation of Church and State (or their entanglement), the relevance of EU policies in shaping Greek state policies towards Muslims and the overall framework of immigrant and minority integration policies are reviewed. Last but not least, the national, ethnic, demographic and socio-economic features of the native and immigrant Muslim populations of Greece are taken into consideration as a set of both cultural and structural factors that affect their position in Greece.

This chapter thus tries to show how the national-political, socio-historical and institutional context (and the discourses developed therein) have been a dividing or a unifying factor between native non-Muslim majorities and Muslim groups (native or immigrant). Considering the negotiation of these structural and cultural elements in public and political debates I seek to cast new light on the issues that Muslim minorities face in Greece beyond deterministic accounts of historical or institutional path dependencies and beyond culturally deterministic accounts about religious diversity and the impossibility of accommodating it.

In the section that follows, the demographic and socio-economic profiles of native and immigrant Muslims in Greece are presented. The main socio-economic and historical features of the native Muslim minority of Western Thrace are outlined in section two. Attention is paid to the complete, albeit 'fossilized', framework of cultural and religious autonomy that native Muslims enjoy in comparison with the dearth of provisions in place for the accommodation of individual or collective religious needs of immigrant Muslims. As regards Muslim immigration to Greece, attention is drawn to its multinational composition (including Albanian, Middle Eastern, Asian and even African Muslims) and the specific socio-economic, cultural and religious features of the different groups involved. The question of mosque building and related issues concerning the religious education of immigrants and their children are investigated as notable instances where the reluctance of the Greek state towards accommodating Muslim claims becomes salient. The fourth section outlines the structural and cultural factors that organize Greek national identity understandings generally and with special reference to the Muslim presence in Greece. It thus looks at current debates addressing notions of identity, citizenship, multiculturalism or assimilation, and what it means to be Greek in the twenty-first century. The ways in which the aforementioned structural and cultural factors are reconstructed in public discourse in order to influence the interaction between Muslim immigrants and the national majority are highlighted.

Native Muslims in Western Thrace

Native Greek Muslims number about 85,000 (Tsitselikis 2004a: 109) and inhabit the region of Western Thrace (in the north-eastern corner of Greece), together with a Christian majority. With its strategic location between three states and two continents, Western Thrace, and its Muslim community, marks a particular kind of geographical and cultural-historical boundary between East and West. In Europe's southernmost corner, the region of Thrace borders with Turkey to the east and Bulgaria to the north. Across the northern border, Bulgaria's southern and south-eastern regions are also home to large and territorially concentrated Turkish communities, part of the country's sizeable Turkish minority. Western Thrace is a 'double periphery' region in terms of per capita income and overall development (Ioannides and Petrakos 2000), although the situation has significantly improved during the last 20 years.

The Muslim minority of Western Thrace inhabits the Rhodope mountains in the prefectures of Ksanthe and Rhodope and also the small urban centres of Komotini and Ksanthe. They are predominantly employed in agriculture, particularly the tobacco and cotton cultivation of the region. They have also been employed in the past (until the arrival of immigrants) in seasonal work at harvest time across northern Greece as a mobile and cheap labour force (Vaiou and Hatzimihali 1997). The minority includes a small elite of professionals who until recently received university education in Turkey (as access to Greek universities was virtually impossible until 1996). The mountainous communities in the Rhodope sometimes lacked access to basic facilities such as electricity and running water, and EU structural or regional development funds were used in these areas to provide for such basic infrastructure. Overall, the native Muslim minority of Greece is an insular population with relatively low human and social capital (see also Anagnostou and Triandafyllidou 2007).

As a result of legacies dating back to the country's Ottoman past, Thrace's Muslim community was exempt (along with the Greeks of Istanbul), from the mandatory population exchange between Greece and Turkey that followed from the Treaty of Lausanne (1923). Signed in the aftermath of Greece's military debacle in Anatolia, the international Treaty of Lausanne includes a section on the 'Protection of Minorities', a bilateral agreement between Greece and Turkey containing a series of provisions to guarantee the rights of the exempted minority populations. In fulfilment of the Lausanne Treaty provisions, the Greek authorities also established a bilingual (Greek–Turkish) minority education system. Greece and Turkey signed two bilateral agreements in 1951 (*morfotiki simfonia*) and 1968 (*morfotiko protokolo*) to decide educational policy vis-è-vis the minorities (Baltsiotis 1997: 321–2), which are valid to this day. Reform of the bilingual education system and improvements in its quality have been implemented during the past ten years with important positive results (see http://www.museduc.gr).

Native Muslims of Western Thrace have suffered various forms of discrimination and have been greatly affected by the tensions in Greek–Turkish relations since the mid-1970s. However, the situation has improved markedly since 1991. Members of the Muslim minority in Thrace have seen their individual citizenship rights restored and relationships between the two communities have improved. Native Muslims in Thrace mobilize politically along the lines of a Turkish ethnic identity but do not show signs of radicalization. Their actions are integrated into the Greek political system,[1] even though they show a certain level of distrust towards Greek political parties. Furthermore, their religious and cultural needs are fully regulated by the Lausanne treaty (Anagnostou and Triandafyllidou 2007).

The Lausanne treaty provides that issues pertaining to the 'family and personal situation' of Muslim Greek citizens in Western Thrace will be managed in line with their traditions but does not state explicitly that Sharia law should prevail. However, from 1920 onwards (see Law 1920/1991, article 5(2)) Greek laws have provided that the Mufti, the spiritual and religious leader, has legal power to decide among Muslim Greek citizens of his district on matters of marriage, divorce, alimony, child custody and inheritance.

Yet there are two sets of problems related to the implementation of the Sharia legal system in Greece. Regulated by Law 2345 of 1920, Islamic law in Thrace is a judicial subsystem, in which the Mufti arbitrates matters related to family, inheritance and child custody, thereby giving 'opinions' (*fetwas*) on the basis of Islamic law rather than the civil code which applies to Greek citizens in general.[2] Thus, in Greece, there is confusion between the role of the Mufti as a spiritual and religious leader who can interpret Sharia law, and the Qadi who is the religious judge who applies the law and resolves any arising disputes. Normally the opinions given by the Mufti are not binding for the Qadi (Ktistakis 2006). Moreover, there is a dispute between the Greek state and the Muslim communities of Western Thrace over whether the Mufti should be elected by the community (as its spiritual leader) or appointed by the Greek state (as a civil servant, paid by the state). Thus, since the 1970s there are two Muftis in Ksanthe and two in Komotini. One is appointed by the Greek state and is a civil servant and a second Mufti is elected by the community. The matter is still unresolved and certainly has not helped in facilitating the socio-political integration of the native Muslim minority into Greek society.

On the other hand, Sharia law presents a number of special features that are in open or implicit conflict with the provisions of the Greek civil law (Ktistakis 2006; Rehman 2007). These relate mainly to the unequal situation of women and the regulation of family law matters such as divorce, child custody, polygamy and inheritance. Although decisions about child custody or divorce may vary depending on each case examined, in principle, Sharia explicitly puts women in an inferior position in matters of marriage, divorce, alimony, child custody and inheritance. Moreover, Sharia runs counter to several international agreements protecting children's rights, including issues of underage marriages and marriages decided by the families without considering the will or interest of the children to be married.

Overall, the divergent nature of Sharia law has not contributed towards the social integration of the native Muslim minority in Greece; while it may have strengthened Muslim civil society through the resistance to the appointed Mufti, it has done so in direct opposition to the Greek state and hence to the detriment of the overall integration of Muslims in their regional and national context. The conflation of Mufti and Qadi roles in one person has endangered the civil rights of Muslim Greek citizens and has failed to produce a mutual *rapprochement* and accommodation of Muslim specificities within the Greek legal order. In contrast, the controversy over the election or appointment of the Mufti has politicized a cultural and religious issue, further contributing to the alienation of native Muslims from the Greek state and to their being labelled as 'backward' by other Greek citizens in the region. Ktistakis (2006) notes that the Sharia legal system in Thrace has been 'frozen' by its isolated geographical and geopolitical context – its regulations have not corresponded to developments in matters of marriage, divorce or inheritance laws taking place in Muslim countries such as Pakistan, Tunisia or Iran. At the same time, recent anthropological research (Demetriou 2004 *inter alia*) documents the emergence of urban identities among younger people living in the city of Komotini for instance. For some of Thrace's younger Muslims, religious marriage under Sharia law is seen as a cultural tradition rather than as a whole value system that institutionalizes gender inequality.

Native Muslims in Thrace have not been able to negotiate the accommodation of their special needs or claims with the Greek state because of the entanglement of their religious and cultural rights with Greek–Turkish relations and because of their wish (since the 1970s) to identify themselves as an 'ethnic Turkish' rather than 'religious Muslim' minority. The Greek state has resisted this claim, reiterating the religious rather than ethnic categories in the language of the Lausanne Treaty, out of concern that an ethnic identification may give way to Turkish nationalist claims in the region. As a consequence, the Greek state has become an important defender of the Lausanne Treaty provisions despite their anachronistic nature and questionable effect on the social well-being of the minority. The minority, on the other hand, also prefers to stick with the Lausanne Treaty provisions because of its mistrust of the Greek state authorities and its fear that if the Lausanne Treaty no longer applies, general rules of religious freedom as enshrined in the Greek Constitution and the Council of Europe regulations on human rights will not provide a sufficient basis for the honouring of claims for special treatment on religious and cultural matters.

Muslim immigrants

The 1989 geopolitical changes and Greece's EU membership converted the country into a target destination for several hundreds of thousands of – in the vast majority – irregular immigrant workers from eastern and central Europe (and to a lesser degree from Africa and Asia). These initially undocumented migrants have, to a large extent, settled permanently in Greece and through repeated regularization programmes (1998, 2001, 2005) have come to constitute a predominantly legal immigrant population.

Between 1991 and 2001 (2001 national census), the immigrant population of Greece grew exponentially from under 2 per cent of the total population to estimates that range between 10 and 12 per cent (www.statistics.gr). Data from the national census of 2001 show that nearly 750,000 foreigners from non-EU15 countries were residing in Greece at the time (including both legal and undocumented immigrants). Another 150,000 co-ethnic returnees from the former Soviet Union (Pontic Greeks) were registered in a special census in 2000. In April 2008, there were a little less than 500,000 residence permits for third country nationals in effect, plus an estimated 250,000 permits that were still being processed by municipal or regional authorities. In addition, there are in Greece 185,000 ethnic Greek Albanians with Special Identity Cards for Co-Ethnics (EDTO) of variable duration (between three years and indefinite stay) on top of the 150,000 Pontic Greeks from the former Soviet Union. This brings the total number of economic and co-ethnic migrants in Greece in 2008 to 1.1 million, not including irregular migrants who are estimated at approximately 200,000 (Maroukis 2009). Greece thus finds itself at one of the top positions in Europe in terms of immigrant percentage in the whole population as at least 10 per cent of its residents, about 15 per cent of its school population (www.ipode.gr) and more than 12 per cent of its labour force are immigrants (including co-ethnics).

The various national constituencies of this aggregate immigrant population divide into the following: over 0.6 million of Albanian citizens (including those of Greek ethnic origin), 150,000 Pontic Greeks who have become naturalized through a preferential channel, an estimated 110,000–120,000 Asians (40,000–50,000 Pakistanis, about 20,000 Chinese and Filipinos, and about 10,000–15,000 Bangladeshis and Indians (Tonchev 2007: 17)) and around 40,000–50,000 Poles (Christou 2008). According to 2008 data from the Ministry of Interior, there are also 30,000 Bulgarians and 20,000 Romanians, 13,000 Georgians, 11,000 Russians and nearly 20,000 Ukrainians legally present in Greece. It is estimated that the actual size of these groups is at least double the reported number, but there is currently no reliable data available.

Muslim immigrants in Greece include people from Pakistan, Bangladesh, Arab countries (including Egypt, Syria, Lebanon and Palestine), Kurds and other Turks and, increasingly, Iraqi, Afghan and Iranian citizens. While most of these groups started settling in Greece in the 1990s (Tsitselikis 2004a: 406–7), their number has increased only recently. Tonchev (2007: 15) notes that some Asian immigrant communities like the Pakistanis first came to Greece at the beginning of the 1970s and were employed in shipyards. Overall, however, Muslim migration from South-East Asia is quite a recent and, indeed, increasing phenomenon in the country.

South-East Asian immigration is predominantly male (over 90 per cent) and typically in search of blue-collar jobs in the agriculture, construction, transport and catering industries (Triandafyllidou and Maroufof 2008). The vast majority of them have been smuggled into the country with the help of organized networks across the Greek–Turkish borders (in the Aegean Sea or in the north-eastern land border with Turkey), using fake passports or tourist visas. Some had relatives living legally in the country. Others have simply taken advantage of the loopholes in national border control: after crossing the borders illegally, those who are caught by coastguard patrols or police forces spend a short period of time at local detention centres (up to three months); after this, they are usually set free with a deportation order. At this point, however, many manage to 'disappear' into the informal economy of Athens by making use of family and ethnic networks to find accommodation and employment (Triandafyllidou and Maroufof 2008).

A number of South-East Asians and other Muslim immigrants have managed to regularize their status during the regularization programmes adopted by the Greek government in 1998, 2001 and 2005. New migrants continue to arrive through the traditional routes: undocumented, with tourist visas, with fake passports, or indeed through other European countries. A recent study suggests that smuggling networks are almost completely responsible for the arrival and creation of these communities (Triandafyllidou and Maroukis 2008). There seems to be a profound dependence of South-East Asian immigrants on these illegal networks, both for bringing relatives/friends into the country, and then for the economic benefits of serving in these very networks.

Asian and Arab Muslims in Greece are a migrant population with relatively few skills that gets absorbed in specific niches of the informal Greek labour market. Pakistanis, Iraqis and Afghans are predominantly employed in the construction sector and in agriculture. They take up manual jobs that require little expertise or experience (Tonchev 2007). Those working during harvest periods in agriculture endure especially harsh working conditions: they work for low wages (since most of them are undocumented) and live in barracks provided by their employers which often lack the most basic facilities. They are scattered throughout Greece (Nodaros and Daskalopoulou 2008; Kasimis and Papadopoulos 2005). The 2008–2009 economic crisis has only made things worse since there is dire competition and daily wages have decreased, especially for irregular migrants.

Bangladeshis are predominantly employed in restaurants in the Athens area. Some of the Pakistani population also engages in immigrant-based business in central Athens setting up corner shops that specialize in long distance phone calls, ethnic food and other types of small trade. Despite their low numbers, Asian immigrants are particularly active in the small business sector in Athens (Tonchev 2007; Kolios 2004).

A large number of nominal but not practising Muslims residing in Greece come from Albania. The majority of these belong to the Bektashi order (Zhelyazkova 2000). Albanian Muslims fall somewhat outside the scope of this study as they have not become an organized group, have not identified themselves as Muslims, nor have they raised any claims regarding the accommodation of their religious needs. This is the case because religion under the long rule of the brutal Hoxha Communist regime grew to occupy a minor place in the lives of Albanians. Indeed, recent studies on Albanian immigration indicate that religion is not a distinguishing feature of the lives of Albanians in Greece (Mai and Schienders 2003; Tsitselikis 2004b).

Muslim migration challenges and policy responses

The native and immigrant Muslim populations of Greece share a common socio-economic profile: they are, on average, poorly educated, employed in low skill, low paying, unstable and often uninsured jobs, speak poor Greek and, overall, have limited interaction with the national Greek majority. However, they are also characterized by important differences. Native Muslims live in villages in mountainous regions or in the cities of Komotini and Ksanthi (of under 100,000 inhabitants each). Some Thracian Muslims have migrated to Athens to work in the industrial zone of the city – particularly in Lavrio, Aspropyrgos, Drapetsona and the more central area of Gazi where a natural gas production industry was located in the 1970s. The factory has been closed for more than 20 years but about 3,000–4,000 members of the community stayed on in the area. They are, on the whole, a poor community, and currently at risk of collective eviction as the Gazi area is becoming gentrified (Antoniou 2005). When living outside the region of Thrace, these native Muslims are not entitled to their special religious and cultural rights.

Some Muslim migrants come from the Pakistani, Bangladeshi or Afghan countryside while others come from cities like Dhaka (in Bangladesh) or Karachi (in Pakistan). A large part of these populations live in the Athens metropolitan area. Those who work in construction or catering live usually in central Athens, close to Omonoia and Ag. Panteleimona squares. Some live in eastern Athens (Koropi or Markopoulo) where they obtain jobs in greenhouse cultivation. Some are also employed in agriculture in the Peloponnese or in mainland Greece at greenhouses and other intensive crop cultivation (see for instance Kasimis 2008).

The Muslim population of Greece is ethnically and religiously diverse. The main dimension of difference is ethnic: native Muslims are of Turkish, Pomak or Roma ethnicity (but largely self-identify as Turkish); Muslim immigrants come from mainly South-East Asia and to a lesser extent from Iraq, Afghanistan or Egypt. Religious difference between the two populations, and also within the Muslim immigrant population itself, is important since the communities that comprise it have different traditions regarding mosque attendance, gender and family issues, or Ramadan observance. Besides, even Muslims from the same country (e.g. Pakistan, Iraq or Turkey) may follow a different religious doctrine and hence belong to the Shia, Sunni or other religious order.

This internal diversity is not taken into account by the Greek authorities who organize their policies only in reference to one distinction: between the native Muslims of Thrace who are protected by an international treaty and have extensive legal, religious and educational rights, and the 'other' Muslims who have no collective rights. It is difficult to speak of a set of institutions or laws that provide for the accommodation of Muslim immigrant claims in Greece as they do not exist. In this section, I shall therefore discuss two sets of issues: the issue of mosque building that has become emblematic of the accommodation of Muslim claims in liberal democratic societies (see also Cesari 2005), and the overall Greek paradigm for integrating religious diversity, and in particular Muslim needs, into the national structure.

Mosque construction

There are over 300 mosques operating in Greece today. Most of these are in Western Thrace, while a few are found in the Dodecanese islands of Kos and Rhodes where about 7,000 native Muslims live. Since Greece's independence from the Ottoman Empire in the nineteenth century, there has not been a single mosque in official operation in Athens and the wider Attica region. However, recent demands for the establishment of a mosque are not new (Tsitselikis 2004b). The first provision for a mosque to be built in Athens dates from 1880 (Law AONA' of 1 June 1880). The issue was discussed again in 1913 and relevant legislation was passed for the construction of a mosque in Athens and four more in other areas of Greece. These legal provisions were essentially ignored and the promised mosques were not built. In 1934 (Law 6244 of 25 August 1934), plans were made for the construction of an Egyptian mosque and the creation of an Islamic Foundation for Egyptian students who held Egyptian government grants. However, this law also remained solely on paper while its main aim was to improve Greek–Egyptian relations with a view to protecting the Greek diaspora in Egypt. It is also worth noting that the legal framework created in Thrace with the Treaty of Lausanne in 1923 made it more difficult in the post-1923 period to build mosques in other areas of Greece (Tsitselikis 2004b: 281–3).

More recently, in 1984, Sudanese students of Muslim faith asked for the building of a temple in the Goudi area, in central Athens, to serve their needs. Greek authorities refused to grant a permit but allowed mosques to function so as to serve the needs of the Muslim population of Athens. Over the past two decades, with the arrival of increasing numbers of Muslim immigrants, prayer rooms have proliferated in Greece's capital (Tsitselikis 2004b: 285). Informal sources put the number of prayer rooms at over 100, mainly located in private apartments, basements, shops or storage facilities. In June 2007, an Arab Hellenic Centre for Culture and Civilization was inaugurated in the Moschato neighbourhood in Athens, which, although not an official place of worship, is functioning as one. Ambassadors from Arab states have been lobbying the Greek government to construct a mosque in the capital for over three decades. However, significant public discussion on this matter was provoked less by the request of Muslim immigrant communities to have an official place of worship, than by the advent of the Athens 2004 Olympic Games and the expectations that came attached. The need to provide a space for athletes and visitors belonging to the Muslim faith effectively brought the 'Athens mosque' issue to the forefront of the political agenda and the press.

Although a law (2833/2000) was voted in 2000 providing for the establishment of a mosque in the eastern Athens suburb of Peania, stipulating that the mosque would be constructed with the collaboration of the Greek public authorities and representatives of Arab countries, this never happened. A bill on the subject of establishing a mosque was submitted to parliament in late 2006 by the ruling conservative party New Democracy (parliamentary proceedings, 12 November 2006: 1230–1231). This bill proposed the establishment of a mosque in Eleonas, near the city centre of Athens. It stipulated that the Greek Ministry of National

Education and Religious Affairs would be exclusively responsible for constructing and financing it, and it would be managed by an Administrative Board appointed by the same ministry. The mosque would be constructed on public premises – i.e. the ministry would make available state property in order to provide a space for its construction, and would be responsible for all related expenses. To this date, however, this plan for a new mosque which was met with satisfaction by all parties at the time, has remained on paper only. Thus, informal prayer rooms continue to serve the religious needs of the Athens immigrant Muslim population.

Mosque building has not acquired wide media visibility in Greece as it has in other countries, nor has it raised important political debates (Cesari 2005). The overall question of constructing a mosque acquired some visibility during the Olympic Games period and in 2006 (Gropas and Triandafyllidou 2009) but died out soon afterwards. There is no mobilization on the part of immigrant groups regarding the building of the mosque in Eleonas, nor is there any formal request for dialogue between Muslim immigrant communities and the state. Such claims are raised at academic conferences and workshops but have not been the subject of an organized and/or massive social movement. In a typically Mediterranean style of accommodating difference and protest, mosque construction is forbidden as a general rule, and the only mosque conceded has not yet been built, while in practice prayer rooms proliferate and are allowed to function. The only interest that public authorities appear to take in these matters relates to the potential for radicalization and concerns for national security (Triandafyllidou and Maroukis 2008) rather than the effective integration of Muslim immigrants into Greek society.

The overall paradigm for recognizing religious diversity

While Greek society is becoming de facto multicultural and multi-ethnic through immigration, efforts at encouraging immigrant acceptance by Greek society are largely predicated on a model of assimilation rather than recognition of cultural diversity (Gropas and Triandafyllidou 2009). With special regard to religion, the dominant approach is one of *tolerating* individual difference while ignoring collective aspects of religious life such as the need for alternative burial practices or Muslim burial grounds,[3] or any other claims that address the collective and public aspect of the religious life of immigrants. Thus, for instance, children who are not Christian Orthodox can be exempted from religious classes upon the request of their parents but there are no alternative modules for them such as other religious or philosophy classes. Greek Orthodox religion is also generally present in school life through the daily morning prayer (from which, again, pupils of different faiths can be exempted but must stand in line with the rest of their class) and in religious ceremonies signaling the start of the school year. Priests in possession of a theology degree can be appointed as teachers of religion at high schools. Church schooling also remains an aspect of school life. There is no consideration given to the fact that children belonging to minority religions might feel pressurized to conform or feel the are discriminated against because of their exclusion from several aspects of school life.

From an institutional point of view, it is also worth noting that the establishment of non-Orthodox places of worship is subject to a government permit issued by the Ministry of National Education and Religious Affairs. This government permit is issued following a non-binding opinion provided by the Orthodox Church of Greece (OCG). This situation offers rather extensive room for the executive to evaluate what constitutes a 'known' religion, whether there is a necessity to establish a religious venue, or what constitutes proselytism.

This discussion shows the ambivalence of Greek state policies towards Muslim difference. Native Muslims enjoy an advanced degree of cultural and religious autonomy although in an isolated and fossilized context that remains deeply entangled with foreign policy concerns. Immigrant Muslims enjoy only passive provisions for their special religious or cultural needs such as the tacit toleration of informal prayer rooms or the possibility of children being exempted from religious classes. Basic requests such as the establishment of one official mosque in the capital city and the creation of a Muslim burial ground are met with refusal or half-hearted acceptance that results in non-implementation. Any more substantial issues concerning religious education of children are addressed through their exemption from religious classes, which applies to all students of non-Christian Orthodox background. Thus the principle of religious freedom enshrined in the Greek constitution is applied with regard to the individual child but no provision is made for allowing a public and collective expression of religious belief. There are no provisions for issues regarding religious festivities, dietary and dress requirements at the workplace, or public services (e.g. hospitals). There is no institutional dialogue between Muslim communities and the state, with the arguable exception of policemen (in uniform or plain clothes) visiting informal mosques and observing attendants (Triandafyllidou and Maroukis 2008). In short, public recognition policies are not on the agenda.

Structural conditions for Muslim integration in Greece fall short of actually promoting their incorporation in Greek society. They either favour their marginalization within the Thrace enclave in the name of their historical rights or they ignore their religious and cultural needs, as happens with Muslim migrants in Athens or other areas of Greece outside Thrace. In the following sections I argue that the marginalizing rather than integrating effect of policies for Muslims (native or immigrants) is closely related to the discursive construction of the Muslim as the 'other' and in particular as the 'enemy from the East' (notably Turkey and Turks) in the dominant national narrative.

Citizenship and diversity

Difference in Greece is understood at two inextricably connected levels: ethnicity/nationality and religion. The ethnic dimension is incorporated into the Greek notion of national citizenship which is based implicitly on *ius sanguinis*. Only children born to Greek parents acquire Greek citizenship. Children born in Greece to immigrant parents to this date have no preferential access to naturalization. Immigrants need to have lived in the country for at least ten years to apply for citizenship. Between 2000 and 2006, approximately 50 people (among roughly 1,000 applicants) per year were granted naturalization (Ministry of Interior data, April 2008). It was only in 2007–2008 that ethnic Greek Albanians who had lived in the country for more than ten years were explicitly encouraged to apply for naturalization so that citizenship grants to ethnic Greek Albanians reached 7,000 in 2007 and more than 8,000 in 2008.

The ethnocultural definition of Greek citizenship is at odds with the presence of a native Turkish Muslim minority in Western Thrace. The Greek authorities reject the minority's claim for ethnic self-definition as Turkish and only accept the existence of a religious minority in line with the provisions of the international Treaty of Lausanne between Greece and Turkey. The difficulty of accommodating the minority's claims stems largely from the complex web of Greek–Turkish relations but also has to do with an implicit view that the Greek nation should remain culturally, religiously and ethnically homogenous (Anagnostou 2001, 2005; Anagnostou and Triandafyllidou 2007).

As regards religion as a dimension of difference, it is worth noting that the Orthodox Church of Greece is constitutionally recognized as the 'prevailing' religion in Greece,[4] while Islam is recognized as the religion of the autochthonous Muslim minority[5] of Western Thrace. This distinction has restricted religious freedom in Greece and has led to a series of discriminatory legal and administrative practices. Such practices do not conform to European human rights standards and provisions and have led the European Court of Human Rights to a series of decisions condemning the Greek state on laws and practices that relate to Muslim community rights (Psychogiopoulou 2007).

Constructing the national self and Muslim 'otherness' in public debate

In this section, I analyse the dominant national self-understandings and how identity/difference is organized within them. I argue that ethnicity and religion are the most important dimensions that structure Greek national self-understandings and hence define who belongs and who does not. The dominant narrative of the nation that was constructed by Greek historiographers in the late nineteenth century, was founded on Greece's classical past; it continued with Christianity and the Byzantine Empire, and concluded with Greece's subjugation to the Ottoman Empire and the national resurrection in 1821. The Greek national community was thus presented as *unique* in both its singularity and universality. The belief in a united and unique national community was further reinforced through state policies in military conscription, education and culture throughout the twentieth century.

Greekness has been defined as an amalgamate of (belief in) common ancestry, cultural traditions and religion. This self-definition provided also for a triple boundary distinguishing Greeks from neighbouring nationalities. Greeks were differentiated from Muslims and Jews in the East because they were Christian Orthodox. They were also distinct from the Slavs in the north based on their claim to classical Greek culture. Modern Greece saw itself as the natural heir to Ancient

Greek civilization – as though culture were an object, and the nation its rightful owner (Handler 1988: 142). This feature made this relatively small and economically underdeveloped country in the south-eastern periphery of the continent a central symbol of the construction of European civilization (Tsoukalas 2002). Although territorial and civic features have also gained importance through the consolidation of the national territory in the late nineteenth and early twentieth centuries, Greekness has often, even today, been defined as a transcendental notion in Greek public discourses (Tsoukalas 1993).

During the 1990s, we witnessed an increased fetishization of Greekness and an increasing emphasis placed on ethnic and cultural features of national identity. This form of nationalism may be defined as defensive, reacting to real or perceived cultural and territorial threats to the national integrity (Triandafyllidou, *et al.* 1997). Not surprisingly, when the Greek parliament voted in 1998 to abolish article 19 of the Greek Citizenship Code which discriminated against Greek citizens of non-Greek ethnicity (notably members of the Muslim minority of Western Thrace), Greek national identity took a defensive and nationalist overtone. The law for the abrogation of article 19 was voted in full *patriotic* ethos as a measure that had served the national interest but did so no longer (Anagnostou 2005). The related government initiatives and parliamentary discussions as analysed in Anagnostou (ibid.) pointed to a very limited opening of the national political elite's debate towards a civic and territorial definition of Greek national identity that would accommodate the Turkish Muslim minority within Greek society on the basis of equality and respect for cultural diversity. While Anagnostou (2005) argues convincingly that European Union norms and values, and concern that Greece would be exposed to the European Court of Human Rights, were important factors engineering a change among experts in the Ministry of Foreign Affairs, she also shows that in parliamentary debates, MPs were mainly concerned with justifying their views in terms of national interest rather than European values or norms.

More recent studies that look into the first years of the twenty-first century note that a more flexible understanding of Greek national identity among citizens and elites has been emerging during the past decade. Kokosalakis (2004) and Anagnostou and Triandafyllidou (2007) suggest that the increasing salience of European policies and symbols, such as the European currency, and the actual experience of belonging to the European Union (for example Turkish Muslim minority respondents in Western Thrace who had been recipients of EU funds (Anagnostou and Triandafyllidou 2007)) reinforce a civic and political value component in Greek national identity. Although the EU is often understood in instrumental terms, both minority respondents in Western Thrace (ibid.) and majority respondents in other parts of Greece (Kokosalakis 2004) emphasize that Europe provides a model for respect of cultural diversity, indeed one that can and should be applied within nation states. In sum, the dominant discourses of defensive ethnic nationalism registered in the 1990s have gradually given way to more open definitions of the nation in this present decade, where civic and territorial elements play an important part.

The entanglement of Muslim difference with Turkish ethnicity has been highlighted by Gropas and Triandafyllidou (2009) in an analysis of press discourse and parliamentary proceedings regarding the construction of an official mosque in Athens. The majority of the Muslim population in Athens is neither Turkish nor of Turkish origin, but this demographic 'detail' was barely noted in the development of the mosque debate in the Greek parliament during the winter of 2006. The construction of the mosque in Athens was associated with Greece's Ottoman past, the Cyprus and Aegean disputes, Turkey's aggression towards Greece (in political and military terms), and the situation of Hagia Sofia in Istanbul. These issues were sewn into the press debate even though they have no direct relevance to the issue.

By contrast, the main political parties and institutional actors (Ministry of Education and Religious Affairs and Ministry of Foreign Affairs) framed the mosque construction as a matter of respect for religious freedom and a fundamental constitutional obligation for Greece. However, the argument was not limited to a rights-duties value level. The practical necessity of the mosque was framed in patriotic terms, as supporting national interest. The Minister of Foreign Affairs, for instance, argued that for Greece to have the authority to pressure Turkey for the reopening of the Halki Theological School in Istanbul, Greece cannot deprive the right to religious worship in an appropriate venue to hundreds of thousands of legal residents. The inconsistency of not authorizing the construction of a mosque was pointed out less as an ethical question than as a negotiating weakness which would prevent Greece from successfully promoting its national interests.

This patriotic framing of the mosque bill was complemented by media debates on religious freedom as a core value and a right that ought to be able to be exercised freely by all. In other words, there was support for the rights of Muslim immigrants in principle. However, such declaratory statements were not followed up by concrete proposals to speed up the establishment of the mosque. Moreover, they were usually associated with qualifying statements regarding practical concerns (e.g. location, funding, security issues) that, in effect, hampered the process and demonstrated a significant degree of 'Muslimophobia' (see also Erdenir in this volume).

Cultural and religious plurality is still presented in media and political discourse as a reality that has befallen Greek society and that has to be accommodated as a necessary evil, out of respect for the constitution as well as Greece's own national interest. In short, while some studies have documented a certain degree of openness in Greek national identity discourses in recent years, suggesting that a civic understanding of the nation has gained some ground and European identity has started to become relevant to citizens as, among other things, a notion of pluralism, the mosque construction issue and related debates testify to a continuation of the exclusionary definition of citizenship and national identity along mono-ethnic and mono-religious lines.

Concluding remarks

In this chapter I have sought to explore both structural and cultural factors that condition the interaction between Muslim populations and the national majority in Greece. As regards cultural factors and their influence on Muslim integration, the situation is rather bleak: the Greek nation remains predominantly defined with reference to common ethnicity and a common (Christian Orthodox) religion despite the large-scale economic immigration during the past 20 years that has significantly altered the demographic and ethnic composition of the Greek resident population. The history of the nation's formation (through a war of independence against the Ottoman Empire and subsequent war with Turkey) has also made a strong imprint on national self-understandings. Muslims are largely construed as 'others'. Islam is often seen as synonymous with Turkey (and Turkish foreign policy), and native Muslims are often construed as the 'other within' (Anagnostou 2005; Antoniou 2005). The ethnocultural and religious definition of the nation equally leaves little room for the incorporation of immigrants in general and Muslim immigrants in particular. Citizenship policies are highly restrictive: not only are the requirements difficult to meet by immigrants, but in practice citizenship is granted almost exclusively to immigrants of Greek ethnic origin and Christian Orthodox religion.

When it comes to structural factors, Greece is marked by a complex situation: native Muslims, while construed as 'others within' the nation, are recognized as a religious minority and enjoy a special status that guarantees a high level of collective autonomy in culture, religion and education. However, this status does not emanate from a recognition and acceptance of their cultural and religious difference. It is rather the outcome of an international treaty signed nearly a century ago between Turkey and Greece as a result of the Greek–Turkish war in Asia Minor.

Muslim immigrants are faced with a different situation. Their own religious or cultural needs are not connected to those of native Muslims. There are no policy provisions for the operation of mosques, Muslim burial grounds, religious education or the accommodation of Muslim religious holidays in working life. By contrast, the Orthodox Church remains not only Greece's official religion but is also consulted when a permit for the establishment of a place of worship of another religion is to be issued by the Ministry of Education and Religious Affairs. Church and State functions are not clearly separated – an issue that makes the accommodation of Muslim claims even more difficult. There are no consultation structures or practices in place for immigrant Muslim communities to enter a dialogue with the Greek state and there are no initiatives on the part of the state to discuss with Muslim migrants anything pertaining to their special needs.

Looking at the socio-economic and demographic profiles of native and immigrant Muslims we also note important differences. Native Muslims are a largely agrarian population engaged in tobacco and cotton cultivation, with relatively low levels of education and relatively high unemployment. They are, at the same time, a population with a high demographic growth rate, a low average age and an elaborate system of family networks. Immigrant Muslims are a population with a strong gender imbalance: they are, in the vast majority, young men who have come to Greece to find work, while leaving families behind in their home countries. Many have received secondary education and while some come from rural areas, others have an urban or city background. The low socio-economic status of either group does not favour their integration. The family situation of Muslim immigrants (i.e. the fact that their families are left in the countries of origin) makes integration even more difficult. They do not have a real, at least initial, intention to stay and their interaction with the host society, given the added problem of a language barrier, is very limited.

The two groups are faced with significantly different conditions of life and work: native Muslims are concentrated in the region of Thrace while Muslim immigrants reside mainly in the Athens metropolitan area or in the mainland Greek countryside where they find employment in greenhouses and intensive forms of cultivation. In Athens they work in the service sector (cleaning, catering, small industries, and agriculture in the city outskirts), often in the underground economy. Interestingly, the Pakistani and Bangladeshi communities have created their own associations and migrant organizations, and in comparison to their size and relatively recent arrival in Greece show a high level of political and civic activism concerning migrant integration issues and migrant rights. The lack of policies and of structures for intercultural and inter-religious dialogue, however, prevents their ability to channel this activism into an official dialogue for the benefit of both migrant and native Muslims. Security remains the main policy concern of the Greek state with regard to its Muslim immigrants.

In conclusion, from a structural perspective, the low socio-economic status and marginal socio-economic position of both native and immigrant Muslims in Greece does not favour their incorporation into Greek society. At the same time, the incomplete separation of Church and State in Greece, the non-existence of a legal and institutional framework for the integration of immigrant Muslims and the fossilized character of the special status of native Thracian Muslims do not offer the opportunity for effective dialogue between Muslims and non-Muslims in Greece, especially one that would facilitate the acceptance and accommodation of the special needs and wishes of Muslims.

From a cultural perspective, the major obstacle to Muslim integration (both native and immigrant) remains the ethnocultural definition of the nation and of national citizenship. Although there are signs that the European model, with its internal pluralism, is becoming an integral part of Greek national identity, Greek national citizenship and related policies and practices remain largely informed by an ideal of a mono-ethnic, mono-religious, compact and united nation within which there is no room for multicultural citizenship policies for integrating native or immigrant minorities. At the same time, Muslim communities of Greece remain very diverse (coming from different countries and adhering to different Islamic traditions), which makes it harder for them to mobilize together in demand for a common framework of recognition. This is also related to the fact that native Muslims mobilize mainly along ethnic lines while Muslim immigrants appear mainly concerned with religious issues. Moreover, the two groups come from countries with different Islamic traditions regarding, for instance, traditions of prayer, mosque attendance and gender relations. While all groups belong to the same religion, informants interviewed (Triandafyllidou and Maroukis 2008) note a strong sense of difference between South-East Asians and Turks.

This study suggests that it is the formidable combination of these structural and cultural factors that pushes the Muslim populations in Greece to the margins, both socio-economically and symbolically. While economic marginalization may affect immigrants in general, Muslim immigrants are particularly affected, as most are recent arrivals and have an insecure legal status. While the country's native Muslims are trapped in the nexus of Greek–Turkish foreign relations, the Muslim migrants experience difficulties in getting their own needs and differences accommodated, as the boundaries of Greek public space remain closed to both passive individual difference but also to active collective diversity.

Notes

1 There is always at least one minority MP elected in the national election within one of the two large parties (New Democracy/conservative party or PASOK/socialist party). Minority candidates would not be elected to the parliament if running the election as a member of an ethnic party since there is a 3 per cent national vote threshold for smaller parties that cannot be reached by minority votes alone.

2 The situation is quite complicated regarding the compatibility and function of Islamic law within the framework of Greek civil law. Decisions of the Mufti are *fetwas* (opinions) (Anagnostou 1997) and are supposed to have a consultative and compromising role; however there are no remedies against such opinions (Tsitselikis 2004a). At the same time, decisions of the Mufti that violate the constitution or international human rights cannot be enforced (Basiakou 2008: 15). In practice, however, as Tsitselikis notes (2004a: 116–17), the legal jurisdiction of the Mufti for members of the Muslim minority in Thrace has become obligatory. It is worth noting that in Turkey citizens are not subject to Sharia law but to Turkish civil law (Soltaridis 1997: 178).

3 To this day Muslim immigrants collect money from one another to raise money to send back to the country of origin (e.g. Pakistan) the body of a friend or relative who has died in Greece but cannot be buried there because there are no provisions for non-Christian burial (see also Fokas 2009).

4 http://www.parliament.gr/politeuma/syntagmaDetails.asp?ArthroID=3 Greek Constitution, First Part: General Provisions, Relations between Church and State, Article 3.

5 The only other recognized minority under public law is the Jewish one.

References

Anagnostou, D. (1997) 'Religious Freedom and Minority Rights in the New Europe: The Case of the Muslim Courts in Western Thrace'. Paper delivered to the XV Modern Greek Studies Association International Symposium 1997 on Modern Greece, Kent State University, Kent, Ohio, 6–7 November.

Anagnostou, D. (2001): 'Breaking the Cycle of Nationalism: The EU, Regional Policy and the Minority of Western Thrace, Greece', *South European Society and Politics*, 6 (1: Summer): 99–124.

Anagnostou, D. (2005) 'Deepening Democracy or Defending the Nation? The Europeanisation of Minority Rights and Greek Citizenship', *West European Politics*, 28 (2): 335–57.

Anagnostou, D. and Triandafyllidou, A. (2007) 'Regions, Minorities and European Integration: A Case Study on the Muslims in Thrace', in D. Anagnostou and A. Triandafyllidou (eds), *European Integration, Regional Change and Minority Mobilisation*, Special Issue, *Romanian Journal of Political Science*, 6 (1): 101–26.

Antoniou, D. (2005) 'Western Thracian Muslims in Athens: From Economic Migration to Religious Organisation', *Balkanologie*, IX (1–2), available at http://balkanologie.revues.org/index579.html (accessed 17 November 2009).

Baltsiotis, L. (1997): 'Ελληνική Διοίκηση και Μειονοτική Εκπαίδευση στη Δυτική Θράκη' [Greek Administration and Minority Education in Western Thrace], in K. Tsitselikis and D. Christopoulos (eds), *Το Μειονοτικό Φαινόμενο στην Ελλάδα* [The Minority Phenomenon in Greece], Athens: Kritiki & KEMO, pp. 315–48.

Basiakou, I. (2008) 'Religious Freedom and Minority Rights in Greece: The Case of the Muslim Minority in Western Thrace', GreeSE paper, no. 21, Hellenic Observatory Papers on Greece and Southeast Europe, December, The Hellenic Observatory, The European Institute, London School of Economics and Politics.

Cesari, J. (ed.) (2005) 'Mosque Conflicts in Europe', Special Issue, *Journal of Ethnic and Migration Studies*, 31 (6).

Christou, A. (2008) 'Agency, Networks and Policy: The Case of Poles in Greece', *Journal of Immigrant and Refugee Studies*, 6 (3): 312–26.

Demetriou, O. (2004) 'Prioritizing "ethnicities": The Uncertainty of Pomak-ness in the Urban Greek Rhodope', *Ethnic and Racial Studies*, 27 (1): 95–119.

Fokas, E. (2009) 'Thiva Case Study', prepared for the European Research Project *Welfare and Values in Europe* (*WaVE*), presented at a seminar on 10 February 2009, Panteion University, Athens.

Greek Parliament (2006) Parliamentary proceedings, 12 November: 1230–1, available at www.parliament.gr (accessed 7 August 2009).

Handler, R. (1998) *Nationalism and the Politics of Culture in Quebec*, Madison: The University of Wisconsin Press.

Ioannides, Y. and Petrakos, G. (2000) 'Regional Disparities in Greece: The Performance of Crete, Peloponnese and Thessaly', *European Investment Bank Papers*, 5 (1): 31–60.

Kasimis, C. (2008), 'Employment Structure and Occupational Mobility of the Immigrants', paper presented at the conference *Employment and Inclusion of Immigrants in Local Societies*, organized by the Agronomic University of Athens, Athens, 31 October.

Kasimis, C. and Papadopoulos, A. (2005) 'The Multifunctional Role of Migrants in the Greek Countryside', *Journal of Ethnic and Migration Studies*, 31 (1): 99–127.

Kokosalakis, N. (2004) 'Εθνική Ταυτότητα και Ευρώπη. Στάσεις και Διαθέσεις των Ελλήνων Πολιτών' [National Identity and Europe: Positions and Attitudes of Greek Citizens], in Koula Kassimati (ed.), *Εθνική και Ευρωπαϊκή ταυτότητα. Συγκλίσεις και αποκλίσεις* [National and European Identity: Convergence and Divergence], Athens: Gutenberg, pp. 57–100.

Kolios, N. (2004) 'Social Capital and Immigrant Entrepreneurship in Central Athens', paper presented at the 5th ENGIME conference, Athens 19–20 January 2004, available at http://siti.feem.it/engime/ (accessed 3 August 2009).

Ktistakis, Y. (2006) *Ιερός Νόμος του Ισλάμ και μουσουλμάνοι Έλληνες πολίτες, εκδ. Π.Ν. Σάκκουλα, Αθήνα-Θεσσαλονίκη.*

Mai, N. and Schienders M. (2003) (eds) 'Albanian Migration and New Transnationalisms', *Journal of Ethnic and Migration Studies*, Special Issue 29 (6).

Maroukis, T. (2009) 'Greece', *CLANDESTINO Project Report*, available at http://clandestino.eliamep.gr/category/projects-reports/country-reports-reports/ (accessed 17 November 2009).

Nodaros, M. and Daskalopoulou, D. (2008) 'The Strawberries of Tzamal', *Eleftherotypia*, Sunday edition, 30 March, Epsilon Review Issue no. 885, available at http://mnodaros.blogspot.com/2008/04/blog-post_02.html (accessed 5 March 2009).

Psychogiopoulou, E. (2007) 'JURISTRAS State of the Art Report: Strasbourg Court Jurisprudence and Human Rights in Greece: An Overview of Litigation, Implementation and Domestic Reform', available at http://www.eliamep.gr/eliamep/files/Greece.pdf (accessed 4 August 2007).

Rehman, J. (2007) 'The Sharia, Islamic Family Laws and International Human Rights Law: Examining the Theory and Practice of Polygamy and Talaq', *International Journal of Law, Policy and the Family, Advance Access*, 21 (1): 108–27.

Soltaridis, S. (1997) *Η Ιστορία του Μουφτή στην Δυτική Θράκη* [The History of the Mufti in Western Thrace], Athens: Nea Synora.

Tonchev, P. (ed.) (2007), 'Ασιάτες Μετανάστες στην Ελλάδα: Προέλευση Παρόν και Προοπτικές' [Asian Migrants in Greece: Origin, Present and Perspectives], Institute of International Economic Relations, Department of Asian Studies, January 2007, available at http://www.idec.gr/iier/new/asian_migrants_en.pdf (accessed 17 June 2007).

Triandafyllidou, A. and Gropas, R. (2009) 'Constructing Difference: The Mosque Debates in Greece', *Journal of Ethnic and Migration Studies*, 35 (6): 957–75.

Triandafyllidou, A. and Maroufof, M. (2008), *Immigration Towards Greece at the Eve of the 21st Century: A Critical Assessment*, Project Report, available at http://www.eliamep.gr/en/migsys (accessed 7 August 2009).

Triandafyllidou, A. and Maroukis, T. (2008) 'Muslim Immigrants in Greece: Marginalisation, Radicalisation and the Role of Religion'. Report prepared for a project on best practices in cooperation between authorities and civil society with a view to the prevention and response to violent radicalization, London, Change Institute, May.

Triandafyllidou, A., Mikrakis, A. and Calloni, M. (1997) 'New Greek Nationalism', *Sociological Research Online*, 2(1), available at http://www.socresonline.org.uk/2/1/7.html (accessed 5 August 2009).

Tsitselikis, K. (2004a) 'Personal Status of Greece's Muslims: A Legal Anachronism or an Example of Applied Multiculturalism?' in R. Aluffi and G. Zincone (eds), *The Legal Treatment of Islamic Minorities in Europe*, Torino: FIERI and Peeter, pp. 109–33.

Tsitselikis, K. (2004b) 'Η θρησκευτική ελευθερία των μεταναστών. Η περίπτωση των μουσουλμάνων' [The Religious Freedom of Immigrants: The Case of Muslims], in M. Pavlou and D. Christopoulos (eds), *The Greece of Migration*, Athens: Kritiki, pp. 267–303.

Tsoukalas, C. (1993) 'Greek National Identity in an Integrated Europe and a Changing World Order', in H. Psomiades and S. Thomadakis (eds), *Greece, the New Europe and the Changing International Order*, New York: Pella, pp. 57–78.

Tsoukalas, C. (2002) 'The Irony of Symbolic Reciprocities: The Greek Meaning of "Europe" as a Historical Inversion of the European Meaning of "Greece"', in M. af Malmborg and B. Strath (eds), *The Meaning of Europe*, Oxford: Berg, pp. 27–50.

Vaiou, N. and Hatzimihali, K. (1997) *Με τη ραπτομηχανή στην κουζίνα και τους Πολωνούς στους αγρούς* [With the Sewing Machine in the Kitchen and the Poles in the Fields], Athens: Exantas.

Zhelyazkova, A. (ed.) (2000), *Albania and the Albanian Identities*, Sofia: International Centre for Minority Studies and Intercultural Relations.

Index

Note: page numbers in **bold** refer to figures and tables.

eupdates
Taylor & Francis Group
Want to stay one step ahead of your colleagues?
Sign up today to receive free up-to-date information on books, journals, conferences and other news within your chosen subject areas.
Visit
www.tandf.co.uk/eupdates
and register your email address, indicating your subject areas of interest.
You will be able to amend your details or unsubscribe at any time. We respect your privacy and will not disclose, sell or rent your email address to any outside company. If you have questions or concerns with any aspect of the eUpdates service, please email eupdates@tandf.co.uk or write to: eUpdates, Routledge, 2/4 Park Square, Milton Park, Abingdon, Oxfordshire OX14 4RN, UK.
Mail